PERGAMON INTERNATIONAL LIBRARY
of Science, Technology, Engineering and Social Studies

The 1000-volume original paperback library in aid of education, industrial training and the enjoyment of leisure

Publisher: Robert Maxwell, M.C.

SCHIZOPHRENIA

(PGPS — 90)

THE PERGAMON TEXTBOOK
INSPECTION COPY SERVICE

An inspection copy of any book published in the Pergamon International Library will gladly be sent to academic staff without obligation for their consideration for course adoption or recommendation. Copies may be retained for a period of 60 days from receipt and returned if not suitable. When a particular title is adopted or recommended for adoption for class use and the recommendation results in a sale of 12 or more copies, the inspection copy may be retained with our compliments. The Publishers will be pleased to receive suggestions for revised editions and new titles to be published in this important International Library.

Related Titles

SCHIZOPHRENIA

Medical
Diagnosis
or
Moral
Verdict?

Theodore R. Sarbin

Adlai E. Stevenson College,
University of California,
Santa Cruz

James C. Mancuso

State University of New York
at Albany

Pergamon Press

New York ☐ Oxford ☐ Toronto ☐ Sydney ☐ Frankfurt ☐ Paris

Pergamon Press Offices:

U.S.A.	Pergamon Press Inc., Maxwell House, Fairview Park, Elmsford, New York 10523, U.S.A.
U.K.	Pergamon Press Ltd., Headington Hill Hall, Oxford OX3 0BW, England
CANADA	Pergamon of Canada, Ltd., Suite 104, 150 Consumers Road, Willowdale, Ontario M2J 1P9, Canada
AUSTRALIA	Pergamon Press (Aust.) Pty. Ltd., P.O. Box 544, Potts Point, NSW 2011, Australia
FRANCE	Pergamon Press SARL, 24 rue des Ecoles, 75240 Paris, Cedex 05, France
FEDERAL REPUBLIC OF GERMANY	Pergamon Press GmbH, Hammerweg 6, Postfach 1305, 6242 Kronberg/Taunus, Federal Republic of Germany

Library of Congress Cataloging in Publication Data

Sarbin, Theodore R
  Schizophrenia, medical diagnosis or moral verdict?

(Pergamon general psychology series)
Bibliography: p.
Includes index.
1. Schizophrenia. I. Mancuso, James C., 1928-
joint author. II. Title.
RC514.S315 1979   616.8′982   79-20222
ISBN 0-08-024613-3
ISBN 0-08-024612-5 (pbk.)

Printed in the United States of America

dedicated to
Genevieve and Susan
with affection and gratitude

Contents

Foreword

It was with mounting excitement that I read the Sarbin-Mancuso book in manuscript form, in my role as co-editor of the Psychology Series. I felt that this book would be a major contribution to the field of psychology. But even more important, their approach to "schizophrenia" through an analysis of metaphoric language reinforced my own bias against the popular and professionally ubiquitous disease model of deviant behavior.

This book emphasizes contextualist approaches to the study of human action. The work itself must be placed in a number of different contexts, including the history of the "mental illness"/"disease" concept, current research in psychiatry and "abnormal psychology," and the current development of alternative paradigms for explaining human behavior. This text reflects the growing trend in psychology, and in all of the behavioral sciences, which will take researchers and investigators away from conceptualizing in terms of fixed entities. The overall contextualist view of this book promotes an awareness that the practice of discussing desirable or undesirable human behavior with terms such as "disease," "mental illness," "aging," "schizophrenia," "neurosis," "adolescence," "infancy," etc., has had its historical origins in the context of a specific time, place, and social milieu.

Sarbin and Mancuso did not invent the method of root metaphor analysis, but they help us recognize that we, as participant-observers in the study of human behavior, are dealing with metaphoric language far more frequently than we usually acknowledge. They cite the strong evidence of the need to be aware of the *contexts* and *consequences* of the creation of such descriptive and explanatory metaphors by behavioral scientists, psychologists, psychiatrists, sociologists, and other "experts" on human behavior.

What I find particularly attractive about Sarbin and Mancuso's approach is that they go beyond a historical analysis of the origin of "schizophrenia" as a metaphoric term into a systematic analysis of contemporary "schizophrenia" research. This multitudinous research, in the name of *science*, has been so instrumental in transforming the metaphor of "schizophrenia" to a myth. Sarbin and Mancuso play fairly in that the "schizophrenia" research is analyzed within the context of the rules of the scientific game. They demonstrate unequivocally that the research is deficient. To demonstrate with detailed scholarship and research sensitivity in the field of "schizophrenia" that "the Emperor has no clothes" is indeed a major accomplishment.

An important aspect of the "schizophrenia" situation, which the authors touch upon in Chapter 6, is that of the "schizophrenia Industry" which is an important element in the maintenance of the current situation. It would be an interesting exercise in economics and occupational sociology to show in detail how "schizophrenia" as a disease metaphor has spawned thousands of jobs, not only for the psychiatric team (psychiatrist, clinical psychologist, and social worker), and other mental hospital employees, but also for the pharmaceutical, publishing, hospital supply, and related industries. The first task of any industry is to perpetuate itself and then to expand.

The noted economist Robert L. Heilbroner has recently illustrated (in the *New Yorker*, October 8, 1979) the dangers of the "disease" metaphor as it is being used to apply to the American political and economic scene: ". . . we regularly use the metaphor of illness to describe the problem of inflation. But the metaphor is wrong, and worse than wrong, it is deceiving. It conveys the idea that inflation is some sort of sickness we have contracted, the way we might catch a cold or pick up some other infection, and that we can get rid of this sickness by taking the appropriate medicine. Even more important, the metaphor of illness suggests that there exists such a thing as a 'healthy' economy in which there are no problems, just as there are healthy persons who have no ills or disorders" (p. 121). Heilbroner then carefully spells out the consequences to our economic system that follow from the use of the "disease" metaphor.

It is the failure of planners, economic or therapeutic, to realize that they are dealing with a metaphoric use of language rather than with "reality" that has had less than desirable effects on the economy or on the targeted labelees. It is the "thinking" and behavior of the planners, designers, therapists and "healers" which can, should and must be influenced by the "revelations" of such authors as Heilbroner/Sarbin/Mancuso (and of others, such as Szasz, discussed in this book). It is ironic that the word "revelation" is so appropriate to describe what amounts to an elementary lesson in language usage and grammar. But the consequences of understanding and utilizing language on the lives of all of us, and on our society, are enormous.

I believe that the "cure" of schizophrenia lies not in any new dramatic psychotherapeutic technique, even a behavioral one, nor in the development of a new "magic pill" medication that will alleviate both "symptom" and underlying "pathology," nor even in a drastic restructuring of society that will reduce the stress and strain of everyday living hence recreating warm, viable family life. Rather the hope for extirpation of "schizophrenia" lies within the process of educating the "mental health" professional in our society, particularly the "team" (psychiatrist, clinical psychologist and social worker). The full implications and consequences of the Sarbin-Mancuso alternative conceptualizations should, could, and must be developed by the current generation of scientists, practitioners, and students.

In this book the authors have taken the initiative in putting forward an alternative paradigm and recognizing the research and conceptual contribution of those investigators who are laying the scientific basis for this alternative paradigm. Thus we were particularly impressed that the audience for this book covers the full spectrum of those involved in the mental health industry; research investigator, practitioner, interested layman, and those entering the system either through the process of being trained as providers or the process of becoming a labelled consumer.

Two issues, among others, follow from the acceptance of the Sarbin-Mancuso approach. How does one (author, teacher, psychotherapist, or any other professional) go about influencing society (lay and professional) to accept the desirability of using a contextual approach rather than the "disease" metaphor, and what will be the consequences of such a paradigm shift? My own orientation to human behavior, "environmental design," is conceptually very compatible with the Sarbin-Mancuso approach, particularly in that both viewpoints stress the reciprocal relationship between the healer and the healee, the labeler and the labelled, the therapist and the patient, the judge and the judgee.

After reading the Sarbin-Mancuso book, the reader must go on to ponder a central social and political question. To view as a *moral verdict* the assignment of a person to the class "schizophrenia" may well change the rules of the game. It may undo the legitimacy of medicine and its professional allies as the officially sanctioned social institution for dealing with "problems in living." In slaying one myth, the reified "disease" metaphor, are we participating in the process of creating a new myth?

Are we about to find ourselves preparing an expedition to find a new unicorn? In a democratic, pluralistic society, *who* indeed will be socially sanctioned to make *moral judgments* on *whom* and under *what circumstances*? The readers are invited to consider these questions and to participate in forming guidelines for assigning moral judgments to the actions of their peers and of themselves.

—Leonard Krasner

State University of New York
at Stony Brook

Acknowledgments

As authors writing a critical review of a large body of work, we acknowledge the sincere efforts of the investigators and theorists who carried out the often tedious and exhausting labor required to complete the reports, articles and books which we have consulted. Though we frequently write sharp negative commentary on some of that work, we do not intend to denigrate the commitment to concept elaboration which underlies these authors' efforts. We hope that our work complements their contributions to a continuing change in explanations of unwanted conduct.

In the same vein we thank all those students who have given us their attention, time and labor as we thought about the many issues that surround the schizophrenia concept. Others have stimulated us to consider points which they have raised, and others have patiently listened to our audible efforts to rearrange conceptualizations.

The senior author's work has been helped along by so many former students and colleagues that it would be impossible to list them all. Those whose contributions have been especially memorable include, among others, Vernon L. Allen, Ki-taek Chun, William C. Coe, Daniel B. Goldstine, Joseph B. Juhasz, Rolf O. Kroger, Robert Nation, and Karl E. Scheibe. The last named is co-author of a paper which serves as the basis for Chapter 11. The Center for the Humanities, Wesleyan University, graciously provided the senior author with a fellowship that helped bring this book to a conclusion.

We also take this opportunity to acknowledge the positive value of those who gave us a base for building contextualist models for psychology. Many important teachers would deserve mention. We name five—E. Brunswick, J.R. Kantor, G.A. Kelly, G.H. Mead, and S.C. Pepper. These scholars worked in an ambience in which contextualist models could not easily grow. The worth of their commitment is now more apparent.

Several lengthy quotations have been reprinted by special permission. The long quotations in Chapter 7, from M. Bleuler, are reproduced with permission of

Pergamon Press, Elmsford, N.Y. The material in Chapter 5, for M. DePorte's *Nightmares and Hobbyhorses*, 1974, is reprinted by special permission of the Henry E. Huntington Library and Art Gallery. The section in Chapter 10, from Ulric Neisser's *Cognitive Psychology*, 1967, pp. 98-99, is reprinted by permission of Prentice-Hall, Inc., Englewood Cliffs, N.J. John Wiley and Sons, Inc., has granted permission to reprint the long quotations in the epilogue, which are taken from K. Salzinger, *Schizophrenia: Behavioral Aspects,* 1973. The sonnet by R.M. Rilke, reproduced in the epilogue, is reprinted by permission from Hogarth Press, London. The poem appeared in *Sonnets to Orpheus,* 1949.

Among the helpful students and friends who undertook some of the time-consuming work of recording references, locating articles, and so forth, we single out Victor Greco and Jesús Salazar for their involved contributions. Though every writer must be grateful to an efficient typist, we owe a special debt to Pat Jones. Her rapid grasp of our subject matter and her skill at making appropriate judgments relieved us of many burdens.

1
Introduction

The title, *Schizophrenia: Medical Diagnosis or Moral Verdict?* is intended to serve as a metaphorical framework to sensitize the reader to an increasingly important problem in the modern world. The basis of our treatise may be seen in the disjunctive question: Should certain kinds of conduct (variably defined) be discussed within the thought and language structure of medical diagnosis; or, should that conduct be discussed within the thought and languages of the morality of custom and juristic institutions?

In the following pages, we try to avoid polemics by taking seriously the disease theory of schizophrenia. The diagnosis of schizophrenia, like any other medical diagnosis, is an implicit statement of a theory, namely, that the signs and symptoms of the disease can be reliably located and are related in some systematic way to antecedent genetic, biochemical, neurological, or psychological antecedents. In the science of medicine, the theoretical statement—the diagnosis—is tested through laboratory or clinical procedures designed to identify the etiological factor or factors. The medical diagnosis becomes more credible as supporting data from laboratory and clinic accumulate.

The ultimate credibility of schizophrenia as a medical diagnosis—as the statement of a disease homologous to diabetes, tuberculosis, and pneumonia—resides in published research reports. In the chapters ahead, we examine critically and fairly the research reports of investigators who have subjected the disease hypothesis to numerous tests.

To anticipate our later argument, our analysis leads us to reject the schizophrenia hypothesis as generally encountered. Instead, we are directed to a competing hypothesis: that schizophrenia is a moral judgment, and like all moral judgments, is conditional upon time, place, and person, and upon identifiable social features of the persons who declare the moral verdict.

We begin our journey with a penetrating question: Within what context does a person enter the category labeled *schizophrenia*?

We can confidently predict that our master question will call out widely disparate conceptions among representative educated readers who live in the Western

1

cultures. We can also predict that a large segment of our readers would unreflectively translate the question to read, "What is the cause of the illness that is diagnosed as schizophrenia?" To explore the differences between the initial question and the transfigured question is the purpose of our journey.

The term *schizophrenia*, by all accounts, comes into use in discussions of unwanted, perplexing conduct. We explore the differences between becoming diagnosed, categorized, or classified as schizophrenic and *becoming ill*. A specific instance provides the entry into the exploration.

Lucille becomes a "schizophrenic."
Lucille had been married for eight years. During those eight years, she and her husband, Andrew, had conducted themselves along a course that could be taken, quite in total, as a description of the course of the life of a typical, American, lower-middle-class family of young married persons. They had three children, and were along their way in amortizing the mortgage on their suburban tract house.

Lucille totally occupied her time with her small children and maintaining the household routines. Andrew was a route salesman for a food items firm that served stores and supermarkets. The family's social life was quite restricted. When time permitted, the family exchanged visits with Lucille and Andrew's parental families, giving more of their time to visits with Lucille's rigorously devout, Irish Catholic family. Andrew was able to socialize through his work. His schedule was flexible, enabling him to determine the amount of time to devote to each of the stores he serviced; he would, if he wished, slacken his pace and cut corners where he needed in order to devote more or less time to such things as coffee breaks, relaxed lunches, etc.

Whenever Andrew did stretch out the social aspects of his life, he could report to Lucille that he had been occupied overtime with the chores of his work. Though he worked on a commission basis, Andrew had evolved a pattern of work which produced a rather regular income rate, and Lucille had no criteria by which to gauge the extent to which he had, indeed, involved himself with his work. Thus, should he not arrive at home for the regular dinner hour, Lucille had to accept Andrew's report of the reasons for his delays.

When he was at home, Andrew offered little relief to Lucille's burdens with the children. He found it offensive to change diapers or to feed the children, and did not comtemplate the possibility that he could be of any help in accomplishing the household chores. As a result, the couple had very little interaction, often passing whole days without engaging in anything that might be regarded as conversation.

The beginnings of this scenario could easily be taken directly from one of the current books that discuss the modern role of women. Lucille and Andrew each had adopted a well-defined, sex-linked role. The female enacts her role by caring for the children, managing the household, and arranging the family's social events. She has access to few other roles that she might enact. The male also fills his role relative to the family. He is the source of the financing of the family's affairs. He has certain other functions in the household, but interactions with the family members is not required by the role definition. Additionally, he has access to other roles outside the family. Psychologically and physically, owing mainly to the role relationship she had developed with Andrew, Lucille has little power to evade her mother-wife role. She is restricted from seeking a role as a worker. Financial considerations prevent her from adopting a role within the kinds of social groupings that support varied cultural and social activity.

If Hollingshead and Redlich (1958) had tried to place this family on a level of socioeconomic status, there would be a problem about assigning them. They would no doubt have been placed in Class IV, but it could be argued that they would better fit into Class III, since they already had begun to live out "the good life," having moved into a single family suburban dwelling. It could be said that Lucille was trapped in that house.

As they entered the ninth year of their marriage, Lucille began to spend less and less time in maintaining physical order in the home. Similarly, she began to become less and less concerned about regulating the day-to-day activity of the children. Gradually she engaged herself with her family and home only to the extent that she met minimal requirements of the children.

Additionally, Lucille accused Andrew of carrying on extramarital sexual activity. She questioned him about details of where he had spent his day and declared her suspicions that he was spending time with other women. As she became more and more disorganized and more and more accusatory, Andrew did, in fact, contrive to spend less and less time at home. He gradually diminished his sexual activity with Lucille, and would spend nights away from home with other women.

It is easy to hypothesize that Lucille had begun to disengage herself from her wife-mother role. There is no verifiable explanation of how this transition evolved. Some suggestions are readily available. In our society, the wife mother role has lost its place as the prime female role definition. Andrew might have been the kind of husband who would not easily validate Lucille's enactment of that role. In fact, his relaxed coming and going, coupled with his low level of communication, might reduce the positive strength of continuing to enact the role.

At the point where Andrew had begun to find Lucille's behavior troublesome, he might have thought about roles, role enactments, and validation. He might also have tried to shape his responses in terms of moral judgments. Lucille could have been classed as a poor housewife, or an unsatisfactory sex partner, or as a shrew. There was little reason to regard her as *ill*.

Had Andrew taken a standard college course in abnormal psychology, he might have thought about "mental illness." The terms *depression* or *paranoia* might have seemed applicable. Perhaps Andrew, like the wives in the study reported by Yarrow, Schwartz, Murphy, and Deasy (1955), would have hesitated to take Lucille into the mental health world until it had become impossible to interact with her. Additionally, Class IV persons are usually reluctant to adopt a mental health ideology toward deviant behavior (Dohrenwend & Chin-Shong, 1967; Hollingshead & Redlich, 1958). If Andrew's response to Lucille had been consonant with that of most of his social peers, he would not have hurried to consult a psychiatrist or psychologist.

On top of the problems created by the diminution of Lucille's involvement in her role as mother and wife, Andrew found it more and more difficult to deal with Lucille's outlandish verbalizations. She repeatedly declared that her body was malodorous. She said she understood why Andrew was not interested in sex so long as her body reeked as it did. The odor, she stated, was also permeating the house, and it seeped up from the dirty and spotted rugs that covered the floor.

During the period of this transition in Lucille's conduct, the frequency of visits to their parental families was cut to a minimum. Andrew did not discuss the changes with anyone in his family, and although Lucille's parents were vaguely aware that things had been changing, they did not explore matters in depth. When they became more aware of the changes, they hesitated to make a thorough inquiry, fearing that the young couple would regard their inquiries as intrusion.

Andrew finally turned to the family to express his concern about the bizarre character of Lucille's communications. He knew that "something was wrong," and felt that her parents could help by trying to convince Lucille that she should resume her previous role as a proper mother to the children.

When the family went to Lucille's home, they were appalled at the level of housekeeping, and were alarmed at the strange unconcern Lucille showed when they expressed their view that things were not right. Further, they found it hard to follow the allusions in Lucille's speech, and could not understand what had generated these strange beliefs. They did understand, having been exposed to TV, magazines, and movie accounts of disturbed and disturbing relationships, that a mental health professional should be consulted.

At this point, people observing Lucille could take any one of a variety of perspectives. One person might say she was bad, that her behavior offended universal rules. One could say that her behavior was linked to a disease. Another observer could say that she had been abandoned by God. Someone else might say that her body had been occupied by an evil force. As we already have noted, an educated reader of these paragraphs would be well prepared to think of *mental illness* in conjunction with Lucille's behavior. If, for no other reason, Lucille's family could consider "mental illness," for very practical reasons. The society has financed the organization of formal institutions under the jurisdiction of medical bureaucracies. Financing of services depends on having been diagnosed as ill. And, as indicated, the lay public has been exposed to a stream of information that establishes the claim that medical diagnosis and prescriptions will alter unwanted behaviors. Thus we have the basis of the family's early responses to Lucille's behavior, her "offense against some arrangement of face-to-face living—a domestic establishment, a work space, a semipublic organization such as a church or store, a public region such as a street or park" (Goffman, 1961, pp. 133-134). She has entered the prepatient phase of her "career" as a schizophrenic.

One of the family members had become acquainted socially with a clinical psychologist. The family called upon this psychologist, who arranged a meeting with Lucille. In this meeting, Lucille expressed her position rather directly. She declared that Andrew looked upon her as "nothing more than a whore." By this she meant that his only concern, within their relationship, was his sexual activity with her. She had accumulated a great amount of "evidence" for this view, including the fact that he actually left cash payments on the dresser top after each sexual encounter. Lucille was quite troubled about this development, but she was more troubled by the gradual diminution in the amount of money that Andrew had been leaving. She declared that after one of their most recent encounters, he had left only 15 cents, an event for which she had an explanation: After all, she reasoned, her sexual attentions could not be worth more because she gave off so putrid an odor.

She explained her neglect of her home partially in terms of her anger with her husband's view of her, and partially in terms of her general malaise and lack of energy. She showed little concern about the lack of available social verifiability of her views and declarations. She expressed no interest in resuming her previous life style.

She did, however, accede to the psychologist's view that she take some action that would assure that her children would receive a minimally adequate level of care. Playing on her expression of malaise and general feelings of disquiet about responsibility to her children, the psychologist obtained Lucille's consent to accompany him to the emergency room of the medical center, where it had been arranged to haver her meet with himself and a psychiatrist.

Even if the psychologist had been intellectually committed to an alternative, nonpsychiatric view of deviant conduct, he could not easily decide to advise the family to avoid entry into the mental health world. To do so would require willingness to confront the weight of the sociology of knowledge that guides the mental health ideology. Through allowing the legal action of civil commitment of those who show troublesome deviant conduct, the society lends its endorsement of the mental illness approach to these behaviors. Institutions to sequester and supervise these people are organized as hospitals. Physicians, and not other behavior-change experts, are charged with the supervision of these institutions. We are reminded here of how the author of Don Quixote constructed a professional role to return the hero to his senses. One would be tilting at windmills if one opposed referring Lucille to a psychiatrist, our current society's expert on madness.

During a short meeting with the psychiatrist, using the leads the psychologist was able to provide, Lucille reiterated her views of her current situation. The psychiatrist acted promptly. He could draw upon his professional training to conceptualize Lucille's stated belief that Andrew viewed her as a whore and her report that she could smell her own body and the odors arising from the rugs. These reports of happenings that could not receive social verification would be seen as the classic symptoms, *delusions* and *hallucinations* respectively. Such symptoms are taken by many practitioners as the hallmark of schizophrenia. The diagnosis, taking into account these symptoms as well as the content of the delusions, could be entered on her medical chart as 295.3, *Schizophrenia, Paranoid type* as defined by the Committee on Nomenclature and Statistics of the American Psychiatric Association in 1965.

A significant event had taken place. Whether or not Lucille "had" a disease before this point, she now had entered the class of events grouped under the term *schizophrenia*. She now *is* a schizophrenic, and people will respond to her in terms of this categorization. It must be made clear that the psychiatrist's belief system is a major aspect of this context. Psychiatrists do not do blood tests, take pulses, analyze urine samples, or study histological specimens. This one heard some words from Lucille *and* from Andrew and conferred a special form of the sick role on Lucille.

Because the psychiatrist's conferral of the sick role via psychiatric diagnosis evolved from an ambiguous and vague belief system, a critic of our work might assert that this example is not valid because the psychiatrist might have erred, that is, misdiagnosed the case.

The matter of correct diagnoses and misdiagnoses could occupy the remainder of this volume, and will be further discussed in later sections. It would be difficult to argue that Lucille's psychiatrist inappropriately applied classification 295.3x of the current proposed revision of the American Psychiatric Association's *Diagnostic and Statistical Manual*. The "essential feature" of paranoid schizophrenia "is a clinical picture dominated by the relative persistence of, or preoccupation with, persecutory or grandiose delusion or hallucinations. . . . In addition, there may be delusions of jealousy" [American Psychiatric Association Task Force on Nomenclature and Statistics, 1978, p. C:13]. The revised manual also includes a broad classification for Paranoid Disorder, under which there is specific reference to "Conjugal Paranoia" in which, "without any clear persecutory theme . . . a spouse will become convinced that his or her mate is unfaithful [p. D:1]." It seems, however, that believing that one is being treated as a whore would represent a "persecutory theme."

Whether or not "schizophrenia" is a correct or incorrect diagnosis in this case is irrelevant. What is important is that conduct was categorized as a medical diagnosis. The conferral of the diagnosis of schizophrenia was made, and society's response will be framed in these terms.

> Lucille was admitted immediately to the psychiatric ward of the medical center. After a period of observation, the staff conducted a diagnostic conference and decided to transfer Lucille to a state mental hospital. There she received treatment in the form of electroconvulsive therapy and neuroleptic medications. She remained sequestered for four months, engaging in regular diagnostic interviews with the hospital psychologist and psychiatrist. In addition, the ward personnel entered a running commentary into Lucille's hospital record, producing a chronicle of her verbalizations, social interactions, and general conduct.

An observer who came upon the scene described in the last paragraph, bringing no experience in assessing behavioral science concepts and a sound background in medical practice, would have little reason to differentiate the mode of treatment from that used to eradicate an unseen cancer. From another perspective, a person could see a woman being forced to adopt a degraded social role. It could be said that someone had judged Lucille's behavior to be bad, and that she was being exposed to rituals to convince her that her bad behavior was under the control of outside forces which could be removed by the powers available to medical scientists.

The perception of what is being done with Lucille depends upon the belief system the observer brings to the scene. One such system is integrated around the term *diagnosis*. The other broad view is integrated around the term *verdict*. The idea of diagnosis fits into the framework of etiology→symptoms→diagnosis→ treatment→prognosis→cure. The idea of verdict fits into the framework of rule→rule violation→verdict→reprimand→conduct control. Obviously, the two contrasting cognitive systems create vastly different worlds.

> After four months at the hospital, Lucille behaved in ways that convinced the decision-making staff that her disorder was an acute episode, and that she had recovered sufficiently to return to the community. Lucille returned to her family, and continued her treatment at the community mental health center. Treatment was a matter of continuing Lucille on daily doses of medication, and having her participate in weekly group therapy with other women.
> In the months that followed her hospitalization, Lucille managed to maintain the home and children at a level above minimum standards. She resumed a strained relationship with her husband, who carefully avoided extramarital activity and provided some solicitous attention to

Lucille's needs. Lucille's parents kept a special watch on the affairs of the couple, and their lives progressed reasonably satisfactorily. As the family settled into a routine, Andrew began to devote more and more attention to his job and found that he could not pass up his frequent opportunities to spend time with his women friends. As his time away from home began to expand, Lucille began to report a return of her body odors, and found it more and more difficult to sustain her attention to home duties. In a conference with the social worker at the community mental health center, Andrew reported the changes in Lucille's conduct. In personal interviews, Lucille readily revealed the return of some of her previously held beliefs and concerns. Lucille was readmitted to the psychiatric wing of the medical center, and was again given a round of electroconvulsive therapy and heavy doses of psychotropic medications. Lucille reported no outlandish beliefs and was discharged after an 18-day stay at the hospital. She returned home, where she resumed a position not generally unlike that which she had resumed after her first discharge.

On the whole, the family has managed to continue to function at a reasonably adequate level. Lucille took prescribed drugs on a regular basis for eight years. The children passed into adolescence. Andrew continued to provide the family with reasonable financial support. As he passed into middle age he spent more time completing minor home improvements, and less in outside social activity. On the whole, this family appears to be similar in form and content to its neighbors.

From a medical perspective, Lucille had been cured of her morbid condition. From another perspective, Andrew and the family had made adjustments in their reactions to Lucille, so that she did not experience negative validations of her role enactments. In turn, Lucille had no need to adopt unusual explanations of her self-perceived failures in social role enactments.

A RETURN TO THE INITIAL QUESTION

How did Lucille enter the category *schizophrenia*? Did she contract a disease that produced a thought disorder, which in turn produced outlandish conduct, which a highly educated professional could recognize as the symptoms *delusion* and *hallucination*? Did the treatments—electroconvulsive therapy and psychotropic drugs—cure the disease, thus eliminating the thought disorder and the conduct that was counted as symptomatic?

Perhaps Lucille did not "really" have a disease. Perhaps the process of her adopting unwanted behaviors was a process that could be interpreted as being *like* a disease; perhaps, that is, something caused the maladaptive behaviors, just as something is the efficient cause of bodily malfunction. These maladaptive behaviors, having been caused by as yet unidentified etiological variables, not necessarily physiological, could be eliminated by inducing convulsions, a process which in some mysterious way eliminates the cause of the perplexing conduct. Perhaps, one might say, the psychotropic drugs abolished the as yet unidentified causes of the symptoms. The end effect, however, was that the unwanted conduct was eliminated through treating Lucille *as if* she had a disease, so that the use of the disease model provided the key to arranging Lucille's life.

The disease hypothesis is not the only way of looking at Lucille's entry into the category *schizophrenia*. Before exploring an alternate view, we shall probe the enterprise of treating unwanted and perplexing conduct as symptoms of an actual or metaphoric disease.

2
Problems of the Disease Paradigm in Psychological Science

Dating from the appearance of Kraepelin's influential work (1896), the disease paradigm has enjoyed over 80 years of high status in the study of that portion of norm-violating behavior tenuously designated as *schizophrenia*.[1] Contemporary scholars publish elaborate reviews of the fruits of this prodigious scientific effort. (See, for example, Blatt & Wild, 1976; Magaro, Gripp, McDowell, & Miller, 1978; Salzinger, 1973; Snyder, 1974; Wynne, Cromwell, & Matthysse, 1978.) Reviewers have tried to make sense of the welter of claims and counterclaims, but their efforts have been futile. *Chaotic* is the most fitting term to describe the literature on schizophrenia.

THE PARADIGM AS A GUIDE TO PUZZLE SOLUTION

To help bring order out of chaos, we shall make use of the concept of paradigm as elaborated by Kuhn (1970). We begin with the general proposition: A successful scientific paradigm generates puzzles, the solutions to which elaborate the paradigm. When sticky puzzles remain unsolved, a summary of contradictory conclusions is enough to demonstrate the sterility of that paradigm. The schizophrenia model, as we shall elaborate, developed from the disease paradigm, and it has now attained a status in which contradictions are commonplace. Recent reviews of research point to the fruitlessness of hypotheses derived from the schizophrenia model. The following paragraphs illustrate the usual sequence of events—first the introduction of a hypothesis generated by the schizophrenia model, and then its rejection through the publication of contrary findings. (The illustrations do not exhaust the variety of hypotheses.)

1. The hypothesis that schizophrenia is a disorder that embodies a loosening of associations was first advanced by Bleuler (1911). It gained vitality in connection with stimulus-response associationist learning theory, which capitalized on the ancillary concept of "drive level." Schizophrenics were regarded as persons whose stimulus-response associations had been disrupted, because high drive (anxiety) raises the excitatory potential of responses that are irrelevant to the presented stimulus (Mednick, 1958). Investigators have followed a direct technology to study disrupted associative processes. The scientist first assumes that each word a person uses has been attached, through reinforcement processes, to other words or to inner representations of events. Each word, in fact, is attached to a hierarchy of terms, each having stronger or weaker associative bonding to the target word. Researchers have developed lists of words evoked by common words. Among people who use the same language, persons commonly report the same associations to a single word. These commonly reported words are considered "close associates," whereas less commonly reported terms are "remote associates." Thus, persons who are asked to respond immediately when given a term, are expected to report a "close associate." Reporting "irrelevant responses" would demonstrate the kinds of disrupted association believed to be symptomatic of schizophrenia.

Studies by Mednick and his associates (Higgins, Mednick, & Philip, 1965) supported the proposition that "high drive" disrupts the verbal response system of schizophrenics. However, Dokecki, Polidoro, and Cromwell (1965), also assessing the idiosyncratic character of word associations as a measure of associative dysfunction in schizophrenia, conclude that only their "poor premorbid" schizophrenic sample shows significant idiosyncracies. Moreover, Spence and Lair (1964) found that a schizophrenic sample and a control sample did not differ when they were compared on the basis of irrelevant intrusions into responses to lists of words on which there was a high probability of associative intrusion. That schizophrenics do not differ from general medical and surgical patients on two types of associate learning tasks has also been demonstrated by Gladis and Wishner (1962).

Likewise Fuller and Kates (1969) were unable to show that schizophrenics differed from normals in terms of their use of high or low frequency associates or in terms of giving personalized responses. A review of such straightforward studies led Schwartz (1978) to conclude, "The support that these data provide for the hypothesis that schizophrenics give rare word associations is illusory [p. 250]."

These conflicting results notwithstanding, the journals publish reports of various efforts to connect disrupted associative processes to the diagnosis of schizophrenia. Perhaps the assumed associational interference represents an inability to filter out inappropriate responses (Cohen & Cahmi, 1967; Rosenberg & Cohen, 1966). Perhaps the assumed deficit represents a general rise in the activation of all competing, related responses, whereupon less appropriate responses competitively replace desirable responses (Broen & Storms, 1966). Perhaps the schizophrenic gives the same incorrect associated responses that normals would give, but that they do it more frequently (Chapman, Chapman, & Miller, 1964). Then, when the mounting evidence provides little clarity, investigators may alter their formulations and hypothesize that associative disruption may not apply to "acute" or to "reactive schizophrenics," but that they do apply to "chronic" or "process" schizophrenics (Hirsch & DeWolfe, 1977; Kantorowitz & Cohen, 1977).

Other investigators have tried to introduce novel ancillary conceptualizations to resolve the puzzles related to the theory of disrupted associative processes among schizophrenics. Atkinson and Robinson (1961) concluded that schizophrenics performed less well than normals on an association task; but that erring schizophrenics who were punished eventually functioned more effectively than did schizophrenics who were not punished for errors, but instead were rewarded for success. They intended to show that the disruptions of the associative processes of schizophrenics were the effect of social censure. On the other hand, Goodstein, Guertin, and Blackburn (1961), using improvement in reaction time as a measure of performance, showed that schizophrenics and normal subjects performed more efficiently after having been told that their performances were something of a failure. Such studies, then, have continued to add contradiction upon contradiction to the major hypothesis which states that anomolous associative processes represent a distinctive feature of schizophrenia.

2. Another widely used hypothesis was explicated in 1957 by Rodnick and Garmezy. They held that schizophrenics are unusually sensitive to social censure, and that mild social censure improves task performance. As we noted above, Goodstein, et al. (1961) demonstrated improvement in performance following "failure" evaluations of previous performance. In addition, Cavanaugh, Cohen, and Lang (1960) reported that schizophrenics' performance on a reaction time task improves with verbal social censure, as well as with neutral information. A few years later, other investigators (Goldman, 1965; Spence, Goodstein, & Lair, 1965) presented contrasting findings: censure or praise has no particular differential effect on the performance levels of schizophrenic subjects. Farina, Holzberg, and Dies (1969) refined the censure hypothesis. They first exposed their schizophrenic subjects to a parental conflict situation, then had them work out an anagram task using "censure words." Nothing in the results supported the expectation of poorer schizophrenic performance in these conditions. Streiner (1969) followed a very complex design to test varied aspects of the censure-sensitivity hypothesis. Streiner's work supports these conceptions only if one adopts the unconventional practice of assigning credibility to differences that would be found by chance in 9 of 100 replications. Magaro (1972), using a highly complicated design that was based on questionably useful measures, concludes that "the present results found little support for the social censure hypothesis [p. 65]." The contradictory findings raised serious questions about the fruitfulness of the social censure hypothesis, and predictably, the hypothesis currently receives little attention.

3. Another circle of students of schizophrenia has searched for "prelogical" or "paleological" processes of thought in the schizophenic. The strongest support for this thesis has come from clinical investigators (Arieti, 1948; Kasanin, 1964; von Domarus, 1964) who have theorized that schizophrenics follow crude logical operations to derive conclusions. At least two studies (Gottesman & Chapman, 1960; Williams, 1964) show that schizophrenics cannot be differentiated from normals in their use of "paleological" thought processes. Williams (1964) gave fine attention to the numerous issues that must be considered in research on cognitive and logical processes. His study solidly refuted the claim that schizophrenic thought processes can be characterized as prelogical or paleological. Current journals give little space to further explorations of this hypothesis.

4. Another example of the contradiction of conclusions in schizophrenic research relates to the hypothesis that schizophrenics function inappropriately in their categorizing behavior. Goldstein and Scheerer (1941) firmly established the use of the vague hypothesis that schizophrenics are deficient in their ability to function "abstractly" while classifying; and that, instead, they tended to function "concretely." The hypothesis derives special vagueness from the footless character of the terms "abstract" and "concrete." Nevertheless, *abstraction-concreteness* versus *schizophrenia-normal* became the variables in a large number of doctoral dissertations. In an effort to extract value from these works, McGaughran and Moran (1957) proposed that rather than ascribing abstractness-concreteness to the classifying activity of schizophrenics, one might profitably view the classes used by schizophrenics as being *open-closed*, and *public-private*. McGaughran and Moran found that schizophrenic patients more commonly classified objects into sets better described as "open" and "private." A few years later, Sturm (1964) concluded that on his classification tasks "schizophrenics" do not differ from normals. One could conclude that schizophrenics and normals produce like quantities of "open-private," and any other type, classes.

Attention to the classifying behavior of schizophrenics has led investigators into other channels of research. Payne and his associates (see Payne & Caird, 1967; Payne, Hochberg & Hawks, 1970; Payne, Matussek & George, 1959) worked out a series of hypotheses, proceeding from the assumption that schizophrenics "overinclude" classifiable stimuli. These investigators used a procedure for defining overinclusion which had been designed by Payne (1962) and Payne and Friedlander (1962). With this defining measurement, Payne and his collaborators produced a string of studies to demonstrate the relationships between overinclusive classifying behavior and the diagnosis of schizophrenia. Kopfstein and Neale (1972) present data collected from all types of patients, using two of Paynes' overinclusion tests. They calculated correlations of these measures to 15 individual differences variables, producing 30 correlations, only 3 of which would not be found by chance in less than 5 of 100 repetitions of the study. The correlation of both tests to the *schizophrenia-nonschizophrenia* variable proved to be identical, $r = .12$. Consider further: Kopfstein and Neale report that the correlation between the two Payne-used tests is represented by a coefficient of .14, when calculated on data from schizophrenics. Further contradiction of the work led by Payne comes from Bromet and Harrow (1973). Following up earlier work (Harrow, Tucker, Himmelhoch, & Putnam, 1972), these investigators assert that Payne's measures of overinclusion "are based on what might be considered excessive behavioral output or overproductivity" (Bromet & Harrow, 1973, p. 345). Using an analogous measure, they find no differences between schizophrenic samples and other samples. Thus, to postulate that schizophrenics are marked by inappropriate classifying behavior has led to no better a definition of schizophrenia than have the hypotheses that schizophrenics are marked by loose associations, by a high sensitivity to social censure, or by paleological thought.

5. Just as new hypotheses related to the psychological functioning of schizophrenia are repeatedly proposed and repeatedly contradicted, so are hypotheses related to its supposedly biological character (see Kety, 1969; Luchins, 1976). Following the introduction of reserpine as a treatment for those labelled schizophrenic, one after another pharmacological product has been acclaimed for its ability to regulate the symptoms of the disease. Concurrently, one after another investigator reports a physiological state that relates to the assumed disease condition, whereupon other researchers fail to implicate the discovered condition.

Despite 25 years of liberal use of behavior-regulating chemical substances, there has been little success in modifying the conduct of those who have been labelled chronic schizophrenic (Paul, 1969; Tobias & MacDonald, 1974). Those validating reports which affirm the "antipsychotic" properties of the regulating drugs (Davis, 1965) can be matched by reports that contradict the reported successes of tranquilization (Little, 1958).

In a "special report on schizophrenia," Mosher and Feinsilver (1970) describe studies that could stand as a prototype for numerous chains of investigations that have proposed that biochemical variables play an etiological role in schizophrenia. Other investigators (Hoffer & Mahon, 1961; Hoffer & Osmond, 1963) studied the "Mauve Spot" in chromatographs of the urine of schizophrenic patients, a sign thought to be helpful in diagnosis. Yet other investigators (Ellman, Jones, & Rychert, 1968) report that with withdrawal of certain tranquilizing drugs, the "Mauve Spot" disappears. Thus, it would appear that the "Mauve Spot" is a metabolite of the drugs often given schizophrenic patients rather than a factor in the so-called illness. (Besides medications, hospital diets have been found to be responsible for other special characteristics found in blood and urine samples of hospitalized mental patients.)

More recently, biologically oriented schizophrenia investigators have advanced sophisticated theories concerning the metabolism of pharmacological substances involved in neurotransmission (Carlsson, 1978; Meltzer, 1969). The early claims that the finding of creatine phosphokinase (CPK) in the blood serum of schizophrenics implicated CPK in the etiology of schizophrenia were countered by confounding and contradictory explanations of the early propositions (Gosling, Kerry, Orme, & Owen, 1972; Warnock & Ellman, 1969). Similarly, the hypothesis that the neurotransmitter substance, dopamine, is implicated in the development of schizophrenic symptomatology (Carlsson, 1978; Wise, Baden, & Stein, 1974) has failed to gain support when other investigators (Nasrallah, Donnelly, Bigelow, Rivera-Calimlim, Rogol, Plotkin, Rauscher, Wyatt, & Gillin, 1977) have tried to relate dopamine to the behavior of people diagnosed as schizophrenic. The CPK and the dopamine theories of schizophrenia appear to be following on the heels of the "Mauve Spot."

HYPOTHESIS FAILURE AND MODEL TENACITY

Although it would appear that experimental hypotheses emerging from the schizophrenia model have a half-life of about five years, the notion of a disease entity called schizophrenia remains as a cornerstone of the mental health edifice (see Szasz, 1976). It is this model which most commonly serves to explain why a person like Lucille, the young woman in our introductory case study, would report her imagined smelling of her own putrefaction. It would be instructive to try to account for the persistent popularity of a model that produces little more than a steady stream of unstable hypotheses.

When a model produces a series of contradicted hypotheses, it behooves a scientist to consider the feasibility of employing a model generated by another paradigm. The scientific status of the schizophrenia model, a model constructed by applying the mechanistic disease model to norm-violating behavior, clearly points to the need for a paradigm revolution.

However, the model is tenaciously retained. Investigators reveal an implicit belief that an entity has been identified by having named a varied set of behaviors with the term *schizophrenia*. They continue their normal science activity as if hoping to refine techniques to measure dependent variables that will be reliably correlated with the independent variable, *presence or absence of schizophrenia*.

It is not difficult to identify the hopes that keep alive the interest in this traditional science activity. Since unwanted conduct has been cast into the disease model, researchers try to locate a *single, significant, salient,* and *crucial difference* between those who presumably harbor the disease schizophrenia and those who are free from the disease. In this way, the "cause" of the disease can be identified. Knowing the "cause" is prerequisite to a search for the "cure." The belief is widely held that once the "cure" is achieved, mankind will be relieved of the social and personal costs of the disease.

THE STATUS OF THE MECHANIST PARADIGM AND THE DISEASE MODELS

We have presented material to suggest that the everyday science of deviant conduct is being guided by a paradigm-in-crisis. The following characteristics define a paradigm-in-crisis (Kuhn, 1970): (1) A confusing multiplicity of variables is introduced into the paradigm. In the course of repeated failures in puzzle-solving, new concepts are offered with the hope that they will facilitate the scientific enterprise. (2) Failures in puzzle-solving are reflected in constantly recurring counterinstances. One puzzle-solver will embarrass the efforts of other scientists by showing that the puzzle was not properly solved. (3) The defenders of the crumbling paradigm offer a variety of conflicting articulations of data. Each counterinstance is the signal for the creation of more and more vague *ad hoc* modifications of the paradigm, so that the theory becomes gross and inaccurate. These features now characterize the paradigm that has been employed in that realm of deviant and perplexing behavior often designated by the term *schizophrenia*.

One might argue that the events known as "abnormal conduct" have never been represented by a science-guiding paradigm and that no crisis exists. Most historians of science would agree that *general psychology* is in a preparadigm state, awaiting the development of a paradigm within which the "normal science" of behavior would operate (Kuhn, 1970, p. 164). In general psychology, competing viewpoints are pressed upon students early in their careers. No single paradigm is assumed to have developed in a straight line out of the diligence and genius of such psychologists as Wundt, James, Woodworth, Skinner, Lewin, and Piaget. Textbooks are written to present the student with the multiplicity of problems that face the profession, rather than to describe a special paradigm within which puzzle-solving can be accomplished.

Unlike general psychology textbooks, textbooks of psychiatry and abnormal psychology make clear that an identifiable paradigm is employed. Deviant behavior is accounted for within the illness-diagnostic vocabulary, a direct application of the mechanistic paradigm that has successfully guided the biological study that forms the basis of the practice of medicine. The disease model, as we shall see, derives directly from mechanism.

Most current textbooks are organized around the diagnostic-classification approach. Although these texts may mention that some writers have cast doubt on the adequacy of answers given to the paradigm's puzzles, discussions are structured within the disease model, particularly in discussions of the psychoses. Textbooks intended for medical students (e.g., Coleman, 1972; Kolb, 1977; Millon & Millon, 1974) raise few questions, if any, about the appropriateness of the puzzle solutions. Syndromes are presented with a deceptive clarity, suggesting that diagnosis would be reliable. Investigators (Gottesman & Shields, 1972; Kety, Rosenthal, Wender, Shulsinger, and Jacobsen, 1975; Snyder, 1974) have earned international reknown through their phrasing and rephrasing of genetic and biochemical causal connections to madness. Furthermore, the abundance of literature about norm-violating behavior gives patent evidence of the effectiveness with which the disease model guides the world view of its users. And finally, the well-articulated criticisms of the illness-diagnostic model (Goffman, 1961; Krasner & Ullmann, 1965; Sarbin, 1967a, 1969b; Scheff, 1975; Szasz, 1961, 1970, 1976; Ullmann & Krasner, 1975) place in clear focus the fact that the model for the study of deviant behavior is derived from the disease model, a direct offshoot of the mechanistic paradigm.

An ever-expanding circle of criticism, incidentally, helps to validate our assertion that a crisis exists in the disease model in psychological science. The presuppositions (1) that the mechanistic disease model has been the basis of the illness-diagnostic model used to structure thought about deviant conduct, and (2) that the paradigm is in crisis, encourage efforts to hasten a needed paradigm revolution. To do this, however, requires some further analysis of the disease model and the mechanistic paradigm in the current traditional science of deviant behavior, particularly as it applies to behaviors that have been classified as schizophrenia.

MECHANISM AND FORMISM IN BEHAVIOR STUDY

The troubles of the medical model in abnormal psychology reflect a trouble that besets much of psychological theory. Traditional workers in abnormal psychology, despite their devotions to mechanistic models where it is preferable to specify all causes as *efficient* causes, have unwittingly slipped into the use of *formal* cause statements.

Psychology has earned its high scientific status by using the mechanistic models that successfully guided the natural sciences during the nineteenth century. The root metaphor of the machine (Pepper, 1942) is applied to building models to explain human behavior. Human beings as machines are denied the ability to specify and pursue their own unpredictable goals. Within this model, causes of behavior originate in forces outside the organism, and the specification of causes should be organized by systematic statements linking antecedent and consequent variables, that is, efficient causal statements. Furthermore, behavior scientists look for efficient causal relationships in order to avoid the temptation to follow naive introspective experience, which may suggest that people act because they "want to" do something—that the *final* goal is the cause of a person's behavior. Furthermore, *formal* causal statements are to be avoided as assiduously as are final causal statements. Little scientific value follows from being able to say, "He smokes a great deal because he is an oral character;" or "He hates minority groups because he is a 'Fascist.' " Mechanists have believed that if the behavior sciences are to emulate successfully the natural sciences, the highest priority must be given to the search for causal statements that line external, observable manipulations of environmental events to observable behaviors. One should be able to make statements of the form: "An extract from the cerebrospinal fluid of schizophrenics, but not of normals, resulted in convulsions when injected into rats." In such statements the result—convulsions in rats—is regarded as the inevitable consequent of the administration of the antecedent—the injection of cerebrospinal fluid. In such statements, the consequent can be treated as having a specific functional relationship to the antecedent variable. The formulation of efficient causal statements of the type illustrated is the objective of those who work from the root-metaphor of mechanism.

Within this ambience of a new, status-conscious science in 1911, Bleuler (1950) a German physician, undertook to explain negatively valued, deviant behavior within a mechanistic disease paradigm. His model promised to replace earlier, theologically tinted, explanations of disordered conduct. The history of Bleuler's model, and its gradual reversion to a moralistic formal causal framework can easily be traced.

Bleuler gave appropriate credit to Kraepelin (1896) for having introduced the possibility that dementia praecox represented a true disease concept. Bleuler substituted the term *schizophrenia* for the term *dementia praecox* and, of course, attempted to improve on Kraepelin's statement:

> We have to try to prove then: 1. That the various other diagnoses under which the Kraepelinian dementia praecox is usually classified do not represent any real concepts of disease. 2. That the concept of dementia praecox substitutes something far better, a genuine concept of disease for the clinical picture and we must prove at the same time that his concept corresponds to what we can actually observe [Bleuler, 1950, p. 272].

The definition of schizophrenia was to follow the prescribed disease paradigm. To describe a syndrome such as schizophrenia was not a simple matter of locating a single salient symptom, about which one would say no more. That was the paradigm that medicine once had followed and then abandoned. In the old paradigm, a medical diagnostician, for example, noted that there were disruptions of kidney function, any one of which identified the patient's illness as "Bright's Disease." To identify the *form* of the condition, however, did not truly describe a disease syndrome. A careful study could reveal a different efficient cause for each of the kidney dysfunction symptoms that identified Bright's Disease.

> The establishment of the dementia praecox concept has brought clarity and order into this confusion. The Kraepelinian dementia praecox is an actual disease concept. The concept includes symptoms which occur only and always in dementia praecox. Thereby the disease group is provided with concrete delimitations [Bleuler, 1950, p. 272]

Believing he had demonstrated that dementia praecox represented a true disease, Bleuler recognized some further implications. It now became a task for normal science, the everyday science practiced in laboratories all over the planet, to solve the puzzles arising from the necessity of stating efficient causes. He did not want to rush a proposal that the efficient cause was a determinate physicalistic entity. He offered guidelines for the activity of normal science, and in doing this he furthered the concept of a singular physiological or anatomic efficient cause of strange, unwanted behavior.

> It is not yet clear just what sort of entity the concept of dementia praecox actually represents. . . . It is true, we have been able to establish the diagnosis in schizophrenic-like cases of organic brain disorder; at least, we were able to see that there was something 'atypical' about the patients. Yet we cannot exclude the possibility that certain mild organic disturbances bring forth symptom complexes which we now designate as dementia praecox. As long as the real disease process is not known to us, we cannot exclude the possibility that various types of autointoxication or infections may lead to the same symptomatic picture [p. 279]. . . .
> Complete justice to all these factors can only be done by a concept of the disease which

assumes the presence of (anatomic or chemical) disturbances of the brain; the course of the cerebral disorder is chronic, for the most part, but there are also phases of acute forward thrusts or of standstill; the disturbance of the brain determines the primary symptoms (disconnection of association, perhaps the disposition to hallucinations and stereotypes, a portion of the manic and the depressive syndromes and of the states of clouded consciousness, etc.) [p. 463].

At a later point he draws up a picture of the syndrome of rheumatic arthritis, and in doing so he intersperses these cautious comments:

. . . Furthermore, it must be remembered that several schizophrenic thrusts are often preceded by an acute infectious disease. Therefore, we cannot reject the idea that schizophrenia may be an aftermath of certain infections . . . The course of schizophrenia is identical to the course of rheumatic arthritis. However, the only conclusion to be drawn from this parallel is that the possibility of an analogous infection exists [p. 470].

As cautious as he was about proposing a somatic efficient cause of the disease, Bleuler could not resist a metaphoric extension of his disease model. The mechanist paradigm had led to a huge payoff in investigations of somatic diseases, why should it not be extended to the study of "mental diseases?" Within this paradigm, the normal activity of science would puzzle out the relationships between variables. What precisely are the symptoms? How do symptoms interrelate? What are the causes of the disease?

Bleuler's specification of the primary symptom of the disorder immediately provided a promising variable to fit into further explanations of the disease. Pavlov (1927) wrote of conditioning; Freud (1901) had written of displacement, and Watson (1916) could offer associationist principles that had the potential to explain "loosened associations." To Pavlov, disordered associative activity was the result of disorders in cortical excitatory-inhibitory function. Inhibitions built up to the point where they "overflowed" to create sudden bursts of disordered associative processes (Pavlov, no date). Freud (1940) would see disrupted associations in psychosis as the effects of regression to primary process functioning. Latter-day Watsonian behaviorists viewed loosened associations as having their efficient cause in heightened drive states, which raise the excitatory potential of tangential responses, which then intrude upon the appropriate associated responses (Mednick, 1958).

The process of clarification could continue. What caused a buildup of cortical inhibition? Why does a person regress to primary process functioning? What is the origin of high-drive states?

As the paradigm is repeated over and over, and as it finds its way into textbooks, it assumes yet another characteristic of paradigms.

. . . Textbooks, however, being pedagogic vehicles for the perpetuation of normal science, have to be rewritten in whole or in part whenever the language, problem-structure, or standards of normal science change. In short, they have to be rewritten in the aftermath of each scientific revolution, and once rewritten, they inevitably disguise not only the role but the very existence of the revolutions that produced them. . . . For reasons that are both obvious and highly functional, science textbooks (and too many of the older histories of science) refer only to that part of the work of past scientists that can easily be viewed as contributions to the statement and solution of the texts' paradigm problems [Kuhn, 1970, p. 136f.].

We shall not overextend this discussion by writing a history of medical psychology. Suffice it to say that the repeated use of the schizophrenia model obliterated the distinction between the metaphoric use of the term *illness* and an immanent event. Scientists forget, as they tend to do with all paradigms, that their world view is shaped by the paradigms that have become a part of their discipline. Thus, a half-century after Bleuler wrote nearly 500 pages to advocate the applicability of the paradigm, Meehl (1962), in his presidential address to the American Psychological Association, asserted that it was time to call a thing by its proper name.

> Granting its initial vagueness as a construct, requiring to be filled in by neurophysiological research, I believe we should take seriously the old European notion of an "integrative neural defect" as the only direct phenotypic consequence produced by the genic mutation. This is an aberration in some parameter of single cell function, which may or may not be manifested in the functioning of more molar CNS systems, depending upon the organization of the mutual feedback controls and upon stochastic parameters of the reinforcement regime. This neural integrative defect, which I shall christen schizotaxia, is all that can properly be spoken of as inherited. The imposition of a social learning history upon schizotaxic individuals results in a personality organization which I shall call, following Rado, the schizotype [Meehl, 1962, pp. 829-830].

With this problem out of the way, the paradigm users can proceed to explain the development of the disease that is surely there. No question is raised about the ontological status of the disease—especially after the paradigm has been unequivocally propounded in textbooks of abnormal psychology and psychiatry. Meehl asserted that the disease "schizophrenia" is revealed by *cognitive slippage, interpersonal aversiveness, anhedonia,* and *ambivalence.* Meehl advances his search for the basis of the disorder (the etiology) because he (in 1962) was apparently convinced of something about which Bleuler (in 1911) was uncertain. Bleuler was obliged to argue about the nature of the "symptoms." Meehl was the heir to 50 years of normal behavioral science activity. The "symptoms" had become reified into symptoms. Meehl spoke as if he knew that his audience of psychologists—reared in the disease ambience—could recognize *symptoms;* and, further, that he could proceed to describe the development of a disease, "schizophrenia," arising from a neurological deficit, "schizotaxia."

This thorough acceptance of the disease model of schizophrenia exposed its metaphysical structuring to an assault from which mechanistic models must constantly be protected. When the model of the machine becomes reified to the point where people begin to draw its blueprints, then the machine begins to take on the characteristics of a Platonic form. The root metaphor of the paradigm becomes the metaphor of a *form.* Metaphysically, then, schizophrenia became a form, an idiograph.

As we have noted, the most desirable laws of causation in the mechanistic models are efficient causal laws. Mechanistic paradigms are best served by laws that state the necessary functional relationships between antecedent conditions and an assumed consequent. Formist paradigms regard statements of *correspondence* as adequate truth statements. When behavior scientists identified schizophrenia as a Platonic form, and declared that some persons behave as they do because they are exemplary of the form of a schizophrenic, they unwittingly rejected the mechanistic metaphor which has directed modern science.

When Bleuler asserted that "several schizophrenic thrusts are often preceded by an acute infectious disease [p. 470]," he was offering the kind of efficient causal statement that blended well with his mechanistic paradigm. He had tried to dissociate himself from the kind of formism (idiography) which had been a common causal explanation in older theories of deviant behavior (pp. 289-293). He wanted to avoid confusing his concept of schizophrenia with concepts of moral *degeneration*. He held that by previously diagnosing norm-violating behavior as degeneration, many cases were included whose symptoms were those of schizophrenia, and that no gain followed the confusing of the concepts. That is to say, diagnosticians should not assume that they had achieved a satisfactory explanation of the true disease, schizophrenia, when they were able to declare only that their schizophrenic patients behaved as they did because of their degenerated nature. This latter kind of idiographic causal explanation is as scientifically useless as saying that an object sways in the breeze because it is in the form of the object—in the nature of the object—to sway in breezes. Mechanistic science demands efficient causal explanations, and Bleuler implicitly recognized this demand when he tried to dissociate his concept from the older concept of degeneration, particularly, *moral degeneration*.

Bleuler's caution, however, was overruled by later users of the dementia praecox concept. Idiographic causal statements are too tempting to persons who are delegated to explain deviant conduct. After all, deviant behavior is readily assimilated to *bad* behavior. Needless to say, members of our society find it useful to locate every possible behavioral concept along an evaluative dimension (Osgood, Suci, & Tannenbaum, 1957; Rosenberg, Sedlak, 1972). If one can identify behavior as bad behavior, and if that bad behavior is a concomitant of schizophrenia, then the very *form* of schizophrenia must be evil. An idiographic causal statement becomes a simple matter. What is the cause of hallucination? The cause of hallucination is schizophrenia. What is the cause of assaultive behavior? Schizophrenia. What is the cause of unrestrained religiosity? Schizophrenia.

Where efficient cause is sought, one would be required to search out an antecedent condition that has a specific functional relationship to the observed event—hallucination or assaultiveness or religiosity. In the metaphysics of idiography, causal statements assert that a person hallucinates or is assaultive or is unrestrained in religious behavior, because the person has the *form* of *a* schizophrenic—a form which is idiographically represented in the knower's cognizing system. If we successfully "diagnose" a person—that is *identify* the person as a schizophrenic, the identity provides the causal nexus of the unacceptable (read: *bad* or *evil*) behavior. Although it provides scant scientific utility, this technique of adducing formal causes has traditionally paid off handsomely in terms of social and political outcomes—a proposition illustrated by the Soviet practice of hospitalizing dissident scientists and intellectuals whose public utterances were regarded as madness.

A recapitulation is in order here: (1) The normal science of abnormal psychology—the study of negatively valued, deviant behavior—has been guided by the disease model. (2) The model represents an application of the mechanistic world views, or paradigms, of the successful natural sciences of the latter half of the nineteenth century. (3) The most accepted causal explanations within the approved mechanistic paradigms are efficient causal explanations. (4) The model of disease, as employed in the study of abnormal behavior, is based on a paradigm-in-crisis. (5) Evidence of this crisis is obtained when one measures the state of the current science against the criteria of a paradigm-in-crisis. (6) In addition to meeting the criteria of a paradigm-in-crisis, we observe that the schizophrenia model, derived from the mechanistic disease model, now makes use of causal statements based on the metaphysics of idiography—a kind of causal statement which leading users of the model have explicitly rejected.

The discussion which follows will elaborate the argument. We shall show that the main body of current research into schizophrenia has the following characteristics: (1) Hypotheses regarding schizophrenia derive—sometimes unwittingly—from the disease paradigm. (2) The research and theory of the normal science of deviant behavior reflect the extreme confusions of variables introduced into the schizophrenia model. (3) Studies done within the model and within variations of the major model have produced little save counter-instances. (4) Hidden variables confuse and challenge the official solutions of the model's puzzles. (5) The continued use of the model often reflects a reliance on formal cause statements.

3
Analysis of Current Research

The normal science of deviant conduct, like other sciences, focuses upon: (1) *gathering facts* which the paradigm suggests are particularly revealing of the "true" state of affairs, (2) *clarifying facts* for comparisons with predictions emanating from the paradigm, and (3) *investigating facts* that resolve some of the ambiguities and recurrent puzzles that prevent sound articulation of the theory. Theoretical writing in normal science is directed toward these same foci, with the first activity less important. Theorizing is mainly concerned with clarifying facts and investigating facts so their articulations may be spelled out.

We have already reviewed how the mechanistic disease model operates as a background for the fact-gathering aspect of the study of normviolating behavior. We now turn to the task of clarifying and investigating facts. We shall demonstrate how the disease model guides these activities. As we proceed, we shall point to unquestionable signs of the failure of the mechanistic paradigm and its derivative, the disease model.

To clarify and investigate facts, we turned to published research on schizophrenia. We examined reports that appeared in the *Journal of Abnormal and Social Psychology* (*JASP*) during the years 1959-64, and in its successor, the *Journal of Abnormal Psychology (JAP)*, during the years 1965-78. A study was included for review if its authors selected (and used as a separate category) subjects who had been classified as schizophrenics. By this criterion, 374 studies were identified. The number of experiments on schizophrenia could readily be multiplied by looking into other journals. In our exposition, we frequently refer to sources outside of *JASP* and *JAP* when necessary to clarify a point. Our aim however, is not explicitly to evaluate the specific worth of the multitude of individual hypotheses that have emerged in the effort to understand schizophrenia. Nor do we seek primarily to analyze the specific shortcomings of the numerous research tactics and statistical analyses that have been used to study schizophrenia. Our aim is to identify the current crisis in the general use of the disease model applied to deviant behavior. To do this, we concentrate on a select group of studies—those that have appeared in a prestigious journal that represents the best efforts of the normal science of abnormal psychology as it is practiced in the United States.

The articles we have chosen fill 2,472 pages and represent 15.3 percent of the publication space of *JASP* and *JAP,* during the twenty years from 1959 through 1978. (References to *JAP* in succeeding chapters include *JASP.*) In 1959, articles that studied schizophrenics occupied 9.7 percent of the journal pages. In 1964, such articles filled 12.9 percent of the total space, while in 1970, articles on schizophrenia took 17 percent of the space. In the fifteenth year covered in this analysis, 1974, articles on schizophrenia occupied 20.7 percent of *JAP* and in 1978, 138 pages, or 20 percent of the journal's space. This prodigious effort reflects an avid, continuing interest in solving the problems of schizophrenia.

We selected the *Journal of Abnormal Psychology* because of its known high standards in accepting manuscripts. The average rejection rate for the years 1974-79, for example, was 80 percent. To be sure, *JAP* would not be the favorite outlet for scientists who work with biochemical and genetic hypotheses. For this reason, we shall review (in Chapter 7) selected studies in biochemistry and genetics that are frequently cited as support for the schizophrenia model.

FROM PARADIGM TO MODEL TO HYPOTHESIS

Kuhn states, "In a science, a paradigm is rarely an object for replication. Instead, like an accepted judicial decision in the common law, it is an object for further articulation and specification under new or more stringent conditions [Kuhn, 1970, p. 23]." Our usage speaks of the schizophrenia *model*, a variant of the disease model, emerging from the mechanistic *paradigm*, and of *hypotheses* emerging from the model. Within this terminology, the model is an object of replication. Other models can be drawn from the disease model, each playing out the mechanistic paradigm to get its greatest possible specificity and cohesion. The schizophrenia model, grounded in the disease model, makes the following claim: Norm-violating behavior is the effect of disturbed psychological and/or somatic processes associated with a disease, schizophrenia. Schizophrenia, like glomerulonephritis, tuberculosis, and mumps, is a model created by employing the mechanistic paradigm. The following paragraphs illustrate attempts to apply this model to those unwanted, norm-violating behaviors that prompt diagnosticians to employ "schizophrenia" as a diagnostic category.

Symptoms

Both the schizophrenia model and the nephritis model follow the most general disease model in that they instruct the scientist to work out a symptom picture. Among other things, glomerulonephritis presents the subjective symptom of pain in the lumbar region, along with the more objective signs of edema, fever, and blood cells in the urine. In the same manner, it is assumed that there are symptoms of schizophrenia. Even Bleuler (1911) expressed some uneasiness about the specification of these symptoms:

> As far as the true schizophrenic symptoms have been described up to the present, they are not *nova*, as for example, a hallucination or a paretic speech disturbance. They are distortions and exaggerations of the normal process.
>
> Thus, the individual symptom in itself is less important than its intensity and extensiveness, and above all, its relation to the psychological setting. In the multitude of psychological paths there are many that lead to the same goal. It is of no pathological significance if someone draws stereotyped 'doodles' on the paper in front of him during a boring lecture; but when the same 'doodles' are included in a serious letter, they may assure for themselves a diagnosis of schizophrenia [pp. 294-295].

Sixty-nine years later, one finds little support for the belief that the activities of behavior scientists have reduced uncertainty about symptoms in the disease of schizophrenia. Phillips, Broverman, and Zigler (1968), after extended research into the topic, summarize their report:

> This article in conjunction with the authors' earlier findings that psychiatric diagnosis is related to attained level of social competence (Phillips, Broverman, & Zigler, 1966; Zigler & Phillips, 1961) indicates that psychiatric diagnosis is essentially a complex indicator of at least three general dimensions of human behavior, namely, dominant mode of expression, social role, and general competence. It should be noted that the findings of this and earlier studies have indicated that while these three general factors all share a certain amount of interrelationship, they are each somewhat independent of each other. In the final analysis, the fact that each plays a role in determining diagnosis may be of less importance than the way in which these three variables independently or in combination are related to such important aspects of psychopathology as etiology, prognosis, and the efficacy of particular forms of treatment. Approaching these basic issues in psychopathology in terms of such style variables would appear to be a far more promising avenue for investigation than the more general practice of exploring the correlates of Kraepelinian diagnosis [p. 312].

Nonetheless, the entrenched model of schizophrenia parallels the disease model in that it provides the basis for exploring the characteristic symptoms of the disorder. Phillips, Broverman, and Zigler (1968) speak of the subjective symptoms—"Feels going crazy," "Feels perverted"—as well as the objective symptoms—"rape," "robbery"—which are listed in the records of hospitalized patients [p. 308]. As they make this distinction, they allude to problems suggested in Bleuler's reference to symptoms as "distortions and exaggerations of the normal process." The diagnostician must rely heavily on subjective assessments of behavior in order to determine that a particular behavior is a symptom of a disease. The reliance on the diagnostician's judgment is particularly troublesome in applications of the schizophrenia version of the disease model.

A consideration of the work of the various committees on nomenclature which have worked under the auspices of the American Psychiatric Association (1968,

1978) suggests how the diagnostician's subjectivity defines the symptoms that will place a person into a disease category. Ten years of experience with the American Psychiatric Association's (1968) Diagnostic and Statistical Manual (DSM-II) has shown the need for a replacement, DSM-III (American Psychiatric Association, 1978). DSM-III is designed "to provide clear descriptions of diagnostic categories [p. vii]." If clarity will be achieved it will not be because DSM-III succeeds in eliminating the diagnostician's subjective assessments. To identify a "disturbance in language and communication [p. C:2]," a diagnostician must judge, for example, whether or not the person makes "statements which are incomprehensible [p. C:2]," or whether or not "the speech is adequate in amount but conveys little information because it is vague, overabstract or overconcrete, repetitive, or stereotyped [p. C:2]." It stands that the diagnostician's skill in making these kinds of judgments will determine the scientific success of the reclarification of the symptoms of schizophrenic disorders.

Causes

It is important to emphasize the point that a classic mechanistic disease model offers the possibility of seeking out efficient causes. Sometimes one of the symptoms of a disease is suggested as the efficient cause. Finding a rampant streptococcus in the urine of a patient could encourage an investigator to identify this organism as the "cause" of glomerulonephritis. In schizophrenia, *disturbed association* has been declared the sufficient cause of the disease (Sommer, Witney, & Osmond, 1962). (Parenthetically, Bleuler had listed disturbed association as the primary *symptom* of the disease.)

To have settled on one cause as the efficient cause is not the final step. There are other parts to the puzzle. Though the streptococcus bacillus can be looked upon as the cause of nephritis, the question of what caused the bacillus to become rampant remains. Each of us might be exposed to an invasion by the same streptococcus, but each does not develop a case of nephritis. The disease model alerts investigators to other aspects of the disease process, for example, the chemical or mechanical condition of the target organ, an aspect that might yield a more significant efficient cause of symptoms. In schizophrenia, perhaps, one might eventually find the efficient cause of the primary symptoms to be a bacillus. After all, do not microorganisms cause the disturbed associations in general paresis? And even if a bacillus has not been found to be the efficient cause of the schizophrenia disease, intricate mysteries of brain and neurological chemistries are yet to be explored. The hope of locating a causal chemical agent has spurred, in recent years, the study of the relationships of schizophrenic symptoms and the neurochemistry of creatine phosphokinase (Meltzer, 1973) and dopamine (Carlsson, 1978; Wise & Stein, 1973), as well as other substances.

It should be emphasized that in the search for causes, the paradigm acts as a guide for the traditional science. It need not specify that any one efficient cause is more "scientific" than another. Other efficient causes, such as anxiety (Higgins

& Mednick, 1963), or schizophrenic mothers (Mitchell, 1968), or troublesome unconscious sexual impulses (Arey, 1960)—in fact, any number of early experiences (see Schofield & Balian, 1959), can be studied as causes of schizophrenia within the hypothesis-guiding mechanistic paradigm.

During recent years, psychologists have reported numerous studies of possible information-processing anomalies as a part of the schizophrenic process. Neufeld (1977), for example, "investigated whether schizophrenics would display central processing stage deficit on a reaction time task with complex stimuli [p. 60]." Subjects were required to read a statement that described a visual display. The visual display might contain four red dots. The statement might say, "It isn't true that the dots are red." The subjects were to determine if the statement was true or false, and then to report their decisions. The experimenter had calculated the number of comparisons that would be needed to make the determination. The number of comparisons was used as an index of task complexity. The data yielded evidence that, though schizophrenics required more time to make decisions, they arrived at decisions as valid as those of the comparison groups. Furthermore, the schizophrenics showed the same relative difficulties with the complex tasks as did the comparison groups. Thus, though information-processing deficit eventually might be found to be a symptom of schizophrenia, Neufeld, as well as other investigators (Russell & Beekhuis, 1976; Russell & Knight, 1977; Schneider, 1976) was not able to establish this deficit as a cause of the problematic behaviors of so-called schizophrenics.

By implication, selective *reinforcement* might be taken to be a cause of schizophrenic symptoms. For example, one group of investigators (Ullman, Forsman, Kenney, McInnis, Unikel, & Zeisset, 1965) undertook to eliminate "sick talk." People who engage in sick talk report bizarre ideation, a behavior that would be taken as a symptom of schizophrenia. Ullmann's group reported that people reinforced for healthy talk decreased the percentage of sick talk; whereas those reinforced for sick talk showed a tendency to increase their percentage of sick talk. One might infer that similar reinforcement could account for the person's original acquisition of the conduct of reporting bizarre ideation. A theorist following this inference chain would add reinforcement to the list of proposed efficient causes of the putative symptoms of schizophrenia.

Intensity

The mechanistic disease model specifies other aspects for the propositions it generates. Diseases can be graded along a continuum of intensity. The disease can be acute, or it can be chronic. These concepts, too, have been employed for the schizophrenia model.

In our sample of studies, seven investigations differentiated acute schizophrenics from chronic schizophrenics on the basis of their performances on the various experimental instruments. (See, for example, Cegalis, Leen, & Solomon, 1977; Draguns, 1963.) Other investigators reflected their use of the "intensity" feature of the disease paradigm by indicating that they had studied *only* chronic schizophrenics. The purpose of this declaration appears to have been to notify readers that the subjects were persons in an advanced state of the disease. Thirty other researchers used one or another tactic to order the level of severity of the schizophrenics used as experimental subjects. (See, for example, Blumenthal, Meltzoff, & Rosenberg, 1965; Heilbrun & Heilbrun, 1977; Weinberger & Cermack, 1973.) Usually the grading is a simple matter of time in hospital, or time since first hospitalization. In 28 of the reviewed studies, the schizophrenic subjects were differentiated along a continuum labelled *process-reactive*, with the strong implication that the process schizophrenic was a long-term, "sicker" person. (See, for example, Davis & DeWolfe, 1971; Hirsch & DeWolfe, 1977; Meichenbaum, 1966.) Forty-eight studies of schizophrenia reported in *JAP* from 1959 through 1978 have used the good-premorbid versus bad-premorbid dimension to imply the level of illness. (See, for example, Farina & Holzberg, 1967, 1968; Fenz & Velner, 1970; Ritzler, 1977; Zigler & Levine, 1973.) The distinction between these two variables remains obscure. Some investigators report that they used the Ullmann-Giovannoni scales (Ullmann & Giovannoni, 1964) to delineate the process-reactive continuum. Most investigators (see Cancro & Sugarman, 1969; Knight, Sherer, & Shapiro, 1977) indicate that they used the Phillips (1953) scale to differentiate process from reactive schizophrenics. At any rate the process-reactive and the good-premorbid—poor-premorbid dimensions have been used in a fashion that indicates that researchers have been taking into account the "severity of illness" concept in the schizophrenia model.

Complications

A fourth characteristic of a disease is that it can produce complications. During serious glomerulonephritis, when salt exchanges are not properly taking place, hypertension can develop. Similarly, one should expect complications in the application of traditional science categories to the schizophrenia model. In clinical lore, "intellectual deterioration" is a concomitant of schizophrenia. Several studies, in fact, do look into the question of the nature of this particular "side effect" (Lane & Albee, 1963; Haywood & Moelis, 1963; Moran, Gorham, & Holtzman, 1960). A particularly interesting twist is given to this matter by Hamlin and Ward (1973), who raise the possibility that the drop in intellectual functioning skill induces the adoption of compensating symptoms. The schizophrenic symptoms, then, would be the complications of the intelligence loss.

Prognosis

The total enterprise of applying a disease model to deviant conduct is brought to focus in predicting the course of the disease. The cognitive activity of scientists, like all cognitive activity, leads to the anticipation of events. The fruits of their work would allow them to foretell the course of the condition—with or without intervention. In our society the scientist earns high esteem by accurately describing the outcomes of specific efforts to alter the progress of an unwanted condition.

Within this context, delineation of *prognosis* becomes the key function of applications of the disease model to that unusual behavior that earns an actor the diagnosis of schizophrenia. The major object of it all is to *cure*, that is, to prescribe an intervention that will consistently allow the prediction of a positively valued outcome. It follows, then, that investigators report numerous studies in which prognosis is considered.

In the central samples of studies here under consideration, there are relatively few studies of prognosis. Treatment and its relationship to the prognosis of schizophrenia seem to gain little attention from psychological investigators. This sampling of 374 schizophrenia studies contained only four studies (Goldstein, Acker, Crockett, & Riddle, 1966; Rosen, Freedman, Margolis, Rudorfer, & Paley, 1972; Saretsky, 1966; and Vestre, 1961) of the therapeutic effects of drugs. In one study, DeMille and Licht (1966) considered the effects that previous lobotomy treatment had upon the problem-solving ability of long-term schizophrenics. About 11 percent of the sample of 374 studies were investigations of variables involved directly in changing the continuing behaviors of schizophrenic subjects. Several investigators (Lerner, 1963; Lerner & Fairweather, 1963; Spohn & Wolk, 1963) reported techniques by which schizophrenics can be led out of their social withdrawal. Other investigators (see, for example, King, Armitage, & Tilton, 1960; Sherman, 1965; Ullman, Krasner, & Collins, 1961) reported the use of behavior modification technology to change the behavior of schizophrenics.

Observations of the trend in *JAP* would lead one to conclude that there has been a diminution of investigations of prognostic and treatment issues. About 35 of the 205 schizophrenia studies (18 percent) that appeared during the years 1959-69 attempt to delimit variables associated with change of the course of schizophrenia. During the years 1970-74, five of 94 studies (5 percent) are aimed at clarifying the means of changing the general course of the behavior of schizophrenics. During the years 1975-79, only one (Chapman, Cameron, Cocke, & Pritchett, 1975) of the 73 relevant research reports was addressed to the topic of the changes of the behavior of schizophrenics.

One might offer a variety of explanations for the decline in publication of treatment and prognosis articles in this journal. Perhaps such articles are being published in other journals, where editors are more receptive to applications of psychological principles. Perhaps the decline in the hopes centered around the use of psychoanalytic or other psychotherapeutic techniques has pervaded the entire psychiatric field so that there has been a general decline in studies of nonmedical approaches to the problems of prognosis in schizophrenia. Perhaps a general change in psychological science is reflected here. Psychologists (Jenkins, 1974; Sampson, 1977; Sarbin, 1977) have been explicit about the shortcomings of the mechanistic metaphors that have been the guide to large segments of the traditional science of psychology, and have recommended consideration of the utility of contextualist metaphors. This awareness would promote some disenchantment with the conceptions that would allow one to speak of specific and absolute causes of a disease. Diagnostic practice (see Blum, 1978; DePue & Woodburn, 1975) might, for example, change, so that a particular segment of conduct would no longer be regarded as a symptom of a disease in an altered paradigm. It would follow that, as a contextualist perspective spreads through psychology, fewer propositions would be advanced to identify *specific* causes of changes in specific behaviors.

The psychiatric journals, on the other hand, contain ample evidence of the continued effort to alter the schizophrenic condition through the administration of drugs. Such effort is complicated, however, by the necessity of making a troublesome assumptive leap. The treatment requires the prescription of drugs. The expected outcomes, on the other hand, are not chemical variables. Results are measured by observing changes in the behavior of those who have been diagnosed. Thus the specifics of the prognosis do not readily fit into the kinds of formulations that a disease model would ordinarily follow. Diagnosticians are left with a special judgmental task: They must make a decision about the extent to which the unwanted behavior has diminished. Thus issues of prognosis hinge on what shall be viewed as the symptoms of the disease. Until the matter of symptoms is resolved, followers of the disease model will remain unsettled in specifying the prognosis of schizophrenia.

Summary

The disease paradigm has guided over sixty years of research into deviant behavior sometimes diagnosed "schizophrenia." The part played by the disease paradigm is obvious in the work covered by this review. First, "symptoms" have been specified. Second, efficient causes have been investigated. Third, the schizophrenia model has allowed efforts to define gradations along a dimension from *intense* to *mild*. Fourth, complications have been proposed and studied. And, finally, the model has provoked attempts to define the prognosis of the disease, with or without appropriate treatments.

MAJOR PROBLEMS IN TESTING HYPOTHESES DEVELOPED WITHIN THE MODEL

The Ontological Status of the Independent Variable—Schizophrenia

Whatever the experimental design of the studies, schizophrenia-nonschizophrenia constantly appears as the independent variable to be related to a (questionably reliable and frequently esoteric) dependent variable. This almost universal feature would require little notice if the disease model were an entirely appropriate framework for making hypotheses relative to unwanted behavior. Fact gathering that uncovers the correlates of the presence or absence of clear and definable mental disease, schizophrenia, would eventually elaborate the model and then theoretical articulation could advance. Investigators would eventually demonstrate the relationship between the causal anomalous functions, symptoms, and prognosis.

However, the unreliability of psychiatric diagnoses (see for example, Mehlman, 1952; Spitzer & Fleiss, 1974; Zigler & Phillips, 1961) and the expediency with which they are applied (Blum, 1978; Miller & Schwartz, 1966; Wenger & Fletcher, 1969) are now a matter of record. One older study may be used as an illustration (Schmidt & Fonda, 1956). Board certified psychiatrists agreed with the tentative diagnoses made by resident psychiatrists in 84 percent of the cases when the board diagnostic categories—organic disorders, psychotic disorders, and characterological disorders—were used. Within the psychotic disorders, which include involutional types, affective types, and schizophrenic types, the residents agreed with the staff psychiatrists in only 51 percent of the cases that were finally diagnosed as schizophrenic. These authors suggested that the low degree of agreement could be attributed to the fact that the residents were inadequately trained, and that better trained personnel would likely show greater inter-rater agreement. These results, however, are consistent with previous studies (Hunt, Wittson, & Hunt, 1953) and do little to alter the conclusion that there is reasonable agreement on very broad classifications, but that classification within these broad categories reflect high levels of diagnostician idiosyncracy. In fact, a current analysis by Spitzer and Fleiss (1974), applying corrections for the probability that diagnosticians would agree simply by chance, suggests that even results like those of Schmidt and Fonda (1956) had been inflated.

Whether or not training improves diagnostic skill, as Schmidt and Fonda suggest, is a moot question after extensive comparisons of diagnostic practices in the United States and the United Kingdom (Professional Staff of the US-UK Cross-National Project, 1974). A part of the project was given over to comparing the diagnoses made by psychiatrists in New York to those made by specially trained project diagnosticians. Similar comparisons were made between the project psychiatrists' diagnoses and those of a sample of London psychiatrists. By comparison, New York psychiatrists assign the schizophrenia diagnosis at an astonishing rate. The project staff is aware of the problems of unreliability of diagnosis, and is also aware of the professional embarrassment it creates. "Unreliability arising from random variations in the use of diagnoses is a different issue and, though possibly it is the issue that most stigmatizes diagnosis, it is not the most crucial consideration for achieving international consensus on diagnosis [p. 96]." The issues again, according to the project writers, will approach resolution when diagnosticians have been taught reliable techniques of gathering, storing, and interpreting information. The project staff might also have considered the role of ideological differences between psychiatrists working in different social structures.

A study by Fitzgibbons and Shearn (1972) is pertinent to our argument. They investigated the beliefs of mental health professionals about phenomenology, etiology, and prognosis in schizophrenia, using a factor analytic method. The disease model was strongly reflected in the respondents' thinking about schizophrenia. Eight factors emerged from the patterns of responses, among them *interpersonal etiology, Bleulerian phenomenology,* and *disease concept in schizophrenia.* Of special interest is the relationship between professional identification and endorsement of specific factors. For example, psychiatrists tend to endorse *disease concept in schizophrenia* and to reject *interpersonal etiology.* Psychologists and social workers tend to endorse the latter and reject the former. The work setting was also a significant variable. For example, professionals in private hospitals tend to endorse Bleulerian phenomenology less often than professionals in state hospitals or in community mental health clinics. The study warrants the inference that much of the disagreement (confusion?) in theories of schizophrenia is traceable to variables that have little to do with the conduct of the target person, such as professional identification and the work setting of the diagnostician.

The problems, of course, stem from a constant lack of agreement concerning which, and what levels of, residual deviances should earn a person the diagnosis. After 70 years of medicine's acceptance of the concept that schizophrenia is a disease, psychiatrists—those who eventually define the dimension *schizophrenia* which serves as the independent variable in the kinds of studies here considered—remain troubled about the characteristics of the disorder. Ritzler and Smith (1976)

> . . . call attention to the careless manner in which the paranoid diagnosis is designated and reported in contemporary research in schizophrenia. M. Strauss (1973) has demonstrated the confusion created when a dimension of the schizophrenia diagnosis (i.e., chronicity) is not applied with a standard, carefully specified definition. . . .
>
> Neglecting operationally defined diagnostic criteria is poor research practice, particularly in the light of reports like that of Abrams et al. (1974) where careful rediagnosis using standard operational criteria left only two of 41 previously diagnosed paranoid schizophrenics eligible for inclusion in a research design [pp. 209-210].

Other investigators have recognized the paradox that Ritzler and Smith so clearly identify. "It is ironic that most authors carefully detail their hypotheses, research designs, and statistical analyses while leaving their diagnoses without adequate specification [p. 215]."

Spitzer, Endicott, and Robins (1978) have carried on the most intensive program toward correcting the situation. Yet their "operational criteria" remain infused with allusions to subjective moral judgments, thereby allowing the continued contributions of the individual diagnostician who has one or another view on moral matters. They suggest as one criteria for schizophrenia, "(3) Somatic, grandiose, religious, nihilistic or other delusions without persecutory or jealous content, lasting at least one week [p. 7]." Would an environmentalist who attends rallies to block the building of nuclear plants and who frequently writes articles predicting catastrophe, be regarded as showing nihilistic delusions? Then consider the subjectivity problems associated with making decisions about the following criteria "(8) Definite instances of marked formal thought disorder (as defined in this manual) accompanied by either blunted or inappropriate affect, delusions or hallucinations of any type, or grossly disorganized behavior [p. 7]." Even if one were willing to ignore the immense latitude allowable in determining the *markedness* of the thought disorder, the *inappropriateness* of the affect, and the *grossness* of the disorganization, one could discount the utility of these criteria by raising questions about the ontological status of terms such as *thought disorder, affect,* and *hallucination* (Sarbin & Juhasz, 1978).

The work of J. Strauss (1973, 1975) and his collaborators (Bartko, Strauss, & Carpenter, 1974) further illustrates the concerns, problems, and proposed solutions to matters of reliability in diagnosing schizophrenia. Their analyses are extensive and thought-provoking. Yet Strauss (1975) must recognize that he describes the work of a moral philosopher or an industrial efficiency expert when he describes his system of noting, evaluating, and recording the "quality of the personal relationships [p. 1194]" and "level of work function [p. 1195]" of a candidate for the schizophrenic label. Strauss's system, like that of Spitzer et al., holds little promise of removing the diagnostician's social perception structure and ideological biases from the process of assigning a person to the schizophrenia category.

As the evidence mounts, one becomes more and more aware of the workings of these biases. Earlier studies (Dohrenwend & Dohrenwend, 1967; Scheff, 1964; Temerlin, 1968) have pointed to the vagaries of the use of the label *schizophrenia.* In fact, Scheff's (1964) work raises questions about the basic ethical practices that enter psychiatric diagnosis as it is practiced in courts of law where commitments to hospitals take place. The practices of segregating, incarcerating, and depersonalizing certain members of the collectivity—the schizophrenics—leads to the inference that sociopolitical purposes, rather than medical purposes, provide the backdrop for the diagnosis of schizophrenia. Further, one may suggest that such social, political purposes are more easily met if the defining characteristics of "schizophrenia" are kept fluid.

As the analysis of the diagnostic process continues, one finds more direct references to bias in the clinician's practice of the mental health professions. Sarbin, Taft, and Bailey (1960) pointed out that the clinician's cognizing processes could be analyzed in the same way as are the cognitive processes of any judge. It follows, then, that the clinician's inferences would depend, in large part, upon the basic postulate system that guides the individual diagnostician. Clinicians who hold professional status through claiming the ability to find illness will, not unexpectedly, find illness.

Langer and Abelson (1974) show how completely these postulate systems can be evoked. They presented a videotaped "interview" to groups of persons trained to work with problems of deviant behavior. The groups were differentiated according to the theoretical commitments they had made during professional preparation. One group was composed of "behavior therapy" advocates, while two other groups had made commitments to "more traditional, analytic or psychodynamic approaches to behavior.'' The investigators informed some subjects that they were observing a job applicant and informed other subjects that they were observing a patient. As expected, theoretical commitments represented a major source of differential judgment. Traditional clinicians made very strong negative assessments of the interviewee as "patient." The psychoanalytically oriented clinicians readily used terms like "tight, defensive person," . . conflict over homosexuality," and "frightened of his own aggressive impulses [p. 8]" Even though these traditional psychodiagnosticians were operating in a situation where they had little power over the person, and where their livelihood and professional reputations were not endangered in any way, they could find "illness" where the behaviorally oriented clinicians would hesitate to do so. When a mental health practitioner operates in a hospital situation in which the incoming person has already undergone the extensive process of degradation before being assigned to the hospital's admissions ward, the circumstances are far more conducive to evoking the "illness bias" than was the bland atmosphere of the research room. And indeed, this expectation is confirmed by Rosenhan's (1973) far-reaching report of the ease with which the label of schizophrenic is attached to a person—though that person be "normal"—once the person enters the mental health system.

One last study illustrates the ways in which biases enter the diagnostic process to determine who shall become one of the schizophrenics in the samples used to investigate the condition. Blum (1978) analyzed a sample of the 2,134 male psychiatric patients who had been discharged from one hospital during 1954, 1964, and 1974. He made an attempt to equalize the number of persons in each year's sample. He then catalogued information on 13 variables, such as diagnosis, age, race, symptoms, life events, and so forth. He showed that, between 1954 and 1974, there were dramatic changes in the relative proportions of patients in the eight diagnostic groups into which the patients were fit. These were largely changes in the numbers of patients diagnosed as having affective disorders, those diagnosed as neurotic, and those diagnosed as schizophrenic. For example, while the proportion of patients in the neurotic category dropped from 25 percent to 4.5 percent, the number of persons diagnosed as having affective disorders rose from 7 percent to 22 percent. At the same time, the percentage of schizophrenic patients increased from 24 percent to 32 percent.

Blum then analyzed the patient age pattern, the life events information, and the symptom information in order to assess the possibility that these variables would account for the changes in diagnostic trends. Blum's conclusions are strong:

Inasmuch as one would expect symptoms to predict diagnosis accurately, it was surprising that changes in patients' primary symptoms could account for only about one-half of the trend in the three largest diagnostic groups: schizophrenia, affective disorders, and neurosis. In brief, the diagnostic pattern seems to be changing in ways not fully justified by the symptoms the patients are presenting; it would seem that other factors are impinging on the clinician's diagnostic decisions. Comparisons of primary symptoms versus total symptoms, furthermore, strongly suggested that different aspects of a patient's symptom cluster become more important at different historical times [p. 1028].

Blum's writing is also valuable for its speculations about the ideologies of diagnosticians as they relate to the findings he reported. The study's data, relative to this essay, highlights the ephemeral character of the independent variable *schizophrenia-nonschizophrenia* used in the multitude of completed studies. A researcher in 1974, taking an experimental sample of persons with a hospital diagnosis of schizophrenia, would have in the sample roughly one person of every three who would not have been included in a similar sample chosen in 1954. In other words a schizophrenic in 1974 would have been something else in 1954.

The state of the independent variable. Considering the state of affairs relative to diagnosis, what can be said about research into schizophrenia, where the independent variable—presence or absence of schizophrenia—is defined by hospital diagnosis? Researchers and clinicians must agree that psychiatric diagnosis is unreliable. The evidence has accumulated to convince the scientist that diagnostic practices are ridden with moral and professional bias. Yet, of the 374 reports in our review, only 42 made any effort to define schizophrenia by means other than the fallible declaration of hospital or clinic staff practitioners.

The tacit acceptance of the validity of the schizophrenia model is blandly echoed in many of the reports' discussions of subject selection. Over and over we are assured that the diagnosis was established by "two psychiatrists," "one psychiatrist and one psychologist," "the attending psychiatrists," etc. Many investigators disclose their convictions when they assure their readers that their experimental subjects were definitively "ill" persons—"chronic schizophrenics." Weidenfeller and Zimny (1962) used 18 subjects who "possess" one of the major types of schizophrenic illness. Lane and Singer (1959) report that their subjects all showed a "clear cut break with reality," therefore unquestionably properly categorizing them as schizophrenics. This assurance is small comfort when one troubles to question the ontological base of the concept "reality contact" (Sarbin, 1967a). The casual and uncritical acceptance of the hospital diagnosis reveals the extent of the professional's avoidance of concern with the ontology of the schizophrenia model. One needs to be reminded that the diagnostic personnel categorized their patient on the basis of hearsay and/or observations of a small sample of behaviors, any set of which would have allowed them to infer that the person was "suffering from schizophrenia."

Specification of the relationship of the independent variable to the dependent variables. Overlooking the impropriety of choosing a poorly founded variable, we must consider the intent of a hypothesis that specifies schizophrenia as the independent variable. Does schizophrenia causally precede the dependent variable, for example, the biochemical abnormality? Or, is it "associated with" the dependent variable? Or perhaps the dependent variable is to be placed on the "causal" side of the equation. It is not unreasonable to expect a researcher to express a conceptualization of the relationships between the independent variable, schizophrenia-nonschizophrenia, and the dependent variable, be it genetic, biochemical, neurological, or behavioral.

When one employs a disease model, wittingly or not, cause (etiology) is implied. The use of opaque language does not fully hide the presupposition of a "cause of schizophrenia," or of "schizophrenia causing a behavioral outcome," or of a hidden common "cause" of both schizophrenia *as well as* the conduct under study. The disease paradigm's articulation would be greatly enhanced if its users would be forthright in connecting their hypotheses and conclusion statements. The inherent and perhaps incurable vagueness of the schizophrenia hypothesis embarrasses any effort to tie together the puzzle solutions.

Sommer, Witney, and Osmond (1962), assert that

> disturbance in association is the primary symptom of schizophrenic thought disorder and "from it can be derived the majority of secondary symptoms" (Bleuler, 1911, p. 355). If methods for improving schizophrenic association can be developed, this should have practical significance for the rehabilitation of schizophrenic patients [p. 58].

Here "disturbance in association" is clearly identified as a "symptom" of schizophrenic thought disorder. The reader is led through the metaphoric framework to the inference that schizophrenic association represents a "disease." Sommer et al. claim that they would have achieved a medical breakthrough had they demonstrated that schizophrenics could be trained to give less idiosyncratic responses in a work association situation. But we are left in the dark about whether their success would have represented a "cure" for schizophrenia. If an investigator of glomuleronephritis could eliminate the symptom from which arise the "majority of secondary symptoms" of the disease, we would be correct in inferring that the investigator had come close to finding the "cure" for the disease.

Consider Sommer et al.'s report from another aspect of the schizophrenia model. Phillips, Zigler, and their collaborators, working within the everyday science of deviant behavior, have focused their fact-gathering activity on problems of diagnosis and symptomatology. They list behaviors such as "eating a lot," feeling "perverted," committing a "robbery," and being "suspicious" as symptoms of psychiatric illness (Phillips, Broverman, & Zigler, 1968). Had Sommer et al. successfully tightened up the "loose associations" of their subjects so that they gave more common associations to stimulus words, would the "symptoms" identified by Phillips et al. also have been eliminated? In pursuing the science of deviant behavior, a contemporary scientist would set out to verify a prediction—a direct implication from the disease paradigm—that by eliminating the "disturbance in association" (the "primary" symptoms), one would eliminate, say, suspicious behavior, robbery, or overeating.

Should this statement appear exaggerated, the reader is asked to consider the logical and psychological obstacles to formulating a cohesive theory that uses schizophrenia as the independent variable against such unconnected dependent variables as "overinclusiveness," "exaggeration of normal response style," and "absence of nystagmus." It is difficult to find a common class for these variables and the derivation of efficient causal statements would be well-nigh impossible.

These last paragraphs direct attention to serious flaws in the use of the disease paradigm to study negatively valued deviant behavior. The diagnosis, the inferred presence or absence of the "disease," is the independent variable. On the surface, this tactic could facilitate the gathering of facts. However, the absence of sound criteria by which to establish the validity of classifying a person as schizophrenic or not schizophrenic renders disastrous the transformation of the diagnosis into the independent variable in an experimental hypothesis.

A number of investigators have reported chains of studies following from extensive programmatic research. Invariably they conclude their reports with statements expressing conviction that their variables had a meaningful relationship to schizophrenia. To observe this practice, one may look at studies (Chapman, 1961; Chapman & Taylor, 1957) on "conceptual disfunctions;" Shakow (1963), on "the inability to retain a segmental set;" Payne and his associates (Payne & Caird, 1967; Payne, Caird, & Laverty, 1964) on "overinclusiveness," and Gur (1978) on "left hemispheric dysfunction." One would expect that in subsequent studies the correlated variable would be employed to define schizophrenia. In theory, such experimentally derived measures, refined and endorsed by noted researchers, should be preferred to the subjective definition of the elusive independent variable. Certainly, a test for, let us say, overinclusiveness that consistently differentiates schizophrenics from normals would better define schizophrenia than taking a poll of the opinions of a psychiatrist, a psychologist, and a social worker.

In this connection, Crumpton (1963) used a measure of abstraction-concreteness to grade her schizophrenic subjects. She also went beyond the usual procedure of assuming the validity of the diagnosis in the hospital record, and asked two psychiatrists to rank 70 patients on "extent of schizophrenia." From the original list of 70, she was able to choose 30 patients who had been ranked quite similarly by the two psychiatrists. Unfortunately, the two presumed orderings of patients on the schizophrenia dimension—concreteness scores and psychiatrist's ratings—yielded a correlation coefficient of .15. In other words, the psychiatrists agreed that 30 of the 70 people were schizophrenic, but their rankings of the 70 patients on a severity scale did not show correspondence; and their ratings had little relationship to a presumed measure of an indicator of "schizophrenia."

Grading the intensity of the independent variable. Crumpton's approach to the definition of the independent variable suggests a second way of elaborating the nature of the undefined independent variable. If one accepted schizophrenia as an independent variable, some interesting design possibilities would follow from grading schizophrenia along a dimension such as "serious" to "mild;" just as one would rate a case of nephritis, tuberculosis, or mumps. Using this ordering, one would be able to relate severity of schizophrenia to severity in the assumed dependent variable. The disease paradigm allows the expectation that severity of schizophrenia would be correlated with intensity of frequently employed dependent variables, such as "overinclusiveness" or "inability to maintain a segmental set."

A ranking of severity is implied when an investigator classifies schizophrenics along certain often-used dimensions. Many of the studies in the sample sorted schizophrenic subjects into classes *acute or chronic, process or reactive, good premorbid or poor premorbid, paranoid or nonparanoid*. These dichotomies, each with a large penumbra of ambiguity (Herron, 1962; McCreary, 1974; Zigler & Levine, 1973) could be interpreted as an effort to make a statement about the severity of schizophrenia. Such interpretation dissolves when the inherent inconsistencies of the mensural definitions of these dimensions are brought into the open. The acute-chronic dichotomy assumes that persons recently admitted to a hospital are acute schizophrenics, whereas those who have been in the hospital for long periods of time are chronic schizophrenics (see, for example, Draguns, 1963; Spohn, Thetford, & Woodham, 1970; Weinberger & Cermak, 1973; Yates & Korboot, 1970). What classification rule is used to determine that a patient is not being initiated into an extended hospital stay? Chronicity, after all, is a *post hoc* determination. More often than not, the researcher accepts the label that was applied by the usual professional polling in the diagnostic staff conference. Thus, the independent subvariable, acute-chronic, is established, not through systematic behavioral observations, but by assuming that the recorded diagnosis represents some characteristic of the disease process. Needless to say, the polling process, while useful for political affairs, cannot be taken seriously as a legitimate way of assessing gradations of the independent variable. Second, the scales used to grade the process-reactive and the good-premorbid-poor-premorbid dimensions are loaded so that they tell about the behavior exhibited by the patients prior to their earning their current diagnostic classifications. To be classed as a process schizophrenic, one must engage in those behaviors which, as a rule, violate the normative expectations of the middle class, the class from which are drawn most of the mental health professionals. For example, a subject who has engaged in "proper" heterosexual activities is moved toward the good premorbid or reactive end of the scale.

Two variables can be inferred from acute-chronic and process-reactive dimension measures regarded as scales that grade the intensity of the disease process: (a) length of hospitalization and (b) acceptability of behavior prior to the subject's labelling. These variables have the potential of being gradable independent variables in studies of mental hospital inmates. A moment's reflection will convince the reader that they are not gradations of schizophrenia. (The place of these variables in the study of the deviant behavior is discussed below.)

How representative are samples of schizophrenics? Study after study in our sample includes the claim that "cooperative" schizophrenic subjects were included in the experimental sample. One is not sure whether this statement intends to inform us that the group is a "more pure" sample or a "less pure" sample of schizophrenia. Lack of cooperativeness, after all, is a basis of much of the "symptomatology" of persons tagged with the label *schizophrenia*. By dropping uncooperative subjects, the investigator guarantees that the character of the patient population will not be fully represented in the study sample. Studies that use highly complex experimental techniques always turn up some subjects who are unable to complete the experimental procedures. A survey of current schizo-phrenia research suggests that though investigators have chosen to study people who have been diagnosed as schizophrenic, the exigencies of the research proce-dures have forced a selectivity that restricts the range of the independent variable to cooperative patients.

Despite the apparent importance of the issue of patient selectivity, investiga-tors inadvertantly show their thorough reification of the independent variable by telling us only that, for example, "schizophrenics were chosen as subjects." About 200 of the 374 studies in this review make no mention of how selection factors might have influenced the choice of subjects. Such a strategy suggests that all these investigators, along with the readers of their reports, believe that one schizophrenic in a sample is equivalent to another schizophrenic. About one-third of the surveyed studies note only that patients were preselected on the basis of cooperativeness and/or ability to carry out the experimental tasks.

In considering cooperativeness among subjects, we must also consider that there has been sufficient evidence that subjects in psychological research can anticipate and seek to produce the results that the investigator has predicted, along with the findings that schizophrenic subjects are also adept at this process (Braginsky, Braginsky, & Ring, 1969; Zarlock, 1966). Is a group of "coopera-tive" schizophrenics, then, a sample of people who can be expected to anticipate and produce the concomitants of schizophrenia that are being explored? In the mysterious atmosphere of the laboratory, do the cooperative schizophrenics cooperate by conducting themselves "as if more ill?" Furthermore, by excluding the noncooperative subjects, the proponents of a special state of schizophrenia are perhaps taking short change on their hypotheses. Shouldn't we expect that the noncooperative schizophrenics are more "seriously diseased," than are coopera-tive patients?

Investigators should meet at least two expectations about the representatives of their study samples. First, the effect of excluding noncooperative subjects should be assessed as precisely as possible. Second, the factors that influence the selec-tion of subjects must be a matter of public record. Needless to say, the canons of research would direct the experimenter clearly to state reasons for dropping subjects.

Two of the studies covered by our survey investigate the characteristics of untestable patients. Wilensky and Solomon (1960) compared a group of schizo-phrenics regarded as untestable to a group judged testable. Their breakdown was further refined by dividing the untestable sample into a *refused* segment and a *confused* segment. Though unfortunately they had no way of actually assessing the ways in which the groups might have shown performance differences, they found that a number of demographic features did distinguish the classifications. The untestable-refused group appeared to be older, hospitalized later in life, and more likely to have been diagnosed as paranoid. The untestable-confused group was likely to have been hospitalized for longer periods and to be less sociable and poorer in "mental health." Klein and Spohn (1964), using the same groupings as Wilensky and Solomon, found that the untestable-confused group differed from other patients in having less verbal interaction in their ward behavior, while the untestable-refused group were like other patients on this dimension. From these studies we see that the untestable group is quite likely to be more "ill," but we do not have evidence of how they might perform on the kinds of tests that are used to measure the variables that are studied as concomitants of schizophrenia.

In the absence of information on test performance differences, scientific protocol requires the investigator to indicate the selectivity factors that operated in the study. Even where the investigator does allude to selection factors that might have played an important part in the choice of subjects, the discussion is generally nonilluminating. As noted above, the usual statement is that the patients were "cooperative," and when this statement is made, we are left to assume that selection has taken place. Even when this kind of statement is given, it is unclear whether lack of cooperation might have meant, for example, that the patients were unable to read a complex set of instructions or to read the material to which they were to respond. In a study by Williams (1964), the task set before the schizophrenic group is one that has taxed the cognitive efforts of at least two nonpatient Ph.D.'s. Subjects were asked, for example, to choose the valid conclusion that can be drawn from the following syllogism:

Some of my wishes are fulfilled
Some of my wishes are small, therefore:
1. All small wishes are fulfilled;
2. Some fulfilled wishes are not small;
3. No valid conclusion possible;
4. Some small wishes are fulfilled;
5. Some fulfilled wishes are small.

Even the nature of verbal instructions would seem to promote some selectivity. Anyone who has attempted to explain to an undergraduate class the concept development task devised by Bruner, Goodnow, and Austin (1956), would wonder at the absence of a report on selection factors where this task was used (see Moriarty & Kates, 1962). When Weckowicz (1964) reports that he used only those patients able to understand instructions for a form constancy task, he has obviously restricted his schizophrenic sample drastically.

Other researchers use a research tactic in which samples are drawn by inspection of the psychology department files (Baxter & Becker, 1962; Zigler & Phillips, 1961). Query: Are all incoming patients referred to the psychology department, or does the attending psychiatrist have a selective bias in referring some patients for diagnostic study and not others? One study purported to explore the defensive style of families of schizophrenics (Baxter, Becker, & Hooks, 1963). The parents of discharged patients were required to return to the hospital and expose themselves to the perplexing and perhaps degrading process of being "evaluated" by the use of a Rorschach test. Cheek (1964) likewise used a tactic of recalling patients and their families to cooperate in a study. The question must be raised: Are parents of ex-patients who submit to these procedures representative of the class *parents of schizophrenics*?

Studies in which selectivity of subjects has occurred cannot be regarded as studies of schizophrenia. At best these are reports about samples selected from a larger pool of people who have been called schizophrenics. One cannot know whether selectivity has contributed to the results that either confirm or disconfirm the hypotheses of the study, so there is no way of knowing that one has contributed to a definition of schizophrenia.

Measures of Dependent Variables

In the schizophrenia model, an important part of securing theoretical connections depends on assurances that experimental variables are reliably measured. A researcher working with a measure of generalization of a conditioned response, for example, and having hypothesized that generalization effects are more apparent among schizophrenics, must be able repeatedly to locate the subjects in the same relative position on a scale that assesses generalization effects. Without establishing the reliability of the dependent variable, it would be difficult to conclude that excessive levels of this effect, generalization of response to a conditioned stimulus, are a feature of schizophrenia. Despite the transparency of this introductory psychology homily, none of the investigators who explored the relationships of generalization to schizophrenia has reported data on the reliability and validity of "generalization." To our knowledge, such data have never been presented in the psychological literature.

The schizophrenia model depends heavily on the identification of specific behavioral characteristics, classifiable as symptoms. "Thought disorder" for example, is a "symptom" of schizophrenia. It has been listed as one of the salient operational criteria for assigning the diagnosis of schizophrenia (Spitzer, Endicott, & Robins, 1978). To test the claim that "thought disorder" is in fact related to schizophrenia, it would be necessary to demonstrate that a putative patient consistently across time and situations would show evidence of thought disorder. If one diagnostician were to detect incoherence (listed as one form of thought disorder by Spitzer, Endicott, & Robins, 1978) under some conditions, and another diagnostician failed to detect incoherence in the person, then it would be difficult to evaluate, let us say, the effects of a drug on this symptom. One would want to be able reliably to characterize the person as incoherent or as coherent.

Since the model works on the assumption that behaviors follow patterns that allow them to be represented as exemplars of different classes, then it must be shown that instances of the target person's behavior can reliably be placed into the class they are assumed to represent. That is, if one investigator sees thought disorder in a certain kind of performance relative to certain kinds of stimuli, other investigators must also see that performance as thought disorder. This must be true of those behaviors which are measured as the experimental (dependent) variables in studies that use the schizophrenia model. Yet, of the 374 studies in our selected sample, 286 of the studies make no statement to indicate that the reliability of the measures of the dependent variable had been a matter of concern. Twenty-four of the studies used measures that had an extremely compelling face validity. For example, Spohn and Wolk (1966) studied the increases in social participation that would arise from arranging a living situation that included schizophrenics of varying social responsivity. Their measure, obtained by rating the person's social participation, compels one to agree that they measured what they claim to have measured. Similarly, one would agree with Turner, Dopkeen, and Labreche (1970) that being divorced or being married is a valid and reliable measure of marital status. A skeptic, however, can often take the liberty of refuting the claim of face validity. Kane, Nutter, and Weckowicz (1971) measured the point at which subjects reported that they could no longer tolerate heat applied to their foreheads. This measure could be accepted as an obviously valid and reliable measure of " 'sluggishness' of their [the schizophrenics'] response to many kinds of biological, chemical and physical stimuli [p. 52]." An alternative explanation would suggest that the subjects who failed to report pain, even after tissue damage, were attending to stimuli other than those being applied by the investigator.

An experimenter who creates a new test is expected to perform the necessary operations and report the usual information. Furthermore, few investigators use precisely the same procedures as other investigators. To be sure, references are made to other investigations, often with clear implications that the same variables are being measured, but without assurances of comparability of measures. Investigators, for example, have studied the question of whether or not schizophrenics respond to different levels of emotional intensity in the speech of other persons (Levy, 1976; Shimkunas, 1972). Willingness to reciprocate by self-disclosure is assumed to be affected by the level of a speaker's emotionality. Levy's procedure required that participants listen to an "emotional speaker." Levy tells the reader that she manipulated the level of emotionality somewhat as did Shimkunas (1972). Shimkunas obtained his levels of emotionality by having ten senior-level psychology students judge the expression of feeling in a written sentence. From those sentences clearly seen to express feeling, Shimkunas constructed narratives believed to be high in the expression of feeling. Levy's speakers could be heard via tape recording, reading narratives of different levels of emotionality. Participants heard the reading, and then, responding to instructions, talked about the topic addressed by the speaker. One of the measures used by both Shimkunas and Levy was a measure of *self-disclosure,* following Jourard's (1971) work. The object of the study was to assess the effect of the level of the speaker's emotionality on the participants' self disclosure. Shimkunas (1972) had shown that there is high rater agreement in judging self-disclosure, and Levy (1976) reevaluated rater agreement on the self-disclosure measure. But is self-disclosure in this work in any way related to self-disclosure in Jourard's (1971) work? Do the very unusual conditions of this laboratory situation reliably produce a kind of conduct that would be called self-disclosure as it takes place in a cocktail lounge or in adjoining seats in an airplane? One may believe that Levy has not provided information about self-disclosing practices of schizophrenics so long as her measurement procedure has not been shown to be a valid index of such conduct.

These experiments affirm a long-standing notion in psychology: to wit, instruments presumably measuring the same quality on examination proved to be unreliably intercorrelated. (See, for example, the work on creativity [Stein, 1968], which once was one of the most highly worked concepts in psychology.)

Twenty-eight of the 374 studies indicated that there had been some kind of direct reliability check of the dependent variable, while 18 others reported that the reliability of the measure had been checked through a form of inter-rater agreement. Nineteen of the reports used measures that had been developed for widespread use, and a reader could assume that reliability of the instruments had been previously analyzed. In about three-quarters of the cases, then, the researcher devised new tests or revised other instruments and reported results without assessment of reliability. In the absence of this assessment, we cannot know that a subject would obtain a similar quantitative ranking if measured in a qualitatively similar situation. The canons of traditional science require that experimenters use tests that have been adequately standardized, reviewed, criticized, factor-analyzed, etc. Failure to observe these canons leaves open the possibility that experimental measures are empty of meaning and unrelated to conduct outside the laboratory.

The reliability of concept formation skills. The overworked concept of loosened associations logically leads to hypotheses about the concept development activity of schizophrenics and to efforts to develop reliable measures. Persons are able to control and anticipate events in their world by classifying objects and treating all members of a class as similar. The verbal expressions of a schizophrenic that are identified as "incoherent" by an investigator could reflect an anomolous form of categorizing behavior. Needless to say, the validity of tests of hypotheses about categorizing behavior would depend heavily on whether an investigator was reliably measuring a single, consistent entity when measuring categorizing behavior.

Essentially, one who studies conceptual functioning is studying the use of classes and categories. For example, a person's use of the concept *triangularity* might be of experimental interest. One could ask, for example, what stimuli a person would include in the category *triangles*. Triangularity, for a particular person, might be defined by the spatial features "straight sides," "three distinct angular turns," and "three sides." Yet that person might use the label *triangle* when speaking of a referent with three distinct angular turns, and three sides, one or two of which were distinctly curved lines. If the lines describing the sides were drawn as sharply arcing curves, so that the distinct angular turns became blended with the overall arc of the sides, then, a person might not call the figure a triangle. Persons may vary in their tolerance of discrepancy from their personal, prototypical triangle. One person might refuse to class the figure as a triangle as soon as the sides were shown as slightly arcing curves. Another person might include figures whose sides arc very sharply.

If we wished to describe "overgeneralization in conceptual functioning," or "overabstraction," and "concreteness," we might use a task related to the process described in the preceding paragraph. We might hypothesize that schizophrenics are "overinclusive." We could then design sixteen figures ranging from "strict triangularity" toward "strict circularity." Then the experimental subjects, the schizophrenics, would be asked to "put into a pile all the figures like this one," whereupon they would be shown the experimenter's prototypical, perfect triangle. Normal subjects might also be asked to complete a similar task. Suppose we then add together the number of figures each schizophrenic classed as a triangle, and we find that the schizophrenics, on the average, classed seven figures as triangles. At the same time, the normals, on average, classed four figures as triangles. This finding might encourage us to speak of "overinclusiveness" in the conceptual functioning of schizophrenics.

It is important to ask, is the test reliable? Would, for example, the person who today puts nine figures into the "triangle" category also put nine figures into the "triangle" class when given the same task tomorrow? Equally important is the problem of whether a person who "overincludes" on this task would "overinclude" on a different task. Is the test a valid test of overinclusion? Would this person include heads of endive in a group that is supposed to match a prototypical head of escarole?

Zaslow's (1950) test of concept functioning, designed much like the "triangle test" described above, was used to assess the concept functioning of schizophrenics. Kugelmass and Fondeur (1955) carefully examined Zaslow's test. The reliability of Zaslow's test was found to be so low as to be insignificant in most cases. In other words, the test scores could not be used to predict conceptual functioning scores from one time to another. Following a statistical maxim that the validity of a test cannot exceed its reliability, and viewing findings like those of Kugelmass and Fondeur, one cannot dismiss questions of reliability of measurements in the study of concept functioning in schizophrenia. One cannot, for example, find utility in the claim that schizophrenics show overinclusiveness if one cannot be convinced that they "overinclude" on a variety of tasks and repeatedly over time.

These old warnings about the reliabilities of measures related to conceptual functioning seem to have had a mixed reception, insofar as they have influenced recent investigations. Shimkumas (1970) explores the possibility that "abstract thinking" and "concrete thinking" are not necessarily reciprocal; that is, that abstract thinking can advance, despite the stability of concrete thinking, as the schizophrenic moves toward "clinical improvement." He uses the Gorham Proverbs test (Gorham, 1956) to extract measures of abstract and concrete thinking. In a proverbs test, a person is asked to explain the meaning of a proverb. For example, after a brief explanation that proverbs are intended to be metaphoric, a person hears the proverb: "The burnt child dreads fire." A person who can communicate the metaphoric meaning of the proverb is judged to be "abstract." A person may say, "Someone who has had one bad experience with something will avoid that thing." This response, being an essential retranslation of the metaphor embodied in the statement, would be taken as indication of the person's ability to use abstraction, or expanded categories. An example of a concrete response would be: "Experience teaches a child not to play with fire." Using a proverbs test, Shimkunas compared the status of his "disturbed schizophrenics" before and after treatment. Three measurement facts stand out in Shimkunas's article: first, he reports no correlations of measures of the abstract and concrete functioning before and after treatment. Second, he expresses no notice that the reliability of the scores is highly questionable. Third, the variabilities of the abstract and concrete scores are very high. For example, the standard deviation of the pretreatment sample's abstract score is reported as 2.80, while the mean score is 3.26. Considering these facts, a reader might be reluctant to accept the proposition that the measures of abstraction and concreteness had any relation to the events under study. The absence of a report of correlations between the scores obtained from repeated measures on the same persons avoids the matter of the stability of the assumed property—abstract-concrete thinking.

Harrow, Himmelhoch, Tucker, Hersh, and Quinlan (1972) sought to demonstrate a distinction between "behavioral overinclusion" and "conceptual overinclusion." They propose this distinction as a way to clarify the investigations of schizophrenic conceptual functioning conducted by Payne and his collaborators (for example, Payne, Caird, & Laverty, 1964). They suggest that such clarity will be attained through complicating the scoring of a test of a psychological function of questionable stability. Harrow et al. presented subjects with a starting object, for example, a knife, to which could be added other objects that might share common categorizing dimensions with the starting object, spoon, ax, etc. Subjects then chose those other objects which they believed represented instances of the class represented by the original starting object. Subjects' responses were evaluated for four characteristics—behavioral overinclusion, conceptual overinclusion, idiosyncratic thinking, and richness of association.

One first notes that these refinements on Payne et al.'s original test would be difficult to score. For example, a subject is given a fork as a starting object. The subject then chooses a knife, and taking notice of the dimension *sharp-dull*, next places a needle in the grouping. How does an investigator decide that this is an instance of "conceptual overinclusion?" Harrow et al. report that raters could agree satisfactorily on judging the quality of subjects' responses. But, then, no indication is given whether a subject would repeatedly and consistently show one or another type of categorizing behavior. In other words, does the test reliably measure something that can be called "conceptual overinclusion?" Further, since the investigators propose to show the utility of distinctions in types of conceptual function, they report the intercorrelations of subjects' scores on the different tests. These intercorrelations are not impressive and, if anything, would discourage the idea that one should approach schizophrenia intending to show that its victims suffer from debility in "generalized conceptual functioning."

The criticism that measures of "overinclusion" have not measured stable psychological function has been confronted by Payne, Hochberg, and Hawks (1970). They claim that the test-retest reliabilities of their object classification test, object sorting test, and proverbs test offer evidence that they have been measuring a recurring, identifiable function. At the same time, one cannot tell what function is being measured, particularly when one notes the statistically significant, but logically unconvincing intercorrelations between scores on the classification tests and the proverbs tests. These correlations (about .40) do not urge the belief that these two tests are measuring a common, stable quality.

At this point, then, the theory of schizophrenia is not enhanced by the "conceptual functioning deficit" hypothesis. The dependent measures that have been used to test variants of the hypothesis have not been shown to be reliable. And, in the face of failures to demonstrate that conceptual functioning is a general, unitary function, there must be an alternative formulation. Perhaps one's cognitive style is intricately meshed with the context in which one forms and uses concepts. Such behavior cannot be convincingly quantified without simultaneous consideration of the meaning of events that require conceptualizing, the social implications of the cognitive actions, and so forth. Until cognitive scientists (see Lachman, Lachman, & Butterfield, 1979; Neisser, 1976) can prepare the groundwork and offer answers to these questions, there is little need for further investigating the reliability of a unitary cognitive function in order to relate the level of that function to a supposed disease.

Galvanic skin response as a dependent variable. Investigators of schizophrenia can raise questions about the reliability of other interesting measures of psychological functioning used in studies. An examination of these studies shows an apparent high face validity for the experimental measures that have been used. Consider the complex study that Magaro (1972, 1973) has reported. His analysis of variance design included as many as five independent variables. The dependent measures were intended to represent autonomic reactivity and form discrimination skill. Measuring physiological response like the galvanic skin response (GSR) leads one to neglect the matter of reliability. A brief second thought, however, encourages one to question the intrapersonal stability of this measure. When one considers the kinds of intrapersonal variability shown by so-called schizophrenics, there is no surprise in the data reported by Rubens and Lapidus (1978). They found that for the people in their schizophrenic sample, the GSR patterns changed radically from one experimental session to the next. Whereas some of these people were classed as "underresponders" in the first session, they were classed as "overresponders" in the second session. Others reversed this sequence. Rubens and Lapidus were able to say that their schizophrenics "exhibit one of two abnormal arousal patterns, overresponder and underresponder, each of which was distinct from the arousal patterns of the nonschizophrenic subjects [p. 208]." They could not, however, reliably predict that schizophrenics would show one or the other GSR response.

Magaro's measure of "form discrimination" is another matter. After studying a careful work on form perception, such as Rock's (1973), one should be wary of accepting Magaro's measure as a reliable measure of "form perception." Subjects look for one second at a representation of a human figure. After a two-second interval, they are asked to indicate whether or not another representation is the same as the first. The comparison figures had been changed by altering the position, for example, of the figure's arm. Subjects who called the figures similar were charged with having poorer form discrimination. Even a reader who succumbed completely to the easy plea of "operationalism," could legitimately ask for an index of the day-to-day stability of the psychological function assumed to be reflected in this measure.

Some other measures and reliability. Further, if an investigator can justify the choice of variables by appealing to face validity, a critic can justify criticism of that choice by appealing to face invalidity. Lane and Singer (1959) instructed schizophrenic subjects to respond to a questionnaire that assessed attitudes towards family life. The investigators suggested that schizophrenics showed more than normal dependency on their mothers. The conclusions were drawn from responses to such apparently face-valid items as, "Mothers always love their children equally." Can one assume that such responses tell us about how a person views *his or her own* mother? On the face of it, this question must be answered negatively. Only by a series of questionable assumptions can this scale be used to draw conclusions about how the subjects would view their own parents.

Other investigators asked a group of schizophrenic subjects to respond to "oral type" proverbs (Lewinsohn & Riggs, 1962). Here the investigators regarded the following as an example of an "oral type" proverb: "There is many a slip twixt cup and lip." When a patient does less well than a normal person in interpreting these proverbs, what are the causal links that allow the inference of regression to oral functioning? (An inference of equal likelihood would be that the patient is complaining about the quality of food in the hospital!)

DeWolfe (1962) intended to demonstrate that process and reactive schizophrenics can be differentiated on the basis of their reactivity in "emotional situations." His schizophrenic subjects were shown some words which they were to use in constructing a sentence. Some of the words were assumed to be neutral and some were assumed to be affective. The sentence was to contain, in addition to the neutral or "affective" terms, one of the three personal pronouns that were listed with the word. The measures of reactivity in emotional situations were to be made by assessing (1) the reaction times between presentation of stimuli and the subject's response, and (2) the use of pronouns which indicated a first-person reference. That these measures have any relationship to "emotionality"—by whatever definition one wished to make of emotionality—is not apparent. Furthermore, since DeWolfe had two measures of emotionality, he could have argued that his definition of emotionality is operational, being hinged to the two experimental measures. At that point he would have had an opportunity to test the validity of his measures by computing their coefficient of correlation. He did not follow this strategy, and an opportunity to practice the normal science of deviant behavior was bypassed. In the end, his measures did not satisfactorily differentiate his process group from his reactive groups, so that his readers were spared from puzzling over the connections between the frequency of using first-person pronouns and having hospital staff members agree that a person should be labelled schizophrenic.

In summary, a scientist in search of a basic characteristic that demarcates the functioning of schizophrenics receives little help from studies that fail to report on the validity and reliability of tests that measure the dependent variables of the investigation. One might agree that diagnosticians can reliably identify the unusual behaviors that encourage diagnosticians to place persons in the schizophrenic category. In order to proceed from the hospital diagnosis to the conclusion that a basic, unusual, pathological form of psychological or physiological activity is associated with these abnormal behaviors—these ceremony violations—one must be secure in the belief that the objective measures of the anomalous functions reflect a meaningful process.

Schizophrenic Subjects' Variations on Dependent Measures

In the language of one investigator, "the study of schizophrenia has long been hampered by a lack of reliable indicators of the disorder [Braatz, 1970, p. 1]." A researcher who is not sure that an experimental sample is made up of schizophrenics cannot, after locating a characteristic of the members of that sample, confidently claim that the experiment has identified a characteristic of schizophrenia. Suppose an investigator finds that some of the sample's subjects do not show the characteristic. Do they lack the characteristic because they have been incorrectly diagnosed as schizophrenic? Or may some schizophrenics show an absence of this characteristic?

In practice, this specific issue rarely becomes a problem for the majority of investigators who have reported the studies constituting the core of this review. Most of the statistical tests used in these studies are not particularly affected by imprecise categorization of individuals. When one uses the most widely accepted statistical tests of hypothesis about the mean differences between group performances, relative to a dependent measure, it matters little if most of the schizophrenics behave in the same ways as do large numbers of the normals.

The statistical tests used in most of the modern investigations of behavior are not designed to demonstrate differences in cases; they are used to show that the differences between the *mean scores* of the different samples are probably not a function of chance variations in scores. With this approach, there can be near identity between the ranges and distributions of the dependent variable scores yielded by the schizophrenic and the nonschizophrenic samples. So long as the difference between the means of the samples is not likely to have appeared by chance, the investigator is permitted to stake a claim for the validity of the hypothesis of a difference between the two samples. Small mean differences are logically inappropriate in a disease model that posits different behavior for schizophrenics and normals. From the inspection of the data, it is abundantly clear that *most* persons identified as schizophrenics do not function differently from *most* persons identified as nonschizophrenics. To be consistent with the disease model, most of the normals should be different from most of the ill persons on measures such as temperature and white cell count, for example, that supposedly differentiate the sick from the well. The obvious, large overlap between experimental and control samples is not suppressed by showing the statistical reliability of a small difference between the mean score of the "ill" and the mean score of the "healthy."

When analysis of variance tests is used to ascertain that mean differences did not result from chance, there may be high variability in the scores of one of the samples and relatively low variability in the scores of the other sample. At one time, this feature, heterogeneity of variance, was treated as a condition that would obfuscate statistical tests for the confidence to be given to results. Currently investigators work from the reliable assumption that high variance differences do not strongly affect the confidence one may place in the results of analysis of variance tests. Thus investigators may ignore the wide variation in the scores of a sample of schizophrenics, and yet remain confident that the group means have not resulted from sheer chance.

Even cursory observation of the variations in the dependent variable scores yielded by persons in the different samples shows two trends. First, the scores of the people in the schizophrenic samples vary more than do the scores of the nonschizophrenic subjects. Second, among the schizophrenics, the widest variations are in scores that indicate a "poorer" performance. Those tagged *schizophrenic* are unlikely to be found on the "high" side of the mean performance on the measure of the dependent variable. From these observations, one may safely conclude that by eliminating from the schizophrenic sample those whose scores are at the extremes, the investigator would be unable to report a reliable difference between the mean scores of the samples. And following the statistical style of current journal practice, the investigators would be unable to report that they had differentiated schizophrenics from nonschizophrenics. As the everyday science of abnormal conduct is currently practiced, investigators are not expected to follow this practice. They may ignore these important variations in the scores of subjects.

To allow readers to assess the utility of the disease model, however, it would be helpful if investigators were expected at least to report the variances; or, more usefully, the distributions of scores. It is now the rare schizophrenia study that reports the extent to which scores vary from the mean of the sample, and the reporting of distributions appears to have gone out of fashion. In fact, when reporting analyses of variance, current investigators rarely report the means of their study samples. These practices, while saving journal space, leave a reader no choice but to declare that the results of the study can give no information that helps to define a disease entity called schizophrenia.

If one followed the stringent practice of ignoring studies that overlook the significance of variation, the results of 172 of the 374 studies reviewed could be discounted because of lack of mention of score variations around the group means. Another 119 studies report variations , but then proceed as if to ignore the implications of the reported variances. Only seven of the studies actually discuss the overlap of scores. Earlier studies were concerned that group differences in variability should not violate the assumptions that underlie the correct use of analysis of variance techniques. Thus, investigators frequently recognized large differences in the variances of their samples' dependent measures. Frequently the observations of these differences encouraged the investigator to use mathematical procedures that presumably allowed proper statistical testing of hypotheses predicting differences in group means. In this way, the logic of hypotheses derived from a disease model evaporated before the requirements of statistical technique.

Several reports illustrate the foregoing points. In one of the seven studies that detailed the overlap between normals and schizophrenics, Shakow and Jellinek (1965) graphically reproduced the distributions of numbers on unusual responses given by schizophrenics and normals in a word associations task. Thirty percent of the schizophrenic group are below the normals' mean score, and about 50 percent of them are below +1 standard deviation on the normals' distribution. In fact, very few of the schizophrenics produced a greater number of unusual associations than did the person in the normal group who gave the highest number of unusual associations. Flavell (1956), reporting his work on the issue of abstraction and concreteness in schizophrenia, tells us that 33 percent of the schizophrenic patients achieved abstract scores above the normal group mean, and 25 percent of the normals scored below the schizophrenic group mean [p. 209]." Braatz (1970) reports that 65 percent of his subjects overlapped. Using an optimal cutoff score, which is clearly a statistical construct that could hardly be individually useful, Braatz would have been able to classify correctly 78 percent of his subjects by using his dependent measure scores. One other report (Rubens & Lapidus, 1978) presents clear information about distributions, and this study is outstanding in that the data show *no overlap* of the sample's scores on the dependent measures. By taking readings of galvanic skin responses (GSR), Rubens and Lapidus measured the orienting responses of subjects exposed to a novel auditory stimulus. Normal subjects show an orienting response to several of the initial presentations of a tone, and then show habituation so that, with repetitions of the tone, the higher level of response disappears. A response pattern may be abnormal in evidencing no change from resting state GSR during initial presentations of tones. Failure to habituate after numerous repetitions may also be considered an abnormal response pattern. Failure to produce the orienting response would be termed *underresponding*, and failure to adapt would be termed *overresponding*. Rubens and Lapidus report that all schizophrenics would be classed in either the overresponder or the underresponder category. None of the nonschizophrenics showed either an absence of orienting response or a failure to habituate within 15 repetitions of the stimulus tones.

These findings must be interpreted cautiously, owing to the drugged state of the schizophrenics and to the temporal variations in some subjects' response patterns. Nevertheless, the report is exemplary for its findings and for its report of distributions.

In sum, marked variation in schizophrenic subjects' scores on dependent measures is a consistent fact of reported studies. Since statistical experts have shown that variance differences do not critically affect the use of analysis of variance tests, investigators are free to contrast mean scores obtained from schizophrenic and nonschizophrenic samples, despite the apparent variance differences seen in data yielded by the measurements used in an investigation. Comparisons of means, however, cannot be an appropriate method of indicating the "distinguishing symptom" of a "disease." Showing that sample means differ does not satisfy the logical requirement of showing that schizophrenics, as individuals, differ from normals. Consider that the following is offered as the single most reliable prediction to be made in studies of schizophrenic and nonschizophrenic samples: The variability of the scores of schizophrenics will be observably larger than the variability of the scores of control samples. In short, most experimental measures have shown *that schizophrenics are very different one from the other.* Further, one would defy chance if one attempted to differentially diagnose a person from a score taken from one of the dependent measures used in the target studies. The distributions of scores of normals and schizophrenics overlap extensively. One, then, must recognize the logical inappropriateness of conducting studies that try to explain minor group differences as the result of a disease called schizophrenia. Innumerable factors, some of which we have identified, can account more parsimoniously for the small statistically significant group mean differences than can the so-called illness of schizophrenia.

It is clear that everyday research—the normal science—directed toward the behavior that earns one the label of schizophrenia is conducted within the disease model. When we evaluate the outcomes of the normal science effort, we find signs of confusion and attendant questionable conclusions. Some of the practices that follow from inappropriate application of the disease model to the strategies of investigating unwanted behaviors are summarized as follows:

1. Few investigators question the legitimacy of classifying (diagnosing) by professional voting. Investigators appear to be confident that the records of the subject, which name a person as a schizophrenic, validly characterize the subject as an entity that has conceptual substance.
2. Investigators do not state the functional nature of the relationship between the independent and dependent variables. They are guided by a belief that there *is* a relationship. Research reports often suggest that the relationship is causal, but one frequently encounters vagueness on this point.
3. Investigators have not taken up the practice of using as definitions of schizophrenia those measuring devices which they had previously used as dependent variables, and which had been claimed to be useful identifiers of schizophrenia.
4. Investigators have not devised satisfactory techniques to explore the theoretically implied practice of grading the severity of schizophrenia.
5. Samples of schizophrenics are restricted explicitly and implicitly and there is no way of knowing if these kinds of restrictions limit conclusions that can be drawn about the supposed disease.
6. Researchers rarely establish the reliability and validity of measures claiming to assess the psychological functioning of people in the schizophrenic samples.

7. The extent of the variation in the scores achieved by those reputedly suffering from the disease is frequently very large, particularly toward the lower end of the scores on the measuring device. Furthermore, the overlap of the scores of the people in the schizophrenic and nonschizophrenic samples often assures that large portions of each sample are indistinguishable from each other. In other words, one could not tell the "sick" from the "well" by the scores on the dependent measures.

All this leads to the disjunctive question: Is it profitable to continue the search for the elusive disease, schizophrenia, or should we add the concept to the list of abandoned curiosities in the history of science that includes ether, witchcraft, and phlogiston?

Proponents of the schizophrenia model might prefer an affirmative answer to the first part of the disjunction. It is profitable to continue the search, they would declare. Small group differences are found on the dependent variables in so many studies. There must be *something* responsible for these differences! We propose that the "something" is to be found through a careful examination of disguised variables, a task to which we now turn.

4

The Disguised Variables
in the Schizophrenia Model

Experimenters in psychology and psychiatry—the practitioners of the traditional science of deviant behavior—have allowed innumerable variables, some hidden and some obvious, to influence outcomes on their dependent variables. This practice has promoted the illusion that they were observing the workings of a disease, *schizophrenia*. Investigators commonly ignore important variables that may act as sources of variation in performance on experimental tasks. It has been difficult to assess and take into account the cramping limitations of socialization and cognitive development, the humiliating effects of being a failure in the social system, the degradation of commitment procedures and hospital routines, the indoctrination into patient status, and the isolating effects of incarceration. All these variables may enter unbidden into the everyday science, where their effects are inadvertently disguised with the name of a mental disease that bears a Greek-rooted, medical-metaphoric title.

That these disguised variables must be taken seriously is a fact brought out by Hollingshead and Redlich (1958) and others who have unequivocally demonstrated that "schizophrenia" is a property readily deeded to persons of the lowest socioeconomic status (SES). The concept of "intelligence" measurement must be examined as a possible disguising variable. It has become increasingly clear that the utility of the concept of intelligence is based largely on its sociopolitical character (Braginsky & Braginsky, 1971; Dorfman, 1978; Kamin, 1974; Mancuso & Dreisinger, 1969). With this in mind, investigators must do more than declare that their samples of subjects attained the same mean vocabulary score if they intend to assure the reader of matching intelligence. The vagaries of assessing educational level may disguise research outcomes. Merely to state that study samples claim the same number of years in school is no warranty of matching on educational level, particularly since the "Coleman Report" (1966) showed that schools have been essentially impotent in changing the learning achievement patterns that a child has adopted at home. Perhaps most important as a disguising variable is the effect of patienthood. With the availability of the contemporary analyses of the nature of patienthood, (Braginsky, Braginsky, & Ring, 1969; Goffman, 1961; Perucci, 1974) no investigator can justify overlooking the effects of hospitalization as a major variable hidden in the all-inclusive independent variable labelled schizophrenia.

SOCIOECONOMIC STATUS AND SCHIZOPHRENIA

If investigators report that they have matched their groups of subjects on socioeconomic class—and only 13 percent of the 374 core papers even mention consideration of this variable—we are led to believe that the control group has a social background which would, in many respects, match that of the schizophrenic group. Nevertheless, when the control sample is made up of aides in the hospital, or of patients on a general medical or surgical ward, even though they are assigned the same mean SES ratings as those assigned to the experimental sample, there is reason to believe that the groups remain unmatched. Schizophrenic samples are generally drawn from the least valued of our "surplus population." Frequently the schizophrenic is rated as class V simply because no lower rating is available. Hospital aides in a control group, particularly where the mental hospital is one of a town's major industries, are often people who have achieved the stability of maintaining families and holding regular jobs. They would be rated as "good premorbid adjusted" on the scale used in many of the schizophrenia studies (Zigler & Phillips, 1962). When a patient on a general medical or surgical ward of a hospital, chosen to act as a control in a study, reports having worked for 20 years as a floor sweeper in a large factory, that patient expresses a different value system from the mental hospital inmate who drifted from job to job as a skilled auto mechanic. Yet the mechanic would raise the mean SES ratings for the schizophrenic sample, and the floorsweeper would lower the mean SES ratings for the control sample, thus helping to adjust matchings on SES.

Socioeconomic status is an important variable because it crudely defines dimensions like *deprivation-advantage, degradation-esteem, powerlessness-power*, and the value commitments that an individual, as a result of social placement on these dimensions, has woven into the personal constructions of his or her world. Clearly, the variables subsumed by socioeconomic status must be a primary concern of the science of norm-violating behavior. At this juncture, we can only begin to locate the intrusion of these variables into the schizophrenia model.

Good Premorbid and Poor Premorbid Adjustment

As an extended example of the subtle operation of socioeconomic variables in schizophrenia research, we point to the report of Rodnick and Garmezy (1957). They proposed a study of schizophrenia based on differences between schizophrenics who had made good premorbid adjustments and those who had made poor premorbid adjustments. More specifically, they hypothesized that good premorbid (GPM) schizophrenics came from homes that were conflict-ridden but father-dominated. Poor premorbid (PPM) schizophrenics were reared in homes that were conflict-ridden but mother-dominated. This latter group was hypothesized to be very sensitive to social censure, so that their behavior was intensely motivated by a need to avoid censure. Further, PPM schizophrenics were more withdrawn and much harder to rehabilitate. They would be similar to the subjects previously designated as chronic types. The GPM schizophrenics, being less inclined to avoid censure and having previously developed to a more satisfactory level, would recover more quickly from their "illness," and would be more likely to return to a satisfactory level of functioning.

One can see that this modest theory is a bonanza for users of the schizophrenia model. All kinds of hypotheses can be generated. Not the least of the uses of this theory is that one could formulate hypotheses that would predict differences between two classes of *schizophrenics*, the good premorbids and the poor premorbids. This tactic allows a researcher to devote attention to subjects who are conveniently sequestered in hospitals. The theory need not be embarrassed by comparing "schizophrenics" with "normals." (The convenience of this tactic was clearly reflected in the sharp rise in the proportion of schizophrenia studies using subtypes of schizophrenics as comparison groups. In 1970 approximately 50 percent of the annual output of the core articles report studies done exclusively on varied types of schizophrenics. By 1977 this approach was used less frequently, when 73 percent [16 of 22] studies used nonschizophrenic comparison samples.)

The implicit socioeconomic character of the *good premorbid-poor premorbid* dimension deserves more attention than it receives in the many reports that have built this variable into studies of schizophrenia. A ranking of *good premorbid* indicates that before the persons being rated were assigned their schizophrenic label, they had demonstrated success in performances that a middle-class psychiatrist or psychologist would call *good*. Poor premorbid schizophrenics had not demonstrated such *good* behaviors. They had probably been jobless, unmarried, and "irresponsible." In short, their case folders allowed the inference that they did not indicate their aspiration to the status system that our major communication media promote both to patients and to behavior scientists. Without recognizing the intrusion of an ideological premise, the formulators of the GPM-PPM dichotomy tacitly incorporated an evaluation of their subjects' socioeconomic status strivings.

In the end, perhaps, one need not be overly concerned about this insidious use of socioeconomically based value judgments. The studies that have purported to define the characteristics of schizophrenics divided into good premorbid and poor premorbid types have ultimately achieved little of value, even to the schizophrenia model. The results of these studies are at best equivocal. (See, for example, Donovan & Webb, 1965; Farina, Holzberg, & Dies, 1969; Magaro, 1972; Nathanson, 1967.) In the end, a series of studies laid to rest the Rodnick-

Garmezy conception about the relationships between premorbid status and sensitivity to social censure (Cichetti, 1967; Cichetti, Klein, Fontana, & Spohn, 1967; Klein, Cichetti, & Spohn, 1967).

The concept of premorbid social functioning lingers on, however. Seven studies of the 92 core sample studies published during 1974-78 partitioned schizophrenic samples by the GPM-PPM distinction. Sometimes the variable seems to represent an archaism. In the report by Knight, Sherer, Putchat, and Carter (1978), schizophrenics are classified on the GPM-PPM dimension without any logical or theoretical discussion to specify how premorbid social adjustment could possibly relate to having "a deficient [memory] icon such that it is inadequately formed, lower in capacity, or deviant in duration [p. 316]. "Carpenter (1976), with less than thorough theoretical justification, developed the hope that, "there is perhaps some as yet unidentified [schizophrenic] group in which this ability [responsivity to the syntactic structure of sentences] is impaired [p. 42]." On the basis of variegated results in studies of poor syntax in schizophrenics, Carpenter proposed that "perhaps the poor premorbids comprise a schizophrenic group which is insensitive to syntactic structure . . . and produces the conflicting results [p. 43]."

Carpenter tested the participants' syntactical organizational skills by two different procedures, both of which assess how persons use what they know about the organization of verbal communications. For example, the participants heard a sentence through one headphone. A clicker was sounded at different points as the sentence was being read. It has been shown that when the click sound is placed at an organizationally logical position, persons may better recall its location. A click at the end of a clause is accurately recalled, while a click in the middle of the clause is not. Carpenter's data led her to conclude that acute schizophrenia "does not make inroads on this aspect of language usage [p. 49]." Thus her results fail to demonstrate that the quality of a schizophrenic's premorbid existance has some relation to processing verbal information in ways that differ from the processing methods used by nonschizophrenics; and, as scientists, we need not speculate about how the GPM-PPM variable relates to data outcomes.

It would be instructive to point to one possible source of confusion in using premorbid adjustment as a variable in the study of schizophrenia. Investigators appear to have been unclear about how to categorize persons along the GPM-PPM dimension. As examples, we refer to the work of Fenz and Velner (1970) and Rice (1970), reported in articles that appear in the same issue of *JAP,* Fenz and Velner report that they used the Phillips scale as the "behavioral measure because it evaluates a person's ability to relate to other significant persons in his life. Chronicity on the Phillips scale implies a severely retarded premorbid 'social maturity,' . . . [p. 27]." They indicate Zigler and Phillips (1962) as the source of the scale. Rice (1970) employed Phillips (1953) as her source for what she calls the Phillips scale. She too was attempting to obtain "detailed information on premorbid social and sexual history [p. 51]." Rice indicates that subjects who attained a score of 13 to 27 were classed as *reactive.* McCreary (1974), in a later study, states that persons attaining a score of *15 or below* are to be classed as reactive on the Phillips Premorbid History Rating Scale (Phillips, 1953). At the same time, Fenz and Velner indicate that they followed the same rule as that used by McCreary and classified as reactive persons scoring below 13 on the Phillips Premorbid Rating Scale. This kind of methodological arbitrariness in assigning subjects their place on the GPM-PPM dimension must be in part responsible for the equivocal findings relating premorbid adjustment to the so-called "illness" of schizophrenia.

Social Role Definition and Premorbid Social Status

Our immediate interest in theory about premorbid status, we repeat, comes not from its predictive value, but from its tacit use of an ideological premise: a premise that socioeconomic status is related to outcome variables. Zigler and Phillips (1962) openly studied the issue of "social competence" in relation to the GPM-PPM dichotomy. Their data showed that the person who was more articulate, who had been committed to the "good life," who was more "socially competent" behaved differently from the PPM person after they became patients—i.e., after their respective failures to maintain their "normal" social roles. In the language of the schizophrenia model, these groups show different "symptoms." The PPM shows self-indulgence, that is, assault, rape, lying, murder attempts, avoidance of others, suspiciousness, or depersonalization. The GPM schizophrenic, on the other hand, "turns against himself." He or she expresses body complaints and contemplates suicide. Zigler and Phillips's findings, if one can extricate them from the schizophrenic model, point out the huge influence that socioeconomic strivings have in shaping the behaviors of people at the point where they become social failures. Good premorbid schizophrenics, as people who have "bought the system," are more prone to see their failures as *their own* responsibility. They declare *their own* weakness and inadequacy. Schizophrenics who show poor premorbid adjustments, who do not overtly aspire to the status system of the middle class, are declared mentally ill by psychiatrists, police officers, social workers, magistrates, and other representatives of the social system. Rather than submitting themselves to "treatment," complaining of self-inadequacy, they maintain a life style marked by "symptoms" reflecting alienation from the dominant social norms—symptoms grouped into the broad category *self-indulgence*.

These observations about the relationships of the PPM-GPM dimension in relation to SES prepare one to see an ironic quality in the work of McCreary (1974) and Strauss, Foureman, and Parwatikar (1974). McCreary takes up the running debate around the matter of what precisely is being measured by the premorbid adjustment measures. In the end, he finds that by simply referring to marital status, one has available a reasonably valid estimate of whatever is meant by premorbid adjustment. In other words, his report leads to the belief that persons who have entertained and acted upon all the values that lead young people to launch into marriage and commit themselves to raising a family, would undoubtedly be rated as having lived through a "good" premorbid history. Strauss,

Foureman, and Parwatikar (1974), having been exposed to the considerations about marital status as the defining criterion of premorbid status, chose to use marital status to differentiate their schizophrenic subjects. These investigators were trying to determine if premorbid history had some effect on the accuracy of estimating the size of comparison geometric figures to the size of an original standard geometric figure. Their experimental design and results allowed the conclusion that marital status was not related to this rather arcane exercise. The everyday science of schizophrenia moves forward.

Some investigators have looked into the probability that SES is a major factor in the schizophrenia research that includes the GPM-PPM continuum. Nuttal and Solomon (1965) recognized that schizophrenics of middle class origin are likely to be rated as good on their premorbid adjustment. Chapman and his coworkers (Chapman & Baxter, 1963; Chapman, Day, & Burstein, 1961), who have investigated the relationship between socioeconomic status and GPM-PPM ratings, reported the paradoxical finding that in state hospitals, a GPM group is predominantly of lower-class origin, whereas a poor premorbid group is predominantly of middle-class origin. On the surface, this appears to contradict our argument that the GPM group subscribed to middle-class values. The contradiction is dissolved when we point to the reluctance of the middle class to sequester its members in state hospitals (Hollingshead & Redlich, 1958). Only those middle-class subjects who had not espoused middle-class values are likely candidates for state hospitals. The "more deserving" middle-class schizophrenics, the GPM group, are sent to private hospitals or to psychiatrists for "treatment." Magaro (1967) found it difficult to find middle class GPM subjects in state hospitals. Although the disease model of schizophrenia is supposedly democratic, the foregoing analysis helps make clear that social class membership is a hidden variable in schizophrenia research.

Cognitive Skills

Approximately 31 percent of the studies in this survey report efforts to make an independent assessment of the level of cognitive skill (intelligence) of the subjects. Nearly two-thirds of these studies give no attention to the manner in which cognitive skills may participate in the definition of the independent variable, schizophrenia. Common sense suggests that the verbal conceptual skills of hospital oldtimers ("chronics") would be less efficient than those of hospital newcomers ("acutes"). One group of investigators studied the correlation between chronicity in schizophrenia and the nature of idiosyncratic responses to a word association test (Higgins, Mednick, & Philip, 1965). No assessment was made of the level of verbal concept development of the subjects. The authors and the editors apparently overlooked the fact that it is meaningless to study relationships of adjustment level to such variables as "persistence," "ego-involvement," "interest" and "complexity" without estimates of the conceptual skill status of the subjects at the different levels of adjustment (Blumenthal, Meltzoff, & Rosenberg, 1965). And what is being compared when the experimenter contrasts the functioning of a "schizophrenic" sample with a sample of persons drawn from those perennially available "subjects," college sophomores (see, for example, Cartwright, 1972; Nolan & Anderson, 1973). While the variable of conceptual development is ignored where it must be important, another investigator went to the trouble of matching a schizophrenic and normal group on intelligence and educational level when testing his subjects on a binocular rivalry task (Fox, 1965).

Gottesman's (1964) study of schizophrenia is illustrative of how a restricted use of concept development notions confounds interpretation of results. He hypothesized that schizophrenics would perform like children on a forced choice word association test. The Freudian regression hypothesis to explain schizophrenia is called to mind here. He found that, on the average, schizophrenics made relatively fewer choices of "contrast" terms. On the surface, this finding suggests that the conceptual development of schizophrenics is more like that of pre-seven-year-old children than are the performances of the control subjects. In the interest of articulating his finding with the contemporary work on children's language, the investigator could have related schizophrenia theory to the penetrating studies of children's use of language (Brown & Berko, 1960), or to the absence of bipolarity in the concepts that young children use (White & Johnson, 1968). Had the investigator made articulation of "child-like quality" with the exciting work on the development of conceptual skills, his conclusion would have been revised to a straightforward statement that the schizophrenics in his sample were simply "unintelligent"—hardly a surprising finding.

Lane and Albee (1963, 1964, 1968) have reported that throughout their lives schizophrenics were less "intelligent" than their peers. It is commonplace to point out that SES and intelligence test scores yield positive correlation coefficients. It is also common knowledge that level of SES is negatively related to the incidence of being tagged with the schizophrenic label. These commonplace findings would lead to the expectation that candidates for the diagnosis "schizophrenia" would have low intelligence test scores. Why then expect anything but poorer performance on any psychological task that is used to contrast "schizophrenics" to "normals?" And, when a difference is shown, why not derive the simple conclusion, "People who are low in cognitive skill development are likely to exhibit conduct that, under some conditions, encourages the use of the diagnosis schizophrenia?"

Cognitive Skill Deficit or Cognitive Processing Deficit?

The disease model would gain considerable credibility from a demonstration that schizophrenics use an identifiable, distorted approach to processing information. One could then claim that the outlandish verbal and behavioral constructions used by these deviants reflect the convoluted thought processes that might be attributable to a biological disorder. It is not surprising, then, that some of the most intense and prolonged efforts are directed toward showing that schizophrenia is marked by cognitive processes qualitatively different from those of nonschizophrenics.

A long chain of studies has attempted to demonstrate, for example, that schizophrenic samples use concepts differently. Yet, by appealing to current conceptions of intelligence (Resnick, 1976), the finding that schizophrenics function inefficiently on concept utilization tasks demonstrates only that the schizophrenic group is "less intelligent" than the comparison groups. In short, these studies show only that persons diagnosed as schizophrenic appear to be less skilled in using concepts required to solve specialized experimental problems. We assume that low efficiency in concept utilization reflects lower development in concept use skills, and that "lower concept development" is synonomous with "low intelligence." Our conviction is that an intelligence test measures a person's facility in applying a particular, limited range of information-processing strategies. In order to be generally administered, intelligence tests must restrict the range of tasks presented to subjects. To include tasks that can be successfully solved only by persons who have had a specialized set of experiences would subvert efforts to achieve the normal distributions that have been of paramount importance to intelligence test builders. The most widely used intelligence tests, then, compare an individual's skill to the standards derived from test scores earned by an acculturated segment of the population as they solved problems through use of a restricted set of concepts. It therefore becomes procedurally illegitimate (1) to equate a schizophrenia group and a normal group on the basis of total scores achieved as they work with a restricted set of general concepts (intelligence test items); (2) to predict that these two groups will show a null difference as they perform on the esoteric kinds of concept-use tasks that investigators invent; and (3) to conclude that observed differences are to be attributed to a variable called schizophrenia. The esoteric experimental tests might reflect nothing more than concept-use skills available only to persons who have had somewhat specialized experiences. Matching the schizophrenic subjects to the control subjects on their use of a generally available set of concepts is irrelevant to predicted differences on the experimental tests. Where differences in experimental test performances appear, the most appropriate conclusion would be that some members of the schizophrenic sample simply have not learned to use the kinds of concepts assessed by the experimental test. A person (schizophrenic or other) who is inept in "translating" a proverb might be one of a large number of persons with limited experience in hearing and using proverbs (Sarbin, 1970).

Chapman and his associates (Chapman & Chapman, 1973a, 1973b; Chapman, Chapman, & Daut, 1974) have recently devoted their attention to some of the confusions created by failure to take into account differing levels of skills on the specific tasks used in investigations. In one article, Chapman and his associates make the following statement:

> The usual way that investigators have attempted to rule out generalized deficit as a source of differential performance deficit has been to match schizophrenic and normal groups on "intelligence." This has been an estimator either of premorbid intelligence (usually education or

vocabulary score) or of current functioning intelligence (usually an IQ test). The rationale is that such matching rules out a differential deficit. Such matching of groups is also intended to rule out an explanation of differential deficit in terms of a difference between the two tasks in their correlation with intelligence. None of these methods of matching groups is a very effective control for generalized deficit. Both education and vocabulary are only modestly successful estimators of premorbid intelligence, and current functioning IQ score is often severely affected by pathology [Chapman, Chapman, & Daut, 1974, p. 618].

These writers continue to complicate their discussion with the "deterioration hypothesis," but they recognize that using a global measure of intelligence cannot support the belief that subjects have been matched on cognitive skills relevant to the assigned experimental tests.

In the study from which the above quotation is taken, Chapman and his colleagues investigated the old idea that schizophrenics respond inefficiently when they try to define "affect-laden" terms. They argue that to investigate this hypothesis, one must be certain that the difficulty level of the affect-laden test items matches the difficulty level of the affect-free test items. Affect-laden terms would be terms like *nurture, whore, torture,* and *puke.* These terms would represent, respectively, dependency, sex, hostility, and oral aggression. The investigators created two tests—one for the affect-laden items and another for the affect-free items—so that the difficulty levels of the tests were matched. By this method, the cognitive deficit would be determined, simply and directly, by comparing performance on an affect-free vocabulary test to performance on an affect-laden vocabulary test of equal difficulty. If the schizophrenic group made lower scores on the affect-laden items, it could be concluded that their ability to work with affect-laden terms has somehow been disrupted by the schizophrenia process. Further, if the schizophrenic subjects reached one level of success on one test and another level of success on the other test, while, for example, normal subjects succeeded equally on both tests, then the response pattern of the schizophrenics could be attributed to a deficit related to the material on one of the tests. With these careful efforts to eliminate results that could come about simply through acquired conceptual skills, Chapman's group was able to conclude that "these findings provide no support for the widely held belief that schizophrenics are less accurate in dealing with affect-laden stimuli than with emotionally neutral stimuli [p. 621]."

Building on this earlier work, Chapman and his associates (Chapman, Cameron, Cocke, & Pritchett, 1975; Chapman & Chapman, 1975; Chapman, Chapman, & Daut, 1976; Raulin & Chapman, 1976) have continued to provide evidence that the difficulty of the items that measure the experimental variations must be equated. Otherwise the schizophrenic subjects could be handicapped by reason of their inability to perform on the experimental task, whereupon the investigators could erroneously claim that they had shown a cognitive process deficit in the functioning of the schizophrenics. A review of one of the more recent studies reported by Chapman's associates will highlight the workings of intelligence variables in the study of schizophrenia.

Raulin and Chapman (1976) first review previous efforts to show that schizophrenics do not function like normals with respect to a phenomenon known as *contextual constraint*. Miller and Selfridge (1950) showed that the choice of a particular word in a word string depends on the words that precede it. If a word string has *high constraint* on a particular word, a person will more easily recall that word in a word list learning task. This concept and the neat technology of conducting associated studies would readily provide a way to demonstrate the "cognitive deficit" of schizophrenics. As usual, one group of investigators showed that schizophrenics do not benefit from high contextual constraint, whereupon another group of investigators failed to replicate the findings.

Raulin and Chapman (1976) go on to make the following cogent statement:

> The discriminating power of a test refers to the power of the test to yield a difference in mean score between more able and less able subjects. If two groups of subjects of different ability levels are given two tests of different discriminating power, the groups will differ more on the more discriminating test [p. 152].

Raulin and Chapman recommend that tests be matched, at least, for their discriminating power among normal subjects. In the case of the contextual constraint assessments, this process becomes particularly necessary. A low-constraint list of a certain length would be harder to learn than would be a high-constraint list of the same length. High-constraint lists are, by definition, easier to learn.

If a schizophrenic group and a normal group are compared on a low-constraint task, they could perform equally. Low-constraint lists would be equally difficult for both groups. On high-constraint tasks, the schizophrenics might perform worse than normals, and this result might be attributed to the level of complexity of the terms in the high-constraint list. The normals might simply be more familiar with words in that list, and that factor would raise the contextual constraint of the list, making the task easier. The results, however, might prompt an incautious investigator to conclude that schizophrenics do not profit from high constraint.

When Raulin and Chapman took considerable pains to achieve the almost impossible task of equalizing the low-constraint task and the high-constraint word lists, they found that the schizophrenic sample performed equally well on both tasks. The normals also performed equally on both tasks. The investigators were not satisfied with the precision of their matching of the two tasks, particularly since the schizophrenics did score lower on both tasks. To evaluate further the hypothesis that schizophrenics do not profit from high contextual constraints, they selected out a group of low-scoring normals, and evaluated their performances on the low-and high-constraint tasks. It was now found that the low scoring normals, relative to schizophrenics, do not profit from contextual constraint.

Raulin and Chapman derive a thoroughly sensible conclusion from this complex process: "The simple hypothesis that schizophrenics cannot profit from increased contextual constraint is inherently untestable because difficulty level varies with constraint [p. 155]." Their work and their conclusion are of particular value to our treatise. The search for the cause and the symptoms of schizophrenia has not been advanced by studies that ignore the cognitive functioning level of the subjects of the study, particularly if the subjects labelled schizophrenic are at lower levels of cognitive development.

Schizophrenia and Intelligence as Crossed Biological Models

The use of models of intelligence, within studies of schizophrenia, reveals the influence of another biologically based, mechanistic model in the behavior sciences. What is implied when investigators claim to have matched their groups on "intelligence" by means of a vocabulary test, for example, and then conclude that they have revealed the effects of a disease when schizophrenic subjects show relative ineptness on a proverb test? This argument presupposes that the intelligence measure, the vocabulary test, measures the "G" factor of intelligence. (The level of "G," incidentally, is another subtle indicator of the *goodness-badness* character of the organism. See Andersen, 1978.) In other words, to assess overall intelligence by assessing vocabulary follows an assumption that those being assessed have developed equally, in all areas, the cognitive skills needed to approach any and all types of problems. This outmoded assumption lingers from the era during which investigators argued about whether persons inherited general intelligence—the "G" factor—or specific intelligences. If one's intelligence can be characterized by "G," then one measure is as good as another; vocabulary is chosen as the best measure, because it correlates best with total intelligence test scores.

The hospital inmates, presumably having been matched to the control group on the "G" factor, are judged to have an equal level of general goodness. The intelligence test, or a truncated substitute, is assumed to have demonstrated that the schizophrenic and the normal group ultimately must function equally well in *all* conceptual areas. If the schizophrenics' performance is inferior to the normals' on the proverbs test, then—according to normal science practitioners—the process that underlies function on this test is the process that underlies "schizophrenia." It is as if one gets a measure of the quality of one's "intelligence knob" by getting a general measure of intelligence, and a discovery that part of the knob is atilt points to the presence of the disease, *schizophrenia*.

The biological logic of these models forcefully intrudes into the work of investigators who talk about "deterioration" of intelligence as a complication of schizophrenia. Lane and Albee (1963, 1964) checked the grade school records of a group of people who had been diagnosed as schizophrenic. They found that this group had had intelligence scores lower than those of their grade school peers. Because schizophrenics score low on intelligence tests, it becomes difficult to find suitable control subjects for a study that matches groups on a general measure of intelligence. But practitioners of the normal science hold that since the schizophrenics are suffering from a disease, their lower intelligence might be attributable to "deterioration." After all, a physical disease is related to a "wasting away" of the body, and surely if one has a "mental disease," ones "mind" must also "waste away"—thus, the invention of the concept "intellectual deterioration." With this premise, one can contrast a schizophrenic group to any normal group. One merely argues that the "premorbid" intellectual level of the schizophrenia group was equivalent to that of the control group. In this connection, it is instructive to note that in an early study, Chapman (1960), whose recent work totally abrogates this procedure, used a schizophrenic group with a mean estimated IQ of 86, and a nonschizophrenic "control" group with a mean estimated IQ of 113, a difference of 27 IQ points. At that time, Chapman argued (unconvincingly) that the last-answered item on the vocabularly test could be used as an indicator of "premorbid" intelligence level, and that on this basis his groups were equivalent. Burstein (1961) compared a schizophrenic group with a mean IQ of 91 to a normal group with a mean IQ of 117, a difference of 25 IQ points. Despite this difference, he declared that because the groups were similar in mean age and years of education, the "premorbid" intelligence of the schizophrenic group was equivalent to that of the normal group.

Were one to accept these arguments for equivalence on original "G," a logical flaw would still remain within the very system employed by these researchers. What is the relevance of the schizophrenic's premorbid intelligence to present functioning? Once we accept the assumption of deterioration, it would follow that all psychological functioning had deteriorated. Granting that the schizophrenics are indeed matched on premorbid functioning, and having shown that they perform less well than the nonschizophrenics, we can now conclude little else than that their performance on the specific task has deteriorated concomitant with the deterioration that has taken place in their general intelligence. Clearly, this shaky assumptive scaffold rests on a bed of sand. Did the persons identified as schizophrenics indeed have an equal "premorbid" conceptual development? The reader is reminded again that Lane and Albee (1963, 1964, 1968) produced a series of studies demonstrating that life circumstances that account for one's being identified as a schizophrenic also have functioned to retard, in contrast to one's peers, one's general conceptual growth. The reader is also reminded that persons of low SES, that is, persons who do not use the same concepts as professional diagnosers, psychologists and psychiatrists, are far more likely to have been declared schizophrenic by the diagnostic team.

A related matter deserves note. Heffner, Strauss, and Grisell (1975) show that people with low assessed IQ are likely to remain in the cohort of persons that bear the label schizophrenia, whereas higher IQ persons exit from this group. This process helps to account for the inappropriate conclusion that schizophrenics show a deterioration in intelligence. A clinician who views a particular hospital population at any one point in time will observe that the long-term inmates are less conceptually developed, in comparison to the newcomers. Should we follow the careers of a single sample of new admissions, however, we would be able to predict that the cognitively limited person will remain in the system eventually to earn the title *chronic*. Heffner and his associates reviewed the records of 91 males who had been diagnosed at one clinic over a five-year period. Of the 46 high-ability persons (>95 IG) in the sample, two had been successively rehospitalized during the follow-up interval; of the 45 low-ability persons, 10 had been repeatedly rehospitalized. Seventy percent of the high-ability group was never rehospitalized, whereas only 50 percent of the low-ability group enjoyed this status.

The Major Significance of Intelligence Differences

Eventually the long-term residents of hospitals, like those in the study reported by Heffner, Strauss, and Grisell (1975), will appear in samples of schizophrenics that an investigator will use to show that schizophrenics process information anomolously. The investigators will fail to take into account levels of cognitive skill relative to the task. If they do consider skill levels, they will most likely use an outmoded concept of general intelligence, so that the logic of biology applied to intelligence will compound difficulties in studying "schizophrenia." It should be added that the scientific value of biological models of intelligence is under attack. As other models are introduced (Inhelder & Piaget, 1969; Resnick, 1976; Riegel, 1973) investigators of schizophrenia may reconsider the place of cognitive skills relative to unwanted behavior.

As more psychologists use a concept of intelligence as equivalent to cognitive skills, and recognize that such cognitive skills are specific to the kinds of information being processed, there will be a clearer awareness of the inappropriateness of declaring that an "IQ test" has been used to equate people who are later asked to perform on a test that measures a specific cognitive skill. From the direction of current research, we predict that investigators of deviant behavior will more consistently report conclusions like those developed by Chapman, Chapman, and Daut (1974) and by Raulin and Chapman (1976). The ultimate effect of such consistently reported conclusions of "no difference" should, if one follows rules of evidence, lead to the rejection and abandonment of the schizophrenia model.

EDUCATION LEVEL

Ninety-nine studies, about 26 percent of the papers covered by this review, leave the reader to infer that the educational level, usually reported in terms of years of schooling, reflects the intellectual development of the subjects under study. Considering our current educational practices, we know that two high school graduates cannot, by any means, be assumed to be equal in their cognitive development. Where there is a mandatory attendance law, many persons who leave school at age 16 have been marking time for the greater part of their last years of school. The famous "Coleman Report" (1966) requires that we look beyond the face validity of the argument that years of school are an appropriate index of cognitive development. School treatments have little effect on learning rates and achievement patterns. These patterns instead strongly correlate with the familial background of students. Again, socioeconomic status, which determines the esteem and opportunity offered to a growing child, seems to regulate what the child takes from the years of schooling.

In an era of compulsory school attendance, the number of years of attendance tells us little about a person's cognitive development, unless we also know the developmental opportunities offered through that person's family background. Thus nothing can be gained from matching subjects according to educational level and then drawing the conclusion that the individuals have developed equal cognitive skill levels. It is more compelling to recognize that a schizophrenic sample population of drug-free schizophrenics. In some hospitals, special research conclude that this hidden variable could account for the small differences on experimental tasks.

DRUGS

In the past 20 years, as the use of potent drugs has increased, the supply of undrugged, hospitalized subjects has diminished. Investigators must devise very special strategies to overcome standard hospital procedure and thereby create a sample population of drug-free schizophrenics. In some hospitals, special research wards have been created so that investigations can be conducted with drug-free inmates. Raulin and Chapman (1976) reported a study in which such subjects were used. They took a strong view regarding the effects of drugs in relation to previous studies of schizophrenic cognitive processes. "Since the effects of these drugs are often as dramatic as the effects of the illness itself, and just as unpredictable, the results of earlier studies could have reflected the effects of medication as well as the effects of schizophrenia [p. 155]."

While Raulin and Chapman take their emphatic position, other researchers propose that drug effects are of little concern to the function under study. When the hypothesis is concerned with the autonomic responses of schizophrenics, the following argument is taken to be an unsatisfactory dismissal of drug effects:

> The control for medication effects is difficult under the best circumstances. Little is known of the individual differences in reaction to drugs, 'untranquilized' psychiatric patients are rather rare, and withdrawal of patient medication for research purposes might introduce an even greater source of error than ignoring the variable would introduce [Ward & Carlson, 1966, p. 11].

In the same year that Ward and Carlson published their article in *JAP*, Goldstein, Acker, Crockett, and Riddle (1966), reported an extended study into the effects of mellaril on the autonomic nervous system responses of schizophrenics. Their results strongly suggest that one should be very cautious about drug effects when trying to distinguish, for example, process from reactive schizophrenics on the basis of their autonomic nervous system activity.

Responses to tests of psychological functioning, particularly when the alertness or the rapid physical action of the subject might be involved, similarly could be affected by the commonly used drugs. Oltmanns and Neale (1975) asked schizophrenic and control subjects to repeat numbers that had been read to them, via tape recorder. Some strings of numbers were read in straightforward, nondisruptive fashion. Other strings were read by a female voice, and each number was separated from the next by a male voice reading a "distraction" number. In comparison to the normal sample, the schizophrenic sample showed problems responding to the six-item digit strings containing the distractors. They showed no loss on five-item distractor-laced lists. Oltmanns and Neale discuss deficits in the schizophrenics' ability to use input grouping strategies to facilitate later recall, and speak of deficient "chunking" as a possible schizophrenic deficit. At the same time, they noted that all the schizophrenic subjects were receiving antipsychotic drugs. Obviously, the control groups were not. The experiment was set up so that conclusions could be drawn about the effect of drugs on chunking. The experiment, carried out precisely as it was carried out, was indeed a suitable study of the hypothesis that links chunking behavior and drugs.

Similarly, Davies-Osterkamp, Rist, and Bangert (1977) find some evidence that schizophrenics show a slowed reaction time in a complex information processing task. All the schizophrenics were taking phenothiazines. Levy (1976) studied the level of self-disclosure as shown in the presence of an "emotional" or a "nonemotional" interviewer. She concludes that "schizophrenics do not disclose very much intimate information about themselves," and "they also revealed themselves to be sensitive to the structure of the interview [pp. 442-443]. Virtually all the schizophrenics were on phenothiazines, and the control subjects (alcohol- or drug-abuse patients) were not. Why does one conclude that *schizophrenia* is the differentiating variable in these studies? It would be as defensible to conclude that phenothiazines influence reaction time and self-disclosure.

Do Drugs Eliminate the Schizophrenic Deficit?

Hamsher and Arnold (1976) tried to replicate findings reported by Boland and Chapman (1971). The latter researchers had proposed that schizophrenics show a deficit in reporting word associations. The deficit represents a propensity to report the strongest associate, rather than the "correct synonym" or the semantic associate of the stimulus word. When Hamsher and Arnold tried to confirm Boland and Chapman's proposition, they could show only that the schizophrenic sample performed very much the same as a sample of nonschizophrenic psychiatric patients. Hamsher and Arnold noted that 89 percent of their subjects were receiving neuroleptic drugs; whereas none of Boland and Chapman's schizophrenic subjects were on drugs. They then state that "the possibility that these drugs very much improved the test performance of our schizophrenics does not appear to be a possible explanation [p. 300]" of the results.

By raising this issue, they reverse a common coin. In most instances, drugs are assumed to debilitate behavior. When one assesses the place of drugs in schizophrenia studies, however, one must consider the alternative. The phenothiazines, according to a common current designation, are "antipsychotic." Thus, if one is to take the use of drugs as "true therapy" for the disease called schizophrenia, then investigators who use drugged subjects are not able to assess a deficit associated with schizophrenia. In effect, the behavior scientists who seek out the basic psychological processes of schizophrenia, and who do so using drugged patients, are logically contradicting their fellow scientists who describe the current crop of most-favored drugs as having a "true antipsychotic action [Carlson, 1978, p. 164]" or as having an "antischizophrenic potency [Snyder, 1974, pp. 238-246]."

These points cannot be trivial in the face of the status of the last ten years of schizophrenia research. (The last ten years are used as a baseline for this discussionof drugs, since it is the rare schizophrenic who has not been given drugs during this period. Indeed, some researchers [Hirt, Cutler, & Genshaft, 1977] note that drug-free subjects could not be used because of the ethical issues involved in withholding drugs.) During the years 1969-78, 193 reports used schizophrenics as subjects. In 23 of these studies, we judged that drug effects are not germane to the outcomes. In another nine studies it was not clear whether drugs were being used. The reports of 45 studies (23 percent) made no mention of the drug status of the subjects. About 50 percent (97) of the studies do indicate that the subjects used in the study were taking prescribed drugs, usually phenothiazines. Fourteen of these 97 studies used one or another technique to assess the possible effects of drugs on experimental task performances. (The assessment was commonly made through correlating drug levels with test performance outcomes.) Only 19 of the 193 studies clearly reported that the schizophrenic samples were not taking drugs at the time of the study.

Since drugs are so widely used, and since the information about their effects is unformed and contradictory, one cannot be confident about what is happening in a study that shows small differences between the mean scores of the schizophrenic samples and the mean scores of the control group samples. Some of the drugs now being used have clearly been shown to create serious motor neuron dysfunctions. These drugs appear to affect motor neuron function by interfering with systems that involve dopamine as a transmitter substance. At best, there is only rudimentary information concerning how dopamine dependent systems are involved in psychological function. While this state of affairs exists, the conclusion is undeniable: Drug effects are involved as an uncontrolled variable in a large number of the studies that attempt to define schizophrenia.

PATIENTHOOD AND HOSPITALIZATION EFFECTS

About 95 percent of the studies covered by this survey can be regarded as studies of hospitalization and patienthood. By focusing research on the schizophrenia model, all but 19 of the 374 studies in this review used as schizophrenics only subjects who were hospital residents. By following the research strategies of the disease paradigm, experimenters have infused every study with the multiple effects that indoctrination into patienthood and hospital residence have upon the behavior of their research subjects.

Theorists (Szasz, 1961; Goffman, 1961; Sarbin, 1969b; Scheff, 1966, 1967, 1975) and novelists (Kesey, 1962) had discussed the effects of hospitalization before research psychologists (Braginsky, Braginsky, & Ring, 1969; Silverman, Berg, & Kantor, 1966) began their explorations of this important variable. These writers have expanded the hypothesis that labelling and then placing persons in a hospital has a deleterious effect on their thinking and actions. Scheff is a proponent of this view:

> *Among residual deviants, labelling is the single most important cause of careers of residual deviance.* This hypothesis assumes that most residual deviance, if it does not become the basis for entry into the sick role, will not lead to a deviant career. Most deviant careers, according to this point of view, arise out of career contingencies, and are not directly connected with the origins of the original deviance. . . . The dynamics of treated mental illness could then be studied quite apart from the individual dynamics of mental disorder [1963, pp. 451-452].

Being initiated into the hospital, then, enters one into the "training ground for schizophrenic behavior [McReynolds, personal communication]." The findings of Hollingshead and Redlich (1958), which clearly show that the second admission of a low SES person marks the beginning of a lifetime career, informs us that the hospital process trains one for the vocation of patient—a vocation for which persons were prepared during their first admissions and during their subsequent encounters with an out-of-the-hospital vocation for which they were ill-prepared.

Playing the Patient Role

No studies in our survey apprise us of the beliefs that patients hold about themselves as they face repeated failure in their efforts to solve the problems in their prepatient lives. Perhaps they are prepared to adopt a variant of the "generalized badness" theory, and apply it to themselves. Perhaps they are willing to believe that they are suffering from a "mental illness." After all, the mental hygiene propaganda is widely disseminated, and under highly reputable auspices (Rabkin, 1974; Sarbin & Mancuso, 1970). Would a belief that one is a potential or actual patient affect the ways one would respond to experimental tests or to interviews? Do practitioners of the normal science of schizophrenia validate one's enactments when one adopts a patient role (Sarbin, 1969b)?

Studies have systematically documented the ability of patients to play their roles to suit varied demands of the environmental situation (Braginsky, Braginsky, & Ring, 1969). Zarlock's (1966) observations are pertinent. Zarlock obtained the participation of thirty hospitalized persons who had been designated as schizophrenics by a variety of proceedings. These men were on a ward in which they were allowed few personal liberties. Each person was introduced, along with nine fellow patients, into settings that were cast as recreational, occupational, social, or medical. In the recreation setting, for example, the participants could play games such as darts, chess, and so forth. In the medical setting, the room contained only chairs in a circle, and the staff wore their professional uniforms. In each of these settings, the patients addressed issues relevant to the setting. In the occupational setting, for example, patients spent 90 percent of their time on projects, and about 50 percent of their conversation was addressed to work activity. In the medical setting, 90 percent of the time was devoted to discussing personal problems. These findings are not surprising, unless one expects schizophrenics to be irrelevant under most circumstances. It is noteworthy, however, that the number of statements judged pathological increased markedly in the medical setting. Bizarre body expressions, genuflecting, and praying aloud were more frequent occurrences in the medical setting, and not in the other settings. Raters judged thirty-three medical setting incidents to be pathological, while only eight incidents, of all activity in the other settings, were judged pathological. When the doctor is in the context, the patient knows that "pathology" becomes the area of common interest.

Other studies complement Zarlock's findings and considerations of the role-playing skills of schizophrenics. Manis, Houts, and Blake (1963), showed that those patients who profess an espousal of a "psychiatric point of view" regarding "mental illness" are more rapidly discharged from the hospital. Is this dismissal brought about by a "cure," or does it represent a social reward for skills in assessing the value of adopting a particular role? Do the same kinds of skills revealed in these studies intercede to affirm differences between schizophrenic and normal groups in studies of perception or cognition?

Studies of schizophrenics have asked patients for information about their parents or family situation (see, for example, Garmezy, Clark, & Stockner, 1961; Fontana, Klein, & Cicchetti, 1967; Farina & Holzberg, 1967). As would be expected, schizophrenics report their parents to be somewhat more objectionable than normal patients report their parents to be. Garmezy, Clark, and Stockner (1961) found that schizophrenics report more negative characteristics than do normals, with the poor premorbid subgroup evaluating their parents, particularly their mothers, most negatively. The effects of patient status could be as effective in producing these results as were the actual family situations of the patients. Consider that schizophrenics have participated in interviews with psychiatrists, social workers, and psychologists, who hold theories about "schizophrenic mothers," and are empowered to reward particular declarations that are evoked from the patient. We expect that the professionals' reinforcements can influence the patients to produce specific verbal patterns (Salzinger & Pisoni, 1958, 1961); that the patients have some ideas about psychiatric theory (Manis, Houts, & Blake, 1963), and that they can manipulate their responses to meet their own needs (Braginsky, Braginsky, & Ring, 1969). A sophisticated investigator would not overlook the fact that some patient might find it useful to make their parents appear to be malevolent.

Effects of Low Stimulation

In addition to evidence that assuming the patient role affects behavior in experimental testing, there is still another way that patienthood influences performance on dependent variables. The extended social isolation that is a part of hospitalization appears to have deleterious effects on a variety of cognitive and motor tasks. Silverman (1964) gave his experimental tests to short- and long-term felons, rather than to acute and chronic schizophrenics (Silverman, Berg, & Kantor, 1966). He found that the performance of these prisoners, as well as their performance in contrast to the normal group, paralleled the performances of the schizophrenics. Sollod and Lapidus (1977) administered a series of tests to chronic and acute schizophrenics. These tests were based on Piaget's studies of qualitative changes in developing cognitive functions. On five of the 11 tests, the chronic sample performed less adequately than did the acute samples. Sollod and Lapidus did not report mean hospitalization time for their samples, though they say that none of the "acutes" had been hospitalized for over one year, whereas the members of the chronic group had been in diagnosis for at least five years and each had spent at least two years in hospitals. Knowing, among other things, that Silverman (1964) could not differentiate long-term incarcerated felons from chronic hospital inhabitants, there is reason to conclude that Sollod and Lapidus (1977) offered a further demonstration of the deadening effects of hospital residence.

The Patient Trying to Control Outcomes

When researchers report that they have worked with chronic or acute schizophrenics (see Cegalis, Leen, & Solomon, 1977; Draguns, 1963; Karras, 1962; Lewisohn & Riggs, 1962; Yates and Korboot, 1970), they silently and perhaps unwittingly weave hospitalization effects into the fabric of their hypothesis. This inclusion of patienthood is in the context of studying another variable. When results show that acute schizophrenics—patients who have been recently hospitalized—are slower to respond in a categorizing task (Draguns, 1963), can this slowness be accepted as a valid sign of instability of conceptual functioning? The newly admitted patient, in contrast to the "oldtimer," may be concerned about the effect of test results on staff decisions. New patients may believe that poor responses may extend incarceration. The oldtimers, on the other hand, like the older subjects in the Braginsky, Braginsky, and Ring (1969) studies, seem less concerned about their continued stay in the hospital. These hospitalization-produced factors, rather than a presumed psychological state, must be further explored for their effects on dependent variables in schizophrenia studies.

Knowing that a patient could be second-guessing an experimenter, where else can we look for this factor in schizophrenia studies? What happens to the responses of hospital oldtimers who are told they are being evaluated to see how well they can be prepared for jobs outside the hospital (Gladis, 1964)? What if they were told, instead, that they were being evaluated for placement on a locked ward? Spence and Lair (1964) investigated the hypothesis that there is greater associative interference in association learning in schizophrenics. Participants were to learn to recite the response word that was presented following the presentation of the anticipatory stimulus word. Each learning test contained eight pairs of words. Though the stimulus word was not paired with a word that would be commonly associated with that word, the common associate did appear as the response word for one of the other stimulus words. For example, *chair* was not the response word for *table*, but the word *chair* could have been the response word for *black*, while *table* would have been the response word for *white*. In this way, there were possibilities for high associative interference as participants tried to learn to anticipate correctly which word would follow the presentation of the stimulus words.

Rather than scoring only the incorrect responses given in the learning of the lists, Spence and Lair sorted out the number of responses that could have been intralist interference responses and the number of incorrect responses that were words that standardization samples give as common associates to the words in the list. Schizophrenics, during the learning trials, gave no more of the kinds of responses showing associative interference than did the control group, thus contradicting expectations based on the interference hypothesis. Schizophrenics did, however, give more responses that were simply errors. If errors alone had been used to assess the hypothesis of associative interference, the schizophrenics would have shown greater associative interference. Perhaps, however, the schizophrenics simply gave more responses because they were motivated to maintain their role as "cooperative patients"—a highly valued role—than they were motivated to be "correct."

Another example of how a "cooperative" subject can gain a higher score on a "pathognomonic measure" is found in the extensive work of Payne and his associates (Payne & Caird, 1967; Payne, Caird, & Laverty, 1964) who have used the dependent variable "overinclusiveness." They have reported significant associations between schizophrenia and "overinclusiveness." Looking closely at their operational specification of "overinclusiveness," as have Bromet and Harrow (1973), we find that someone who is "garrulous" or "overproductive" would be labelled "overinclusive." Price (1968) carefully investigated the relationships between concept identification and pathology level. Unfortunately he did not report hospital length, but his data show that as level of pathology (longer time in hospital?) rises, so does the number of "yes" responses to incorrect items, particularly as the item difficulty increases. A patient, then, who is trying to be "nice," who cooperates with instructions, or who agreeably responds "yes" to questions will be regarded as more pathological, rather than as more garrulous or more agreeable. Again, the role that patients believe they must assume, and not the esoteric independent variable, intervenes in the testing of hypotheses.

The Researcher Renames the Cooperative Patient

Broen and Nakamura (1972) created an experimental situation in which schizophrenic subjects were given instructions that required them to attend to two different tasks simultaneously. The subjects were told specifically that it was far more important to follow a rotating target than it was to listen for a tone that was presented through a head set. The chronic schizophrenics apparently obeyed these instructions; and, at the same time, lost some of the accuracy with which they were able to detect the presentation of the tone. The most parsimonious interpretation of this finding is that chronic schizophrenics were following instructions, playing out a compliant, "good patient" role. Broen and Nakamura, however, offer the esoteric and tortured conclusion that "the sensitivity of chronic non-paranoid schizophrenics to a simple auditory signal was shown to be attenuated more than that of acute paranoids when auditory monitoring was of secondary rather than primary importance [p. 110]." When scientists are committed to the "schizophrenics-are-in-a-bad-way" philosophy, they simply cannot perceive the blighted schizophrenic performing positively.

Thornton and Gottheil (1971) offer another excellent example of how to make schizophrenics into "bad guys," when they are only trying to be "good guys." These investigators used Kuethe's (1962) felt board figures to test, among other things, the hypothesis that schizophrenics "do not organize their perceptions according to the schema that 'people belong together' and thus will more often replace human figures farther apart than nonhuman figures [p. 192]." Subjects viewed, among other sets of stimuli that were presented in separate trials, sets of human figures placed 60 centimeters apart on a felt board. Subjects were instructed to replace the figures "exactly where they were," after they had been told that the study was concerned with "how well people can judge distance [p. 193]." Thornton and Gottheil conclude "The normal males, then, displayed the expected bias and replaced the human figures closer together than the nonhuman figures, while the schizophrenic males showed no reliable bias in either direction [p. 193]." Following the canon of parsimony, the most appropriate conclusion is that the schizophrenics followed instructions while the normals did not. These schizophrenics, after all, had spent anywhere from two weeks up to 27 years in their present hospitalization. Over half of these subjects had at least one year of training at their "total institution" (Goffman, 1961). They were well aware of the need to play the role of the "good patient."

Some Other Hospital Effects

Another aspect of "playing the patient" has been suggested by Magaro (1973). Patients live out their lives by following very routinized formulae. What are their silent ruminations and reflections when the experimenter calls on them to carry out strange tasks devised to produce dependent measure data? Do they regard it as a dramatic intrusion into monotonous hospital routine? Do they see it as a new diagnostic procedure? Do they have hopes of becoming one of the guinea pigs in that one great and significant experiment that will unlock the secret of schizophrenia? Do they think of it as another of those strange things that the psychologists and the psychiatrists do to entertain themselves? Magaro concludes that his complex study is best interpreted in terms of the novelty of the laboratory situation for people who have been socially isolated in a stimulus deprivation condition. Whatever the subjects' reactions, their approach to the tasks must be different from the approach of the "normal" subjects who usually serve as the control sample. Whatever the differences in views, one could conjecture that the normal subjects are more sympathetic to the unspoken wishes and desires of the investigator; and, if this is the case, we can expect, following Orne's far reaching analysis (1962), that they will do what they can to help the experimenters discover what they need to discover.

And yet another point: All of us have watched adults alter their behavior as they approach different persons who occupy different roles. People are more simplistic as they interact with children. They are more cautious when they interact with strangers. People are more deferent when they interact with notable figures. Experimenters who have carried out the studies under our current scrutiny know that they are approaching schizophrenics—those strange, alien creatures, ridden with a mysterious disease that causes attentional deficits, cognitive deficits, loss of contact with reality, loosened associations, and perhaps even inability to make a reversal shift. When they approach these creatures, do experimenters enact the same role as when they approach the normals of the control sample? Or do they behave in an "understanding and sympathetic way"? In other words, experimenters can unwittingly influence their subjects, perhaps alienating them, helping to create a set that would influence the schizophrenics as they respond to the dependent measure tasks. Brown (1973) commented, following his three-week exploration of places frequented by schizophrenics, that though he never heard anything childlike in their speech, he "fairly often heard patients spoken to with what I call nursery school intonation, a kind of prosody that most adults use with small children [p. 397]." Such observable, demeaning reactions might better account for an experiment's small mean differences than does the patient's "schizophrenic state."

In short, when Ph.D. candidates set out to do their doctoral dissertations, using as captive subjects the "old hands" on the wards of U.S. Veterans' Administration hospitals (where most of the schizophrenic studies have been completed), are they studying "schizophrenia" or "patienthood?" After a decade of research attention to the matter of patienthood, and having available the series of studies devoted to investigating its relevance, we can see that it has hardly been considered in the 374 core studies. Two hundred and eight studies in this review report the length of time the schizophrenics had spent in hospitals. In most cases, length of hospitalization is reported in order to assure readers that anyone who has spent the stated time in hospitals is clearly and correctly diagnosed as mentally ill. In the majority of the studies where length of hospitalization might be relevant and where it is reported, there is no effort to analyze the effects that patienthood might have upon the results. Only 61 studies analyzed the relationship of length of hospitalization to the dependent variable or eliminated it as a variable. Occasionally an investigator will report the use of a correlational technique, which has the intent of showing that scores do not rise or fall in direct relationship to the length of hospital stay (see Bernstein, 1970; Draguns, 1963; Ham, Spanos, & Barber, 1976; Larsen & Fromholt, 1976). This technique would be useful only if patienthood were to develop linearly as a function of time spent in hospital.

The Importance of Patienthood in Identity Definition

Before closing our remarks about patienthood, some comments are in order about the effects of becoming a "mentally ill" person. If behavior scientists explicitly recognize that diagnostic labelling is confounded by the person's assuming patienthood as a self-definition, then they can entertain hypotheses about the social and cognitive effects of becoming a mental patient (see, for example, Perucci, 1974; Price & Denner, 1974). Sarbin (1962), interested in "language and thought disorders" in persons identified as schizophrenic, argues that such "disorders" may be products, resultants, or outcomes of certain identifiable social events associated with the labelling of a person as mentally ill and with the concomitant instrumental acts and degradation rituals performed by medical, police, and court personnel.

To advance this argument, five sequences in the career of the mental patient are noted. These sequences are placed on a time dimension as follows:

Sequence I: remote ecological events, postulated genetic and constitutional events
Sequence II: prepatient role
Sequence III: unsettled patient role
Sequence IV: stabilized patient role
Sequence V: posthospital patient role.

In the present analysis, Sequence V is not discussed. Identifiable contingencies during Sequence V will influence whether a person assigned the posthospital patient role will continue in that role, will act so as to repudiate the role assignment, or will return to Sequences III and IV [Angrist, Lefton, Dinitz, & Pasamanick, 1968; Freeman & Simmons, 1963]). In most of the 374 studies reviewed, the experimenters compared the performances of persons in Sequence IV with the performances of "normals" or of "nonschizophrenics." (The exceptions to this generalization are those studies that compared two categories of persons in the stabilized patient role, such as "good premorbids" and "poor premorbids.") If differences are found between the means of the schizophrenic and the nonschizophrenic samples, and if the investigator is interested in articulating the findings with some general theory, then the investigator will relate the fact of mean difference to events of Sequence I drawn from retrospective accounts or from records. For example, mean differences in interpreting proverbs are related to such Sequence I ecological events as having a schizophrenogenic mother, death of one parent before the patient's thirteenth birthday, disorganized family, etc., or such genetic and constitutional events as having a lunatic grandfather or a mother who took drugs during pregnancy. That events of Sequence I may enter into the texture of antecedent events is undeniable; however, an examination of Sequences II and III may yield more appropriate antecedent variables for Sequence IV conduct, at least for the kinds of performances required in the typical experiment.

At least for a large proportion of persons who ultimately are hospitalized and classified as schizophrenic, it seems clear that attention deployment is the primary adaptive technique. In a social ecology that provides inputs that the person cannot instantiate or assimilate, strain may be reduced through attending to inputs that are assimilable (that make sense), even though similar input would not necessarily be of interest to coresidents, friends, neighbors, and others. To disengage oneself from the disturbing social ecology without engaging in proscribed or doomed-to-failure instrumental activity requires a shift in attention from inputs derived from the confusing, ambiguous social ecology to other kinds of inputs. This maneuver is often labeled *withdrawal*. The effect of disengaging oneself from the relevant social ecology is to focus on fantasy creations or pseudocommunities, where the input can be silently matched with cognitive structures of unknown consensual validity. It is important to emphasize that withdrawal and redeployment of attention to a pseudocommunity are not by themselves taken as sufficient evidence for classifying a person as a prepatient. One can cite ample evidence of effectively functioning persons who—at one time or another— have engaged in attention redeployment as a means of symbolically removing inputs that were noninstantiable and hence stress-producing. Everyday occurrences may be cited: reading a romantic novel, having daydreams of glory, attending a movie, watching TV—in short, any action where the person focuses on symbolic constructions. It is when an audience of relevant others declares a valuation on the *overt* side effects of attention redeployment that one observes the conditions for assigning the person the role of prepatient.

Before this time, the person enacts the social roles appropriate to the statuses he or she has been assigned in virtue of membership in age, sex, occupational, family, and other groups. Insofar as the audiences regard the public enactments as appropriate to the positions the person occupies, there will be no question of assigning a prepatient role, even though the person may make frequent use of attention redeployment as a way of neutralizing the effects of strain. Only when relevant others judge overt role enactments to be incongruent with suitable identity definitions are the conditions present for considering such enactments a part of another role—the sick role—or, in the present analysis, the prepatient role. At this point, the person, mirroring the actions of well-meaning doctors, may begin to take the sick role as a metaphor for his or her identity. However, the audience of relevant others—family, relatives, friends, neighbors, clergymen, and teachers—may change the picture by modifying their own role behaviors, thereby modifying inputs, or adding inputs from the social ecology that make sense to the potential patient. If the efforts of the audience are successful, then the dependency upon a pseudocommunity may be broken.

However, the audience of relevant others may not be successful in its efforts at modifying the socially dysfunctional conduct, or may not at first place a negative value on the role enactments of the distressed person, in which case the adaptive technique of attention deployment is reinforced (through strain reduction). When the actor's invalid role performances disturb the primary or secondary social groups, a condition similar to societal anomie is found. Members of the family of the actor generally have no norms for dealing with counter-expectational events. They cannot resolve the incongruence between the identity definition they perceive in the prepatient and the role enactment they observe. They too experience the effects of epistemic strain. The functioning of the group is threatened. If the group has no resources for changing the stress-producing ecology, then available social institutions are sought. In modern times in the Western world, the institutions are there and so is a ready made social identity—the mental patient, the mentally ill person (Rothman, 1971). But before one is inducted into acting the role of institutional inpatient, there is a period when one plays, sometimes unwittingly, prepatient roles (Goffman, 1961).

A prepatient role is a variant of a sick role. The person who is assigned the adjective "sick" or "ill" is excused from performing most of the other customary roles. At the same time that the person is considered sick by family and associates, there is an obligation on them, or on their surrogates—social workers, physicians, police, etc.—to see that the sick role is enacted in the proper setting. The institutional resource for sickness is, of course, managed by physicians. In enacting their assigned roles, the physicians practice their craft and find that the patient is not sick in the usual sense of having aches, pains, chills, fevers, sweats, itches, or other subjectively felt complaints. However, any of the patient's performances allow the physician to enact the diagnostician's role and to offer a diagnosis of mental illness—the diagnosis being influenced by a prediagnosis given by responsible relatives and neighbors and further supported by a "mental status" examination.

Important in this phase of the development of the sick role is what Goffman (1961) calls the "betrayal funnel [p. 140]." It is often the case that responsible relatives conspire with the court, the police, the district attorney, and the doctor to have the patient removed to a psychiatric hospital or state hospital with a minimum of fuss and disturbance to the community. Even where the person is told forthrightly that he or she is mentally sick and must go to a hospital for care and treatment, the probability is great that certain conspiratorial efforts have preceded the announcement.

Lemert (1962) had convincingly demonstrated the influence of conspiratorial efforts in the production of paranoid disorders. The prepatient sequence has this special characteristic—members of the person's significant audiences have begun to look and act as if the person could only enact roles with minimal obligations. Any role requiring more than these minimal obligations is quietly taken away. The upshot of reducing the number of roles that persons play is to reduce the size and complexity of their social ecology, and thereby force them to depend more and more on inputs from their private worlds. The usual standards of competence in role enactment are modified to take into account the injunction that these persons are to be held responsible only for the minimal social performances of the sick person. In short, their claims to being valid persons are challenged. They are subject to subtle degradation rituals, the effect of which is to eliminate their claims to being actual persons—to having a social identity that can be communicated by self-chosen role enactments.

Further, the failure to have their enactments taken as suitable representations of their social identity repeatedly deprives them of the consensual validation that confirms their identity. They experience further the effects of epistemic strain, and they are driven to further experimentation with "metaphors" by which they may represent their now degraded social identity. It is unlikely that the newly constructed role enactments will be accepted as valid representations of "real" (other-attributed) identity, and the prepatients are more actively motivated to accept the sick role. By accepting that role, they resolve the incongruities between social expectations and role enactments, and relieve the epistemic strain developed by their own persistent failure properly to instantiate (by role enactments) their identity.

But the prepatient role is not easily enacted. In the first place, the usual referent for sickness is pain or malaise. Since these persons cannot support their assignment to the sick role through phenomenal experience of pain or other somatic dysfunction, their audience or their surrogates must induct them into the niceties of the role of mental patient. If they accept this role and the explanation that they are emotionally sick or mentally ill, they must then learn the behaviors appropriate to the role. The focal item is to believe the doctors and nurses "that whatever they do is for your own good." Such an answer, of course, if accepted, removes any semblance of criticality from patients and they are made to take on the role behaviors of a trusting child, the same enactments that they offer in the presence of the investigator who chooses them as a subject in a study of schizophrenia. If they do not accept the definition of their role and put up a fight, then the relevant audiences may point to such resistance to reinforce their belief that the patients are ill. The bureaucratic wheels of medicine and law turn unyieldingly and persons who will not give up their roles without a fight find themselves heavily drugged in a locked ward of a mental hospital, where they too may become subjects in a study of schizophrenia.

This sociological description is preparatory to the argument that the mean differences in performance on experimental tasks may be accounted for in the effects of stripping away persons' roles in order to make them fit the profession's image of the mental patient.

Sequence III is characterized by the further stripping away of the patients' usual roles. In some communities, they are locked in a psychiatric ward for observation for a few days. They are subject to commitment procedures where a judge or magistrate "commits" them to a mental hospital on the basis of the reports of relatives or police and the examination of a physician (Miller & Schwartz, 1966; Morse, 1978; Wenger & Fletcher, 1969). Their civil rights are taken away and so are their accustomed claims to being a person, of having a

valid identity. Their entry into a state hospital is marked by rituals and ceremonies which can only be likened to degradation ceremonies in other institutional contexts (Garfinkel, 1956). There is no need here to detail the various
mortifications practiced on new patients in order to convince them that they are
sick and that their proper performance of the sick role is required before they can
achieve a state of health and grace. Unlike somatic illness, where the events
associated with a known disease entity are catalogued and fairly reliable, the
events associated with mental disease may include everything the patient does or
does not do. Every employee of the hospital, in principle, may record and even
interpret any act of omission or commission as evidence supporting the diagnosis
of schizophrenia. The fact of large numbers of inpatients and small numbers of
staff together with the ubiquitous power of the disease paradigm create a climate
in which administration of the routines of the hospital can only be carried out
through the cooperation—voluntary or not—of the inpatient in the sick role. This
role calls for docility, submissiveness, and abasement. The efforts of most hospitals produce a kind of nonperson role, one that pushes patients further into the use
of the adaptive techniques that may have started them on their careers in the first
place—excessive attention to fantasy creations. If the social ecology of the
extramural world produced inputs that made no sense within the construct system
of the prepatient, certainly the social ecology of the mental hospital has the
potential for producing even more nonsensical inputs for the patient. Since instrumental acts designed to right the threatening conditions are quickly demonstrated to be invalid (by condescending reprimand, assignment to disturbed or
cooling off wards); and since other forms of adaptation are in short supply or
proscribed, patients may find themselves seeking out and responding to inputs
that are classifiable, that make sense, given their structure of knowledge. They
generate pseudocommunity, a fantasy ecology. Here, as in the previous sequences, contingencies may disrupt the preference for enacting fantasy roles.
The interest of relatives, other patients, and professional personnel, the shift
from the ambiguous outside world to one that has clear dimensions, and so on,
may lead the patient into a search for other adaptive techniques, including the
modification of the belief-value structure through programmed or unplanned
learning.

   Needless to say, some patients return to the community after a short stay in the
hospital and are able to resume validatable social roles—particularly if the social
community can accept the claim that the patients have been "cured of their
illness." If the positive contingencies are not present, then the shaping processes
of the hospital housekeeping and medical routines turn the patients from the
unsettled inpatient role—that is, a role to which they are not attached and
committed—to the stabilized inpatient role. The patients who accept this role
assignment have a minimum of rights, responsibilities, obligations, and duties.
Their role enactments are shaped through segregation, supervision, surveillance,
lack of privacy, limited opportunities for interaction, and so on. With Goffman
(1961), we underscore the fact that the stabilized patient role in the hospital is in
essence a nonperson role, one in which reciprocity of interaction is extremely

limited. The removal from a social ecology in which reciprocity of function characterizes even roles of the lowest prestige ranks to a nonperson role again places a strain on patients to fill their cognitive space with inputs. These inputs are most readily drawn from their imaginal constructions.

The legal, bureaucratic, and medical processes involved in disengaging persons from their roles in the social ecology are frequently effective. They result in individuals who play parts in a hospital setting where they are looked upon as "cooperative schizophrenics;" cooperative because they give the staff no trouble, schizophrenic because they emit behavior that sometimes fits the vague, multiple, disjunctive defining characteristics of a presumed disease entity called schizophrenia. By and large, it is this group of persons enacting a stabilized patient role that provides the pool of subjects in experiments designed to illuminate the independent variable, schizophrenia-nonschizophrenia.

We do not take the position that these social processes are the only avenues for acquiring the cognitive behaviors that show up as small mean differences identified in experimental studies. The same effects may be produced in certain family and community settings where some opportunities exist for stripping away roles from persons who are deviant in one way or another. Because the community is usually not a total institution (Goffman, 1961), the opportunities for producing desocializing conditions are fewer and less extreme than in that special kind of total institution, the mental hospital. The culture of poverty may be seen as having many of the characteristics of total institutions. Because some minimal opportunities are present for breaking out of the degradation sequences, the totalism is not complete and the range of conduct alternatives includes more than attention-deployment to fantasy products (Sarbin, 1968).

To summarize, in the prepatient and patient sequences, certain social psychological events make no sense, and attention redeployment to inputs created by an active fantasy life helps form answers and reduces epistemic strain. These language and thought solutions are by-products of role changes imposed on the person by the social community and by the processes of commitment and degradation. This is not to say that at the time of admission to a mental hospital patients show no unusual conduct, language, or thought. Rather, the systematic study of conduct, language, and thought occurs after the person has become stabilized in the role of the hospital patient, that is, after the person has become "cooperative."

We have already alluded to the impropriety of constructing generalizations about "schizophrenics" when the supporting data are provided by the selected performances of preselected, cooperative patients.

REPRISE

This chapter contains data and arguments to support claims that hidden variables can account for the small mean differences between test performances of hospitalized "schizophrenic" and nonschizophrenic samples. The small differences that emerge from the comparisons of mean scores on dependent variables can, in principle, be attributed to disguised aspects of the experimental context, to wit: (1) socioeconomic status, (2) cognitive development, (3) educational level, (4) drug effects, and (5) patienthood. These variables make ambiguous the interpretation of the majority of schizophrenia studies published in the 30 volumes of *JASP/JAP* under review. Many of these variables are not recondite. Some are widely used in the study of behavior development. Many of their correlates are known.

The implications of this chapter are clear: (a) The fact that disguised variables may account for the small mean differences places a great strain on the schizophrenia hypothesis. Thus (b) the scientists of deviant behavior cannot be excused from incorporating these variables into their theories of norm-violating behavior and, of course, into their experiments.

5
Schizophrenia:
A Verdict for Unwanted
Conduct

We have already presented data and arguments to support the proposition that the career of the mental patient *qua* patient begins only after the person is diagnosed. As outlined before, the task of diagnosing ''mental illness'' has been assigned primarily to the medical profession, and in recent times, to the specialty of psychiatry. That the diagnostician plays the central role in the drama of ''mental illness'' is a compelling fact.

The diagnostician occupies a status not unlike that of the professional drama critic. Once assigned to their special status, the role enactments of both the mental health diagnostician and the drama critic serve a kind of tastemaking function. The drama critic evaluates performances of stage actors, the diagnostician, of real life actors. The diagnostician has the task of deciding one day that the actions of homosexual lovers are not symptoms of mental illness and on another day of judging that begging for coins while holding a bank balance of $24,000 is a symptom of mental illness. Before we can present an alternative way of looking at unwanted conduct, the status of the diagnostician as critic of social role enactments needs to be elaborated. We must also examine closely the structure and function of *diagnoses,* the products of the diagnostician's art.

Psychiatrists enacting the role of critic of others' social role enactments were responsible for defining the parameters of the 374 studies that provide the basic data of this treatise. The search for ''schizophrenia,'' or the basic identifying symptom of schizophrenia, is not independent of the diagnostic practices of those who participate in assigning persons to mental hospitals. It is the diagnostician, after all, who willy-nilly defines the independent variable for investigators of ''schizophrenia.''

Each year thousands of potential diagnosticians are exposed to the stereotypes—the ''pictures-in-the-head''—that are to serve as the patterns against which the candidates for the insane role will be matched. Those prepatients who match the patterns become patients, and they are then eligible as subjects for schizophrenia studies. Beginning mental health professionals cannot be given profiles for schizophrenia, like those available, say, to the resident physician studying hematology. The beginning hematologist can place a blood sample profile into a computer; the profile becomes a standard against which a particular patient's blood and other characteristics are matched. Our review of current research clearly demonstrates that no reliable profiles are used to assign the label "schizophrenia." We also conclude that there appears to be no promise of such profiles being made available in the near or remote future. It is reasonable to ask what set of characteristics is given to beginning diagnosticians of schizophrenia in lieu of such "profiles?" When they sit at a desk facing a person who complains that his or her body reeks of rottenness, or another person despondently declares the futility of being, or still another, who complains of being the object of surveillance by government sleuths; or still another, who complains of "hallucinating" a "dull thud," diagnosticians need—as all persons need—a suitable knowledge structure to give them a sense of credibility, or at least lead to actions that may be confirmed by peers and superiors in their social organization.

It is not that the profession has not labored to provide nosological categories and scientific descriptions of "mental illnesses." In an effort to make diagnosis more reliable and more credible, the Committee on Nomenclature and Statistics of the American Psychiatric Association published in 1952 the *Diagnostic and Statistical Manual* (DSM-I). This was designed in part to standardize the nosological language, and, incidentally to reduce the dependence on stereotypes.

The 1952 diagnostician would conduct a diagnostic examination in an effort to match the characteristics of the putative patient against descriptions contained in the *Manual*. Schizophrenia (Code. No. 000-X210) was to be identified in the person who showed "psychotic reactions characterized by fundamental disturbances in reality relationships," and who manifested "emotional disharmony, unpredictable disturbance in stream of thought," or "regressive behavior [p. 26]." A serious effort to define the terms used in the *Manual's* descriptions of schizophrenia quickly reveals the magnitude of the problems of matching the characteristics of the putative patient against the published criteria for schizophrenia. More than half the terms are abstract, ambiguous, or equivocal.

The *Manual* was revised in 1968 by the Committee on Nomenclature and Statistics. The revision might have provided the basis for increasing the precision of diagnostic classification. The new description of schizophrenia (Code Number 295) reads as follows:

> This large category includes a group of *disorders* manifested by *characteristic disturbances* of *thinking*, *mood*, and *behavior*. *Disturbances in thinking* are marked by *alterations* of *concept formation* which may lead to *misinterpretation of reality* and *sometimes* to *delusions* and *hallucinations*, which *frequently* appear *psychologically self-protective*. Corollary *mood changes* include *ambivalence*, *constructed* and *inappropriate emotional responsiveness*, and *loss of empathy* with others. Behavior *may* be *withdrawn, regressive*, and *bizarre* [p. 33].

The added italics show the extent of built-in ambiguity, equivocality, and abstractness that persisted in the new specifications. Needless to say, the revised "profile" of schizophrenia did not reduce subjectivity and unreliability. The American Psychiatric Association appointed a Task Force on Nomenclature and Statistics (1978) to produce DSM-III. R. L. Spitzer, the author of well known work (Endicott & Spitzer, 1979; Spitzer, Endicott, & Robins, 1978) on the research criteria for diagnosing schizophrenia, chaired the Task Force. DSM-III reflects Spitzer's work in its approach to diagnosing "schizophrenic disorders." The diagnostic criteria are headed by six "characteristic schizophrenic symptoms" (American Psychiatric Association: Task Force on Nomenclature and Statistics, 1979). Some examples of these symptoms are as follows:

> (1) Bizarre delusions (content is patently absurd and there is *no* possible basis in fact), such as delusions of being controlled, thought broadcasting, thought insertion, or thought withdrawal.
> (6) Incoherence, marked loosening of associations, marked illogicality or marked poverty of content of speech, if associated with at least one of the following:
>> (a) blunted, flat or inappropriate affect
>> (b) delusions or hallucinations
>> (c) catatonic or other grossly disorganized behavior [p. 30].

The critics of the disease approach to schizophrenia can safely predict that after these criteria for diagnosing schizophrenic disorders become official and are promulgated, there will be continued uncertainty in matching these descriptions to the behaviors of persons who are candidates for the schizophrenic disorder classification. For example, the diagnostic process will be made into a more interesting spectacle by the DSM-III requirement that at least one of the characteristic symptoms shall be present during an active phase of the illness, and that signs of the illness shall have been present "continuously for at least six months at some time during the person's life and the individual now has some signs of the illness [C:11]." How will prospective diagnosticians be taught to confirm, for example, the hypothesis that a person has shown marked loosening of associations for at least six months at some time in his or her life, and that the person now experiences thoughts as being broadcast from the heart, or that the person now holds a patently absurd delusion?

As they have in the past, diagnosticians will employ their own subjective criteria to determine if a person experiences *thought broadcasting*, or if affect is *flat* or *inappropriate*, or if the person is *incoherent*, or if the speech shows *poverty of content*, or if the person's behavior is *grossly disorganized*. These implicitly formed and used subjective criteria will provide the basis for the diagnosticians' work. From this base they will judge success or failure in enacting the role of the "schizophrenic."

THE DISEASE MODEL AS A DETERMINER OF PERCEPTIONS

Before entering the mental health world, it is probable that the young preprofessional recognizes that the identification of a person as sane or insane depends on the total context of the diagnostic enterprise including the diagnostician's own cognitive habits—his or her implicit personality theory. This recognition is, in most cases, transformed by the strength and ubiquity of the mental illness model as it is taught to novices in the mental health professions. For help in explaining the power of this model, we can consider the sociology of knowledge relative to unwanted behavior.

Mental illness, the disease model drawn from the more encompassing mechanistic paradigm, has been, since the decline of demonism, the accepted mode of representing deviant, unwanted conduct. Only a little change in allegiance to the illness doctrine has occurred as a result of the studied objections of Goffman (1961), Sarbin (1967a), Szasz (1960), Laing (1967), Torrey (1974b), and others. Evidence for the strength of the model is found in the marked increase in the number and intensity of professional counterattacks against critics of the medical model. Highly esteemed participants in the mental health world (Kety, 1974; Kubie, 1974; Siegler & Osmond, 1974) have led the reaction. Those who defend the disease model, in addition to calling into question the scientific validity of critiques of the illness model, often employ the kind of polemics that are engendered by such major controversies. Their professional role, for example, prompts them to offer the ever-recurrent counsel to abandon criticism lest the mentally ill be subjected to even more intense suffering than that which is already induced by their ''disease.''

In a paradoxical and revealing statement, Siegler and Osmond (1974) offer the following argument for the preservation of the illness model:

> Since the advent of psychoanalysis, physicians have turned away from applying the medical model to mental illness. They have deprived mental patients of the sick role, and their families of a concise diagnosis of their relatives' distress. In doing so, they have stripped away people's medical rights. Even where there is no wholly satisfactory treatment for an illness, a physician can make certain time-honored moves that will alleviate the suffering of the patient and his family [p. 71].

Siegler and Osmond, we point out, do not argue for the disease model on the basis of its internal efficacy. Diagnosis, they argue, serves primarily to confer the social role ''sick person,'' a role which exonerates one from responsibilities. Diagnosis helps one perceive certain persons as ill, rather than as persons who conduct themselves inappropriately. Having been granted Aesculapian authority, the diagnostician reviews the performances of everyday actors thus helping to shape the ''tastes''—the stereotyped expectations—of the public. The educated public, generally unschooled in the epistemology of models and metaphors, overcomes its confusions about what it understands to be a serious social problem by relying on professionals, and people are then encouraged to view unwanted and perplexing conduct as being representative of ''mental illness'' (Rabkin, 1974). The concerned citizen needs the comforting aid of a credible theory and under some conditions accepts the professional establishment's view of the meaning of events (Sarbin & Mancuso, 1970).

One should expect confusions as a logical consequence of the acceptance of the mental illness doctrine. When the model fails, people do not have the conceptual tools by which to reorganize their thinking about unwanted behavior. This result is illustrated by a series of exposés of New York State's Department of Mental Hygiene (Albany *Times Union,* 1974). These articles attempt to retain the illness model as an unquestioned foundation from which to assess the Department's follies. The reporters are concerned, for example, with the Department's lack of success in treating and curing patients. The series does not question the propriety of dealing with deviant behavior by allotting approximately one billion dollars annually to a medically led bureaucracy. The reporters, some of whom were advised to the contrary, avoided an analysis of the underlying model that guides the expenditure of this huge segment of New York State's budget.

Not surprisingly, the Albany *Times Union's* series (1974) elaborates the thesis that New York State's Department of Mental Hygiene must be viewed as having failed, simply because it cannot meet the criteria of success that derive from the model which, in the first instance, generated a "department of mental hygiene." Workers within the system cannot gain a positive value for their success in "curing" "mental illness." The exposé—no surprise to sociologically oriented observers—suggests by implication that to continue along the lines laid down by the illness model leads the science of deviant behavior, as it has in New York State, into bureaucratic ennui. The reports of rampant "goofing off" among workers reflect the absence of meaning in the lives of professionals whose job it is to "cure mental illness" for the state. Alert young physicians turn down administrative positions at rural mental hospitals, the inmates of which are persons whose conduct has become troublesome to the committing community. Dedicated college graduates, no matter the intensity of their humanistic commitment, lose interest in "caring for the mentally ill" when they find that the illness model inevitably leads to the application of massive doses of drugs. To these young people, *One Flew Over the Cuckoo's Nest* (Kesey, 1962) offers meaningful metaphors, while the standard *Tesxtbook of Psychiatry* (Kolb, 1977) offers scientific formulae that continue to advance the idiographic and mechanistic notions of symptoms and syndrome.

Our association with university undergraduates has led us to the inference that Kesey's colorful protagonist, Randle Patrick McMurphy, draws the understanding sympathy of the young, socially and politically sensitive audience. The same audience responds with incredulity to Kolb's interpretive case histories. It appears that Kesey's use of a contextual model directly appeals to the vision of a large segment of the intellectual community, while Kolb's mechanistic paradigm is judged a sterile academic exercise.

As a result of penetrating critiques of the profession, we expect that diagnosticians *qua* scientists will become analytical about their own implicit personality theory. As a result, they will be able to "diagnose" their own cognitive structures as one of the strands woven into the texture of their current diagnosing activity. A review of a recent study of schizophrenia pointedly illustrates the need for turning attention to an analysis of the diagnostician.

A "COMMUNICATION" STUDY

Cohen, Nachmani, and Rosenberg (1974) reported one of the 374 investigations that provides the empirical base of this essay. We have selected this study for detailed analysis because it is a careful, well planned, and thoughtful study that clearly reveals the operation of the silent assumptions of the schizophrenia model. As we shall point out, these investigators, by their commitment to the disease model, were led to frame questions that focus on one side of the context of a quasi-diagnostic process. A model generated by a contextualist paradigm, with attention to the diagnostician's inference systems and to the implicit communication theory of the speaker and the listener, would have directed these researchers toward different kinds of questions.

Cohen and his associates designed an ingenious method of exploring that part of a person's communication activity which is cognitively processed by the diagnostician who then claims that one of the communicating participants suffers from schizophrenia. They did not, we should add, cast their study in these terms.

Cohen's group went into a mental hospital and chose "twenty-four acute first-admission male schizophrenic patients" and then also found "24 non-patient control subjects [p. 4-5]" to serve as subjects. The schizophrenic diagnosis had been assigned in the usual way:

> The schizophrenics were initially diagnosed by a psychiatrist or psychologist on intake duty at a mental health clinic affiliated with a general medical center in the greater New York area. The diagnosis was later checked by three other professionals (two psychiatrists and a psychologist) at a treatment planning conference for the patient. A schizophrenic was selected as a subject if all three conference members confirmed the initial diagnosis of schizophrenia and agreed that the patient manifested (a) symptoms of language and thought disorder, and (b) a predominantly nonparanoid symptom picture [p. 5].

Note well that a patient, clearly, was assigned to the experimental group because of "symptoms of language and thought disorder."

The experimental subjects (the schizophrenics) and the control subjects then provided a speech sample that was recorded on electronic tape. Each subject was given a variety of specific tasks, all centering upon the requirement that the subject convey a specific piece of information to a nonpresent, imaginary listener. The communicator had a set of varicolored discs, numbering two discs or four discs per set. One of the discs was "the right disc," and the speaker was required to tell the imaginary listener which disc was "the right disc." The problem was relatively simple when the set surrounding the referent disc contained two (or four) colors which were widely separated within the Farnsworth-Munsell 100-Hue Test (Farnsworth, 1957). The task was relatively difficult when a set contained colors that lay adjacent to each other within the Farnsworth-Munsell selection. After the subjects recorded their attempts to designate the referent color chip, the investigators played the taped linguistic productions to a panel of listeners. The members of the panel were required to identify the referent color chip on the basis of having heard the communicator's production.

Cohen, Nachmani, and Rosenberg (1974) intended to validate their view that schizophrenics show

> a deficit, not in the repertoire of referent response associations of meanings from which speakers select their utterances, but rather in a self-editing function (Rosenberg & Cohen, 1966) that screens out the less effective referent descriptions in the speaker's repertoire before they are emitted [p. 1].

They found that listeners easily identified the referent color chip so long as the colors were far from each other within the Farnsworth-Munsell gradations. This finding held for both the experimental and the control sample subjects. Also, as the sets of colors became less distinguishable, both samples produced linguistic statements that were less usefully informative. The subjects in the schizophrenic sample, however, were considerably less understood by the listener panel when the colors were less distinguishable (i.e., closer together), particularly when the sets contained four discs. Furthermore, some of the experimental subjects, when faced with self-perceived failure to express appropriately the color of the referent disc, launched into language that would readily encourage a contemporary diagnostician to use the label ''schizophrenic.'' For example, one subject, trying to delimit a yellow-red referent in a set of highly similar discs, said: ''Shit, shit, shit, shit, shit. All we do turns to shit. You're a shit. Shit, shit, shit. When we shit less, and this one has the least shit in it. So you don't have to do too much [p. 11].'' The researchers conclude:

> As given earlier, this account of schizophrenic speaker deficit assumes a normal sampling stage and a non-deviant repertoire but no self-editing stage. This model is entirely consistent with the communication accuracy findings (self or listener panel). If a speaker samples the most probable descriptions (the common color names) and emits these with no self-editing, he will show high accuracy on the lower similarity displays and progressively lower accuracy as similarity increases. This is because, with increasing similarity, the common color name also describes the non-referent(s), *thus leading to a form of schizophrenic overinclusion.* [Cohen, Nachmani, & Rosenberg, p. 9, italics added].

The assumptions, methods, and conclusions of this study show tacit reliance on the mechanistic metaphysics of the disease model. These investigators, like most of those who produced the 374 studies we have already analyzed, have been poorly served by the disease model in their study of the complexities of deviant communication. Contextualist models (Rommetveit, 1974; Sarbin, 1979) better frame the communication processes. Our critique first emphasizes some points made in the body (Chapter 3) of our critical evaluation.

To begin, Cohen, Nachmani, and Rosenberg propose a schizophrenic deficit—''failure to self-edit.'' The measure by which they wish to operationalize this self-editing process is, essentially, the success of a listener who attempts to identify the referent within a set of possible referents. There is no reason to suppose that the failure to communicate by verbal specification a referent's relevant color dimensions implies failure to communicate the identity of *all* other referents. What if the subjects were required to communicate the identity of a head of escarole while they had before them representative heads of endive, escarole, and dandelion greens? Would "schizophrenics," be they truck farmers or office workers, reliably fail to "self-edit" and thus produce communications that listeners, regardless of their occupations, could not find useful in differentiating the referent among these salad greens? In short, is this color communication task a valid measure of self-editing?

Brown (1973), discussing language function relative to diagnosing schizophrenia, identifies the foregoing point in this way:

> It is as if the assumption were that schizophrenia resulted from an across-the-board, content-free impairment of a basic function like perception, learning, concept formation, or attention. If that were indeed the case, then it would make no difference what task was used to test the function, and convenience might as well dictate the selection. But is this the case? It may be that we have been too much influenced by the disease concept. Lacking psychic organs comparable to the heart, liver, and spleen, we may have made too much of the unity of our functions [p. 402].

Cohen's group refers to each member of their experimental sample with the term "schizophrenic." They give very dramatic examples of the kinds of outlandish verbalizations that one expects from "really sick" persons. From their report, we cannot tell whether *all* these "sick" people gave such verbalizations. We expect that some did not. On the other hand, it would be useful to know how many of the schizophrenics gave responses—in all kinds of situations—that were indistinguishable from those of the normals. In other words, how many schizophrenics behaved no differently from ordinary folks? Is inability to self-edit, indeed, the single identifying symptom of the disease, or at least, one such symptom?

Cohen and his colleagues cannot claim that they were studying, in a modal sense, the conduct of a sample of "schizophrenics." They chose a very restricted sample of people called schizophrenic. Their sample was young (mean age = 25.7 years; SD = 5.8), well schooled (Mean years of education = 13.1; SD = 2.3), and on its first round in the hospital circuit. Their modal subject, at any rate, differs notably from the modal subjects in the other 374 studies covered in our review. They fail to report, as many other investigators similarly fail to report, how they obtained cooperation from speakers; nor do they tell us how many potential subjects refused or failed to cooperate.

Cohen's group does report that their schizophrenic speakers and their non-schizophrenic speakers were matched on age and educational level. They do not report consideration of the socioeconomic status of their samples. They also report that no subject was on drugs while acting as a speaker.

Length of hospitalization does not seem to be an important factor, since the schizophrenics were newly admitted, first admissions. Nevertheless, Cohen and his associates do not mention length of hospitalization, nor do they consider the possibility that people who have been placed in a mental hospital might view the strange doings of the experimenters from a different cost/benefit perspective from that brought into the laboratory by the volunteer medical center employees who formed the control sample.

When Cohen's group so precisely spells out their method of selecting their schizophrenic sample, they show how they biased their study for positive results. They asked their diagnosticians for persons who showed "symptoms of language and thought disorder [p. 5]." Of course, the diagnostician, using existing cognitive structures while hearing the patient's verbalizations, detected "language and thought disorder"—and, thereby, "schizophrenia"—when carrying on the interview in which the prepatient uttered terms and phrases which did not allow the diagnostician to differentiate the referents which the prepatient was trying to denote. Schizophrenia, the independent variable in the study, then, was defined by the diagnostician's prior categorization of the behavior to be assessed by measures of the dependent variable; namely, the patient's inept verbalizations. Schizophrenia did not "cause," nor was it "caused by" the ineffective communication. *It was the prepatient's language that, at least in part, caused psychiatrists and psychologists to employ the category "schizophrenia" to frame the "thought disorder" revealed by the language usage.*

Reconsidering Unusual Communications

Two important references relate to the Cohen, Nachmani, and Rosenberg (1974) study. In 1964, Werner and Kaplan published an important monograph on symbol formation and use. That monograph also reported some measures obtained by instructing a sample of schizophrenics to describe an event so that it might be identified by a hypothetical or an actual listener. Werner and Kaplan report the not-too-surprising finding that the schizophrenics simply say less during a communication. Another aspect of their findings focuses on communication in the diagnostic process. Relatively few of the schizophrenics' communications contained "communal referents." Werner and Kaplan's normal subjects, even when speaking with the belief that their production was for their own use, employ a large percentage of communal referents in their speech. Werner and Kaplan used the material on schizophrenic communication as but one aspect of their overall treatise. They were working out their general theory that in the speech activity of young children there is a relative lack of differentiation between self-address and verbal communication for consumption by others; and that older, and thereby more skillful speakers can distinguish these two types of speech activity.

Another reference would be useful in reconsidering the findings of Cohen, Nachmani, and Rosenberg. Olson (1970) expounded a convincing thesis of linguistics that heavily emphasized semantics and the *role of the listener* in the communication context. In Olson's system, speakers constantly attend to the feedback from their listener, and direct their language productions so that they can locate an event within the *listeners' category systems*. The speaker does this by specifying the socially shared categorizing dimensions that have the most salience to the identification of the event under discussion. In short, one can never separate a speaker's categorizing system and verbal productions from the context that includes not only the event, but also *the listener's construct system*. ". . . [It] is impossible to specify the meaning of a word or sentence unambiguously unless we know the context and hence the set of alternative referents being entertained by the listener [p. 260]."

Olson provides an illustration that strikes at the very center of the problem of differentiating perceived referents. The dictionary meaning of the word *horse* includes such properties as quadruped, mammal, and domesticated. Olson suggests that in an unusual context, properties not mentioned in the dictionary might be the differentiae. If a person were addressed with the task of differentiating between a whale and a horse, an appropriate response would be "the horse is the terrestrial one."

> The feature "terrestrial" may now be considered to be part of the definition of horse; note, however, that the marker "terrestrial" is not given by the dictionary but rather by the speaker's knowledge of whales and horses. Anything else the speaker knows that will permit their differentiation may be used as if it were part of the meaning of the word. The ones that have been frequently used have been listed in a published dictionary but that is a poor indication of what a speaker knows or how he uses the language [Olson, 1970, p. 261].

Brown (1973) employs the implications of Olson's thesis to suggest the events that encourage a diagnostician to categorize a speaker as schizophrenic. Brown first dismisses the hypothesis that these crucial events have to do with grammar or syntax. He states, "clearly, whatever is wrong is in the domain of meaning [p. 399]." Brown indicates that people who participate in our culture share an implicit knowledge of the rules that govern "adequate reality testing"—the rules we are required to follow if we expect others to believe that we are being logical and coherent. His final view is expressed as follows:

> But, I should think that the most relevant efforts to make explicit the notions of rationality on which we operate are the efforts to describe psychological implication, principles of affective consistency, principles of attribution, and the common fallacies of logic and of evidence evaluation. All of these seem to be efforts to describe rules we really use rather than rules we ought to use, and it seems chiefly to be the rules we use that cause propositions to be considered deluded. It is perhaps also departures from these rules that indicate mental illness [p. 401].

Here, then, Brown assumes a contextualist position, particularly since he previously acknowledged that socially shared conceptions of adequate reality testing evolve through historical time. In adhering to the disease model as they try to find "the thing wrong" with schizophrenics, Cohen and his colleagues fail to articulate their theory to this corpus of research on communication. The disease model focuses on the intraindividual relaying of force and counterforce. The contextualist paradigm that frames the work of Werner and Kaplan, Olson, and Brown requires that there be no separation of the speaker and the listener. Although Cohen and his associates are not strangers to Sullivan's (1946) "fantastic auditor," and Mead's (1934) "generalized other;" their use of the mechanistic paradigm leads them to design a study that will demonstrate that the communication failure derives from the speaker's skill in screening out task irrelevant responses. They end writing of the schizophrenic's "overinclusion."

The effort to locate an intraindividual "processing deficit" within the schizophrenic is reflected in the basic design of the Cohen, Nachmani, and Rosenberg investigation. They used the artificial technique of having their speaker address a tape recorder. This method would be justified if one were willing to believe that individuals do not vary their speech actions to accommodate to the variations they perceive in the cognitive systems of their listeners. Or, one might use this method to extend the study to test the hypothesis that schizophrenics do not profit from the presence of a listener, whereas nonschizophrenics improve communications when a listener is in view.

Furthermore the procedure of excluding the listener, in this situation, implicitly defines a significant power relationship. The subject is being given the message: "You have the responsibility to make yourself understood. I (the experimenter) have no responsibility to make myself understand you." This is precisely the message that is repeatedly addressed to patients during the prepatient phase of their careers as mental patients. They constantly have been asked to justify the validity of the content of their communications. The lesson has been repeatedly imparted that they are powerless in the presence of others who have social support to validate their commerce with the world. Patients are well schooled in the social rules by which they are given the onus for failures in the communication game. When they speak into a tape recorder, they know that they surely will not encounter that rare listener who can help them shape their communication so that they may make themselves clear. The mechanistic cultural thought model influenced Cohen's group to study the characteristics of those who "fail to communicate," rather than those who "fail to understand."

Power Distribution and Implicit Personality Theory in Diagnosis

Brown (1973) makes a point relevant to the power distribution in the diagnostic process:

> It is my scarcely revolutionary suggestion that we, as participants in this culture, share also some much more complex notion of what constitutes adequate reality testing and rational coherence, and share it well enough to agree quite closely on whether thought samples are deluded or disordered. And this sharing results *not primarily from professional training but from general enculturation* since naive undergraduates are not much different in their judgments than experienced clinicians [p. 401; emphasis added. See also Agnew and Bannister, 1973, for verification of the lack of differentiation between psychiatrists' lay diagnostic language and their professional diagnostic language].

Members of our society are enculturated to incorporate certain principles within their implicit personality theories (Rosenberg, 1977; Rosenberg & Sedlak, 1972). The professional diagnostician is empowered to certify the marginality of those whose behavior does not conform to the shared metaphysical principles. The layman involved with the prepatient can say, "You have failed to make me (and the rest of us) understand you, and my 'theory' of how people behave does not explain your failure.'' (See Cox, Costanzo, & Coie, 1976, for descriptions of the prepatient behaviors which induce people to refer a prepatient to a diagnostician.) Thereupon, the prepatient is taken to the diagnostician, whose diagnostic procedures are translatable to: ''My implicit personality theory does not explain your failure, therefore you are a special person whose operations are explained by the special principles that define the behavior of a schizophrenic.'' It becomes the task of research-oriented colleagues to find the special psychological or biological deficits associated with the presumed illness. The task is undertaken with the guidance of a belief that such deficits exist independently of the diagnostic context. We again emphasize that a central feature of the context is the diagnostician's implicit theory about the processes by which people create, disseminate, and attempt to communicate the symbolic representations of their personal action systems.

DO DIAGNOSTICIANS IDENTIFY ILLNESS?

We selected for detailed analysis the study by Cohen, Nachmani, and Rosenberg (1974) because it is an exemplar of a large class of studies in which the focus is on diagnosed patients; and in which the social and psychological events antecedent to, or a part of, the diagnostic process is ignored. To uncover the etiology of the restricted vision of schizophrenia investigators, we look further at psychiatric diagnosis.

We have already chronicled the well-established fact that psychiatric diagnosis is not reliable. The degree of correspondence between diagnosticians is sometimes uncomfortably small. Only in highly artificial settings do diagnosticians show a degree of correspondence equivalent to 80 percent. If the classification of a person as schizophrenic or nonschizophrenic could be carried out reliably, would the diagnosis be credible? That is to say, if a panel of diagnosticians could agree that certain persons should be tagged with the schizophrenia label, and others not, would the diagnoses be valid? Would the diagnoses have any truth value? Since diagnosticians can regard any bit of conduct as a symptom of underlying psychiatric disease—a point elaborated by Goffman (1961), Perucci (1974), Rosenhan (1973), Sarbin (1967a), Szasz (1961), and others—the task of establishing a ''profile'' for schizophrenia presents many difficulties. That psychiatrists and other mental health professionals are biased toward psychopathology is also a well established fact.

Building on the work of Goffman (1961) and Temerlin (1968), Rosenhan (1973) has provided us with data that place great strain on the credibility of psychiatric diagnosis. In brief, eight of Rosenhan's associates volunteered to enter mental hospitals as patients. We can speak of 12 cases since some of the volunteers participated more than once. They revealed no ''psychiatric impairment.'' Each volunteer presented a fictitious complaint: an ''auditory hallucination'' that said ''empty,'' ''thud,'' or ''dull.'' This symptom was selected because such an atypical form of conduct does not ordinarily come to the attention of diagnosticians. Indeed, the rarity of this symptom could have seductively enticed diagnosticians to see it as precisely that kind of unwanted deviance that deserves diagnostic labelling. Henceforth, after the draft model of DSM III is wholly adopted, diagnosticians will not easily be misled by malingering patients using this deceptive symptom. A characteristic hallucination must be repeated on several occasions, and "not limited to one or two words [American Psychiatric Association: Task Force, 1979, p. 30]." The volunteers (pseudopatients) were instructed to be truthful about everything except this one symptom. In every case, the pseudopatient was admitted to the hospital; eleven cases were diagnosed as paranoid schizophrenia, and one case was diagnosed as manic-depressive psychosis. On discharge from the hospital, the pseudopatients, it is important to note, were diagnosed as "schizophrenia: improved," or "schizophrenia: in remission" or "manic-depressive: in remission."

The second part of Rosenhan's report, and equally important, was his response to a challenge made by the staff members of a hospital not used in the study. Rosenhan agreed to send one of his pseudopatients into this hospital, but did not identify the date. During the period of the study, 193 patients were admitted. Of these, 21 percent were diagnosed as pseudopatients by at least one staff member, 12 percent were diagnosed as pseudopatients by at least one psychiatrist, and 10 percent were diagnosed as pseudopatients by one psychiatrist and one other staff member. Because of illness, the assigned pseudopatient did not appear during the interval of the study. Rosenhan's conclusion is worth repeating: ". . . we have known for a long time that diagnoses are often not useful or reliable, but we have nevertheless continued to use them. We now know that we cannot distinguish insanity from sanity [p. 257]." The continued labelling of the pseudopatients on discharge as "paranoid schizophrenia: in remission," in the absence of any reliable or valid diagnostic signs, underscores the conclusion that schizophrenia must be regarded as a myth supported by the implicit personality theory that guides diagnosticians.

Rosenhan's study has been criticized by supporters of the medical model. Kety (1974), for one, offered a criticism in the context of deception. He said,

> If I were to drink a quart of blood and, concealing what I had done, had come to the emergency room of any hospital vomiting blood, the behavior of the staff would be quite predictable. If they labelled and treated me as having a bleeding peptic ulcer, I doubt that I could argue convincingly that medical science does not know how to diagnose that condition [p. 959].

It is interesting to note that Kety does not comment on the next stage of his hypothetical experiment. When no bleeding was observed the next day, and when all diagnostic tests had proven negative, would the physician write the discharge note as "bleeding peptic ulcer: improved, or in remission?" In the absence of continued pseudobleeding, the discharge diagnosis most probably would be listed as "unknown." A highly competent internal medicine specialist might even conclude that he had been duped. But Kety leads his readers to believe that the deception of a medical or psychiatric staff officer is easy because doctors are obligated to diagnose and treat people in distress. He overlooked entirely the fact that when a person is diagnosed, or "misdiagnosed," as paranoid schizophrenic in the absence of unequivocal criterial conduct, the diagnostician is illegitimately becoming a "stigmatician."

To challenge further the credibility of psychiatric diagnosis, we point to the fact that the outcome of the diagnostic process may be influenced by "personal tastes" about the appropriateness of certain actions staged during entry into patienthood. Extraneous events, such as social class or political beliefs of the putative patient, may guide the diagnosis. That psychiatric diagnosis, the basis of expert testimony in civil hearings, is influenced by extraneous factors is a fact now well documented. If, for example, "suspected patients" or "quasi patients" appear to be of lower-class origins, they are more likely to be declared psychotic than if they appear to belong to the middle class (Hollingshead & Redlich, 1958). The political stance of the prepatient can serve as another extraneous factor that influences psychiatric diagnosis. The Braginskys and their coworkers have illuminated these rather hazy scenarios (Braginsky & Braginsky, 1974).

In the first two studies, Braginsky and Braginsky assessed certain political attitudes of hospitalized mental patients and mental health professionals in the same institution. They were particularly interested in attitudes toward New Left philosophy and attitudes toward the use of radical tactics. The New Left attitude scale assessed a philosophy of support for social change, the radical tactics scale assessed attitudes toward various strategies to achieve social change. On both these scales, patients scored significantly higher than mental health professionals and, incidentally, higher than a reference group of high-scoring university students. Among the mental health professionals, psychologists and psychiatrists were the most politically conservative.

Having established that mental hospital patients, as a group, are politically different from mental health professionals, the Braginskys and their colleagues undertook a second study to determine whether such an extraneous variable as political attitudes could influence psychiatric diagnosis. Two videotaped interviews between a doctor and a pseudopatient (enacted by a college senior) were put together. Each interview was composed of four distinct segments: Segment 1, *presenting complaints;* Segment 2, *expression of political philosophy;* Segment 3, *expression of political strategy;* Segment 4, *evaluative comments about mental health professions.*

For both interviews, the first segment consisted of complaints made by the patient in response to the doctor's question, "How are you feeling?" The complaints were listlessness and fatigue, poor appetite, restless sleep patterns, irritability with friends, and so on. In the second segment of the tape, the patient expressed either a New Left political philosophy or a middle-of-the-road political philosophy. In the third segment, the patient who expressed the New Left attitudes endorsed the use of radical tactics to bring about social change, while the moderate patient decried the use of radical tactics. Both patients in the fourth segment criticized mental health professionals, but did so from different perspectives. The New Left radical accused mental health workers of being the "handmaidens of a repressive society, labelling, drugging, and incarcerating anyone who disagreed with conventional values.'' The middle-of-the-road patient asserted that ''mental health professionals have done more harm than good by destroying traditional values, by encouraging permissiveness, and by being, in general, too radical.''

Each videotaped interview was shown (on separate occasions) to audiences of mental health professionals who were asked to diagnose and to describe the severity of the illness after each of the four segments. After Segment 1 was shown, the videorecorder was stopped and the observers made their ratings. Then Segment 2 was shown, and so on through Segment 4.

The results of this study clearly indicate that in this situation, political attitudes have a profound effect on psychiatric diagnosis. As the New Left radical's complaints shift from statements about self to statements about society, the patient is regarded as increasingly psychologically disturbed. Suggesting action to correct what is wrong with society, such a patient is perceived as still more pathological. The moderate patient's degree of psychopathology remains stable as he or she vocalizes anti-New Left sentiments, and somewhat decreases with criticism of those who advocate radical change for our social institutions. The judgments of severity of pathology of both the New Left and the middle-of-the-road patients dramatically increase when they *criticize mental health professionals*. Even the politically ''rational'' young man seen as moderately disturbed (despite being presented as a hospitalized mental patient) is diagnosed as being quite psychotic following his attack on the mental health profession.

The most spectacular change in judgments about the patients occurred when they directed their derogatory remarks to mental health personnel. This observation suggested the question: How would the patients be perceived if they uttered flattering comments? That is, if their insults to psychiatry were seen as a function of a ''paranoid'' disturbance, would complimentary remarks be perceived as the functioning of a nonpsychopathological person? The experimenters then constructed a new Segment 4 where the patient emphasized positive aspects of mental health professions. This new Segment 4 replaced Segment 4 of the New Left radical interview. Another group of hospital staff was convened and the same procedure followed.

The results for the first three segments were similar to those obtained before. On Segment 4, however, the very disturbed mental patient was suddenly perceived as without psychopathology—he was judged as having given up his symptoms, of being ''normal.'' The ''cure'' consisted of communicating to mental health personnel that they were helpful, kind, competent, and, in general, very special people.

The studies reported by Rosenhan and the Braginskys support the assertion that psychiatric diagnosis is something other than a scientific enterprise; it is certainly *not* like the diagnosis of pneumonia, cancer, or mumps. The disease model, as we have shown, was borrowed from somatic medicine to explain unusual, perplexing, and undesirable behaviors. The practitioners of the normal science of deviant conduct, despite their failure to account for unwanted conduct as disease, have persisted in their search for disease as the ultimate cause of unwanted conduct rather than turning their efforts more directly to the task of explaining unusual, perplexing conduct. It is instructive to ask the question: Why have so many scientists continued to focus on the diagnosis of disease, at the same time avoiding the study of norm-violating conduct?

As an answer to this question, we suggest that psychiatric diagnosticians *qua* scientists have hesitated to recognize openly that their efforts are directed toward explaining *unwanted* behaviors, that is, behaviors that have been declared violations of moral rules. If such open recognition were the order of the day, the public might demand justification for assigning to scientists the job normally assigned to legislators, clergymen, the judiciary, and other acknowledged authority figures. Such justifications would immediately make clear that behavior scientists are engaging in activities that serve a social control function.

SCIENTIFIC ACTIVITY OR MORAL ENTERPRISE?

Historically, science has abjured interest in value pursuits. To be pure, scientists of behavior prefer to study presumably value-free disease process rather than pursue the study of antecedent conditions for the development of unwanted behavior, that is, conduct that is objectionable to, at least, some powerful segments of the current society. The disease model is employed to legitimize society's support of a search for ways of controlling persons who engage in undesirable behaviors. Diagnosticians can justify their efforts to eliminate unwanted and perplexing behaviors by holding the belief that they have joined a universal crusade against disease. Even when they skirt the practice of referring outright to a somatic disease process, psychologists use terms like "correcting maladaptive behavior," or "racism represents a deep unconscious disorder." Having available the mechanistic disease model, psychologists readily offer their services to explain and eliminate unwanted behavior (see Mancuso, Eson, & Morrison, 1979). We agree with Szasz (1970) that the model lingers on as a subterfuge that disguises social control mechanisms.

The horrifying images used by Bellak, a frequent contributor to the literature on schizophrenia, qualifies as propaganda for the model rather than objective scientific description. Note that he implies the earlier social control concept of dangerous classes.

> Overall, though, there can be no question that schizophrenics constitute a major social problem, not only as patients. . . . It is my guess that the politically fanatic type meeting with other disturbed people in dingy halls, sometimes exploited by more cunning though not much less disturbed ones, may be the special danger of our times [Bellak, 1970, p. 15].

Let us state explicitly: the targets of the diagnosticians (the practitioners of the science of abnormal conduct) are those who engage in actions that offend the moral standards of others—usually others who hold greater power than the offender.

For many offenses against moral propriety, such as larceny, homicide, and auto theft, society has enacted criminal codes and has instituted magisterial procedures. For other offenses against propriety—offenses where a person publicly exhibits conduct that annoys, embarrasses, bothers, perplexes and/or mystifies relevant others—the society has devised procedures that follow from the implicit content of the metaphors of medical institutions. To deal with the first group of offenders, behavior scientists address their efforts to the concept of the "criminal," whereas transactions with the second group of offenders are conducted within the "mental illness" framework. Some contemporary observers find it difficult to be constrained by these peremptory classifications. They consider some "criminals"—e.g., prostitutes, child molesters, peeping Toms, and drug users—as persons who are "mentally ill." The readiness to cross back and forth between the *criminal* and the *mentally ill* classifications is a striking reminder that the conduct of "mentally ill" persons is by definition conduct that violates various moral standards. Some behavior analysts argue against the practice of "overcriminalization," that is the labelling of perpetrators of victimless crimes as "criminals." At the same time, criminal offenders are subject to the practice of "overmentalization." We argue that this tendency to "overmentalize" is found in scientific efforts to use the disease model as explanations of the conduct of persons who have violated uncodified moral proprieties, for example, persons who fail to observe communication norms, or who publicly declare allegiance to unusual religious precepts, or who use strange verbal and motor metaphors to symbolize their personal conceptions, or who assert unusual sources of validation for their beliefs.

Diagnosticians who hesitate to admit they are engaged in a moral enterprise rather than in the objective study of "diseased behavior," face several breeches of scientific propriety. By viewing improper behavior as "illness," they invite confusion about whether they make their pronouncements in the role of scientist or in the role of citizen. It is usually unclear which role is adopted by the behavior scientist who pronounces on the "dangers" of "meeting with other disturbed people in dingy halls" to discuss political matters. It is legitimate to ask: Does Bellak speak as a member of "the establishment" when he begins from a premise that the "sick" people congregating in these meeting halls may constitute "the special danger of our times?" Or, does he speak as a scientist convinced that the political manifestos issuing from such meetings are a product of mental disease, written by persons whose behavior is best regarded within a disease model?

In addition to avoiding role confusion, other gains would accrue from the open admission that mental health practitioners are interested in behaviors that offend moral propriety. To speak of violations of moral propriety rather than "mental illness" forcefully directs our attention to societal variables involved in the processes of norm setting and norm regulation. Upon achieving such an open declaration, the scientist can shift attention from *disease* to *behavior regulation;* from *illness of the mind* to the conditions for *declaring moral judgments;* from *curing* to *selling behavior regulation services.* Such shifts can now be supported by drawing upon the burgeoning literature treating social influence processes and moral judgment skills. The contemporary scientist is now in a better position to account for and deal with perplexing behavior. Neither the idiographic paradigm that gave rise to mentalism, nor the mechanist paradigm that gave rise to behaviorism are adequate for solving the puzzles generated by the declaration of moral judgments, especially moral judgments uttered in the vocabulary of psychiatric diagnosis.

Recapitulating, we see that the "profiles" for schizophrenia are not like the profiles employed by the hematologist for diagnosing disease within the mechanistic tradition. On our analysis, the lack of reliability and credibility of the diagnosis "schizophrenia" is not unexpected. The problem of defining madness has puzzled scientists and moralists for centuries. Madness invariably connotes unwanted conduct. This invariance directs us to examine the relationship between the values of the diagnostician and the values of the target person. The examination has proceeded to the empirical, data-gathering stage; and it can be shown that diagnosis does depend on the valuings of the diagnostician, and that the values of diagnosticians are inseparable from their professional pronouncements.

Diagnosis and Values in Literature

The interplay between the diagnosis of madness and value situations has been a fertile topic for satirists. DePorte (1974) in an analysis of the work of eighteenth-century writers, shows how Jonathan Swift, in his writing, handled the relativity of evaluations.

> It is a concern sometimes expressed as a fear that madness will escape detection if it is common. In Prior's dialogue between Cromwell and the mad porter, for example, the porter insists that the difference between Bedlamites and "Public Madmen" like Cromwell is only that the latter have been lucky enough to gather others round them who share their dementia:
>
> "You all Herd together and it is a very hard thing to catch one of You, but we are fewer in number, divided, unarmed, and different in our principles. If the least disturbance happens from any impetuosity of our Temper the Neighborhood has an Eye upon us, and away we are hurried the next dark Night to Morefields or Hodgdon . . . but you have commonly the majority on your Side, which as your Excellency very well knows, is no small advantage in England [p. 82]"

DePorte continues:

> The problem thus set forth is a perplexing one, and one which since the Nurenberg trials has become especially painful in our own time. What if the norms of society upon which a man models his behavior are unworthy? What if they are base and ignoble? What, in other words, if the common forms sanction a kind of madness? A true skeptic would have to reply that it is not meaningful to speak of madness in any absolute sense since we can have no absolute knowledge of anything, that it is only meaningful to speak of madness relatively, as it is defined by a particular community or group. This answer turns up repeatedly in the 'Digression on Madness.' The narrator tells us that although Epicurus, Diogenes, and Lucretius were honored in their own day, they would, if alive today and separated from their followers, incur manifest Danger of *Phlebotomy*, and *Whips*, and *Chains*, and *Dark Chambers*, and Straw [p. 83].

John Adams, commenting on the writings of the famous medical scientist, Benjamin Rush, was keenly aware of the relativity of the diagnosis of madness.

It seems to me, that every excess of Passion, Prejudice, Appetite; of Love, Fear, Jealousy, Envy, Revenge, Avarice, Ambition; every Revery and Vagary of Imagination; the Fairytales, the Arabian Nights, in short, almost all Poetry and all Oratory; every ecart, every deviation from pure, logical mathematical Reason; may in some sense be called a disease of the mind [Adams, 1774, quoted in Dain, 1964, p. 34].

A Panel of Critics in Subject Selection

A contextualist view of the diagnostic process allows us to claim that Adams's concerns in 1774, are little dispelled by the state of affairs in 1979. We boldly assert that in the 374 studies we reviewed as we tried to assess the current state of research on schizophrenia, we could uncover no instance of the study samples having been chosen on the basis of *diagnosis* such as is traditionally practiced by physicians. When the psychiatrists classified a person as *a schizophrenic* (thus making the person a potential subject for schizophrenia research) they functioned quite unlike physicians constructing a diagnosis within the established disease model; instead they functioned in the manner of a drama critic writing a review of a role enactment. They certified that the target person had turned in a performance that failed to match their (the psychiatrists') script, a script that had been "written" as a guide to *proper* performances on the stage of life. When an unsuccessful role performance is brought to the attention of the "drama critic," he or she may declare that the enactments are more like those of a "character" called "madman" or "schizophrenic."

Shands' (1970) discussion of subject selection points to the ultimate in the use of the metaphor of drama critic. What stratagem is employed when a critic lacks confidence in his or her review? Or when there is more than one drama critic? If two or more critics write differently phrased evaluations of a particular role enactment, how can their differences be resolved?

Shands refers to the work of Shakow as a point of departure. He writes:

[Shakow, 1963] discovered in the early days of his work that if he wanted to get even a modicum of consistency he had to rely upon a *jury* to select his subjects. After an intensive exclusion of the majority of possible subjects because of complicating factors, so that consistency of age, residence in hospital, sex, schooling, and a host of other factors were controlled, it was still necessary for a group of experts to review these patients to identify which ones were 'really schizophrenic.' The significant implication in this methodological maneuver is that what is established by a jury is not a diagnosis but a verdict! In social systems the necessity of spreading the onus of responsibility and delivering any single citizen from the burden of decision in important matters is a reasonable background to legal process—but it is scarcely the ideal road to scientific 'truth.' The principle is that enunciated in a famous statement by the Bellman: 'What I say three times is true' [Shands, 1970, p. 392].

From our claim that psychiatric diagnosis is a thin veil for declaring moral judgments, the juristic expression "verdict" is a most felicitous term.

Popularization of the "Schizophrenia" Role

Szasz (1970), in his intriguing polemic on modern psychiatry, urges the conclusion that psychiatry "manufactures" madness. Drawing a telling analogy, Szasz argues that the process of establishing the condition of "mental illness" parallels the process of establishing the condition of "witchcraft." The psychiatrist and the inquisitor share role enactments in that they judge the existence of an ephemeral state of affairs. Yet, the psychiatrist and the inquisitor each argues that the state of affairs exists and that it can be identified. Furthermore, the psychiatrist and the inquisitor claim the necessity of special techniques to discover the identifying characteristics. At worst (best), the inquisitor relies on the thumb screw and the rack. At worst (best), the psychiatrist relies on response to drugs and the mental status examination to establish the condition of mental illness. Both the inquisitor and the mental health professional, nevertheless, serve the purpose of lending moral authority to the concurrent model for assessing norm violation. They try to teach the public how to use the professional conceptions, and, in this way, everyone can assume the role of amateur psychiatrist. The professionals themselves provide a highly significant strand in the context in which diagnosis is framed.

Failure of a Moral Enterprise

For several decades, workers in the mental health movement have engaged in a moral crusade to induce the general public to adopt the proposition, "mental illness is just like any other illness." The underlying assumption of this moral credo is that the nonstigmatizing attitudes held toward diagnosed somatic illness would transfer to such "mental" illnesses as schizophrenia. Mental health professionals have worked assiduously to convince the public to look at certain behaviors as manifestations of "illness," with the expectation that the sympathetic, nonrejecting valuations usually declared on physical illness would then be automatically declared on conduct deviations.

We employ the term *moral crusade* intentionally. Becker (1963) described a moral crusade as the enterprise of persons who see the need for a particular rule of conduct and who become committed to a social movement that aims to establish that rule. A predictable by-product of such crusading is a professional apparatus first to promote the rule, then to implement it. The history of the mental health movement in America provides abundant data to confirm our adopting this colorful metaphor. Psychiatry, the semiofficial authority behind the mental health crusade, has handed us the rule: *People who exhibit unacceptable conduct are mentally ill.* It does not distort history to suggest that the leaders of the movement are "moral entrepreneurs."

Entrepreneurs of morality, like entrepreneurs of commerce, may achieve success or they may fail. Moral enterprise may be judged as having successfully achieved its goal when the rule of conduct at issue becomes a part of the moral

ᏏᎷᏏᏏᎾ

ideology of the public, and is widely enforced through officially designated agents.

Elsewhere we have reviewed published studies of the public's attitudes toward mental illness and mental health (Sarbin & Mancuso, 1970; Sarbin & Mancuso, 1972; Mancuso, 1979). Our conclusion: the moral enterprise of promoting the "mental illness" metaphor has failed. The general public has not accepted illness as an appropriate metaphor for deviant behavior. In spite of extensive public relations and propaganda programs, the public is not ready to use such labels as "schizophrenia," "psychosis" or "mental illness" to index one or more of those people whose behavior would lead a professional diagnostician to declare a psychiatric verdict. Further, the public does not advocate the use of a special cognitive category to isolate (and to sequester) persons whose performances motivate a diagnostician to employ such categories as "schizophrenia," "psychosis," or "mental illness." On the other hand, if the average citizen is told authoritatively that a target person is schizophrenic or mentally ill, he or she will tend to place the deviantly behaving person in the "reject" category. Our review of the relevant literature available at that time, along with our evaluation of recent publications (Mancuso, 1979), supports the conclusion that, in general, the public tends to tolerate and accommodate to overt conduct which professionals diagnose as "mental illness," but the public tends to see persons who are branded by the label "mentally ill" as stigmatized.

It is important to note that the authors of books and articles on the public's attitudes towards mental illness have been, by and large, *professional* mental health workers—psychiatrists, psychologists, and social workers. These are the moral authorities who declare that the public is "misinformed," that the public holds "incorrect attitudes," that the public has not acquired a "scientific orientation," etc. They frequently recommend "public psychotherapy" in the form of better public education about mental illness, about schizophrenia, about depression, about psychodynamics, and similar topics, even reaching into the secondary schools.

These observations constrained us to ask the question: Precisely what should the public be taught about deviant conduct? The systematic attitude studies lead to the inference that if the public were to classify deviant behavior as mental illness, then the deviantly behaving person would be stigmatized and rejected. The stigmatization and rejection are, of course, decried as an unintended consequence. A second question is pertinent: Could a sustained, powerful propaganda effort succeed in validating the mental illness metaphor, so that labels such as "mental illness" and "schizophrenia" would produce the same neutral (nonstigmatizing) valuational responses as are called forth by the labels "pneumonia," "mumps," "myopia," or "indigestion"? Even if a convention of mental health professionals, jurists, linguists, and educators could resolve the communication problems contained in the multiplicity of definitions of mental illness (Scott, 1968), would it be possible to design an educational campaign that could detach the moral connotations from psychiatric diagnosis? Could mental health organizations and government bureaucracies influence the public to regard "mental illness" diagnoses (verdicts) as having the same moral force as diagnoses of somatic illness? Is the detachment of morality from mental illness a worthy goal?

Our reviews of published studies warranted the conclusion that professional campaigns to promote the mental illness metaphor have failed. Because of the mythic status of mental illness, the campaigns had been foredoomed to failure. At one time, mental illness was a potentially useful metaphor. So were madness, schizophrenia, and dissociation. Like so many other metaphors of mentalism, these were illicitly transformed into myths—guides to action without empirical supports. Once such a transformation occurred, moral valuational components became an integral part of the mythical concept and could not be detached.

The evidence of the failure to convince the general public to adopt the mental illness myth, together with the logical and humanistic arguments against the current usefulness of the myth, demand a reevaluation of the whole enterprise concerned with informing the public on the issue of inappropriate and improper behavior. Our review of studies on attitudes of the public toward mental illness supported three major propositions:

1. The ordinary citizen tolerates and accommodates to extensive conduct deviations.
2. The public is hesitant about using the mental illness label for those behavior deviations and unusual solutions to life's problems which psychiatrically oriented diagnosticians would unhesitatingly label mental illness, schizophrenia, psychosis, etc.
3. If the diagnostic term "mental illness" or its equivalent is attached to a particular behavior, the public will tend to reject and to advocate isolation and exclusion of the person whose behavior is thus labeled.

Rabkin (1972), who appears to approve the dissemination of skills in taking the psychiatrist/drama critic role, has provided an analysis of the propaganda efforts of the mental health enterprise; she records the frequently expressed professional position in relation to the attitudes held by nonprofessionals.

While the delineation of attitudes toward mental illness can be of interest as an end in itself, it is most commonly undertaken in relation to efforts at attitude modification. That is, hospital and clinic administrators, supervisors and instructors are eager to encourage more favorable attitudes among staff and students. They want to be able to ascertain attitudes held when workers first join the staff, in order to modify those which do not fit into the institution's prevailing beliefs and procedures [p. 163].

Mental health professionals appear to be secure in their belief that they are serving a positive function by altering the attitude of outsiders. Mental health professionals are convinced that something positive—for example, tolerance, understanding—is to be gained through programs designed to alter attitudes so they are congruent with those held by the professionals. The dissemination of their stereotypes is held by the professionals to be a part of their duty.

Considering the state of uncertainty that pervades the science of unwanted behavior, one would rightfully feel some discomfort about the knowledge that mental health professionals have been given license to engage in attitude-change adventures. The studies of stereotype distribution support the credibility of

Szasz's claim that the mental health enterprise includes efforts to disseminate the role definitions which are to be used in the judgment of an actor's adequacy as a performer of mentally ill roles. Indeed, one of the studies of popular conceptions of mental health (Manis, Houts, & Blake, 1963) contains evidence that persons who enter a mental hospital tend to change their views toward greater congruence with those of the hospital personnel. (An ancillary finding in this study suggests that longer term residents of mental hospitals *had not* adopted the mental health ideology. Manis, Houts, and Blake found it necessary to confront the disturbing possibility that acceptance of the mental health system's premises is regarded as evidence that the patient is "cured." Consider, again, the analogic comparison to the inquisitor who pronounced the judgment "saved, but burned" on the confessed witch.)

Yaffe and Mancuso (1977) have reported some other aspects of the effects of disseminating a "mental health" view of unwanted behavior. They completed a study in which college students watched a videotaped scene showing a person being interviewed by a mock psychiatrist. The interviewer enacted three versions of the role as follows: (1) low interest in the client's communications, (2) high interest, and (3) overinterest. The low interest and the overinterested role enactments were designed to portray a mental health worker who failed to comply with the popular conception of how a mental health professional interacts with patients. The high-interest interviewer maintained comfortable eye contact and body distance with the client and encouraged the client to tell more, and so forth. In each interview, the client said precisely the same things, in the same tone and with the same emphases. Different samples of students watched each of the scenarios. The students then evaluated the target person so that it was possible to assess the level of psychological adjustment assigned to the client under each of the three conditions. The students who watched the high-interest interviewer clearly attributed greater maladjustment to the client in that scenario. Apparently the observers attributed higher expertise to the interviewer who enacted the role appropriately, and the enactment convinced the observers that they were witnessing an event that could take place in the mental health world context. To authenticate their impressions, they ascribed less power to the client and predicted that the client would engage in behaviors thought to be indicators of poor psychological adjustment.

In effect then, the general public, particularly the educated general public exposed to books on abnormal psychology and psychiatry written under the guidance of the disease model, acquires role definitions that delineate the character of creatures they have never seen. It is the general public who observes the daily behavior of the prepatient, confronts indicators they have been trained to instantiate as *mental illness* (see Cox, Costanzo, & Coie, 1977, for behaviors that raise mental illness concerns), and then funnels the person toward a mental health professional. There one expects a verdict, in the form of a diagnosis. The popular media make an immense contribution to creating the appropriate context for the diagnostic process. When the popular media portray the activities of various and sundry "schizophrenics," or dramatically report that medical science is on the verge of discovering a cure for the disease "schizophrenia," the general public utilizes a conception which, though not satisfactorily congruent with accepted psychiatric conceptions, could be taken as a reasonable facsimile.

We reiterate: the disease model has failed to offer satisfying explanations of unwanted behavior. It is time to turn to a contextualist model to explain unwanted behavior. It is time that behavior scientists freed themselves from the mechanistic paradigm that demands that the current conduct of the actor must be explained in terms of the antecedents of the actor's responses. The conduct of the person declaring the moral judgment and the conduct of the actor are parts of the total context within which verdicts are declared on unwanted behavior.

The science of deviant behavior is in need of a paradigm revolution. "Schizophrenia" will be better explained when psychological scientists employ a paradigm that recognizes "that psychological events consist of symmetric fields in which the acts of persons and the acts of stimulus objects are simultaneously occurring poles [Kantor, 1969, p. 377].

Our advocacy of the contextualist paradigm in these pages has deferred discussion of several large epistemological problems. What, for example, shall we do about the current demand that our behaving subjects shall be predictable? Can we develop a psychology that satisfactorily deals with this demand? A more extended analysis would suggest that behavior science need not predict responses of individuals, instead, we should work toward predicting contexts. An alternate model offers an approach toward discussing an individual in contexts. Specifically, a constructively based social role model of conduct promises to discuss individuals in their social ecological contexts. And more specifically, the role transformation model to be elaborated in a later chapter provides a framework for studying the process by which an individual is assigned to the nonperson status *schizophrenia*.

A proclamation by fiat cannot eliminate the disease model from the study of unwanted behavior. The preparation of this book, however, has led us to believe that it is unreasonable to continue using the disease model of the mechanistic paradigm to understand unwanted conduct. Other paradigms are available. As they are applied, we predict, the "disease of schizophrenia" will disappear, just as the "venality of witchery" disappeared when the specialists in the inquisition removed their services from the public marketplace.

No claim to novelty accompanies this conclusion. Over 50 years ago, Trigant Burrow, an eminent psychoanalyst, physician, writer, and critic of earlier theories of unwanted conduct, wrote a statement that neatly fits our position. (The reader should substitute "schizophrenia" for "dementia praecox.")

Of dementia praecox, the disease, psychiatry is in fact more a cause than a cure, just as mothers and doctors . . . however handy they may be in untoward emergency, are more an occasion than a remedy for disease in general. And so the real disorder, after all, is not dementia praecox, but psychiatry. When the psychiatrist will have come to understand dementia praecox . . . this objective figment of his own disordered consciousness will spontaneously vanish [Burrow, 1927, p. 137].

6
Extrinsic Support for the Disease Model of Schizophrenia: Ideological Premises[1]

It is now time to raise the rhetorical query, since schizophrenia cannot be reliably diagnosed, since no experimental variable has been discovered that would make possible the identification of a person as schizophrenic or nonschizophrenic, since small group differences cannot be taken seriously in the absence of efforts to partial out variables such as socioeconomic status, cognitive skills, and patienthood, what are the conditions that support the entrenched belief that it is possible to diagnose a disease entity called schizophrenia?

The most obvious response to the query would begin from noting the inherent conservatism of scientific paradigms. Although, as suggested before, paradigms appear to be self-supporting, they are in great measure maintained and sustained by forces extrinsic to the scientific enterprise.

It is a matter of common knowledge that a vast bureaucratic network legitimizes and even authorizes "mental illness" explanations of deviant conduct. A mammoth sociopolitical apparatus has been created to label, sequester, and regulate those persons who suffer from "mental diseases." At all levels of the political structure, bureaucracies sustain and support the disease model. Local county medical associations act as lobbies to assure, for example, that health insurance plans cover "treatment" for young adults who trouble their parents by advocating extremely esoteric religious beliefs. The report of a grant-controlling federal agency declared that despite huge previous effort, ". . . schizophrenia remains the most challenging and devastating major mental illness [Mosher, 1969, p. 4]." The National Institutes of Health created a *Center For Studies of Schizophrenia*, complete with its own professional journal. The mission of the center is to give special attention to *diagnosis, etiology, prevention*, and *treatment* of this "dread disease."

Thus a powerful bureaucracy, riding in tandem with the universal conservatism of scientific paradigms, prolongs the life of the schizophrenia model.

It would be instructive to examine the ideological premises that provide cognitive support to the workings of the mental health bureaucracy, and, of course, ideological support for the continuing efforts of scientists to construct reliable methods for identifying schizophrenia.

It is important to recognize explicitly that the assumed entity "schizophrenia" cannot be divorced from the supraordinate category "mental illness." "Schizophrenia" is not studied in the same manner as, say, introversion. Investigators of introversion are not confined to the ambience of mental illness. They have the freedom to pursue their interest almost anywhere. Their subject pool is, in principle, the universe of persons. Not so investigators of schizophrenia. Their subject pool is not the universe of persons, but a greatly restricted subuniverse—the already-diagnosed mentally ill, most often persons who are (or have been) committed or certified to mental hospitals. Very few of the reviewed 374 *Journal of Abnormal Psychology* studies were conducted on nonhospitalized persons. As we stated in an earlier chapter, the scientist of schizophrenia begins work with subjects who have already been preselected on various dimensions. The preselection depends upon the operation of procedures that involve a number of well-entrenched social institutions, among them, legislative bodies, law enforcement agencies, the courts, governmental administrative systems, and the medical profession.

To explain the tenacity of the disease paradigm in the study of unwanted conduct, then, we must look at the larger social fabric. As we noted before, a vast bureaucracy containing representation from law, medicine, police, and government provide "extrinsic support" for the maintenance of the disease paradigm. At this point, the question must be asked, What are the often unrecognized premises, beliefs, biases, and assumptions of the practitioners of mental health and mental illness? What remote and concurrent events have created the background for the acceptance of the entrenched views about madness?

At this juncture, we offer a description of the underlying, often tacit, premises that appear to constrain the study of norm violation, particularly, that part of the study that deals with "schizophrenia." The analysis must perforce enter the sociology of knowledge and employ the notion of ideology.

As Mannheim (1936) has observed, knowledge in the social sciences is in many ways different from knowledge in the mechanistic sciences: Social scientific knowledge is situationally determined. That is to say, the metaphysical perspective and the social status of the knower have an influence on the content of knowledge. The study of ideological premises reflects how an entrenched group or profession can become so bound to a situation that its members cannot recognize facts that would weaken their power.

An ideology is a set of beliefs organized around a small number of values and accompanied by strong feelings. The term *ideology* is ordinarily connected to discussions of authority and to the distribution of power; as such, an ideology is necessarily political. Unlike other kinds of assumptions, ideologies are concerned with the sacred. A challenge to an action based on an ideological premise is likely to invoke a response characterized more by passion than by dialectic.

Our task now is to identify some of the ideological premises that support—often unwittingly—the practitioners of the normal science of deviance. We accent again the caution that unwanted, unacceptable conduct is *not* to be construed as equivalent to psychopathology—the latter term focuses on the abstract individual and gathers its meaning from an illicit joining of a mythical abstraction (psyche) to an enterprise that deals with tumors, toxins, and trauma (pathology).

Unwanted conduct refers simultaneously to the actions of at least two interacting participants: the target person (the identified patient or quasi defendant) and a second person who has declared a negative valuation on the actions, including the reported imaginings, of the target person. We underscore the phrase, *at least two interacting participants*. In actual practice, where the second person, most often a relative, has an interest in the target person and—more important—has legitimate or coercive power to bring the latter to the attention of the local or state mental health establishment, the number of persons involved is much larger than two. For example, a county prosecutor may receive the petition from the interested relative or from a police officer. A probate or superior court judge presides at a civil hearing preliminary to a decision to commit or not to commit to a state hospital. One or more physicians may be called upon to examine the patient and provide expert testimony. In some states, psychologists may be invited to conduct a psychological examination. In addition, the personnel of a hospital or of a county or city jail where the target person is temporarily detained become part of the social system of interest to the social scientist. The actions of any of these persons may provide the contingency for labelling or not labelling a person as a mental patient, thus affecting the person's career.

In examining this social system, two positions are of special interest—the judge and the physician (usually a psychiatrist) called upon to advise the judge. The remarks that follow are pertinent to the beliefs held by the occupants of these positions. Such beliefs help legitimize the enactment of their roles within the civil proceedings for involuntary mental hospitalization.

In order to focus our arguments, we call upon the reader to imagine a courtroom drama but with three roles: the judge, the psychiatrist, and the target person. This drama is perforce fictional—the actual situation, as described in formal research reports (Miller & Schwartz, 1963; Wenger & Fletcher, 1969) may include relatives, bailiffs, hospital attendants, hangers-on, and occasionally a lawyer representing the target person. But the central roles are the three already identified: the person whose liberty is at risk (hereinafter called the "quasi defendant"), the judge who has the legitimate power to deprive the quasi defendant of liberty, and the physician whose expert knowledge or advice may be employed by the judge in arriving at a decision. The actor taking the part of the "quasi defendant" becomes a shadowy figure and the spotlight is beamed on the other two actors. As the scene develops, the spotlight narrows on the physician, the judge joining the "quasi defendant" in the shadows. Parenthetically, the metaphor of "shadowy figure" is an apt one. Unlike criminal proceedings, where the person whose liberty is at risk is identified with a label ("the defendant" or "the accused"), the object of judgment in the civil proceedings has no status, at least no status that can be dignified with a standard title or label. No better example could be cited of the nonperson status of the quasi defendant and its implications for prejudgment.

We have identified a number of ideological premises based on (1) the apparent legitimacy of civil proceedings; (2) the legitimacy of the mental hospital; (3) the belief in the dangerousness of certain types of people; (4) the unique authority of the physician; (5) the concept of the abstract individual; (6) the concept of mind; (7) the *parens patriae* concept; (8) the "genteel tradition;" and (9) the positive value of research. These conjoined premises provide a mute context for the role enactments of judges and medical doctors (and their surrogates) in assigning the status "mentally ill," "psychotic," "insane," "schizophrenic," "manic," etc., to the person whose conduct comes under their evaluative scrutiny.

THE APPARENT LEGITIMACY OF CIVIL PROCEEDINGS

Because the subjects for nearly all experimenters are drawn from a pool of committed patients, it is necessary to examine the context of commitment, the process of depriving persons of their liberty. The judicial procedures for denying liberty are of two kinds: criminal and civil. Dershowitz (1970, 1973) has cut through the legal haze surrounding civil proceedings most convincingly. He outlines two strategies for denying a person liberty: performance-punishment and prediction-prevention. The first is predicated on the premise that an alleged offender has performed certain acts in violation of the law and should be deterred from further violations through punishment or other sanctions; the second is predicated on the premise that an individual is alleged to belong to a certain class of objects. The class possesses the attribute of being potentially violent or potentially disorderly. Merely being a member of the class rather than performing an unlawful act, then, becomes the defining criterion for the denial of liberty. It is the responsibility of the court to prevent the potential offender from engaging in unlawful conduct; therefore, the quasi defendant is prevented from doing harm on the basis of status: membership in a class with certain attributes, that is, mental illness.

It should be evident that the concept of involuntary mental hospitalization is similar to, if not identical with, the concept of preventive detention. Dershowitz pointedly asks whether the United States Constitution permits detention on the ground of a probabilistic prediction that at some time in the future a person *may* engage in harm-doing. His answers to the constitutional question in part hinge on the arbitrary decision by prosecutors to label a proceeding as criminal or civil. If the proceeding is "criminal," then certain constitutional safeguards must be observed. If the "civil" label is invoked, the court is not constrained by due process and equal protection safeguards. We quote Dershowitz:

> . . . prosecutors have succeeded with the help of the court, and all too often, without the opposition of "defense" attorneys, in attaching the civil label to a wide range of proceedings

including commitment of juveniles, sex psychopaths, the mentally ill, alcoholics, drug addicts, and security risks. Likewise sterilization, deportation, and revocation of parole and probation proceedings are regarded as civil. By attaching this label, the state has successfully denied defendants almost every important safeguard required in criminal trials. Invocation of this talismanic word has erased a veritable bill of rights [1973, p. 1296].

The arbitrary labelling of a proceeding as "criminal" or "civil" has the effect of an accusatory proceeding similar to those of continental justice systems. The quasi defendant is treated as "guilty until proven innocent." Quasi defendants must in effect establish their innocence of crimes not yet committed. Complaints about the arbitrariness of courts in labelling a hearing as "criminal" or "civil" are parallel to the frequently heard complaints about police officers arbitrarily dispensing "curbside justice" (Skolnick, 1966).

Given the ambiguous status of civil proceedings in a democracy that guarantees due process, it is no wonder that jurists seek the help of experts, namely, physicians. The presence of the expert lends an atmosphere of credibility to the court proceedings. After all, the arbitrary decision to label the proceeding "civil" follows from the premise that the quasi defendant has not overtly violated the criminal code, but may in the future do so. The court looks to possible actions *in the future*. The court implicitly predicts the behavior of the quasi defendant. Since prediction of behavior is a subtle art, especially if the behavior is mediated by "mysterious mental processes," the quasi defendant is presumably protected from arbitrary decisions based on ignorance when a physician provides expert testimony. The physician's diagnosis gives the appearance of scientific legitimacy to the "civil" proceeding. However, the prediction of behavior—by physicians or any others—is no simple matter. It has been a lively topic in the behavior science literature for at least 50 years. In the late 1930s the Social Science Research Council commissioned a panel of social scientists to review the problems connected with the prediction of adjustment (Horst, Wallin, & Guttman, 1941). They recommended, *inter alia,* more research on the relative accuracy of clinical (case study) and actuarial methods of prediction. A series of studies in the 1940s made clear that the clinician was no better, and often worse, than the prediction table or actuarial equation (Sarbin, 1944; Meehl, 1954). Logical and conceptual analysis suggested that the degree of accuracy of the clinical method could be accounted for by a statistical model (Meehl, 1954; Sarbin, Taft, & Bailey, 1960). In their efforts to clarify the clinical-actuarial controversy, the fact was overlooked that neither method provided a degree of accuracy that freed the predictor from the embarrassment of false positives and false negatives. To predict college achievement, for example, the actuarial method was superior to the clinical method, but at best it could reduce error by no more than 50 percent over chance. Parole prediction was less accurate. An important article by Meehl and Rosen (1955) turned attention to the problem of base rates. What degree of error would result from predicting, let us say, that all members of a cohort of applicants for college would satisfactorily complete the course of studies? If the base rate is, say, 70 percent, then the clinical or actuarial forecaster would be obliged at least to match the base rate.

The recognition of the base rate problem has had a sobering influence on those who would eliminate violence by identifying "violence-prone" individuals and incarcerating them or subjecting them to educational, psychological, pharmacological, or surgical treatments. Since, statistically speaking, violence is a relatively infrequent event, the prediction of violence (or dangerousness) from case history material or psychological tests can hardly match the prediction of "no violence" in terms of the number of correctly predicted cases. By predicting "no violence," a small number of false negatives, but no false positives, would be identified.

Even with a relatively "pure" sample of violent offenders and an equal number of nonviolent offenders, Sarbin, Wenk and Sherwood (1968) could predict from a psychological test with an error rate of 27 percent, about half false negatives. The power of any test diminishes when the two groups are unequal in number, for example, when one group is the general population. If the ratio of assaultive to nonassaultive individuals in the general population is five in a hundred, then the prediction "nondangerous" would be correct 95 times in 100. The false positive rate would be five percent.

It is well established that dangerousness, the hidden concern of the judge and the forensic psychiatrist, cannot be predicted by physicians or any other specialists (Cocozza & Steadman, 1976; Steadman & Cocozza, 1974). It is also well established that the mass media mistakenly attribute more violence to mental patients than to others. These facts, ironically, have had little influence on social policy decisions regarding involuntary mental hospitalization (Monahan, 1973; Dershowitz, 1970; Steadman, 1973; Wenk, Robison, & Smith, 1972).

Behind the willingness to call upon the expert to make predictions lies the belief that the expert has developed a sophisticated system into which one can fit the signs that are used in the judgment process. In other parts of this essay, the diagnostician's guiding paradigms are analyzed. In other extended essays (Morse, 1978; Mancuso & Sarbin, 1976) the same kind of analysis is applied to the behavior science paradigms that have been brought into jursiprudential activity. The basic conclusions that may be drawn from these articles are as follows: The behavior scientist has brought a mechanistic conception into the enterprise of judging the motives for misconduct; and the mechanistic paradigm, being inappropriate to all behavior science, has also failed to be useful in juridical proceedings. Morse (1978) made this strong recommendation as he closed his essay:

> Finally, no matter what role craziness may play in legal decision making, it should be recognized that the ultimate decisions are moral and social and that special treatment rests on strong intuition and not on scientific rationale. The role of the experts should be limited and lay decision makers should assume full responsibility for the hard social, moral, and legal decisions that must be made [p. 654].

To recapitulate: The belief in the legitimacy of civil commitment fits the definition of an ideological premise. Civil commitment allows the exercise of power without the constraining influence of constitutional guarantees. The employment of physicians as experts is an ill-conceived strategy to envelop the commitment process with the aura of science. The physician's assistance to the court is concerned with the prediction of dangerousness. Since physicians (or other experts) have no special skill in prediction, their contribution to the magisterial procedure is ornamental. At best, their "scientific" diagnoses give comfort to the judge who has the awesome responsibility of depriving people of their liberty.

THE MENTAL HOSPITAL AS A LEGITIMATE INSTITUTION

Another item in the ideological background of the court and the forensic psychiatrist is the knowledge of the existence and availability of mental hospitals. Needless to say, the purposes of mental hospitals are markedly different from the purposes of institutions denoted by the unmodified word "hospital." It is important to note that the court's decision, which frequently follows upon the expert testimony of the psychiatrist, is conditioned by the fact that there is a *place* to send the person upon whom the role of mentally ill patient has been conferred. Diagnosis, then, is not idle.

Even though psychiatrists may have available the pessimistic statistics on rate of improvement, the knowledge of the stigmatizing and degrading effects of hospitalization, and the knowledge that labelling is pernicious, they conduct their forensic work on the premise that a *place* exists for "mentally ill" patients to be segregated from the rest of society.

It is **instructive** to remind the reader that the state hospital, a standard feature of the contemporary landscape, is the outgrowth of a noble experiment. Its predecessor, the asylum, was regarded by many observers as a reform. On the surface, "it was an obvious improvement not only over existing conditions, but over *other possible alternatives*," the historian David J. Rothman writes. "But such a perspective," he goes on to say,

is bad logic and bad history. There was nothing inevitable about the asylum form, no self-evident reason why philanthropists should have chosen it. Indeed, the subsequent history . . . should make historians somewhat suspicious of any simple link between progress and the asylum. Was an organization that would eventually turn into a snake pit a necessary step forward for mankind [p. 87]?

Rothman's question is worth pondering in the light of counter-productive effects of the mental hospital, repeatedly documented. The question also alerts us to the recent and much belated judicial opinions on the patient's right to treatment when incarcerated. (The prior constitutional problem—the right to noninterference—has not been completely resolved [Kittrie, 1971].)

The promise of the early asylum humanely to regulate the conduct of its inmates has not been fulfilled. Rather the institution became a facility for helping to maintain order. In the middle of the nineteenth century, waves of immigrants entered the United States, industrial and commercial developments changed the economic structure, and cities and slums proliferated. These economic changes contributed to the increase in the distinctions between social classes. Societal strains created the conditions for urban disorder and personal disorganization. Time-honored mechanisms for maintaining order became unworkable. The concept of "dangerous classes" became a slogan for pamphleteers and led to repressive legislation. Under these conditions, segregation and imprisonment became the method of choice for controlling those subsets of the population that were suspected of violating concurrent propriety norms. The reform movement of the early nineteenth century had created the asylums, their subsequent utility as centers for custody made them indispensible. When, through accidents of history, medical superintendents were appointed to administer these custodial centers, "asylums" became "hospitals," but their basic function remained the same: the maintenance of public order through the incarceration of actual and potential norm violators.

The fact of the mental hospital, then, is a necessary feature of the ideological premises of those charged with determining whether a putative quasi defendant should be assigned the status of inmate in a mental hospital.

CERTAIN TYPES OF PEOPLE ARE MORE DANGEROUS THAN OTHER TYPES OF PEOPLE

A third source of ideological bias may be found in expectations tied to social class. In 1958, Hollingshead and Redlich published their monumental study of social class and mental illness. Among other things, they demonstrated the docility of psychiatric diagnosis to indicators of social-class membership. Persons identified as lower-class were overrepresented in the diagnostic class "schizophrenic," those identified as middle-class were more often diagnosed as "neurotic." Recent reports give experimental support to the conclusion that a silent assumption about social-class membership guides the practitioner in the use of diagnostic labels. Various experiments have been reported that demonstrate that when the stimulus persons are presented as lower-class mental patients, they are consistently diagnosed as being more pathological and having a poorer prognosis (Trachtman, 1971). In their review of epidemiological studies of mental illness, Dohrenwend and Dohrenwend (1969) concluded that being poor was the single most important attribute of persons diagnosed as mentally ill.

What is the ideological source of this bias? The readiness to attribute mental illness to members of the lower class (with the attendant high risk of depriving them of their freedom) has been interpreted by Rotenberg (1975) within the context of the Protestant ethic. Concern with success and failure in meeting life goals, especially economic goals, had its origins in the writings of the influential sixteenth-century theologian, John Calvin. The essence of his teachings is contained in a sentence that declares favorable destinies for some people and not for others. "Eternal life," he wrote, "is foreordained for some, and eternal damnation for others." The doctrine of predestination was widely circulated in Protestant countries. Max Weber (1930) has shown that Calvin's doctrine of the pre-destination of the elect and the damned was the object of great political and cultural struggles of the sixteenth and seventeenth centuries. Calvinism provided the motive force for the Puritan movements in England and America. Calvin's writings became part and parcel of the credo of Protestant Bible readers. Roten-berg noted that all English Bibles, at least from 1574 and for many years after-wards, contained the Calvinistic catechism, the pages bound between the Old and the New Testaments. In this way, there was imparted to the Calvinistic doctrine an authority that was almost a part of the inspired word of God.

For our present analysis, it is not enough to subscribe to Weber's analysis of the extensive influence of the Protestant ethic. It is not enough to show the similarity between Calvin's doctrine of predestination (with its attendant cate-gories of "elect" and "damned") and the readiness of mental health profession-als to assign labels equivalent to "damned" to the system's failures. In the context of diagnosis leading to involuntary mental hospitalization, the identifica-tion of a person as one of the damned carries with it the belief that the damned person may be dangerous. We have not outgrown the beliefs of the nineteenth and early twentieth centuries that poor people, especially recent immigrants and blacks, besides being "damned," were to be regarded as members of "danger-ous classes" and in need of control. Danger is a relationship and is not the same as violence, an instrumental act. An etymological analysis suggests that "danger" derives from "dominium," a power concept. The "dangerous classes" of late nineteenth-century writers were the powerless poor who might engage in actions to change the "dominium," i.e., to challenge the current distribution of power; thus, the concern with facilities that would help control the potentially dangerous (Sarbin, 1967b).

In order for psychiatrists or other professionals to declare a person "danger-ous" in the absence of clear-cut instrumental acts, they must first construct an inference of dangerousness. This may be accomplished through cognitively equating sixteenth-century Calvinistic damnation with twentieth-century mental illness. Being mentally ill or psychotic, then, is a variant of being forever damned. And the mentally ill could be "dangerous" to the elect and to their social institutions.

The origins of the connection between mental illness and dangerousness is obscure. Certainly the brutality to persons imprisoned in public madhouses in the seventeenth and eighteenth centuries created caricatures of dangerousness. In Bedlam and in LaBicétre, for example, inmates appeared to show little or no socially appropriate conduct. Rather they were considered little better than wild beasts or savages.

White (1972) has written a fascinating account of the origin of the myth of the "wild man within." In earlier times, when large areas of the globe were still unexplored, Europeans nurtured the belief that these unknown lands were peopled by unsocialized, untamed, wild savages. Their beliefs followed from assumptions of how human beings would look and act without benefit of civiliza-tion. The world has shrunk, and no wild man of Borneo, of Africa, of Asia has been found. From Lombroso's atavism to Freud's impulse-ridden Id, the myth of the "wild man within" lingers on.

Imaginings of self as governed by unmodulated passion are the probable source of the ancient hypothesis that the denizens of unexplored lands are wild. Under conditions of imagined or actual frustration, privation, insult, or adversity, almost any of us can create a fantasy in which we "lose control of the self," in which we act without benefit of reason. It is as if the imaginer peels off the thin veneer of repressive civilization.

The lingering myth is supported in part by the Wild Beast theory of insanity drawn from early English law (Platt & Diamond, 1966), and in part by the entrenched position of Freudian doctrine in psychiatry. To the diagnostician it provides a silent ideological premise to support the belief that the "mentally ill" person has failed to become fully socialized or civilized, and may not be able to contain the "wild beast within," and is, therefore, potentially dangerous. A further conclusion is implied: Dangerous persons should be removed from society.

THE UNIQUE AUTHORITY OF THE PHYSICIAN

A fourth ideological premise has to do with the role of the physician in civil commitment. In the light of contemporary knowledge about the difficulty of predicting conduct, a reasonable question may be asked: Why are physicians (rather than other professionals) identified by statute or by custom as having the appropriate expertise to participate in commitment proceedings? To be sure, the assimilation of so-called mental illness to somatic illness, discussed in detail in Chapter 3, would be a partial answer to the question. However, the repeatedly demonstrated fact that psychiatric diagnoses lack reliability and credibility ought to have influenced the courts and legislatures to review their reliance on psychiatric testimony.

The reader is asked to recall the rhetorical device of the imaginary courtroom and its three leading figures: the untitled quasi defendant in the shadows, the judge and the physician under lights. The focus is now on the judge, who must make a decision based on a fallible prediction that the quasi defendant may in the future engage in harm-doing if not restrained. A judge who incarcerates a quasi defendant who would not have engaged in harm-doing (false positive) or who dismisses one who would then injure or harm others (false negative), is liable to criticism and even to public sanctions. Judges need assurances that their predictions contain as few errors as possible, especially false negatives.

Our spotlight now shifts to the physician whose authority to provide expert testimony has until recently gone unchallenged. Physicians, unlike other professionals, possess a unique kind of authority. Paterson (1966) noted that conventional categories of authority (or power) failed to describe the special features of the authority of the physician. He had previously identified five types of authority: expert, moral, charismatic, personal, and structural. The medical doctor, unique among professions, exhibits a combination of expert, moral, and charismatic authority. Paterson adopted the label "Aesculapian" (after the Greek god of healing) for this combination.

Siegler and Osmund (1973) elaborated this conception. The medical doctor's unique authority resides first in the claim to being taken seriously in virtue of knowledge or expertise. Physicians possess expert power because they are assumed to have knowledge of anatomy, physiology, chemistry, pharmacology, etc. The second aspect of Aesculapian authority is moral authority. It is based on the belief shared by both doctor and patient that the doctor intends to do good, to alleviate pain, to prolong life, to defeat death. The third element is charismatic authority: this kind of authority entitles the doctor to order and control others reminiscent of the times when priestly and healing functions were undifferentiated. The physician is perceived to have a god-given grace and to function in a quasi-priestly role.

Charisma is the quality of certain individuals that sets them apart from others. They are treated as if endowed with exceptional powers. The quality is lost if the individual is recognized as *not* having special features or powers. In short, charismatic authority depends upon doctors conducting themselves in ways that are consistent with the attributions that others assign to them. They make use of their Greco-Latin vocabulary, their technical skills, and their rituals to confirm this charisma. Siegler and Osmund regard the Aesculapian authority as necessary in order to confer the sick role. They go on to say that without Aesculapian authority, "one cannot function as a doctor, and indeed cannot even be a successful medical imposter [p. 51]." The similarity of this description to that of shamans is striking (Lévi-Strauss, 1963). It also calls to mind the caveat of Judge Bazelon (1974) in a paper entitled the "Perils of Wizardry." He warned psychiatrists against the unrestrained use of power especially in the area of diagnosis. If physicians go beyond their level of expertise, they may be perceived as wizards rather than doctors.

Nearly everyone comes into contact with this unique form of authority early in life. The judge, no less than other mortals, is socialized into the belief that the physician has special powers. To reduce their own uncertainty, judges call upon physicians to apply their skills to diagnose the suspected "mentally ill." In a sense, the court authorizes the doctor to do the work of a jury, that is, to arrive at a verdict that denies liberty to a man or woman suspected of future law violations.

The employment of physicians as expert witnesses has a long history. Pertinent to our concern with the power of physicians in influencing court decisions is the celebrated case of the Lowestoft witches in 1664. In principle, the work of the expert physician as witness in our time is no different from that of 1664.

Two women, Amy Duny and Rose Cullender, were accused of witchcraft. Some young girls had "fits" that were attributed to the witchery of these two women. The accused denied the charges.

SirThomas Browne (an esteemed physician)was consulted as to whether the children's fits could be caused by witchcraft, and replied that though in his opinion the fits were probably due to hysteria, they could be "heightened to a great excess by the subtility of the Devil,co-operating with the Malice of these which we term Witches, at whose Instance he doth these Villanies." The views of so learned a man naturally carried great weight, but there were some dissentient voices.Mr. Sergeant Keeling was not satisfied with the evidence and declared roundly that if such testimony were accepted no one would be safe. He thought it more than likely that the children were acting a part and . . . he arranged a practical test. A bewitched person was usually supposed to react violently to the touch . . . of the witch. . . . One child was therefore taken to a room where Amy Duny was and blindfolded. She knew that the witch was there but she could not see either her movements or those of any other person. A bystander then touched her and she, assuming it was Duny, immediately fell into a fit. For Sergeant Keeling and those with him this was sufficient; . . . "But," says the author of *A Tryal of Witches*, "Mr. Pacy's arguments and those of the learned [sic] Dr. Browne . . . prevailed." The jury returned a verdict of guilty, and in due course the two women were hanged [Hole, 1945, pp. 142-143].

While Aesculapian authority may have utility in the doctor-patient relationship, the use of such authority in civil commitment proceedings is to be deplored. The decision to deprive a quasi defendant of liberty requires attention to cold, hard facts, not to the effects of the magico-religious features of the healer.

THE CONCEPT OF THE ABSTRACT INDIVIDUAL

In a brilliant essay on individualism, Lukes (1973) has analyzed the concept into five subordinate notions: the dignity of man, autonomy, privacy, self-development, and the abstract individual. The last-named notion is of special interest as an ideological premise that helps support the schizophrenia model.

The premise operates as part of the epistemic framework for diagnosticians who place the locus of causality of unwanted conduct within the individual and for magistrates who are empowered to pass judgment on such individuals. The boundaries of interest are the boundaries of the individual. Such boundaries are borrowed from traditional somatic medicine that addresses organs and organ systems located inside the skin. The "individual" is conceptually partitioned from the milieu and from the social systems of which he or she is a member.

Individuals are regarded as abstract entities, and social organizations (such as family, clan, nation) are perceived as "arrangements" aimed at satisfying the needs of such individuals. Lukes (1973) points out the most significant aspects of this conception:

> . . . the relevant features of individuals determining the ends which social arrangements are held (actually or ideally) to fulfill, whether these features are called instincts, faculties, needs, desires, rights, etc., are assumed as given, independently of a social context. This *givenness* of fixed and invariant human psychological features leads to an *abstract* conception of the individual who is seen as merely the bearer of these features which determine his behavior, and specify his interests, needs, and rights [p. 73].

The ideas that together comprise the concept of individualism—including the machismo subconcept—*rugged individualism*—silently lend support to the notion of trait as the unit of the abstract individual. The search for traits, both by the psychiatrist in the mental status examination and by the psychologist in the psychometric laboratory, is guided by an unexamined belief in the axiomatic nature of the abstract individual. In a subsequent chapter we shall point out that trait theory conceals the operation of a metaphysic of "forms" underlying the performance of the individual. In quoting Marx, Lukes raises for the reader the necessity of considering a different premise from that of the abstract individual. We repeat Lukes's quotation from Marx:

> The further we go back into history, the individual, and therefore, the producing individual seems to depend on and constitute a part of a larger whole: at first it is, quite naturally, the family and the clan . . . ; later on, it is the community growing up in its different forms out of the clash and the amalgamation of clans. It is but in the eighteenth century, in "bourgeois society," that the different forms of social union confront the individual as a mere means to his private ends, as an outward necessity. But the period in which this view of the isolated individual becomes prevalent, is the very one in which the interrelations of society (general from this point of view) have reached the highest state of development. Man is in the most literal sense of the word a *zoon politikon*, not only a social animal, but an animal which can develop into an individual only in society. Production by isolated individuals outside of society—something which might happen as an exception to a civilized man who by accident got into the wilderness and already dynamically possessed within himself the forces of society—is as great an absurdity as the idea of the development of language without individuals living together and talking to one another [Marx, quoted by Lukes, 1973, p. 76].

THE CONCEPT OF MIND

Related to the metaphysical ascent of individualism is the dualistic philosophy usually attributed to Descartes. "Mind" is given an ontological status parallel to that given the body. When physicians conduct a "mental status examination," they operate on the implicit assumption that they are examining a "mind" but employing different skills and technology from the ones they would employ were they examining a "body."

The actions of legislators and jurists, not to mention the ordinary citizen, are influenced by this entrenched philosophical tradition. Needless to say, the vocabulary of mentalism permeates our language. Statutes and court opinions that contain terms such as "mental disease or defect," "mental illness," "of sound mind," "*mens rea,*" and so on, illustrate the operation of the venerable premise that minds exist, and, like bodies, can be sick or healthy, and further, can be the responsible instrumentality of action.

Gilbert Ryle's influential book *The Concept of Mind* (1948) demonstrates with some force the "category mistake" that led to "mind," a term used to denote such actions as thinking, imagining, and feeling, being transformed into a substantive. Arguments can be sustained to demonstrate that "mind," at one time a useful metaphor, was reified, that is, given literal status (Sarbin, 1964, 1967a, 1968b).

The concept of mind is contained within Bleuler's coinage of "schizophrenia" (split mind). The combining form *phrenia* is found in other psychiatric concepts, such as hebephrenia, phrenology, phrenitis, frenzied, and frenetic. Jaynes (1976) has pointed out that one of the antecedent concepts for mind was the Homeric *phrenes*, located in the region of the diaphragm. Although the brain has displaced the diaphragm as the seat of mental activity, one of the Greek forms for mind has been retained.

The tenacity of the belief in mind can be in part understood when we recognize its historical relation to the theological concept of soul. From the middle ages and well into the age of Enlightenment, the soul was an incontrovertible fact of existence. With the rise of science and the decline of ecclesiastical authority, the concept of soul was replaced by a term with fewer theological implications. The dualism "body and soul" was displaced by "body and mind." The superempirical nature of both soul and mind has allowed the transmittal of the older, religious connotations of soul to the concept of mind.

The reluctance to drop the concept of mind from jurisprudence has been in part responsible for the continuing confusion in dealing with issues of responsibility and accountability. Without the concept of mind, no case could be made for calling upon specialists (usually forensic psychiatrists) to establish the condition of a defendant's mind—presumably a necessary datum for establishing accountability.

THE PARENS PATRIAE CONCEPT

Seldom questioned is the premise that the court (or its surrogates) is in a position to declare what is "good" for the quasi defendant. The modern concept is descended from ancient common law that granted monarchs the wisdom to determine what was good for their subjects. That the interests of the quasi defendant may coincide with the interests of the public is an interesting hypothesis. The courts and legislatures tend to treat the hypothesis as if it were a well-documented, demonstrated principle. *Parens patriae* can be employed to legitimate the actions of petty bureaucrats, probation and parole officers, child-saving professionals, as well as the actions of legislators and jurists in creating a therapeutic state (see Kittrie, 1971).

Many of the men and women who serve as subjects in studies of schizophrenia have been committed through the use of the *parens patriae* power of the court. The power relations between the quasi defendant and the judge (and the medical advisors) correspond in many ways to the power relations between subject and monarch. We need only mention again the fact that the candidate for the ascription "schizophrenia" is most often poor and powerless. The judge, of course, has legitimate power in virtue of elective or appointive status, a status indirectly connected with educational, economic, political, and other indicators of power.

We must also be alert to the possibility that the diagnosis of schizophrenia and subsequent involuntary hospitalization is often justified by an appeal to *parens patriae*, when, in fact, the underlying reason is assumed "dangerousness" from the "wild man within."

THE "GENTEEL TRADITION"

On the surface more a style of life than an ideological premise, the "genteel tradition" influences the cognitive work of magistrates and physicians, as well as the representatives of the mental health establishment. We have borrowed the term from the philosopher George Santayana (1967), who was concerned with the direction of intellectual life in the early twentieth century. The operation of the "genteel tradition" constrains opportunities for entertaining unconventional hypotheses. For example, the life styles of legislators, magistrates, and physicians, governed by social-class norms, would hardly lead to the hypothesis that deviant conduct could arise as the result of political and economic factors. Like the stereotype of the philosopher, the genteel tradition addresses abstractions such as beauty, mind, dispositions, the good, rather than the not so genteel actions of ordinary men and women striving to make sense out of a changing, probabilistic, and imperfect world. A conventional researcher, a magistrate, or other public official brought up in such an intellectual tradition would hardly entertain causal hypotheses openly derived from economic or political doctrines. Such hypotheses would direct attention, for example, to the possible effects of poverty on unrestrained religiosity. The genteel tradition would instead focus on the disordered mind that produced bizarre religious conduct. Genteel psychologists then study the relationships between delusions and oral deprivation, rather than the relationship between poverty and charismatic religious experience.

THE POSITIVE VALUE OF RESEARCH

Young behavior scientists, by their commitment to the intellectual tradition of their profession, show that they place a positive value on research. This evaluation is endorsed and shared by powerful networks that surround them. Additionally, as a behavior scientist, one can express one's altruistic orientations through studying schizophrenia. Any contribution one might make would relieve the burden of thousands of individuals, their families, and the supporting society. As one enters the profession, one rarely meets someone who would invalidate this positive view.

Aside from the value commitment to investigate schizophrenia, a young, aspiring, academically based scholar must establish a career by publishing reports of investigations. Tenure and advancement in rank are assured by the ability to attract research grants and to establish credentials as an expert.

The scholar who is a clinical psychologist will want to find opportunities to make applications of the behavior science concepts he or she generates and elaborates. This practice, too, will enhance the scholar's status at the university. By maintaining an association with local mental health agencies, the scholar can help students gain entry to that world, where they will have access to persons whose behavior is framed in the metaphors of illness. More importantly, the scholar will have access to the subjects who will supply data for his or her research.

It is undeniable that there is an interlock between the valuing of publishing research results, access to subjects, and access to money to finance the research. Research foundations, government agencies, and private industries allocate large amounts of money for research into schizophrenia. Scholars who apply for some of this money find it easier to win grants if they use the language of the mental health world. If they propose to search out basic causal and symptomatic aspects of schizophrenia, their language should coincide with the language used by members of the review panels and boards that channel the flow of money.

Thus, if aspiring investigators express a strong preference for the use of nonmedical conceptualizations, they will find themselves outside the mainstream. They cannot expect a warm welcome from the practitioners, most of whom are physicians, who currently administer the mental health agencies. They stand to lose access to the population whose behavior they hope to explain. Students will avoid associating with persons not closely linked to the organized system that promises employment. And, most importantly, without all of these accessories, grants, accessibility to subjects, publication outlets, etc., the scholars find it difficult to maintain high positive status at their universities.

Of course, the young scholar's students suffer the effects of these constraints. If one hopes to avoid an "antipsychiatry" reputation, one must not profess an alternative nonmechanistic, nondisease model of unwanted behavior. To avoid public espousal of alternative views, one may choose to teach from any one of the standard, widely circulated abnormal psychology textbooks, in which the disease model takes center stage while alternative models are given a bland, by-the-way coverage.

The final effects of these ever-present and powerful constraints, which are almost an unobtrusive ground to the whole academic psychology enterprise, are apparent. The young academic is subject to pressures to add to the literature which gives the appearance that schizophrenia, rather than unwanted conduct, is the subject of study.

In this connection, we note the infrequency of reports of negative findings, that is, findings that reveal no differences between schizophrenics and normal subjects. In doctoral dissertations, the usual explanation given for negative findings is framed in terms of the crudeness of the measuring devices, not in terms of the inadequacy of the underlying schizophrenia model. Even if the experimenter were to submit a report which showed no differences between diagnosed schizophrenics and undiagnosed persons, there is low probability that reviewers would recommend publication. We cannot lose sight of the fact that editors and reviewers are also influenced by the extrinsic supports for the schizophrenia model.

Finally, at the clinics, hospitals, and guidance centers where young professionals consult and do research, they pass the illness model on to the clients or patients. They satisfy students who expect to learn about mental illness so that they may enter the mental health world. And, most importantly, in their teaching, practice, and research work, they participate in promoting the ideology that it is good to investigate the causes of "mental illness."

REPRISE

Earlier, we referred to ideologies as having sacred properties. One would predict that an attack on an entrenched ideological premise would generate passionate response.

For example, in an article reprinted in the *San Francisco Examiner and Chronicle*, October 20, 1974 (Torrey, 1974a), E. Fuller Torrey, M.D., author of *The Death of Psychiatry* (Torrey, 1974b), proposed that psychiatrists were no more effective than nonmedical therapists in dealing with patients or clients who sought help in solving "problems in living." He proposed, without supporting data, that schizophrenia and manic-depressive disorders were neurological and ought to be treated by neurologists and internists. He was especially critical of the economics of psychiatry, arguing that psychiatrists were making too much money. He predicted the death of psychiatry; patients with "problems of living" would consult educators, psychologists, counselors, etc., patients with somatic disorders would consult internists, neurologists, etc.

Torrey's challenge stimulated two practicing psychiatrists, D.W. Allen and E.F. Alston (1974) to reply. The response is only in part dialectical, but mostly passionate. For example, the critics first employed an *ad hominem* argument: They found fault with Torrey's training and experience. He "completed his residency training . . . less than five years ago, and directly after his training became an administrative psychiatrist in the National Institute of Mental Health. His experience in treating patients has been negligible [p. 40]." The critics use the rhetorical device of comparing Torrey's distinction between problems of living and somatic illness with "reviving the idea that the earth is flat [p. 40]," and that the mind-body split is an outmoded concept. Their assimilation of problems in living to "mind" is gratuitous. The concluding remark of Torrey's critics has additional rhetorical clout. It assumes an ontological status for "mental illness," and invokes a concept, "real," that has no firm metaphysical base. They wrote: "anguish and suffering are as real to those with mental illness as they are to those whose ills are of the body. And there is no clear line between the two [p. 40]." These two sentences contain the distillation of unrecognized ideological premises—most of which have been discussed above.

In Chapter 7 we shall discuss the internal supports for the maintenance of the schizophrenia model. Besides the conservatism of paradigms, we suggest that the highly visible programs in biochemical and genetic research confer a specious form of credibility on the schizophrenia model. The credibility is conferred by the well-advertised fact that vast sums of money are spent on research and that tentative findings are occasionally reported (and not confirmed). The credibility does not follow from the reports of rigorous testing of carefully phrased biological hypotheses.

In the present chapter, we have identified a number of ideological premises that provide external support for the continued use of the schizophrenia model. These premises have historical roots in jurisprudence, social structure, political action, metaphysical foundations, conceptions of authority, and linguistic constraints. The operation of ideological premises contrary to those described here could hardly generate and sustain the schizophrenia model.

7
Internal Support for the Disease Model of Schizophrenia: Biological Research

We have tried to illuminate a large section of the scientific enterprise devoted to norm-violating behavior which—under some conditions—is signified by the label schizophrenia. The initial arguments have been directed toward justifying the following five conclusions:

1. The disease model as applied to those variable events known as "symptoms of schizophrenia" has emerged from the mechanistic paradigm, the paradigm that has served modern science. The disease model has become paradigmatic, tacit, conventional, taken for granted. As a result, investigators and theorists uncritically accept ontological assumptions embedded in the use of "schizophrenics" as research subjects. Thus, the majority of reported investigations proceed from the fallible verdicts of mental health professionals, and uncritically test hypotheses as if they contained a concrete, behaviorally defined independent variable—schizophrenia-nonschizophrenia.

2. The application of the mechanistic disease model has produced innumerable puzzles whose solutions require the fabrication of more and more esoteric variables. As variables proliferate, the specifications of theoretical linkages diminish. Research reports fail to meet the scientists' obligation to produce convincing statements of the interconnections of variables. Few studies consider the theoretical and mensural foundations of their dependent variables. Further, it is the rare investigator who writes about the relationship of his or her particular favored variable to public conduct ("hallucinations," "delusions," "mutism," "agitation," "wife beating," etc.) that led to a person's being hospitalized and ultimately to serving as a research subject. The variables employed to keep the sinking disease model afloat have not been convincing in explaining the occurrence, maintenance, or elimination of unwanted behavior.

3. Most of the findings disclosed in our review have been confounded by hidden variables. Among the hidden variables are those which, in themselves, lack the clarity that would allow their proper articulation to an extended behavior theory. So long as disease theorists cannot define and partial out behavioral variables connected with *socioeconomic status, intelligence, patienthood,* and *cooperativeness* there can be little progress in defining the status of presumably salient variables such as *conceptual skill, chronicity, responsiveness to social reinforcement,* or *sensitivity to censure.*

4. The majority of research papers fail to report the extensive overlap of distributions of scores attained by the schizophrenic sample and the normal control sample on dependent variables. Readers are rarely informed that *most* schizophrenics are like *most* normals on the experimental measures and that the differences in group mean scores are often attributable to a small number of subjects in the experimental (or control) groups.

5. Analysis of the literature reveals a strong trend toward replacing the metaphysical assumptions of a machine paradigm with the metaphysical assumptions of an idiographic paradigm. The explanatory principles embedded in current schizophrenia research frequently explain the behavior of those who "suffer from the disease" in terms of an ideal form marked by the term *schizophrenia.* Investigators unwittingly demonstrate loyalty to the idiographic paradigm when they organize their observations on the premise that all varieties of unwanted "bad" behavior will identify those "bad" persons who harbor the "bad" form, that is, the form of schizophrenia. Almost every study in our review, when analyzed within the perspective of our fifth conclusion, ignores relevant antecedent-consequent connections. That is, they fail to consider the process aspects of behavioral development, thus violating the causality requirements of the mechanistic disease model. The retrogression to the metaphysical position of idiography—the metaphysical position that led to ancient demonic explanations of deviance—brings into sharp focus the failure of the disease model.

Additionally, in Chapter 6, we identified external influences on maintaining the schizophrenia model. Ideological premises, bureaucratic power, and cultural thought models help keep alive the schizophrenia model.

THE TENACITY OF THE DISEASE MODEL

For over eight decades, the disease model has served as the official guide to the study of norm-violating behaviors. The evidence is overwhelming that the disease model has been particularly unfit as a guide for explaining behaviors subsumed under definitions of schizophrenia. The evidence notwithstanding, polemical and research-based efforts to vindicate the schizophrenia model appear with regularity. How do scientists justify their tenacious allegiance to the model?

To be sure, all paradigms, ideologies, and myths tend to be conservative.

Changes are more likely to occur in conjunction with a "death-rebirth" experience. Change rarely follows the gradual accrual of facts that question the utility or truth of the belief system.

> . . . The transfer of allegiance from paradigm to paradigm is a conversion experience that cannot be forced. Lifelong resistance . . . is not a violation of scientific standards but an index to the nature of scientific research itself. The source of resistance is the assurance that the older paradigm will ultimately solve all its problems . . . But it is also something more. That same assurance is what makes normal or puzzle-solving science possible. And it is only through normal science that the professional community of scientists succeeds, first, in exploiting the potential scope and precision of the older paradigm, and, then, in isolating the difficulty through the study of which a new paradigm may emerge [Kuhn, 1970, pp. 151-152].

Reasonable investigators need not abandon a paradigm following signs of its initial inadequacies. A useful paradigm, after all, presents its user with puzzles as well as the structures within which such puzzles may be solved. Even when an attempted solution is unsuccessful, a scientist may retain the paradigm, hoping that future investigations will yield the elusive solution.

The mechanistically derived disease paradigm—it may be concluded—fails to illuminate the conditions of unwanted conduct because of its inability to fill its self-imposed task of making efficient causality statements. In the biological sciences, where the disease model has been eminently successful, investigators have demonstrated their success through specifying the antecedent events as independent variables which "cause" the resulting symptoms—the dependent variables in efficient causal statements. But such efficient causal statements cannot be made for schizophrenia. In reviewing the course of the scientific enterprise devoted to understanding schizophrenia, it becomes clear that the proponents of the disease model are aware of its failure, but they continue to hold to the paradigm on the belief that the appropriate independent variable is yet to be discovered and defined. To such proponents, the *cause* of schizophrenia will emerge, in some more enlightened day, from the continuing efforts of puzzle solvers.

The behavior scientist's commitment to the promise of the mechanistic disease paradigm is easily discerned in the writing of Blatt and Wild (1976) as they attempted to integrate a vast segment of the psychological literature devoted to the topic of schizophrenia. Their hope to establish basic causal variables is best expressed in their summary.

> In summary, we have attempted to conceptualize schizophrenia as a developmental impairment in the capacity to experience, perceive, and represent boundaries. While this impairment varies in degree and intensity, both within and between patients, many of the disruptions in cognitive processes and interpersonal relationships in schizophrenia can be considered as manifestations of developmental impairment in the fundamental establishment of boundaries. In some patients, this impairment may be apparent only under conditions of stress, but our review of the research and clinical literature suggests that it is one of the fundamental issues in schizophrenia [p. 246].

Having proposed an impaired function as cause, the scientist then must show that the schizophrenic's dysfunctional behavior originates in an incapacity to work with boundaries. It is necessary, also, to understand what is meant by such impairment.

> By boundary differentiation we mean the capacity to maintain a separation between independent objects and between representations of independent objects . . . We also mean the maintenance of separation between an object and its representation, as well as between self and nonself and between internal experience and external objects and events [p. 6].

To discover the basis of these impairments, one could take the developmental approach. "The developmental approach to schizophrenia—and to other types of psychopathology—may foster a view of psychotic disturbances that will help to integrate the disruptions in functioning with an understanding of their etiology [p. 237]."

The causal chain can be traced through these passages. Disruptions in cognitive processes and interpersonal relationships can be considered "manifestations" of impairment in the fundamental establishment of boundaries. This impairment, in turn, might be found to have its roots in the person's development. But, "developmental impairments do not have to be considered only in psychological terms [p. 237]." One must ". . . allow for the possibility that significant genetic and biological factors interact with environmental influences [p. 237]. As psychologists, Blatt and Wild emphasize the psychological variables, but they would not ignore the causal aspects of genetic and biological factors.

When, after all, scholars think of some kinds of conduct as a disease, it would be practically impossible to avoid the conceptual pull of biological conceptualizations. Meehl's (1962) statement represents one of the clearest affirmations of the utility of mechanistic, biologically defined, causal formulations relative to schizophrenia. He suggests a target for investigators who search within the malfunctioning machine for the elusive physical foundation of the "schizotypic tetrad," that is, cognitive slippage, anhedonia, ambivalence, and interpersonal aversiveness.

> What kind of heritable parametric aberration could underlie the schizotaxic's readiness to acquire the schizotypic tetrad? It would seem, first of all, that the defect is much more likely to reside in the neuron's synaptic control function than in its storage function [p. 832].
> . . . What we are looking for is a quantitative aberration in synaptic control—a deviation in amount or patterning of excitatory or inhibitory action—capable of yielding cumulative departures from normal control linkages under mixed appetive—aversive regimes; but slight enough to permit convergence to quasi-normal asymptotes under more consistent schedules (or when massive repetition with motive-incentive factors unimportant is the chief basis for consolidation). The defect must generate aversive drift on mixed social reinforcement regimes, and must yield a primary cognitive slippage [p. 836].

Those who work with genetic concepts as they relate to schizophrenia similarly reveal their adherence to the mechanistic paradigm, which asks that investigators express their principles in terms of efficient cause and observable effect. Shields (1976), who has reported some of the most frequently cited studies of the relationships between genetic variables and schizophrenia, offers the following at the close of one of his recent papers:

> What is required, if we are to identify genetic factors which contribute to the predisposition to schizophrenia, is a constitutional trait which will show up in an individual whether he is sick or well and is not just a consequence of his being a schizophrenic. Cazzullo, Smeraldi and Penato (1974) hope that the leucocyte antigenic system HL-A may provide a genetic marker for schizophrenia [p. 65].

And in the closely related biochemical tradition, the mechanistic causal formulations are also reflected in Richter (1976):

> In seeking information as to the biochemical factors that may be concerned, we ask how do the symptoms of schizophrenia arise? What are the underlying neurological systems and what transmitter mechanisms are involved? . . . It would appear that the disturbance does not extend to all areas of the brain, but that specific mechanisms are specially involved [pp. 71-72].
>
> One possible line of investigation is to look for abnormal metabolites that cause the symptoms of schizophrenia [p. 72].

Without question, then, the disease paradigm in behavioral science offers the hope that the model will ultimately provide the signs that will direct investigators to the solution of the last, most important puzzle—the histological and/or physiological causes of the unwanted conduct that leads to the diagnosis of schizophrenia. The paradigm cannot be abandoned when it is believed that the search yet holds promise, particularly for a biological solution.

SUPPORT FOR THE SCHIZOPHRENIA MODEL FROM DIRECT BIOLOGICAL INVESTIGATION

The mass media together with professional journals are constantly reminding us of the massive efforts to find the biological "cause" of the putative disease schizophrenia. From such an effort, the public expects to hear the recurrent reports that such biological agents have been isolated. In fact, such reports regularly appear, often coupled with the implied promise that the corrective to the biological dysfunction will follow forthwith. Such reports also give hope to the families of hundreds of thousands of persons who have been declared "schizophrenic."

Such hope cannot be and should not be dissolved by the declaration that the search for biological causes is futile. No one can yet affirm the claim that future scientific efforts will fail to reveal a recognizable biological anomaly which, for example, would cause a woman to report a malodorous vapor arising from her body (not confirmed by persons with normal olfaction), or a man to proclaim that he is Jesus Christ. No one can yet affirm the ancillary claim, further, that anomalous biological conditions that supposedly "cause" undesirable behaviors will be shown not to have a specific genetic basis.

Biological Concommitants of Schizophrenia

The foregoing review of 374 investigations of schizophrenia contains little that refers directly to studies of biological factors associated with the diagnosis of schizophrenia. Having chosen to focus on the reports in a prestigious journal that concentrates upon psychological interests, we have not discussed the direct approaches to biological substrates of the putative disease. A critic might assert that our choice of research literature might bias our analysis against the utility of the disease model. Our encounters with representative biological studies of schizophrenia confirm the conclusions drawn from the review of the psychological literature.

The Schizophrenia/Genetic Transmission Hypothesis

The hypothesis of a distinct biological entity in schizophrenia easily leads to a parallel hypothesis that hereditary factors account for the development of such behaviors. (For summary reviews, see Gottesman & Shields, 1972; Rosenthal & Kety, 1968; Rosenthal, 1970). This latter hypothesis has provided the framework for a number of significant investigations, the enthusiastic and uncritical journalistic reports of which lend further internal support for the schizophrenia model. What is more, highly placed professionals assert that, "if schizophrenia is a myth, it is a myth with a strong genetic component [Kety, 1974, p. 961]," or that "The results of many . . . studies, using increasingly elegant methods, continue to confirm the hypothesis that genetic factors play an important, if still imperfectly understood, part in the etiology of schizophrenia [Shields, 1976, p. 66]." In this way, support is given to those who search out the morphological or histological pathologies that underlie unwanted conduct.

Cromwell (1978), in commenting on a series of papers on genetic factors in schizophrenia (Wynne, Cromwell, & Matthysse, 1978), reflects a point of view that closes out the possibility of any serious challenge to the genetic model of schizophrenia. He says, "This Conference just might be the last one where questions are seriously asked whether genetically transmitted factors play a role in schizophrenia [p. 76]." In another place, he comments, "If this proposition [the genetic model of schizophrenia] were not already true at the time of this Conference, it should certainly be true in the future [p. 81-82]." Such confidence is remarkable given the recognized unsatisfactory state of the diagnostic art as well as the failure to provide a model that would fit the requirements of scientific genetics. In this connection, Gottesman (1978) after reviewing the current status of research reminds us: "Since no corpus delicti has yet been identified that can be equated with a genotype for schizophrenia, the premorbid schizophrenic is currently not identifiable. Hence, ambiguity haunts the attempts to fit specific models of genetic transmission [p. 68]."

To evaluate the concept of genetic transmission in relation to unusual behavior, it is necessary first to establish some basic concepts. It is useful to consider some classic studies that have related genetically determined biology and behavior.

A paradigm case. To discuss the schizophrenia/genetic transmission hypothesis, we draw a paradigm case, not from schizophrenia studies, but from studies of phenylketonuria (PKU), a disorder of metabolism. In PKU, the amino acid, phenylalanine, is not metabolized; instead, it is excreted in the urine in its unmetabolized form. Children in whom this condition is diagnosed often show retarded development of expected basic skills. It has been quite convincingly shown that this anomaly in metabolism can be accounted for by a genetic hypothesis. Thus, PKU provides an excellent three-step model of a relationship between genetically transmitted body structure and the development of unwanted behavior: (1) A distinct physically identifiable anomaly has been located; (2) the presence of this anomaly is clearly related to neurological dysfunction; and (3) the neurological dysfunction can readily be connected with learning difficulties.

Two other points fit into the overall conceptualization. First, when a child can be diagnosed as phenylketonuric, *all* the child's behavior is affected. A PKU victim shows developmental retardation when dealing with number-defining concepts, space-defining concepts, or person-defining concepts. Secondly, if the child is treated, for example, by a diet regulation that eliminates systemic phenylketones, the psychological development is not retarded. A correction of the physical aberration forestalls the nonnormal psychological development.

To preface our analysis of investigations of the schizophrenia/genetic transmission hypothesis, we profitably note a discussion of PKU written by Rosenthal (1970). Rosenthal and his collaborators have extensively reported on and discussed the heritability of schizophrenia, so that his views are valuable to our discussion. Rosenthal says, among other things, the following about PKU:

> This disease has been traced to a single recessive autosomal gene. Its most striking characteristic is moderate to severe mental deficiency, but not all affected children are quite so abnormal, and some may even pass for normal [p. 70].
>
> What is inherited is a disorder in the metabolism of phenylalanine, one of the basic amino acids involved in the building of body proteins. It is important to note that it is this defect that is inherited, not the disease. . . . Since tests are available to identify PKU in infants, when such children are found they are fed diets low in phenylalanine. With such treatment . . . the intellectual impairment is decreased and may be prevented [pp. 72-73].

In his commentary, Rosenthal highlights some essential considerations that must be incorporated into a discussion of genetics and behavior. First, one begins with the explicit postulate that "behavior" and "actions" are not inherited. Instead, "inheritance" applies to physical (somatic) structures. One could even take issue with Rosenthal's statement that the "disorder of metabolism" is inherited. More precisely, genetic determination and ordering of the somatic structure govern the physiology of phenylalanine metabolism.

Rosenthal's commentary highlights another consideration. Even where the inherited structure and its related physiological function are quantifiably present, one may not assume that the unwanted behavior will appear. The environment must react with the structure in specifiable ways in order to generate the unusual behavior. If phenylketones are withheld from the diet, one does not find the behaviors that occur as a result of the debilitating neurological effects following upon the accumulations of phenylalanine. Thus, it would be illogical (1) to stress strongly, as does Rosenthal, the point that a disorder of metabolism is inherited; (2) to say, at another point, that a "most striking characteristic" of the disease is "moderate to severe mental deficiency;" (3) to say, also that "this disease has been traced to a single, recessive autosomal gene." There are arguments against this program: first, if the most striking characteristic of the disease is the mental deficiency (the unwanted behavior), then the *disease* does not "exist" until this characteristic appears. In that case, the condition resulting from the gene action *can* exist, without the appearance of the mental deficiency. By presenting the person with a phenylketone-free diet, the neurological disruption that prevents the person from learning age-appropriate behaviors will not occur. Secondly, if the most striking characteristic of the disease is mental deficiency, then there can be no disease until someone determines a deficiency in the person's "mental functions," which are assumed to underlie the failure to learn age-appropriate conduct. In particular cultures, at particular points in history, and under particular economic conditions, the person would not necessarily be judged to be deficient. A place would be found for that person within the social group, and there would be no thought of the person's being stigmatized as deficient.

In short, a mechanistic disease model is appropriate for discussing the process whereby an anomalous genetic factor *causes* an anomalous morphology, which in turn *causes* the accumulation of phenylalanines. The mechanistic paradigm becomes somewhat nonfunctional, however, when so many of the variables take on meaning only in one or another social context. It requires another paradigm to include in the discussion the cognitive processes of the behavior analyst who pronounces *deficiency*, along with the social organization that shaped the analyst's cognitive processes, and supports the analyst's role-enactment. To formulate statements that will be useful in the foregoing situations, many psychologists are turning away from mechanistic to contextualist paradigms.

Selective exposure and differential susceptibility as contextualist principles. A contextualist formulation includes genetic action, particular morphologies associated with those actions, the environmental interaction with those morphologies, conduct that evolves to maintain reasonable equilibrium between the morphology and the environment, social judgments of the value of the conduct, and personal reenactment of the conduct; all embedded in a multistranded context. Each of these strands has meaning only in relationship to all the other strands. None of the strands can be seen as *causing* any other strand. From a contextualist position one might, for heuristic purposes, speak of the cause of *shifting relationships* between strands in the context. But, as Pepper (1942) aptly observes, change is a given in a contextualist position. Contexts continually flow. A contextualist tries to describe emerging contexts, not single features of the context.

Two principles, presented by Wiggins, Renner, Clore, and Rose (1971, p. 52), exemplify contextualist statements regarding genetic actions. First, one may speak of relationships of behavior and a particular inherited morphology in terms of *differential susceptibility*. In a particular context, one or another aspect of genetically developed morphology will function so that the person will be more or less susceptible to events that occur in the standard environment. For example, in an environment in which it is standard to include phenylketones in food, the person who cannot metabolize these proteins will be more susceptible to failure to develop age-appropriate behaviors.

Second, morphologies may interact with the standard environments so that persons who are characterized by one or another morphology are *selectively exposed* to features of the standard environment. Boys, for example, since they inherit morphology that identifies their "maleness," are traditionally exposed, more than girls, to vigorous physical interactions with the social environment. Such selective exposure allows boys to develop self-definitions in which more vigorous physical activity is construed as socially approved and positive.

Taking a totally contextualist perspective encourages one to avoid saying that a genetically evolved condition, for example, inability to metabolize phenylalanines, *causes* retardation of intellectual development. Similarly, an inherited morphology, externally placed genitalia, does not *cause* more vigorous physical activity. The specific behaviors are discussed only within the total context. Biological parameters relate to the environmental parameters through linkages that affect selective exposure and differential susceptibility. A biological parameter has no ontological status outside the context in which it appears. A different context would give a totally different meaning to any strand in the context.

Biology, genetics, and leadership roles. A long series of studies (see, for example, Ames, 1957; Jones, 1957, 1958; Jones & Bayley, 1950; More, 1953) shows that the development of leadership roles is very strongly associated with the age at which boys develop into adolescent maturity. "Physiological" maturity can be quantified by a variety of measures, such as skeletal maturation, the appearance of secondary sexual characteristics, and the adolescent acceleration in the height curve. Rate of maturity is associated with genetic (Hewitt, 1957) and nutritional factors. A person's leadership status is closely related to the age at which these changes begin and to the pace at which the changes occur. Early-maturing, far more than late-maturing boys, are likely to be accorded more popularity, prestige, or leadership roles by their peers. Early maturers are perceived, by both peers and adults, as behaving like adult males, and they are more frequently assigned roles bearing responsibility and leadership within their peer group. Futhermore, younger adolescents are not able to "catch up," and they remain less sociable and less likely to be assigned occupational positions that require supervision of the work of others.

In speaking of these linkages between leadership and biology, one may more readily understand the necessity of taking a contextualist position. The genetically related early body maturation takes on meaning relative to the leadership role only insofar as early maturing promotes an environmental response that *selectively exposes* a person to assuming leadership roles and to the social approval for the enactment of such roles.

Adults and peers react to early maturers by giving them tasks and prerogatives usually assigned to older persons. Upon validating the role expectations, early maturers confirm the social attribution and assume the "competency" dimension as a self-defining dimension. Thereupon, they maintain equilibrium and avoid cognitive strain only to the extent that their future enactments are confirmed.

None of the investigators who have produced the supporting data for these conclusions has suggested that genetics *cause* leadership behavior. In this context, the tendency to speak of direct causal chains is less important than in discussions of perplexing unwanted behavior.

The foregoing considerations highlight the necessity of undertaking our normal science activity against a clear understanding of the paradigm being applied. Studies of genetic concomitants of socially grounded conduct make sense when viewed from a contextualist perspective. A search for direct, mechanistic causal relations only stands in the way of locating the relations between morphology and behavior. The preceding discussion is a prelude to our discussion of the genetic hypothesis. We have tried to establish that the contextualist principles of selective exposure and differential susceptibility are particularly useful in understanding genetic, morphological, environmental, and behavioral relationships.

Support for the schizophrenia/genetic transmission hypothesis. With the previous paragraphs as background, we comment on the genetic transmission/schizophrenia hypothesis, restricting ourselves to the main arguments advanced by the proponents of the hypothesis. We begin with a direct quotation from Rosenthal's (1970) summary review: "There is a clear correlation between the degree of blood relationship and the incidence of schizophrenia in relatives, but the ratios do not correspond to any simple Mendelian pattern [p. 117]." One of the major problems stems from the inability to establish correspondence between the incidence of schizophrenia in families, as calculated in clinical assessments, and the numbers of schizophrenics who would be predicted by alternative genetic theories. For example, to posit a monogenic theory in a form that specifies that the action of a single dominant gene is linked to the inheritance of schizophrenic symptoms, a theorist would support the position by predicting the percentage of the population that carries the gene. From this figure, one would be able to calculate that the carriers would maintain the eight per thousand schizophrenics that are assumed to appear in clinical situations. But people labelled schizophrenics do not reproduce as actively as do nonschizophrenics. Thus the gene pool would diminish and the genetic base for the disorder should also diminish. Each successive generation would contain progressively less than eight per thousand schizophrenics. But the number of schizophrenics per thousand apparently does not diminish, so that one would retain a monogenic theory like this only by introducing one after another qualifying statements.

To meet such recurring objections to straightforward monogenic theories, polygenic theories have been introduced to account for the genetic correlates of schizophrenic behavior (Gottesman & Shields, 1972). To demonstrate the utility of a polygenic theory, it would be necessary, as with the single gene theory, to compute expected incidence among relatives having different degrees of familial relationship to the diagnosed person, the proband. Thereupon the actual rates of incidence would be compared to the expected rates of incidence. If the computations yield expected rates that approximate found rates, then the polygenic theory receives support. When investigators have proceeded in this manner, however, the outcomes do not strengthen belief in the utility of a polygenic model. Frequency estimates from a polygenic theory are found to be no more, or no less, predictive of actual rates than are the estimates of a monogenic model, whereupon qualifying additions to the model are suggested and explored.

The need for a strong genetic model to discuss the transmission of schizophrenia encourages these kinds of reformulation of the polygenic model. As any alternative model should, the polygenic model may yield answers to questions that its counterpart, the monogenic model, is unable to answer. The polygenic model, for example, could account for the maintenance of the eight per thousand population incidence of diagnosed schizophrenia. When the "trait" is polygenetically maintained, the selection processes associated with lowered reproduction rates of diagnosed persons would work very slowly to eliminate those carrying the multiple genes, and the eight per thousand incidence would remain stable over a few generations before statistical surveys would show the decline.

Strong models of genetic transmission have been employed to describe incidence rates for various disease processes, for example, Tay-Sachs disease. Not to come up with a strong genetic model for schizophrenia has been a source of frustration to scientists who are committed to the disease model. The current state of affairs is expressed in work like that of Kidd and Cavalli-Sforza (1974), who preface their efforts to explicate a genetic model by saying, "The magnitude of environmental effects is such that disbelief or minimization of the role of inheritance in schizophrenia is not uncommon [p. 254]."

Their considerations of alternative models leads them to the summary statement that

data on the inheritance of schizophrenia indicate that both genetics and environment contribute in an important way to the manifestations of the disease. However, heterogeneity of the data makes an accurate analysis very difficult. For this reason, the solution is unlikely to come from statistical techniques alone. Future advances in physiological, toxiological, and biochemical research are more likely to supply a firmer basis to the understanding of the genetic component of this disorder. . . . Though argument about genetic models seems futile when virtually any model can account for the data, the single gene hypothesis is unavoidably more attractive at this stage [p. 263].

In their conclusions, then, they agree with Gottesman and Shields (1972) on proposing a suitable statistical model for discussing inheritance relative to schizophrenia. "However, there is considerable overlap between the two principal models, and the tests proposed to differentiate between them are far from efficient [p. 330]."

A failure to produce a robust genetic model once again reflects the logical absurdity of regarding socially categorized behavior as the syptom of a disease. And, as one would expect, the failure leads to readjustments of the model, rather than to abandonment. One frequently appearing readjustment requires that diagnosticians consider a variety of diagnostic classifications as a spectrum of a single disorder (Heston, 1970), and that the genetic factors relate to the schizophrenic spectrum. And there have been advocates of a converse view: that schizophrenia represents a group of varied disorders inappropriately classed as a single disorder (Wing, 1978). Thus one would need to await the development of more precise diagnostic criteria in order to develop the proper genetic model for each of the separate disorders.

Evaluations of investigations of the genetic hypothesis. The work of Gottesman and Shields (1972) and Kety and his associates (Kety, 1974; Kety, Rosenthal, Wender, Shulsinger, & Jacobsen, 1975) is repeatedly cited as evidence for hereditary factors in schizophrenia. These works, using the twin-study approach and the foster-rearing approach, respectively, seek to demonstrate the role of genetic factors in relation to the development of unusual behaviors. The conclusions of these researchers are accepted as pivotal in establishing the validity of the biological approach. Snyder (1978), for example, introduces his discussion of dopamine and schizophrenia with the following commentary.

> . . . The powerful genetic studies of recent years, especially those of Kety et al. (1968), have established rather unequivocally that at least a portion of schizophrenics suffer from a disease in which the vulnerability stems from genetic factors. It is almost a dogma of modern molecular biology that a genetic disturbance will be reflected in biochemical abnormality. Hence, it is realistic to assume that one or more biochemical abnormalities exist in the bodies of schizophrenics, probably in the brain [p. 87].

Similarly, Kety, Rosenthal, Wender, and Shulsinger (1976) cite Gottesman and Shields (1972) as an important contribution to the clarification of the role of genetics in schizophrenia.

> Gottesman and Shields have reason to be proud of the Maudsley twin study (Gottesman & Shields, 1972), which successfully minimized many of the methodological biases (Kety, 1959; Rosenthal, 1962) of earlier studies and laid to rest the notion that the syndrome of schizophrenia was a myth. [p. 413].

Some basic studies of genetics and schizophrenia. The basic statement that has guided the work on twins would read as follows: Monozygotic twins, that is, twins developed from the union of the same sperm and ovum, would show a higher rate of concordance of schizophrenia than would either dizygotic twins or noncontemporaneous siblings. Monozygotic twins receive the same growth-regulating genetic material, so that they share physical structure, to the extent that structural development can be regulated purely by the basic genetic materials. Insofar as structure influences behavior development, monozygotic twins should develop similar structurally influenced behaviors. Cellular, glandular, and associated physiological function, if it is anomalous in a monozygotic twin, should be similarly anomalous in the co-twin. If one of the monozygotic pair develops schizophrenia in association with a genetically based anomaly, the co-twin should show the same disorder. Such would not be the case for dizygotic twins, who do not share identical genetic material.

Rosenthal's (1970) summary statement on twin findings informs us that the concordance rate is always greater for monozygotic twins than it is for dizygotic twins. One is likely to find four or five sets of monozygotic twins in which both twins have been classed as schizophrenic for each set of dizygotic twins concordantly classed as schizophrenic. Data from a careful long-term study by Gottesman and Shields (1972) promote a similar conclusion. If a monozygotic twin acquires the schizophrenic diagnosis, the other twin, in about 45 percent of the cases, will also acquire that diagnosis. A dizygotic twin diagnosed as schizophrenic will be joined by the co-twin in about ten of every 100 cases in which one of the pair is diagnosed.

A skeptic may cautiously withhold conversion, despite the support given to the genetic transmission hypothesis by the twin studies. One can enumerate many substantial criticisms of the studies that have produced these findings (Kreitman & Smythies, 1968; Kringlen, 1967). Campion and Tucker (1973), for example, point out that monozygotic twins show greater concordance for all kinds of physical anomalies, including early death. Seventy percent of monozygotic twins share the same chorion in the maternal placenta, while all dizygotic twins have separate chorions. Difficulties in adequate blood supply to both fetuses, among other problems, result from the environmental factors created by chorion sharing. Thus, we would expect that of those monozygotes who do survive, proportionately many more will bear physical stigmata that will increase their differential susceptibility and selective exposure to problems that may affect ways in which their public conduct is evaluated by significant others.

Further, one must face the clearly obvious fact that the most careful work done to date (Gottesman & Shields, 1972) has shown that in about half the occasions where one monozygotic twin is diagnosed as schizophrenic, the other is not. In effect, if there is a genetic anomaly, it does not produce effects, relative to acquiring the schizophrenia label, in half the cases of monozygotic twins where it would be expected to work. Such findings would be astounding in cases of cleft palate—a genetically determined anomaly. These kinds of finding promote careful consideration of the principles of selective exposure and differential susceptibility, and have led investigators like Stromgen (1975) to say, "Although family studies and twin-studies tended to show the importance of genetic factors, the only quite unquestionable result of genetic studies, especially the twin-studies, was that environmental factors contribute extensively to the etiology of schizophrenia [p. 17]."

Studies of adopted children. To factor out some of the considerations relative to how the responsive environment interacts with a genetically associated morphological substrate, investigators have conducted studies of the genetic pool from which had come foster-reared children who were, later in life, classed as schizophrenic. The basic assumption and hypothesis of these studies might be summarized as follows: If there is a genetically associated factor in the process of becoming a schizophrenic, that factor will have its effects in a variety of environments. Thus, a child who carries the gene-related condition would probably end up in the schizophrenic sample, despite having been placed in a foster home. Additionally, one could trace the genetic strains backwards from the current schizophrenic. The biological family could be shown to have developed the symptoms, whereas the families of foster-reared, nonschizophrenic comparison groups would show a relatively low incidence of schizophrenia's symptoms.

Rosenthal (1970, p. 127) indicates that findings in this kind of study are in line with genetic transmission theory. Among 150 biological relatives of 33 adoptees assigned a *definite* diagnosis of schizophrenia, Kety, Rosenthal, Wender, and Shulsinger (1968) found 13 diagnosable as "schizophrenia-spectrum" relatives, whereas only three "schizophrenic-spectrum" relatives were found among the 150 biological relatives of adopted control subjects. At the same time, two schizophrenic-spectrum adoptive relatives were found among the families (74 persons) who had adopted and reared the schizophrenics. Three schizophrenics were found among the 83 adoptive relatives of the nonschizophrenic adoptees.

Kety and his colleagues (Kety, 1974; Kety, Rosenthal, Wender, Shulsinger, & Jacobsen, 1975) presented more elaborate analyses of the study of these samples. In later investigations, diagnoses were made from extended interviews with relatives. From these interviews, professional mental health workers then "blindly" made psychiatric diagnoses of adoptive and biological relatives. By depending on this approach to diagnosis, according to Kety's (1974) report, about 14 percent of the adoptive schizophrenics' biological relatives fell into the "schizophrenic spectrum," along with about 3.5 percent of their adoptive relatives. Such data, he concludes, "speak for the operation of genetic factors in the transmission of schizophrenia [p. 961]"

Consider now that of nearly 5,500 adopted persons whose records had been searched, only 33 had entered hospitals to allow the accumulation of records from which the investigators could classify the adoptee as schizophrenic (Kety, 1974). According to official records, seven (4.7 percent) biological relatives of the adoptees were found to have been hospitalized and diagnosed as schizophrenic. (Subsequently, by relying on the blind diagnostic process, rather than hospital diagnosis, the investigators found a total of 24 biological relatives within the "schizophrenic spectrum.") One notes immediately that six-tenths of one percent of the population of adopted persons (33 persons) were given the diagnosis of schizophrenic, and that no more than 5 percent of their biological relatives could definitely be classed as schizophrenic. (Fourteen percent could, according to Kety and his colleagues, be placed within the "schizophrenic spectrum.") These data require special attention when placed alongside Rosenthal's (1970, p. 104) summary of the studies of incidence of schizophrenia in the general population. He notes that the median morbidity risk, derived from about 20 world wide studies, is approximately eight-tenths of one percent (8 of 1,000 persons) of the population studied. The original population from which the Kety group's schizophrenics were drawn, a large portion of all the children adopted in Denmark during the years 1924-1947, seemed to have a low propensity for earning the schizophrenia diagnosis (6 of 1,000 persons), whereas their biological relatives had, relative to the general population, an extremely high incidence of diagnosis (47 of 1,000 persons).

What conclusion is urged by the findings of these approaches to studying the genetics of schizophrenia? Do they "bear directly on the claims of Szasz, Laing and Rosenhan that schizophrenia is a myth, and that it cannot be diagnosed reliably [Kety, 1974, p. 960]"? If they do bear *directly on these claims, they* cannot deliver significant weight. First, these studies simply do not yield data that make good sense within models developed in genetic theory, and proponents of the genetic transmission/schizophrenia hypothesis are required to devote much consideration toward developing a genetic model that will give the data a semblance of order (Fulker, 1974; Kidd & Cavalli-Sforza, 1974; Rosenthal, 1970). The models that can be devised allow no unique predictions of inheritance rates, and there can be no meaningful test of strongly formulated hypotheses, as there would be if strict Mendelian principles were applicable.

Secondly, innumerable familial and other environmental variables can readily account for the findings that a schizophrenic is more likely to be found among the biological relatives of another diagnosed schizophrenic than among the relatives of nondiagnosed persons. Besides, in this study, the numbers of cases that demonstrate this greater likelihood is found to be impressively small. This becomes an important consideration.

In one of the many reworkings of the data collected by Kety and his associates, for example, Kety (1974) reports having found 24 biological relatives of schizophrenics whom they would class within the schizophrenic spectrum. This number represented about 14 percent of the 173 interviewed relatives. Thirteen of the 24 fall into the "uncertain" category. An observer is left with 11 definitely diagnosed cases, six of whom nevertheless are considered "latent." By disallowing this category, the sum reduces to *five people,* or 2.9 percent of the sample relatives, whose conduct is such that a diagnostician can unequivocally call them schizophrenic.

Of course it is clear that the diagnosticians found significantly fewer "uncertain," "latent," and "chronic" schizophrenics among the biological relatives of nonschizophrenic adoptees and among the adoptive relatives of both the control and experimental samples. Kety's (1974) blind diagnosticians found six "schizophrenic-spectrum" persons (3.4 percent) none of whom was declared clearly chronic, among the 174 biological relatives of the nonschizophrenic adoptees. One must also report that the Kety group's 1975 report expands the "schizophrenic spectrum," by justifying the inclusion of "schizoid inadequate personalities." Thus, the number of biological relatives of schizophrenic adoptees in the schizophrenic spectrum expands to 37 persons (21.4 percent). By this manipulation, the number of schizophrenic-spectrum persons among the biological relatives of nonschizophrenic adoptees rises to 19 persons (10.9 percent).

Can these data be used to support the genetic transmission explanation of unwanted conduct? To interpret the often confusing reports of data of this group's investigations, one must reflect on the conditions under which children are removed from their biological parents and placed for adoption with nonrelative parents. Any experience with this process can reveal the often immense ineptitude of some people who become biological parents. One can observe, for example, infants of less than six months who have become malnourished, who have been physically battered and seriously damaged, and who have experienced near total isolation from social contact. It is not unusual to find infants who require months of intensive nursing care following removal from a mother who has created these morbid conditions, a mother who might attract the attention of police or social agencies and ultimately be diagnosed as schizophrenic. And it is such mothers who are counselled to place their children into adoption.

Thus, when the Kety group found an adopted child who, later in life, had been diagnosed as schizophrenic, we would predict the high likelihood that this person is one of those seriously mistreated children who were placed in adoption and had survived its stigma-producing beginnings. Should there be but two such severely battered children in Kety's sample of 33 schizophrenic adoptees, he could easily uncover, in those two children's biological families, five persons who had behaved sufficiently badly to be diagnosed as schizophrenic.

Consider another of Kety's findings relative to reported data on population incidence of schizophrenia. An unexpectedly small percentage of the population of nearly 5,500 adopted persons could be diagnosed as schizophrenic (0.6 percent, compared to an assumed world incidence of 0.8 percent). When one considers the circumstances that frequently surround adoption, this low incidence becomes even less expected. That so few of these children developed unusual self-role definitions while bearing expected stigmata speaks well for the social services of Denmark. Case workers had apparently done an excellent job in screening adoptive families and had placed these children with unusually fine families.

In short, then, the adoptive family/biological family comparisons are of very small value. They show, quite simply, that the social service agencies have suitably done their job. In other words, little can be gained from making a comparison between people who are counselled to place their children into adoption and people who, we expect, had been carefully selected to act as adoptive parents. The social service agencies are designed to facilitate adoption when the natural family is judged to be excessively deviant, and they surely would not serve their function were they unable to arrange far more suitable placements.

An excursus into the genetics of littering. To give the reader another perspective on the genetic transmission hypothesis, we paraphrase contemporary findings employing another variable—littering. The reader is reminded that biochemical and genetic research findings are used to provide internal support, supplementing the ideological premises (discussed in Chapter 6) that give external support to the sagging disease model of schizophrenia. Our fictive investigators begin with 5,500 Danish adoptees whose records were available. Of these, 33 adoptees could be definitely classified as litterers. Among 150 biological relatives of the 33 adoptees assigned a *definite* diagnosis of littering, there were 13 diagnosable as "littering-spectrum" relatives, whereas only three "littering-spectrum" relatives were found in 150 biological relatives of adopted control subjects. At the same time, two "littering-spectrum" adoptive relatives were found among the families (74 persons) who had adopted children who turned out to be litterers. Three litterers were found among the adoptive relatives (83 persons) of the nonlittering adoptees. A later analysis was made from extended interviews with relatives. From these interviews, professional diagnosticians made "blind" diagnoses of littering of adoptive and biological relatives. In this more elaborate study, about 14 percent of the adoptive litterers' biological relatives were assigned to the "littering spectrum" diagnosis, along with approximately 3.5 percent of the adoptive relatives. The conclusion: These data support the operation of genetic factors in the transmission of littering.

Littering is a judgment made about a person's conduct. Whether or not a given bit of behavior is classifiable as littering is related to the criteria employed by the diagnostician. The criteria listed in the Diagnostic and Statistical Manual for littering are not unequivocal and reliability of diagnosis is marginal.

Should one make the diagnosis of littering only if the untidiness is confined to the patient's own room? Should littering refer only to careless disposal of gum wrappers, candy boxes, cigarette packs? Or should the diagnostician include newspapers, old magazines, used envelopes, and discarded book jackets? How about cigarette butts, apple cores, and orange peels? Are two gum wrappers on the floor of a meticulously clean room sufficient for a diagnosis? If the person litters only on highways and not in enclosed places, is the littering diagnosis appropriate? Perhaps such a person should be included in a "littering-spectrum" diagnosis, along with "latent litterers" who are sloppy about their dress or speech and who would probably litter if in the right situation. If the diagnostician is unsure whether a person is a litterer, the uncertainty can be resolved by assigning the uncertain cases to the litterer-spectrum diagnosis. Of course, the littering spectrum should include borderline litterers as well as litteroid personalities. Take the case of a person cited by a police officer for violating an antilittering ordinance and convicted in a local court. The person pays the $50 fine imposed by the judge and apologizes for littering the public roads. Is such a person to be diagnosed as a *litterer in remission*?

By relying on the "blind" diagnoses made from interviewers' records, rather than *definite* diagnoses made by experts and using the litterer-spectrum concept, the investigators could identify 24 biological relatives, about 14 percent of the

173 relatives interviewed. Of these, 13 relatives were classified as "uncertain" litterers. If we subtract the "uncertains," the number of littering relatives is reduced to 11. On further analysis of the litterer-spectrum cases, we find that six were considered latent litterers. Removing these latent cases reduces the sum to five persons, less than 3 percent of the sample of relatives whose conduct was such that a diagnostician could use the litterer category with full confidence.

Although not many definite littering biological relatives were identified, an advocate of the genetic theory of littering would point to the fact that even fewer litterer-spectrum cases were found among the biological relatives of nonlitterer adoptees and among the adoptive relatives of both the control and experimental samples. These data require careful examination. Besides the small (tiny) samples, the vagaries of diagnosis, and the possibility of even a slight degree of leakage of critical information in the blind diagnosis of littering, one must recognize that the adoptive families were screened by social workers. The act of selecting an adoptive home could include standards of housekeeping. Homes where littering was evident would be disqualified—thus adoptive parents were effectively screened so that they could not later be diagnosed as litterers, whether or not the adoptee had become classified as a litterer or not.

A further point: According to one of the most respected investigators on the heritability of littering, the base rate in the population for littering is 8 per 1,000. The incidence in the Danish adoptee study is 5 per thousand. The whole exercise takes on the character of a futile enterprise when the small proportions are compared with the supposed base rates of littering.

The most parsimonious conclusion is that the results on the heritability of littering are due to sampling errors.

Reconsideration of the Schizophrenia/Genetic Transmission Hypothesis

The most acclaimed studies of genetics and schizophrenia are not compelling evidence of a schizophrenia/genetic transmission hypothesis.

In our judgment, the Gottesman and Shields (1972) report of greater concordance among monozygotic twins, relative to dizygotic twins, provides the most striking support for the conception. The study's procedures include a strong effort to forestall the most serious criticisms of this kind of study. Yet the investigation need not be taken as evidence that a *specific* morphological state, or *set of specific* morphological states, underlies a disease process associated with schizophrenia. Monozygotic twins are more likely to bear shared stigmata resulting from prenatal competition. Additionally, monozygotic twins, owing to their concordance for morphological structure, share largely identical risk for *any* physical stigmata. If one twin develops clubfoot, or cleft palate, harelip, or misaligned eyes, the other will develop a similar morphological anomaly. Degraded social status is easily awarded for any of a very large number of small and large physical stigmata. If identical twins, more than dizygotic twins, are at risk for concordant physical stigmata, they also are more frequently at risk for more frequent concordance of identity degradation and the role in security that follows such degradation. It would thus be quite likely that they would concordantly develop self-role enactments that under some conditions lead to the stigmatizing declaration of value on the enactments: schizophrenia.

The principles of selective exposure and differential susceptibility easily allow the possibility that monozygotic twins will develop a similar genetic anomaly, and that such anomalies will be stigma-evoking. The anomalies, however, need not be similar across all twin pairs where there is a concordance for schizophrenia. That is, not every twin pair concordant for schizophrenia needs to have inherited club foot, or crossed eyes, or disordered protein metabolism. Yet clubfoot, like any other concordant anomaly, can selectively expose a monozygotic male pair to exclusion from boys' games, to being treated dependently, to rejection in heterosexual advances, and to constant disconfirmation of adequacy in filling a required male role. It is no surprise to find that this monozygotic pair concordantly develops an unwarranted belief that young women are covertly sexually attracted to them, and that these women are surrepticiously signalling their wild desires. When the police are summoned to the apartment of a pair of young female students, to take one of the college aged twins into custody for forcible entry, it is not difficult for them to deduce that the twins should be referred to psychiatric agencies.

In considering this example, one may refer to Wahl's (1976) conclusions about discordance for schizophrenia. Following a very thorough review of studies of discordant twin pairs he writes:

> The one consistent finding across studies is that people note and respond to early differences in personality between twins later to be discordant for schizophrenia. Common findings include greater childhood psychopathology, submissiveness, dependence, social isolation, and maternal overprotection of the index twin [p. 101].

Consider the assumption, as defined by Pollin and Stabeneu (1968), that the parental response of overprotection is generated by recognition of the poorer physical status of the index twin. Then, when both twins show similar poor, and perhaps genetically determined physical status, we would expect that both would be selectively exposed to role-deforming environmental responses. It would not be illogical to expect concordance for schizophrenic diagnosis.

The general point is as follows: Just as one can use the principles of selective exposure and differential susceptibility to explain the linkages between genetically related morphology and the adopting of leadership behavior, one may also show that genetically related histology and anatomy may be implicated in the development of a schizophrenic role. Shared morphology would raise the probability that monozygotic twins would develop schizophrenic or any other behavior, since they would be similarly selectively exposed to social reactions to their morphology, and they would be similarly differentially susceptible to positive or negative environmental stimulation. Early-maturing monozygotic boys would be selectively exposed to experiences that would induce concordant leadership behavior. Male monozygotic twins, in contrast to female twins, will be differentially susceptible to a cold winter wind during outdoor urination. Yet, no one has tried to prove that leadership behavior or standing while urinating in the snow are diseases, in that they are grounded in biology. And no scientist is seeking the drug that will cure the "symptoms" of urinating in the snow or of nonleadership. Indeed, these actions are not listed as symptoms. An item of behavior, we are reminded, becomes a symptom only in those contexts where another person—usually more powerful than the index person—finds the behavior perplexing and annoying and then posits a disease as underlying the symptoms. The search for direct genetic links completes the folly.

Hypotheses of Biochemical Causality

The CPK hypothesis. Let us look at a recent effort to relate enzyme activity to madness. A series of articles (Martin, Garey, & Heath, 1972; Meltzer, 1968, 1973; Meltzer, Grinspoon, & Shader, 1970; Vale, Espejel, Calcaneo, Ocampo, & Diaz-de-Leon, 1974) reported exploration of the possibility that serum creatine phosphokinase (CPK) activity increases during the initial phase of the psychotic episode among acutely psychotic patients. One of the first publications reporting this possibility (Meltzer, 1969) studied the presence of CPK and aldolase, another enzyme, in blood samples taken from persons who had been sorted into various psychiatric diagnostic categories. Persons who had not been given a psychiatric diagnosis also provided blood samples. Meltzer (1969) reports that, "In ten of 12 acutely schizophrenic patients studied on a longitudinal basis, a significant elevation of serum CPK and aldolase was found at some phase of their clinical course [p. 104]." A table shows that the mean maximum activity of serum CPK and aldolase of *acutely psychotic subjects* was significantly higher than the mean maximum activity of *chronically psychotic, nonpsychotic,* and *normal subjects*.

Meltzer replicated the study, with variations, and so did other investigators. Meltzer, Grinspoon, and Shader (1970) assessed the CPK and aldolase activity of acute schizophrenics, of members of a hospital psychiatric staff, and of members of the schizophrenics' families. They report that only two of the 10 hospital staff members had an abnormally increased enzyme activity in two or more of the blood specimens taken from them. At the same time, 25 of the 39 schizophrenic patients had an abnormal level of CPK and/or aldolase activity. Meanwhile only five of the 22 relatives of the schizophrenics showed a high level of enzyme activity.

The CPK hypothesis was given additional credibility in a report by Gosling, Kerry, Orme, and Owen (1971). They reported that 10 of 20 psychotic patients showed an increase in serum CPK, whereas a control sample of nonpsychotic patients did not show any increase in CPK.

Credibility of the CPK hypothesis was reduced when Warnock and Ellman (1969) reported that only five in their sample of 25 acute psychotic patients showed heightened levels of CPK. They also established that three of these five had received intramuscular chlorpromazine within 72 hours before the specimen was drawn. They proceeded to explore the hypothesis that intramuscular injection stimulates the release of CPK. They found that rabbits given an intramuscular injection of chlorpromazine showed significant increase in CPK activity.

Vale, Espejel, Calcaneo, Ocampo, and Diaz-de-Leon (1974) reported 30 percent of actively psychotic patients showed an increased level of CPK in samples of fluid drawn from the cerebrospinal system rather than from a blood sample. This contradicts the finding reported by Martin, Gary, and Heath (1972), who drew fluid through a lumbar puncture, as did Vale et al., while at the same time taking CPK readings from blood serum samples. Martin et al. report that there was *no* measurable spinal fluid creating kinase activity in *any* patient, while serum CPK was elevated in eight of 11 patients. These contradictory results have no ready explanation.

As a final illustration of studies of the relationships between CPK activity and schizophrenia, we note one of Meltzer's (1973) attempts to bring order out of chaos. Meltzer took up two issues that seemed to have been generated by the stream of research reports. On the one hand, he tried to deal with Gosling et al.'s suggestion (1971) that heightened serum CPK appeared more predictably in manic and paranoid schizophrenia than in other psychotic states. On the other hand, Meltzer explored the temporal relationship between the CPK activity and the onset of the conduct that had initiated the diagnostic process. This issue had been implicit in the entire stream of work, in that Meltzer (1969) had specifically stated (see above) that the increased CPK activity related to *acutely* schizophrenic patients, yet subsequent reports had left unclear the temporal relationships between CPK activity and the onset of inappropriate conduct. For example, in one report Meltzer (1970) indicates that "thereafter, serum samples were obtained on Monday of each week of the patients' hospitalization. The number of samples per patient ranged from five to 41 [p. 553]." Thereupon, Meltzer reports that a subject was rated as having abnormal CPK or aldolase activity if two or more of the specimens were out of the expected range. One may surmise that samples were taken from patients who had spent 41 weeks in the hospital, and that any three samples could have been used as indications of abnormal CPK activity. Does this mean that a patient who had spent up to 41 weeks in a hospital continued to be considered as an *acutely* schizophrenic case? Meltzer's original claim specifically associates CPK presence with *acute* schizophrenia.

Similarly, Martin et al. indicate that they had regarded their patients as acute. Nevertheless, they report that "the subjects were randomly selected without regard to diagnostic classification or previous psychiatric history [p. 727]." Also, they indicate that their subjects ranged in age from 18 to 72 years. Thus, Martin et al. not only confounded Meltzer's original indication that the heightened level of CPK is associated with behavior labelled as schizophrenia (and not with behavior that leads to other diagnostic classifications), but they also leave some confusion about the definition of *acute*. Or, had they considered a 72-year-old patient, whose previous psychiatric history is ignored, to be an acute case?

To deal with the issues deriving from using the term *acute*, as well as to refute Gosling et al. on their observation regarding the relationship between CPK activity and the diagnosis of paranoid schizophrenia, Meltzer (1973) divided his sample into groupings that depended on the estimated number of weeks between the time of the original manifestation of unusual behavior and the time at which the person was hospitalized. In this report, Meltzer takes the position that "serum CPK activity increases are generally present for not more than ten days from the onset of symptoms [p. 592]." If this conclusion were to be accepted, many of the other studies invoking the CPK hypothesis, including Meltzer's 1970 study, would need reinterpretation, since these studies appear to base their conclusions on findings that elevated CPK activity was present at times beyond 10 days from onset of the unwanted behaviors.

By 1976 Meltzer (1976) changed his emphasis and reviewed the state of the CPK hypothesis in a discussion of neuromuscular dysfunction in schizophrenia. By 1978 the hypothesis receives only brief mention in one article (Wyatt & Bigelow, 1978) in a compendium (Wynne, Cromwell, & Matthysse, 1978) of 60 papers given at a noted international conference on schizophrenia. The CPK/schizophrenia hypothesis seems to have exhausted its utility. Other chemical hypotheses are waiting in the wings.

The Dopamine/Schizophrenia Hypothesis. In the decade after 1950, a series of chemicals was introduced into psychiatric practice for use with "psychotic" individuals. Among the most noteworthy of these drugs is a group of phenothiazine-related substances, the most famous of which is chlorpromazine. Chlorpromazine gained its current reputation under the trade name *Thorazine*. In the early years of the widespread use of these drugs, they were commonly known as *tranquilizers*. Currently contributors to the psychopharmacological and the psychiatric literature refer to these drugs as "neuroleptic" or "antipsychotic" drugs. The transition in terminology contains a message. It is an effort to introduce a new, lively metaphor to replace a dying metaphor. *Psychosis,* a term that denotes a disordered psyche, is presumably antagonized by a drug.

The new metaphor, *antipsychotic,* is supported as a replacement for *tranquilizer* by findings that offer some explanation of the neuropharmacological functioning of the phenothiazines. It is asserted that

> regardless of whatever secondary and varied pharmacological properties individual drugs in this group may have, they share one common and probably crucial neuropharmacological property, namely, that they are all antagonists of the action of DA [dopamine] at CNS [central nervous system] receptor sites [Iverson & Iverson, 1975, p. 243].

If it can be asserted that the phenothiazines, which are antagonists to dopamine, are truly antipsychotic (not simply "tranquilizers"), then there is promise of finding the neurochemical basis of schizophrenia. By implication, "it would thus appear that dopamine plays a profound and unique role in inducing schizophrenic symptoms [Carlsson, 1978, p. 170]."

Thus, the dopamine/schizophrenia hypothesis has become the latest in the series of biochemical hypotheses postulated to explain a biological basis of schizophrenic symptoms. This fascinating hypothesis has been built, however, on an assumptive chain that has been stretched to an ultra-high tension. The tenuousness of the conclusions that come with the chain is well expressed by the following closely juxtaposed statements found in an address to the 1977 meeting of the American Psychiatric Association. In the address, Carlsson (1978), a leading investigator of the dopamine/schizophrenia hypothesis, begins by saying, "No biochemical lesion has yet been demonstrated beyond doubt to be linked to schizophrenia. The so-called dopamine hypothesis of schizophrenia rests almost entirely on pharmacological evidence [p. 164]."

After an enthusiastic review of the progress in developing the fine points of the neuropharmacology of dopamine, Carlsson is willing to say, "Nevertheless, the conclusion seems inevitable that a dopaminergic mechanism occupies a very strategic position in functions that are disturbed in schizophrenia [p. 170]." This statement is closely followed by the claim that dopamine plays a profound role in inducing schizophrenic symptoms. Then all the earlier caution and all the earlier enthusiasm are mixed into the following ambivalent statement: "Despite the undisputed role of dopamine in inducing schizophrenic symptoms there is so far no direct support for a primary causative role of dopamine in schizophrenia [p. 171]."

The source of this ambivalence is easy to detect. The value of the dopamine/schizophrenia hypothesis rests largely on the acceptance of the assumption that the phenothiazines are antagonistic to "psychotic behavior." But it is important to assert that *only* the psychotic behavior is removed by the dopamine antagonistic phenothiazines. If the phenothiazines generally produce a sophisticated chemical extirpation of a large group of neural connections—a kind of chemical removal of the human spark plugs—then one could simply say the phenothiazines are antagonistic to *all kinds* of behavior. Then it could be argued that in the process of bringing large segments of the human nervous system into a resting phase, the intensity of the adjudged schizophrenic's unwanted behavior is also diminished. In this way, a "psychosis" is "cured." Among other things, the drug-taker no longer performs the unwanted behavior that initially led to his or her being tagged with a psychiatric label.

Some notes on the effectiveness of phenothiazines. The work of Davis and his colleagues (Davis, 1965; Klein & Davis, 1969) is often cited to support the claim that the phenothiazines can be regarded as something other than a sophisticated tranquilizer. Davis's (1965) review of the literature regarding the efficacy of drugs in the control of psychotic behavior led him to conclude that in treating schizophrenia, a large group of the phenothiazines "were equally effective and clearly better than mepazine and promazine, which were in turn more effective than placebo or phenobarbital [p. 554]." This conclusion is distorted in the writing of Iversen and Iversen (1975) and Snyder, Banerjee, Yamamura, and Greenberg (1974). Davis's conclusion becomes, "Phenothiazine drugs are generally acknowledged to be highly efficacious in alleviating symptoms of schizophrenia [Snyder et al., 1974, p. 1243]." In addition, it is argued that "antianxiety drugs do not alleviate schizophrenic symptoms, so that mere "tranquilization of anxiety" cannot account for the antipsychotic effects of the phenothiazines.

These fragile claims lend little strength to the chain that anchors the dopamine hypothesis. Phenobarbitol has an effect notably different from that of any of the phenothiazines. Comparisons of the dosage levels of the phenothiazines and the barbiturates cannot be made. Phenothiazines can be administered in massive doses without inducing death. Overdoses of barbiturates are frequently fatal. Further, to argue that antianxiety drugs do not eliminate schizophrenic symptoms, whereas the phenothiazines do eliminate such behaviors, puts one squarely into the morass of defining anxiety (Sarbin, 1964, 1968b).

If the problems of specifying the pharmacological linkages to behavior do not cast sufficient doubt on the claim that the phenothiazines work as antagonists to the expression of psychotic symptoms, there remain the unresolved problems of defining the referents for the term *psychotic symptoms*. Pharmacologically oriented investigators cannot claim elimination of symptoms if they cannot first agree on which items of conduct are to be classified as "psychotic symptoms."

Some tests of the dopamine/schizophrenia hypothesis. In its simplest and most incautious form, we could state the dopamine hypothesis as follows: Excessive dopamine is found in the dopamine-sensitive central nervous system centers of those persons who display "psychotic" conduct, whereas such a condition does not exist in the CNS of those who do not show "psychotic" conduct. Wise and Stein (1973) approached this statement when they assessed the brain specimens of 18 deceased schizophrenics for the presence of dopamine-B hydroxylase (DBH), an important hydroxylating enzyme in the metabolism associated with dopamine. DBH converts dopamine into norepinephrine. It is assumed that if there is a low level of DBH, dopamine will not be converted; and one would expect a high level of dopamine to be present in those central nervous system centers where dopamine acts as an effective neurotransmitter. Wise and Stein found a low level of DBH in the brains of deceased schizophrenics, and concluded that these persons were unable successfully to metabolize dopamine, and that the presence of high levels of dopamine is associated with the development of schizophrenic symptoms. The conclusion may then be stated, "The deficit in DBH might therefore be associated with the disease [p. 346]."

Other investigators (Wyatt, Schwartz, Erdelyi, & Barchas, 1975) failed to verify the dopamine hypothesis by direct methods like those used by Wise and Stein (1973). As Carlsson (1978) notes, the dopamine/schizophrenia hypothesis gains support through indirect pharmacological investigation. An example of the way this evidence has been accumulated is taken from a study reported by Nasrallah, Donnelly, Bigelow, Rivera-Calimlim, Regolo, Plotkin, Rauscher, Wyatt, and Gillin (1977). This team of researchers studied the effects of metyrosine, an inhibitor of tyrosine hydroxylase. Tyrosine hydroxylase limits the rate of synthesis of dopamine (DA) and norepinephrine. "If the DA hypothesis is correct, then by decreasing the synthesis of DA, metyrosine should theoretically have a therapeutic effect in schizophrenia similar to that of the neuroleptic drugs that block DA receptors [p. 649]." Since the phenothiazines inhibit the transmission of impulses across the neural receptors activated by dopamine, and since it is assumed that the phenothiazines have an antipsychotic effect, then the administration of metyrosine should have the effect of increasing the antipsychotic properties of the phenothiazines. In short, if metyrosine is administered to a schizophrenic who is already being given a tranquilizer, the "illness" should abate more dramatically.

Nasrallah and his colleagues administered three grams per day of metyrosine to schizophrenics who were already being given a dose of phenothiazines equivalent to 800 milligrams of chlorpromazine every 24 hours. There was little question about the actual neural effects of this experimental drug. "To varying extents, all of the patients developed extrapyramidal reactions with metyrosine. This initially manifested itself in most of the patients by stiff posture, drooling, and shuffling gait [p. 651]." The patients developed, in effect, symptoms of Parkinson's Disease, a disorder associated with deficiencies of dopamine in crucial motor neural centers.

Nasrallah et al. used a variety of behavior change assessments to register the antipsychotic effects of this treatment. They then concluded that this program "does not potentiate the antipsychotic activity of the phenothiazines in these patients [p. 653]." These findings contradict the findings of other studies (Walinder, Skott, Carlsson, & Roos, 1976), and thereby create a situation not unfamiliar to those who observe the process of relating chemicals to those unwanted acts known as the symptoms of psychosis.

Dopamine and unusual behavior. The large problem of the dopamine hypothesis remains: How does one translate fascinating neuropharmacology into psychopharmacology? How does one go from the physiology of single cells to the strange behavior of individual persons? One of the routes to follow is offered by studies of the effects of administering L-dopa to persons suffering from Parkinson's Disease. L-dopa is an amino acid which is decarboxylated into dopamine by the aromatic amino acid called Dopa-decarboxylase. When L-dopa is administered to persons showing the Parkinsonian symptoms, that is, persons assumed to be deficient in dopamine, there is distinct clinical alleviation of the Parkinsonian symptoms. If these persons also develop unusual behaviors that could be the symptoms of schizophrenia, then one might suggest that there is a direct linkage of some sort between unwanted behaviors and excesses of dopamine in central neural centers. Though there are some unsystematic reports of the development of unusual behaviors in persons treated with L-dopa, no convincing data have yet appeared to demonstrate such linkages (Iversen & Iversen, 1975, p. 271).

Another approach to developing arguments for the dopamine hypothesis is to propose a parallel between "amphetamine psychosis" and "excess dopamine schizophrenia." Amphetamine-related compounds are widely available in the illicit drug trade, going under the vivid cognomen *speed*. Persons who have long-term access to D-metamphetamine (speed) have occasionally appeared for treatment showing behaviors that are taken for psychosis. Snyder and his associates (Snyder, 1973; Snyder, Banerjee, Yamamura, & Greenberg, 1974) propose that the amphetamine psychosis is an analogue for the disorder known as schizophrenia. Since amphetamine has been shown to encourage the release of dopamine, it is assumed that the resulting excess dopamine promotes the amphetamine psychoses, and one may assume a parallel between the drug-related psychosis and schizophrenia.

Despite the tidiness of the pharmacology, Snyder and his colleagues recognize that the classification of the drug-related behaviors remains problematic. Snyder (1973) points out, for example, that "the clinical picture, however, differs in a number of ways from that of schizophrenia," and suggests that "the differences are attributable to other 'contaminating' amphetamine effects [p. 62]." Furthermore, the amphetamine psychosis seems to mimic only paranoid schizophrenia. Then, "the auditory hallucinations are very much like typical schizophrenic auditory hallucinations, with vague noises, voices, and occasional conversations with voices [p. 62]." It is tempting to ask; How does one categorize the typical schizophrenic hallucination? What is a hallucination? Do clinicians deal with hallucinations, or do they deal with *reports of imaginings*?

Not only are the problems of defining psychotic behavior in persons taking the dopamine-releasing drugs unresolved, problems remain in interpreting behaviors in animals that have ingested these drugs. Ellinwood, Sudilovsky, and Nelson (1972) speak of studying "psychosis" in cats. Randrup and Munkvad (1970) have studied drug induced psychoses in humans. Behavioral repertoires are reduced and the animals repeat continuously a small segment of their overall range of behaviors. Some of the animals' postures are regarded as catatonic. The practice of considering these animal behaviors as analogues to "psychotic behavior" is obviously facilitated by the ease with which any unusual behavior may be characterized as a symptom of psychosis. To carry forward the analogy does require, in addition, that one think of an animal's behavior within the set of principles that define a person's behavior. One might well believe, then, that if animals could talk in human languages, they would tell us about the "hallucinations" and "delusions" they experience while under the influence of amphetamines. The analogue would be considerably more complete. Then the case for excess dopamine release being a causal factor in schizophrenia would be more definitively anchored. In the meantime, the problems of directly linking dopamine to unusual behaviors have not been solved.

The Place of Biological Variables in Explaining Unusual Behaviors

It is not our position that biological hypotheses be eliminated from the enterprise of building theory about unusual behavior. The science of biology cannot be rejected because of the failure of previously proposed hypotheses. Further, *a priori* argument alone cannot eliminate the data that are collected in studies of behavior-biology relationships. Our scrutiny of the conclusions of the many reports on studies connecting biology and schizophrenia leads to the observation that, so far, biologically grounded hypotheses have added little to the explanation of human conduct which, under some contingencies, earns a person the diagnosis of schizophrenia.

The studies of genetic linkages have not produced findings that point to the inheritance of specific implicated structures. In the absence of ability to point to an implicated structure, there is no means by which to connect the anomalous behavior to the bodily functions that presumably develop from the defect-producing, basic genetic materials. And, there can be no environmental reaction that will either reduce or remove the negative consequences that develop in association with the defective bodily condition. In effect, theoretical linkages are impossible to state. Concretely, the genetic studies completed to date provide no starting point for speculating on the connections between a person's genetic substrate and, for instance, the fact that the person holds esoteric religious beliefs or communicates through strange postures, or speaks in a manner that frustrates attempts at decoding.

The biochemical hypotheses have been similarly unproductive. As with the psychological studies reviewed earlier, the biochemical investigators fail to call their independent variables into question. Kety (1969), one of the most renowned investigators of biological processes associated with schizophrenia, aptly informed his colleagues that "an unavoidable difficulty at the present time is the fact that the crucial processes of diagnosis and evaluation of change are based almost entirely on subjective estimates [p. 165]." A scientist's announcement of finding a relationship between a dependent variable (for example, CPK level) derived through elegant technology and a "diagnosis . . . based almost entirely on subjective estimates" is hardly convincing. Yet, in studies of the CPK hypothesis only Gosling's group (1971) and Meltzer (1973) report the use of other than psychiatric opinion alone for deriving their diagnosis; and Meltzer refuted the utility of one of these alternates to subjective opinion—Lorr and Klett's (1967) Inpatient Multidimensional Psychiatric Scale.

Another grave question remains. How does one explain these two observations: (1) evidence for heightened CPK or dopamine activity, and (2) the conduct of the diagnosed schizophrenic woman who claimed olfactory "hallucinations"? or the acts of the self-proclaimed Jesus Christ? It is no longer satisfactory to begin from an idiographic postulate that *bad* chemical functioning leads to *bad* thoughts and *bad* conduct. There is no reason why unusual CPK function should be associated with unconfirmable claims to being Jesus Christ. No one has yet advanced a theory that links a physiological malfunction to a person's acceptance of unverified imaginings.

Our brief overview leads us to predict, with high confidence, the following: The dopamine-schizophrenia hypothesis will fade into oblivion, like the taraxein hypothesis advanced by Heath, Martens, Leach, Cohen, and Feigley in 1957, the 3,4-dimethozyzpheny-lethylamine (DMPEA) hypothesis proposed by Friedhoff and VanWinkle in 1962, and the CPK hypothesis of recent years. Since the dopamine hypothesis is psychopharmacologically more sophisticated, it is unlikely to be overturned by a discovery that an alteration in diet or in amount of exercise alters one or another chemical condition, as alterations in diet eliminated the compound DMPEA from the urine of schizophrenics.

The endorphine hypothesis has already appeared and stands available to replace the dopamine hypothesis. Substances (endorphins) that bind to "opiate receptors" have been isolated in neural tissues. It has been suggested that behavioral disorders may be associated with an excess of these compounds at specific central nervous system sites. Davis, Bunney, DeFraites, Kleinman, Van Kanmen, Post, and Wyatt (1977) tested the possibility that the use of naloxone, an antagonist to the endorphines, would produce clinical and subjective changes in a schizophrenic sample. Nothing of significance occurred. "Nonetheless, further testing of naloxone in patients with catatonia or other neuromuscular symptoms is warranted [p. 76]."

We conclude our analysis of biologically grounded research with a quotation from Manfred Bleuler (1968). Carrying on the work begun by his father, Eugen Bleuler, he has published the results of a 23-year follow-up of 208 people diagnosed as schizophrenic. After reporting his findings, he sums up his impressions:

It is safe to state: Up to now a somatic background of schizophrenia has not been discovered, neither a brain lesion nor a pathology of metabolism. I do not disagree with any somatic theories of schizophrenia on account of philosophic speculations or on account of overgeneralizations of psychoanalytical theories as others do. I disagree with them just because I am attached to biology and to general medicine. As far as I can see, all the somatic theories of schizophrenia are open to most severe criticism from biologists. As a physician, I feel that we are not allowed to diagnose a somatic disease without somatic findings. It seems not to be good medical policy to maintain that schizophrenia is a symptom of a somatic disturbance, if we cannot demonstrate this somatic disturbance, just as a conscientious physician is not allowed to treat any complaint as a cardiac disease if there is no cardiac symptomatology to be demonstrated. My personal studies with regard to potential somatic backgrounds of schizophrenia have been made in the fields of psycho-endocrinology. They have led to the simple observation: most schizophrenics are endocrinologically healthy and most endocrine patients are not schizophrenic. We can even go further and state: Any psychopathological complications of somatic disturbances are not schizophrenic psychoses.

I have discussed the frequency of improvements many years after the onset of the psychosis. It is difficult to explain it if schizophrenia is an error of metabolism or any brain atrophy [p. 9].

Our analysis should not be taken as a rejection of biologically grounded research. The scientist's search for truth need not be constrained by past failures.

The scientist needs to be cautious, however, lest biological hypotheses be used too uncritically to give support to the disease model of unwanted conduct. The prestige and apparent epistemic cogency of the disease model are lures to biologically oriented investigators. More critically, these hypotheses hold a prestigious fascination and social policy is influenced directly or indirectly. For example, people are excused from crimes because they are regarded as mentally sick. Others perform residually deviant behaviors and are sequestered because they too are regarded as sick and helpless. Since such outcomes as sequestering and excusing proceed from the disease model, the failures of the model might better be taken as an argument for abandoning this conceptualization of schizophrenia.

The repeated disconfirmation of numerous genetic and biochemical models for discussing unwanted behaviors is parallel to the repeated disconfirmation of hundreds of psychological models. The reasons are the same: The independent variable, schizophrenia-nonschizophrenia, is a will-o'-the-wisp.

8

The Task of Articulating Theory: The Idiographic[1] Solution

There has been reference to the mechanistic disease model throughout the discussion of studies of the unwanted conduct that sometimes earns a person the schizophrenia diagnosis. The mechanistic features of the model are most apparent in discussions of causal relationships. Investigators construe outlandish, deviant conduct as "disordered behavior" when they articulate that conduct to a network of assumptions and principles in which the action is treated as the result of an anomalous transfer of energies. If one holds to a strict biological perspective, the disordered behavior can be seen to result from irregularities at the intracellular, that is, the molecular, level. Or the cause might be ascribed to a process that befuddles the transfer of energies at the intercellular level. Biological specifics are not requisite in designs of disease models used to explain unwanted conduct. As noted earlier, Bleuler's version of the disease model for schizophrenia was built largely from Freud's conceptions of the functioning of a "mechanized mind." Disordered thought, in a theory like Bleuler's, would result from inappropriate transfers of mental energies; and such inappropriate transfers would develop as a result of the child-rearing practices that affect the distributions of libidinal energies. The model need not posit a biological base to describe a "diseased mind."

When we have perceived the effort to articulate the data of schizophrenia studies to one or another version of the disease model, we have inferred that the investigator is showing a preference for a mechanistic world view. The preceding chapters of this work include repeated demonstrations of the inadequacy of the mechanistic model as it applies to unwanted behavior. We now venture the observation that investigators are aware of the failures of the mechanistic models, and that some scientists show this awareness, often quite inadvertantly, by drifting into other world views. We agree with Pepper (1942) that paradigm-crossing is illicit, and that

> . . . an eclecticism should be excluded from within world theories . . . in the interests of clarity; otherwise, how can one see just where the maximum of structural corroboration lies? If a world theory partly developed in one set of categories is broken in upon by a foreign set of categories, the structure of the corroboration is broken up, and we cannot clearly see how the evidence lies. For intellectual clarity, therefore, we want our world theories pure and not eclectic [p. 330].

In the next three chapters we will explore the reactions to failures in theory articulation, attempting to show that a clear analysis of paradigms can be of value in avoiding confusing eclecticism.

Bannister recognized and commented on the complications of theory articulation in schizophrenia research. He pointed out that ". . . studies in schizophrenia cannot be additive unless they are carried out within a specific language and series of assumptions—we are not only faced with an intellectual silence as to the 'seat of madness' but an equal silence as to the seat of sanity" (Bannister, 1968, p. 183f). Bannister cites work from the *British Journal of Psychiatry* to illustrate his points. Referring to the work of Begelman (1966) on the performance of schizophrenic and organically impaired patients, he says, ". . . it is clear that 'abstraction' as function is not a concept articulated by some overall theory of psychological process. It is a concept stemming from traditional logic imported into psychology [Bannister, 1958, p. 184]."

Bannister's critique of theory in schizophrenia research extends into two important areas: (1) In the absence of sound theory, the links between the concepts being investigated and the operations that define the concepts are excessively weak. "Unless a series of intervening concepts, each in themselves capable of operational definition and with clear superordinate and subordinate implications, are provided, other research workers are chaotically free to attach almost any operational definition to the original concepts [Bannister, 1968, p. 184]." (2) Little consideration is given the sequence of events involved in the connections between the variables under study and the behaviors that define schizophrenia. "The tendency is for research workers in the field to be preoccupied with the question of defining the "condition' rather than hypothesizing a process—hence the popularity of the group discrimination research designs [p. 185]." Bannister's main points promote several ancillary arguments to which we now turn. The reader is herewith alerted to the ease with which platonic forms (idiographic solutions) are silently intruded into the otherwise pure methods of mechanistic science.

A CASE STUDY OF THEORY ARTICULATION DIFFICULTIES—ATTENTION DEFICIT

The brief review of the series of short-lived hypotheses given in Chapter 2 can be regarded as a sampling of case studies of unsuccessful attempts at articulating theory with the "facts" of schizophrenia. A more extended example will illuminate the kinds of difficulties to which Bannister has directed our attention.

In 1964, Silverman published a review paper in which he drew conclusions such as the following: "Extreme scanning and/or field articulation perceptual dispositions characterize the attention response style of schizophrenics. . . . Long term involvement in the schizophrenic resolution appears to be associated with change in attention response style [pp. 375-376]."

McGhie and Chapman (1961), in an earlier review, had offered an apparently related explanation of schizophrenic function: The earliest reported symptoms of a schizophrenic illness indicate that a primary disorder is a decrease in the selective and inhibitory functions of attention (p. 114).

The investigators conducted studies to explore the extreme scanning dispositions which presumably characterize the attention response style of schizophrenics. Schooler and Silverman (1969), for example, carried out a factor analysis of a variety of types of performance scores, using schizophrenics as subjects. They report a "scanning control factor" that accounts for a large part of the variability in the performances on their tests. The writers go on to speculate about the relationship between scanning anomalies and the behavior used to diagnose a person as *schizophrenic*. For example, "it is apparent that a highly significant relationship exists between extensive visual scanning of the environment and the group of traits that we have interpreted as behavior-guardedness [p. 468]." It is unnecessary to comment on the lack of utility of these loosely stated principles and conclusions, and on the possible implications that would follow from using a term such as "extreme scanning disposition." Rather, we note some additional findings that illuminate the concept "attention response style."

To gather data for their factor analytic study of schizophrenic performance, Schooler and Silverman measured "scanning control" by taking accuracy measurements from subjects who had been instructed to adjust a variable-sized disc so that it "looked exactly like the size of the disc he was holding in his hand [p. 462]." The variable-sized disc was located at a distance from the subject, so that the retinal image projected by a particular disc would be smaller than the image cast by a hand held disc of similar size.

Using the same concept, "scanning control," McKinnon and Singer (1969) employed a size adjustment task as one of the measures for their study. They concluded, "The results failed to support the experimental hypotheses predicting differences in size-judgments and visual scanning behavior of paranoid and non-paranoid schizophrenics and psychotic depressives and control Ss" (p. 247). Some of the samples' score variations appeared to be related to drug effects, and McKinnon and Singer concluded, "The results for drug effects indicated the possibility of confounding drug effects in several previous studies on schizophrenics with tasks taken as indicating scanning behavior [p. 247]."

Spohn, Thetford, and Woodham (1970) set out to explore "relationships between arousal and attention in schizophrenics by concurrent measurement of information processing efficiency, span of apprehension, arousal level, and reactivity to the task in schizophrenic and normal Ss [p. 114]." They connected their work to the attentional deficit hypothesis by the use of measures of level of arousal and reactivity. Span of apprehension procedures were used to assess the "scanning skills" of the subjects in this study. Subjects fixated on an "X" in a visual matrix onto which a six-letter array was then projected. The subjects then wrote into a 3-by-2 matrix those letters which they recalled having seen. Schizophrenics, these investigators conclude, showed constantly poorer performance on this span of apprehension task. The acceptance of this conclusion, however, depends on accepting their assumption that they had statistically controlled for the very high correlation between measures of span of apprehension and measures of vocabulary and memory. The schizophrenic sample was decidedly inferior on the two latter measures. Nevertheless, the findings relative to relationships between measures of span of apprehension and arousal level represent the main concern of this study. The attention deficit hypothesis would have required that the subjects whose performance suggests that they were poor on span of apprehension should have shown unusual arousal patterns, since it was assumed the unusual arousal accounted for the poorer span of apprehension. Spohn, Thetford, and Woodham make the following final statement:

> If the SCL (Skin Conductance Level) and the HR (Heart Rate) level scores are interpreted as reflecting individual differences in level of arousal, then the inference must be that arousal level, within the range of variation obtained in the present samples, and information-processing efficiency are not related [p. 122].

Cash, Neale, and Cromwell (1972), taking up the earlier work of Lawson, McGhie, and Chapman (1967), investigated whether schizophrenics do or do not function less efficiently than do normals on a "full report span of apprehension task." In their study, subjects watched an empty 4-by-4 matrix, over which either four letters or eight letters were randomly spread—that is, either four of the 16 squares contained a letter or eight of the 16 squares contained letters. The subjects then reported the letters they had seen on the display. Scores depended upon how many letters were correctly reported. One notices that this "full report" approach is quite similar—if not somewhat more complex—than that used by Spohn et al. (1969). Recall that Spohn et al. concluded that the schizophrenics performed more poorly than did the normal control subjects. Cash et al. arrive at the following:

> The critical finding in the present study is the absence of a schizophrenic deficit in span of apprehension when assessed by the full report technique. The most parsimonious interpretation of this result is that no deficit is manifested by the schizophrenic group as compared to the control group [p. 325].

Royer and Friedman (1973) continued the study of scanning time in the information-processing activity of schizophrenics. They manipulated two independent variables, in addition to the schizophrenia-normal variable. They varied the complexity of the information to be processed, and they included a hospitalized-normal sample (paraplegic persons) to be compared to the hospitalized-schizophrenic and the nonhospitalized-normal group. An extrapolation of theory relative to information-processing deficit in schizophrenia, coupled with theory regarding short- and long-term memory function in information-processing, led them to predict as follows: First, the schizophrenics would perform poorly, relative to the nonschizophrenics, on both the simple and the complex information displays. Second, the schizophrenics would show a greater loss in function, relative to the loss shown by the normal subjects, in processing the simpler material.

Royer and Friedman's results present the usual interpretive difficulties. First, the hospitalized normal paraplegic subjects performed more poorly than did both the reactive schizophrenics and the nonhospitalized normals, their performance being much like that of the process schizophrenics. Second, the decrements in performance that resulted from introducing complexity into the stimulus display were equal across all the subject samples. In other words, the decrease in effectiveness of schizophrenic subjects, as a result of increasing stimulus complexity, was no different from the normals.

Royer and Friedman conjecture on the possible reasons for the paraplegics' performance being no less "deficient" than the performance of the schizophrenic groups. Among their conjectures, Royer and Friedman suggest that institutionalization might well account for the deficit shown by the paraplegics. We have already discussed the notion of "hospitalization" as a variable that affects performance, perhaps more than does the ephemeral variable schizophrenia. The finding that the complexity of the stimuli did not differentially affect the different diagnostic groups is a direct disconfirmation of the "attentional deficit hypothesis."

Davison and Neale (1974) tried to nail down the source of some of the contradictions of the earlier work on attentional problems in information processing. Neale had been involved in a series of previous studies (Cash, Neale, & Cromwell, 1972; Neale, McIntyre, Fox, & Cromwell, 1969) which showed that schizophrenics might perform differently under different informational and response conditions. Davison and Neale (1974) attempted to determine whether schizophrenics performed more poorly when discriminations during the search process were complicated by distracting stimuli of increasing similarity to the target stimulus. Like Royer and Friedman (1964), Davison and Neale found that normals and schizophrenics were equally handicapped by the increased complexity of the stimulus information. Their findings, however, led them to conclude that the schizophrenics did show a deficit, and they stated, "The deficit occurs because the schizophrenic is simply slower than the nonschizophrenic at carrying out these operations, and as a result processed fewer letters [p. 685]." This conclusion, however, leaves them at odds with the conclusions reached by Cash, Neale, and Cromwell (1972), which indicated that in the "full-report span of apprehension task" the schizophrenics processed as many letters as did the nonschizophrenics. Such contradictions are usually met by the ritual expression: more research is needed. The never-ending search for the "crucial symptom" of schizophrenia continues.

Kopfstein and Neale (1972) had also turned their attention to some basic conceptual problems. First, "the primary aim of the present investigation was to study the relationships among several of the tasks from which deviant attentional mechanisms have been inferred [p. 294];'' and ''the second purpose . . . was to assess the relationships between several dimensions of individual differences and performance on the laboratory tasks [p. 295].'' The parallel conclusions derived from this study were as follows:

> It is clear from the correlation data that the tasks employed in the present investigation share little common variance. Therefore, in contrast to what has become a common assumption, these data suggest that performance on these tasks cannot be subsumed by a general attention construct [p. 296] . . . The individual difference variables (e.g., schizophrenic-nonschizophrenic, good versus poor premorbid adjustment) failed to correlate with our laboratory task variables. Neither classical nosological categories, nor the individual difference variables were strongly related to performance [p. 297].

Alternative Approaches to Attention Deficit

With studies of this kind, Neale and his co-workers (Cash, Neale, & Cromwell, 1972; Kopfstein & Neale, 1972) had support for the conclusion that the span of apprehension concept was not sufficient to encompass an assumed, universal, attentional deficit in the schizophrenic process. The failure to articulate this particular concept to the disease paradigm, however, does not require one to abandon the attentional deficit hypothesis. General experimental psychologists who had been working actively with memory and attention (for example, Craik & Lockhart, 1972; Moray, 1970; Treisman, Squire, & Green, 1974) had introduced a variety of new ways to consider and study attentional processes. Researchers could adapt these novel approaches as they continued the search for the attentional deficit that might explain the crazy thinking attributed to people diagnosed as schizophrenic.

Much experimental work on attention is derived from an everyday observation. As people go about their daily business, they are exposed to vast amounts of change in the distal and proximal, or internal, ecology (Sarbin, 1962, 1969b). Much of this change can activate sensory processes. Yet people do not ''pay attention'' to all of this sensory input. By some principle, some of it is ''selected'' for ''central processing'' whereas the large portion never ''goes on attention.'' Yet, as Broadbent (1971), Moray (1970), Treisman (1964) and others have shown, this ''other information'' is processed relevant to a person's ongoing cognitive and motor systems.

The potential value of ideas derived from these observations immediately attracts someone searching for what is ''wrong'' with people who persist in their ''crazy'' conduct. Perhaps these disordered persons do not keep apart the ''separate channels'' of input? Perhaps they cannot focus on the relevant channel? A variety of technologies and scores of intriguing hypotheses are available. Four studies generated by the selective attention approach are herewith outlined and assessed.

Korboot and Damiani (1976) reviewed the work on signal detection and the processing of separate but simultaneously arriving stimulus input. The research shows that people may "attend" to one chain of information, while psychologically processing simultaneously arriving information. Korboot and Damiani designed stimulus sequences so that they could study patterns of responses in order to describe the nature of "cross channel" interference. For example, subjects were given the task of detecting instances of digits repeated in pairs as they listened to a target string of digits being transmitted to one ear. Meanwhile, another string of irrelevant digits was transmitted to the other ear. The competing irrelevant string also contained instances of repeated digits. By using this arrangement, the investigators expected to determine whether or not schizophrenics suffer from an inability to "filter out" irrelevant stimuli. Such an inability would reflect an "attentional deficit."

Subjects released an electrical contact switch to indicate that they had detected an appropriate two-digit sequence. The reaction time to release this key was used as a measure of processing efficiency. It is assumed that more efficient attentional processes would allow for faster reaction. The mean reaction time of the schizophrenic samples were higher than were the mean scores of the nonschizophrenic samples. The schizophrenics—particularly the chronic nonparanoid schizophrenics—operated much like the nonschizophrenics except that they took more time to respond to target stimuli. Korboot and Damiani persist in perceiving a deficit in schizophrenia. "This [study] suggests that a basic deficit in schizophrenia appears to be a function not of sensory sensitivity but of time taken to process stimuli [p. 294]." The slowing is presumed to reflect "attention-refractory periods," "a protective mechanism against state of information overload [p. 294]."

It is important to note that mixed neurotics also functioned like the chronic schizophrenics, and that these two samples were the lowest educated of the samples and had the lowest mean vocabulary scores. Korboot and Damiani offer no explanations of the "neurotic deficit."

Davies-Osterkamp, Rist, and Bangert (1977) followed a different complex methodology to investigate attentional deficit among chronic nonparanoid schizophrenics. Davies-Osterkamp et al. examined a proposition put forth by Broen (1973) that among chronic nonparanoid schizophrenics there is a narrowing of the breadth of attention. Monitoring of the environment is restricted so that sensory input from a single dimension tends to take over central attention processors, to the relative exclusion of input from competing sensory modalities. Davies-Osterkamp et al. assessed the attentional functioning of schizophrenics by having them respond when one or another of a pair of stimuli was turned off. In some instances, two visual or two auditory stimuli were presented simultaneously. In other instances, one visual and one auditory stimulus was presented. Other conditions of presentation also were controlled and varied. For example, sometimes the subjects were prepared to have the light go off each time it was presented in the tone/light pair. At other times, the subject was uncertain about which stimulus would go off. Davies-Osterkamp et al. measured the time between cessation of stimulus and onset of the subject's response. The schizophrenic sample responded more slowly under all conditions. On the whole, schizophrenics and normals, relative to their basic skill in responding, were equally handicapped when decisions required that subjects take into account information from two different modalities. Davies-Osterkamp et al. are temporarily moved toward adding their conclusions to the interpretation offered, above, for Korboot and Damiani's findings: "From this, it would even be possible to conclude that chronic schizophrenics do not have any specific attentional disorders, and that variance between the groups can be explained solely by the schizophrenics' retardation in information processing [p. 467]."

We must note, however, that they, like so many other researchers committed to the disease model, did not completely endorse this position. They did squeeze out a point of small difference between the schizophrenics' performance and the performance of the normals, and they ended by encouraging further efforts to tease out the schizophrenic deficit.

Oltmanns (1978), who had been associated with Neale and his colleagues, designed a study to isolate the source of the sought-after schizophrenic attentional deficit. Oltmanns was able to make use of elaborations of conceptualizations regarding the processing of sensory input. Investigators like Craik and Lockhart (1972) had described processing of sensory input in terms of short-term memory and long-term memory. The conceptualization requires a formulation in which sensory input is retained in short-term store, where it is matched to a schematic code drawn from existing long-term memory. After appropriate coding, the input is stored in long-term memory. Retrieval from long-term memory then involves "tapping into" the code involved in the storage. Oltmanns wanted to show that the schizophrenic attentional deficit could be attributed to the effects of distraction stimuli which interfered with the coding and storing of information retained in short-term memory.

Oltmanns arranged digit series and letter series into several kinds of sequential presentations. In some cases, digits were presented in series by a female voice while interspersed between the target digits, a male voice presented another digit. The digits read by the male were to be ignored. The digits read by the female were to be repeated at the end of the presentation of the series. Compared to manics and normal subjects, schizophrenics did relatively poorly on those series that were interspersed with distractors. Similarly, when to-be-recalled words were presented in series with distractors, the schizophrenic sample again showed a greater average deficit. Additionally, the average performance of the normal sample was improved by slowing the rate of presentation of items, which was not the case with the schizophrenic sample. Oltmanns concludes: "The most parsimonious explanation for this pattern of results is that the introduction of irrelevant words interferes with the schizophrenic's ability to recode relevant words in short-term memory into a less transient form [p. 223]." Oltmanns attributes this to the fact that this kind of recoding requires an active process which is disrupted and made less efficient by extraneous stimuli.

Oltmanns does note one matter which is also relevant to the Asarnow and MacCrimmon (1978) study of attentional deficit in schizophrenia. Oltmanns claims that "the deterioration in active process is not due to inappropriate coding [p. 224]." Nothing in his study's design seems aimed at isolating the coding categories that the schizophrenic subjects might or might not use. The categories used in the coding process are of major concern, and Oltmanns is correct in noting this issue, though he had no control on coding categories which his subjects might use.

Asarnow and MacCrimmon (1978) assessed span of apprehension and distraction effects in order to analyze schizophrenic attentional deficit. Two tasks were set before subjects. First, subjects watched a screen onto which were projected sets of digits. The sets varied in length, from one digit to ten digits. Subjects were to report each time they observed the 7 in the displayed set. Second, subjects watched the same screen onto which were projected a continuous series of digits. Simultaneously, a continuous series of digits was read through headphones. Subjects were required to indicate each time they heard a 7.

Asarnow and MacCrimmon found that, on the average, acute and remitted schizophrenics succeeded less in identifying the embedded 7 when the series was increased in length. They then speak of "impaired performance on the span of apprehension by remitted schizophrenic outpatients [p. 604]." In making this statement they appear to contradict the conclusions of Cash, Neale, and Cromwell (1972), but their bending of their interpretations allows them to say that their findings parallel those of Neale and his colleagues.

The schizophrenic sample also made more errors in identifying the target digit as they watched the continuously presented series. In this distraction condition, they not only failed to report the 7 when it was present, they also tended to report a 7 when it had not been projected.

Another result from the Asarnow and MacCrimmon study corroborates a finding relative to a basic issue of these studies. These investigators had available the means of assessing the individual variation on three putative measures of attention. One measure was an index of span of apprehension. One measure was the number of digits erroneously identified as 7s during the continuously presented series. Another measure was the number of times the subject failed to identify a 7 that was present. The investigators computed a correlation coefficient between all possible combinations of these scores, for the subjects in the two different schizophrenic samples. "None of the four correlations attained statistical significance. This finding indicates that different kinds of nonrelevant stimuli vary in their effects [p. 603]." This finding also confirms the results of the Kopfstein and Neale (1972) study. These researchers said that their "data suggest that performance on these tasks cannot be subsumed by a general attention construct [p. 296]." Apparently investigators can take very divergent perspectives in their interpretations.

An Effort to Concretize

An extreme example of research guided by idiographic postulates is found in the report of Cegalis, Leen, and Solomon (1977). They carried the attention-narrowing hypothesis to its concrete limits. If one may speak of narrowed attention, then one should be able to relate that narrowing to the narrowing of the visual field. Cegalis et al. devised a procedure in which people were presented information at varied distances from the center of their visual field. These researchers then evaluated the inspection strategies used by schizophrenics and normals as they worked with this information. They conclude that chronic schizophrenics may use strategies that require greater numbers of sampling actions, with more head and eye movements, to acquire the information on the periphery of the visual field. Thus they "may process information in a serial and mechanical fashion [p. 497]." One might also wonder if the factors of the age of the chronic schizophrenics (mean age 47.6 years), their time in hospital (mean, 8.8 years), their lower cognitive skills (mean verbal IQ, 94.5, compared to normals' mean verbal IQ, 100.8), and their levels of medication would cumulatively account for their unusual motor patterns in completing the experimental tasks. (It should be noted that Cegalis et al. did separately correlate age and medication level with response accuracy scores. The individual correlation coefficients were not statistically significant.)

The Status of the Science after Study of the Attention Deficit Hypothesis

This case study of the attention deficit hypothesis reflects the usual state of affairs in the normal science of schizophrenia. A hypothesis—presumably locating the "crucial symptom" of schizophrenia—is advanced. Complicated, contradictory, and nondefining techniques are introduced to provide assessment of the dependent variable presumably related to the disease. The diagnostic category, presented as the independent variable, is confounded by the hospitalization variable. Cognitive skill differences contaminate efforts to differentiate the schizophrenic sample from the nonschizophrenic sample. Numerous extraneous variables intrude to complicate interpretation. There are serious questions about measures of the basic phenomena. Findings are contradicted. More and more esoteric hypotheses flow from the original hypothesis. The phenomena become more and more difficult to articulate to the overall model of the selective and inhibitory functions of attention, a model being fruitfully developed in the laboratories of experimental psychology. Investigators grasp the technology being developed in the laboratories, applying it pell-mell to the problems of the clinic. More confusion results. The laboratory psychologists, meanwhile, move on to different conceptions and technologies which in turn become available to scientists seeking a way to define the hoped-for deficit to explain why some people persist in their unwanted conduct.

Fifteen years of research into the schizophrenic attentional deficit hypothesis shows the power of the disease model. The model operates so ineluctably, with such subtlety, that the prior question is rarely asked: What common features of the conduct of the persons ultimately diagnosed as schizophrenic suggest a deficit in attention? Among the studies reviewed above, we find only one (Oltmanns, 1978) which alludes to a relationship between attentional deficit and "schizophrenics' use of language [p. 213]." "Communication failures result when thought-disordered speakers fail to provide their listener with adequate referents for noun phrases or other links across clausal boundaries [p. 224]." Oltmanns refers to his work on the effect of distraction on processing input from short- to long-term memory. These processes presumably, "allow the speaker to monitor the adequacy of informational links between successive clauses [pp. 224-5]." Thus Oltmanns seems to expect his reader to go through the following theory chain: Attentional deficit—disordered thought—inappropriate speech—communication failure—diagnosis as a schizophrenic. In the long chain of causality, the attentional deficit would be explored as the root etiological variable. Would one be required to look to attentional deficit to explain the communication failure that precedes diagnosis?

IDIOGRAPHIC FORMULAE IN THEORIES OF SCHIZOPHRENIA

Oltmanns (1978), at least, attempts to honor an obligation to explain the social interaction that leads to the schizophrenia diagnosis. He might, as do many investigators, simply recite a litany of other, better known investigators who have tried to show that attention deficit is the basic flaw in the person of schizophrenics. Having pointed out that others had preceded him, Oltmanns could then report his contribution to the discovery of what's wrong with schizophrenics.

At this juncture, it is instructive to remind the reader that the underlying premise of studies into attentional deficit—the premise that schizophrenics are generally inferior—can be traced to an adherence to the idiographic world view, the metaphor of form. Philosophers or scientists who adopt an idiographic world view set out to find the form—the identity—common to two events. They search out the presence of reporting an unverifiable system of beliefs, which is a form of *badness;* and low ability in using syntactical structures, which is also a form of *badness.*

Both of these bad events, then, should predictably appear in a schizophrenic, which is also a form of badness. If both events are present in the bad schizophrenic, then a major truth test of the idiographic world view has been satisfied.

In fine, the idiographic solution is no more than a refined description of the essential *badness,* the flawed form, of the schizophrenic. Rommetveit (1974) refers to the use of such solutions as formist escapism. From the point of view of the advocates of mechanistic science, the science presumed to guide the study of a disease, the absence of reliable antecedent-consequent statements is a cop-out. To say "It's in the very nature of schizophrenics to be flawed in cognition, affect, and action" is to say little that is interesting or useful. To derive a satisfactory mechanistic solution, one must develop formulations to explain the causal linkages that relate to these flaws. As investigators do this, they can be observed to refer back to prior flaws to explain the cause of current flaws. The ultimate, of course, is a bad gene; and one is then left with the most basic kind of idiographic solution. As we suggested in Chapter 7, even genetic action requires a contextualist theoretical frame, but investigators of psychological matters have been constrained from adopting contextualist metaphors. Theory articulation has followed either mechanistic metaphor or, often naively or in desperation, idiographic metaphors.

As we analyze the basic core sample of schizophrenia studies, we conclude that schizophrenia investigators are, in the first place, reluctant theorists. In making judgments about the adequacy of theoretical articulation in the research reports under scrutiny, we recognize the operation of our own bias. How does one decide that the theoretical statements in research reports are adequately drawn out? Should one expect any particular form of theoretical statements in a research report? Applying our judgments as conservatively as possible, we estimated that not more than half the 374 core studies have presented adequate theoretical justification for the hypotheses. In the remainder, the writers made only crude statements, or no statement at all, about the presuppositions (models) from which their hypotheses developed.

It could be that the authors of the more atheoretical papers attempt to serve science by empirically linking events to the disease known as schizophrenia. As an example, Salzinger and Pisoni (1961) investigated means by which schizophrenic subjects can be conditioned to generate high response levels using self-referring affective terms and words, such as "I am satisfied," "I like him," etc. There is no effort to explain why the generation of these kinds of verbalizations are particularly relevant to the study of schizophrenia, nor is there any effort to give a theoretical rationale for having observed hospitalized schizophrenics rather than, let us say, devil-worshippers or self-declared witches. Broekma and Rosenbaum (1975) report their study of cutaneous sensitivity in schizophrenics. Their review of previous studies seems to be written to document the relationship between schizophrenia and sensory receptive deficits. They conclude that "schizophrenics are less sensitive to cutaneous stimuli than are normals," and that these differences "were significantly greater on the leg than on the face and hand [p. 33]." Broekma and Rosenbaum suggest nothing to provide a theoretical linkage between cutaneous sensitivity on one's leg and the common features of conduct that allow a psychiatrist to apply the diagnosis, schizophrenia. Green (1978) says, "Since 1973, evidence has accumulated showing that there are failures to achieve the normal linkages between the cerebral hemispheres in schizophrenia, and it is possible that some schizophrenic symptoms follow from this basic fault [p. 472]." He is able to say that "the relations between interhemispheric transfer deficits and schizophrenic symptoms remain to be investigated [p. 478]."

Such studies follow from adherence to strict positivism; the investigators simply seek to establish linkages. Should this metaphysic be taken seriously as a guide to research on deviance, one could expect scientific journals to publish reports relating the incidence of warts to the incidence of neurotic depression; or the correlation of severity of dandruff to length of hospitalization for hysterical inactivation. One may also concur with the frequent observation that even the strictest positivist does use an implicit theoretical structure. One particular structure is easily revealed as one scrutinizes the foregoing studies. The basic postulate is: People diagnosed as schizophrenic are flawed.

Our analysis further shows that about one-third (133 studies) of the total 374 papers used one common research objective: The research is done simply to show that the mean of the schizophrenic sample's performance is poor or inadequate on some preselected experimental task. The investigators who report these papers satisfy the theoretical demands of their normal science by a variant of the following (sometimes tacit) proposition: "Schizophrenics are generally in a bad way, and therefore they should perform in a bad way on a test of Z." Thus one article states that since schizophrenics are "inefficient" they will show more generalization to homonyms than will normals (Peastrel, 1964). Another tells us that reactive schizophrenics, being more *unstable* than process schizophrenics, show more variability in guessing "heads" or "tails" when asked to guess the outcome of a coin flip (Zlotowski & Bakan, 1963). Schizophrenics will be relatively poor at eliminating inadequate responses after these responses have proved to be ineffective (Crumpton, 1963). Schizophrenics are predicted to show poor ability to shift from functioning within one sensory modality to functioning in another sensory modality (Kristofferson, 1967). Nonparanoid schizophrenics would choose more childlike responses in a word association test than would the paranoid schizophrenics, who are less regressed (Youkilis & DeWolfe, 1975). Another writer says, "It seems clear that some schizophrenics are responsive to syntactical structure and are able to use it to increase the recall of verbal material [p. 42]," then sets out to see if different categories of schizophrenics hear, recall, and process differently (Carpenter, 1976). Or perhaps, "If eye directionality is taken as a measure of (cerebral) hemispheric activation, we may conclude that schizophrenics activate their left hemisphere to a larger extent than do controls [Gur, 1978, p. 234]." The theoretical connections between these somewhat esoteric variables and becoming tagged as schizophrenic are left to the imaginative skill of the readers of these studies. These samplings from the 133 idiographically inclined studies represent the weakest of the "schizophrenics are in a bad way" hypothesis. Again admitting our bias, we generously classified as adequate any report that spoke of linkages between any variable, no matter how vague, that mediated between poor performance on the dependent variable and becoming diagnosed as schizophrenic. We accepted as theoretically adequate, for example, statements that proposed that the schizophrenic has "withdrawn from social contact," and that this condition led to the prediction of inadequate performance on such-and-such a task (Lerner, 1963; Spohn & Wolk, 1963). Another research group theorized that schizophrenics come from family situations that give them poor models. Schizophrenics will, therefore, reflect some of their "badness" by their performance on the dependent variables in the study (Baxter, Becker, & Hooks, 1963). Another frequent proposition holds that schizophrenics are anxious (when chronic, they are no longer regarded as anxious), and as a result, will perform less effectively on any number of tasks. Higgins and Mednick (1963) hypothesized that high arousal will interfere with associative learning, and that this would be reflected in the finding of greater reminiscence among early schizophrenics (high arousal) than among later schizophrenics. Draguns (1963) expected acute schizophrenics to take longer to develop categories and respond to categorizing tasks. DeWolfe (1962) expected that personal references—apparently assumed to be emotional—and reaction times would be less among reactive (more anxious) than among process (less anxious) schizophrenics.

Youkilis and DeWolfe (1975) attempt to make use of "the conceptual sophistication gained in recent years [p. 36]" to revive the proposition that schizophrenics are regressed; that is, that there is an "observed similarity between schizophrenics and children [p. 37]." From this position, of course, we would deduce that schizophrenics should behave like children by showing "frequent selection of word association alternatives more characteristic of children over those more characteristic of adults [p. 37]." LaRusso (1978) showed paranoid schizophrenics two different series of videotaped materials. One series consisted of 40 shots of "genuine facial expressions," whereas the other contained 40 shots of "simulated facial expressions [p. 465]." The theoretical reasons for deriving the expectations are not easily discovered by reading the introduction to LaRusso's article; nevertheless, she hypothesized, among other things, that "a greater sensitivity to nonverbal cues would elicit more conflict in a paranoid subject when he is presented with simulated or posed stimuli, and would result in reduced accuracy if the pose or simulated expression were used as the basis for a correct answer [p. 465]." Though LaRusso's discussion of her study does conclude with a set of agile verbal exercises, the theory articulation does little to take a reader past the proposition: Paranoid schizophrenics simply behave poorly.

Nowhere did the simplistic quality of the idiographic solution—the "generalized badness hypothesis"—of schizophrenia appear more strikingly than it does in studies on concept functioning in schizophrenia. The belief that schizophrenics perform inadequately (badly) in tasks calling for classifying or categorizing, or in tasks involving the extraction of relations, has had a venerable history. Study after study has attempted to support or clarify this hoary belief. The belief, however, fails to articulate "schizophrenia" with the theory construction of correlative sciences (see Feffer, 1961; Harrow, Himmelhoch, Tucker, Hersh, & Quinlan, 1972; Leventhal, McGaughran, & Moran, 1959; Sturm, 1964). For example, a subject is given an object and is then asked to sort from an accompanying group all those objects that belong with the original sorting object. In doing this, an investigator might seek to verify the simple hypothesis that schizophrenics will show a "cognitive deficit." One might also ask about relationships between the proposed deficit and a person's construction and use of those internal representations that function as "prototypes" for classes. Some investigators do provide models into which these kinds of questions may be framed (Hyman & Frost, 1974; Posner & Keele, 1970). Following these available models, and, thereby explicitly attempting to articulate schizophrenic research to this broader line of cognitive studies, investigators not only would avoid the idiographic solution—asserting the general inferiority of schizophrenics—they would also gain from recognizing the utility of a contextualist model that stresses the person's schemata as a context for the stimuli the investigator presents. Such recognition aids in encouraging the view that all personal categories, schemata, prototypes, and implicit personality theories, are essentially "idiosyncratic," and subject to individualized alteration. (See Chapter 10.)

Adapting Advancing Technology to the Search for Schizophrenic Badness

Another feature of the problems of theory-articulation deserves note. In efforts that stem from the objective of locating the "crucial differentiating symptom," investigators try out all kinds of novel technologies to test all manner of hypotheses. We have already noted the use of information-processing technology (see Cash, Neale, & Cromwell, 1972; Royer & Friedman, 1973) to study "attentional deficit." Another model has included the conditioning technology which has been available for a long time; and it would be expected that someone would come along and hypothesize that schizophrenics are "poor conditioners." The investigations continue (Ax, Banford, Beckett, Fretz, & Gottlieb, 1970; Drennen, Gallman, & Sausser, 1969), offering a stream of currently nonintegratable results, which might be coherently interpreted at that time in the future when we are more clear about the events known as the conditioning process.

Experimental psychologists have worked out a very efficient set of techniques to measure the processes by which persons maintain size constancy when dealing with distant objects which project "small" retinal images. Another laboratory-developed technology thereby became available, and investigators could create more hypotheses concerning the scanning process deficiencies that might afflict schizophrenics (Magaro, 1969; Schooler & Silverman, 1969; Strauss, Foureman, & Parwatiker, 1974) to cause them to perform poorly when estimating the size of distant objects.

Langer, Stein, & Rosenberg (1969) found a ready-made dependent measure in a well-known "cognitive interference" task, where subjects were required to recognize words printed in inks of colors that presumably created cognitive interference. That is, the word "black" might be printed in red ink. Of course, the hypothesis stated that the schizophrenics would perform *less* effectively than would the normals.

Though the experimental design known as the prisoner's dilemma has come under harsh negative criticism (Nemeth, 1972), investigators would not avoid this rather clever means of collecting data on schizophrenia. Harford and Solomon (1969) invented a hypothesis predicting differences between the performance of paranoids and the performance of nonclassified persons asked to build strategies for the kinds of interpersonal relationships involved in resolving the prisoner's dilemma.

For many years, the *Cloze Technique* was used in reading research as an index of difficulty. People report on the comprehensibility of text in which words— every third word, for example—have been consecutively eliminated. "Difficult" material is material not comprehended when relatively few terms are eliminated. One is not surprised to find the technique appearing as a means of investigating the "understandability" of the speech of the parents of schizophrenics (Becker & Finkel, 1969). Knowing that people would rather not be exposed to high-intensity sound, one could wonder if schizophrenics report pain on hearing loud sound, and how do these persons compare to normals? What solid theoretical steps would lead to the prediction (Levine & Whitney, 1970) that schizophrenics have a lower threshold of unpleasantness and that they would report unpleasant reactions at lower decibal levels?

Kendler and Kendler (1962, 1969) have worked out a neat technique by which to study how persons develop and use categorizing dimensions. Where a neat technology is reported, can a schizophrenia study be far behind? Studies are reported (e.g., Nolan, 1970, 1974; Nolan & Anderson, 1973; O'Keefe & De-Wolfe, 1973), the objective of which is to show that one or another kind of schizophrenic has one or another kind of difficulty in working with discrimination tasks that require a person to remain within one dimension or move to another dimension to categorize experimental stimuli.

Numerous investigators have explored individual differences in skills whereby relevant, problem-oriented stimuli are separated out of displays containing irrelevant, nonuseful stimuli. This work has promoted a belief that one can observe intraindividual, generalized approaches that allow a person to be described as *field independent*, or *field dependent*. For some reason, field dependency is the "bad" end of this dimension; and we are not surprised to find that it has been predicted (Magaro & Vojtisek, 1971) that the particularly bad schizophrenics would do particularly badly by being more field dependent than are other kinds of schizophrenics.

We note one further illustration of the effort to find what is "wrong" with schizophrenics by using another technological development of experimental psychology. Investigators have followed a model which assumes that one can describe a person's perceptions of social relationships by speaking about how the person places representations of human figures in the two-dimensional space delimited by a felt-board, to which the cutout figures adhere. How can one resist the hypothesis that there is something wrong with the ways in which schizophrenics place these figures (see Thornton & Gottheil, 1971)?

The Conclusions from Idiographic Hypotheses

The list of illustrations could be extended, but the point has been established. So long as one can follow the idiographic hypothesis that schizophrenics are in a bad way, investigators can easily adapt any new measurement technique that allows them to gather data that presumably describes a dependent variable. The main hypothesis is straightforward: Schizophrenics will perform more poorly. It would be useful, of course, to have more elaborate explication of the theory out of which the measurement technique has developed. And it would be even more useful, if one fully subscribes to the disease model, to have means of articulating the disease model to the theory that generated the dependent variable.

Even the briefest involvement with theory-building efforts in general psychology exposes the difficulties in defining everyday psychological functioning. Against this background, it appears futile to mark off the functioning of those people called schizophrenic and then to identify that functioning as a special variant of a poorly defined general human function. What, after all, is the quality of the "normal" functioning relative to the "diseased" functioning which the investigator intends to define?

A report published by Wagener and Hartsough (1974) brings this general issue into sharp focus. These investigators arranged their study so that they compared schizophrenics, alcoholics, and normals—standard procedure in schizophrenic research. They also took another step. They graded all subjects, regardless of diagnostic category, on a measure of previous competence in in-life social situations. This step then allowed them to compare outcomes of measurements in terms of level of social competence as well as by level of diagnosis. They used Magaro's (1967) measure of ability to discriminate figural or spatial differences in either the presence or absence of social censure. Their data allowed the strong conclusion that "schizophrenics, alcoholics, and normals performed quite similarly on this task when social competence was held constant [p. 115]." In short, when the subjects were located on a definable dimension that allowed the conduct of all kinds of subjects to be classed negatively or positively, it mattered little if the subject was called alcoholic or schizophrenic or normal. Performance is related to the defining dimension and not to the gratuitously appended diagnostic label. The thrust of our analysis suggests that such findings will become more common when investigators become fully aware of the necessity of joining explanations of behavior called schizophrenic to explanations of behavior in general. The foregoing analysis supports an obvious conclusion: Efforts to "go eclectic" by appending idiographic formulations to the mechanistic disease model cannot lend clarity to the study of unwanted deviance. Investigators who take recourse to the "schizophrenics are in a bad way" formula have only reaffirmed the negative social judgment that was pronounced when the subjects used in the investigation were officially given their stigmatizing label.

A set of rhetorical questions will help illuminate the implications of this intrusion of idiography. Why have scientists failed to discover a condition that makes a human perform in a fantastically "better" way than most normal people perform? If there is an undiscovered "something" that allows us to predict that thousands of our fellow citizens "suffer" debilitation in countless psychological functions, why is there not an undiscovered "something" that generates massive improvement of psychological functioning? Why do the devils have all the power? Why doesn't some of the evil quality of schizophrenia cause the schizophrenic to do exceptionally well on some psychological function? The fact is that Harway and Salzman (1964) did find that the "abnormals" in their study actually performed more accurately on tasks of size judgment; similarly, Thornton and Gottheil (1971) gathered data that shows that their schizophrenic subjects more accurately reproduced spatial arrangements than did their normal subjects. Wouldn't findings of this kind stimulate other scientists to search out other areas where schizophrenics function "better" than normals? A close look at disease conditions will show that some aspects of physiological function are "better" during a particular illness. For example, waste products can be removed more rapidly. Phagocyte production rises during some illnesses.

The answers to the foregoing rhetorical questions are, of course, obvious. The propensity to make predictions of performance decrements—to ascribe a state of "generalized badness" to people called schizophrenics—reflects the intrusion of idiographic causal explanations into the mechanistic illness metaphor. One always expects poor performance from a schizophrenic because it is in the extant form, in the nature, of a schizophrenic to perform poorly! This then is the precise statement of a law generated by an idiographic paradigm. Having discovered the identical character of two forms, a follower of an idiographic paradigm has defined a *law*. In the case of the study of schizophrenia, one finds an abundance of hypotheses and group discrimination research designs (Bannister, 1968, p. 185), that seek simply to show the identity of schizophrenia and badness. The scientist need not further explain poor performance since it is assumed from the start that schizophrenics are in a *bad* way.

Two citations show how easily investigators invoke the "bad way hypothesis." Gelburd and Anker (1970) begin the report of their investigation by stating that "virtually every reference made to the performance of schizophrenics in the scientific literature alludes to their relative ineffectiveness when compared to normal Ss [p. 195]," and then proceed to search out the concommitants of this pervasive ineffectiveness. Another investigator (Calhoun, 1970) reports the findings from his doctoral dissertation, and offers the following evidence of the utility and unabashed acceptance of the idiographic paradigm: "As used in the present study, psychological deficit refers to an observable behavior that is called defective, that is, poorer than that expected for an adult [p. 485]."

In a paradigm that constantly seeks efficient causes, a behavior analyst, after witnessing poor performance on a task, would ask: "What variables have a functional relationship to that task?" But this question, legitimate in the context of mechanistic science, all too often disappears after the researcher reports a statistically reliable difference between schizophrenic samples. Rather than focus on the functional relationships, the experimenter takes the demonstration of mean differences as a verification of the discovery of the inherent badness of that poor soul, the schizophrenic. The experimenter has unwittingly slipped into an idiographic posture rather than construct an antecedent-consequent statement. It is as if researchers had convinced themselves that the lore of schizophrenia is not without foundation: Schizophrenics *are* in a bad way!

An advocate of the traditional research strategies could claim that the continual effort to show that schizophrenics are bad is totally legitimate since these investigations are defining the concommitants or outcomes of the disease, schizophrenia. This counterargument is unconvincing in the light of schizophrenia researchers' avoidance of the problem of articulating their abstracted variables to general psychology. The task of explaining the efficient cause of individual differences in behavior is the same task no matter whether we are interested in negatively valued conduct or positively valued conduct. With Bannister (1968), we hold that if ''schizophrenia'' is to be defined, the concepts used in its study must be articulated to an overall psychological theory. The obvious neglect of this activity derives from an inadvertant decision to follow an idiographic metaphysic, revealed by the ''schizophrenics are bad'' hypotheses.

Our criticism of theoretical activity in schizophrenia research is helped along by analysis of the variable, socioeconomic status (SES). Hollingshead and Redlich (1958) reported that 77 percent of the persons originating in the lowest socioeconomic class, diagnosed as psychotic, and remanded to psychiatric care had been referred by others—courts, police, social agencies, other professionals, or families. No person diagnosed as psychotic from an SES Class V (poor folk) background was self-referred. In other words, none of the SES Class V—who make up the largest portion of persons diagnosed as schizophrenic—walks into the office of a professional to announce that he or she is ill. This group has not accepted the disease paradigm as a means of talking about their own negatively valued behaviors (see Sarbin & Mancuso, 1970).

Current normal science appears to ignore the puzzle created by the fact that most people diagnosed as schizophrenic enter psychiatric care through the efforts of other persons. How does one make the assumptive leaps that link behavior required to perform an esoteric laboratory task and, for example, the conduct that leads a harried wife to call the police to take her husband out of their home? What are the assumptions that connect poor performance on a concept utilization task and ''withdrawal'' (a symptom commonly reported in the records of schizophrenics)? Such questions were rarely addressed by the authors of the 374 articles covered by this review. By our count, only 100 reports show any effort to link any psychological malfunctioning to one or another of the behaviors that lead a person to psychiatric referral.

None of these studies offers to identify the efficient causes to explain a man beating his wife, or exhibiting exaggerated religiosity, or withdrawing from the company of his peers. This is not to say that writers completely ignore the need to propose linkages between behavior on experimental tasks and assumed schizophrenic behavior. Many writers tell us (for example, Goodman, 1968), that being unable to perform the function evoked by the experimental tasks produces in schizophrenics an inefficiency that makes it difficult for them to live out their lives. This difficulty-producing inefficiency, the argument continues, produces extended anxiety, or tension, or pressure, which forces the incipient schizophrenic to withdraw from social contact. But there is a strange ingredient in the many recipes that depend on this particular notion. The investigator does not aim at describing a functional relationship between performance on the experimental task and *withdrawal*. The usual aim, rather, is to show an identity between *''schizophrenia''* and the *experimental task performance*. No data are supplied to inform the reader whether the schizophrenics in the sample had in fact exhibited ''withdrawal behavior.''

This same fault is embedded in the numerous studies that begin from the hypothesized deficit in the associative processes of schizophrenics. All these studies are noninforming in regard to what strange associations (if any) characterized the behavior that landed the subject in the hospital. The assumption is that the person who would show idiosyncratic associations in some fashion disrupts the communication patterns that are a part of the culture, and that this disruption forces the person to enter psychiatric care. Again, we have no evidence that the samples in the study were handicapped in their associations. Parenthetically, uncommon associations also appear to be a characteristic of creative poets who win Pulitzer Prizes.

These examples could be extended. How does "overgeneralization" lead to hospitalization? How does conflict in a child's family lead to the behaviors that instigate hospitalization when he or she is an adult? What is the relationship between overestimating the size of a standard figure in a size judgment task, and anhedonia or cognitive slippage? What is the connection between reporting less figural after-effect after satiation on a visual task, and the "symptom," *feeling sexually inadequate*? This set of rhetorical questions highlights the ludicrous character of some of the theoretical links proposed in many of the research reports. The typical report makes no attempt at theoretical linkage between public conduct and experimental variables: 274 of the reports presented no theoretical linkages between the public conduct that leads to hospitalization and the sometimes esoteric measurements. The most common practice followed by the writers of these articles was to imply or express a variant of the idiographic "schizophrenics are in a bad way" assertion.

The practice of predicting poor performance from schizophrenics simply because they have a formal structure of badness is constantly revealed even in articles that do propose linkages between assumed schizophrenic behaviors and the experimental tasks. Payne, Caird, and Laverty (1967) claim that the overgeneralization presumably shown on their overinclusion tasks leads to the faulty conclusions of delusions. Query: Why does overgeneralization lead to *faulty* conclusions, and why are faulty conclusions labelled *delusions*? Everyone overgeneralizes. Everyone draws faulty conclusions, by overgeneralization as well as by other illogical procedures. But not everyone is judged delusional or schizophrenic. But the idiographic paradigm directs us to expect *schizophrenia, overgeneralization*, and *delusion*—all "bad" characteristics—to appear together. Research guided by the hypothesis that schizophrenics are unable to "maintain a segmental set" (Zahn, Rosenthal, & Shakow, 1961) has yet to offer a convincing connection between norm-violating behavior and this inability, other than the tacit assumption that norm violation and inability to hold a segmental set are both negatively valued.

Boardman, Goldstone, Reiner, and Fathauer (1962) using a well-developed judgmental task, showed that acute schizophrenics, in contrast to normals and chronic schizophrenics, are more influenced to judge the magnitude of lines in terms of a standard figure that was constantly present during the judging activity.

That is to say, these people were inclined to judge the length of a line in a way that showed that they were using the standard figure as a comparison against which other lines were judged. This kind of anchor effect can be shown in a variety of judgmental tasks. One should have a sound theoretical basis, however, for selecting this task, out of a huge realm of available tasks, to differentiate normals from schizophrenics. In any case, Boardman et al. make the following statement in their conclusions: "This excessive combining of immediate sensory information with established concepts to produce judgments is analogous to the clinical manifestations of disordered thinking represented by delusions [p. 275]." A moment's reflection reveals that the analogy is tortured. Behind the tortured analogy is the paradigm-inspired belief that, like the Devil who is the master of many disguises, *badness* is a form that may have multiple appearances—being influenced by an anchor in a judging task is *bad*, reporting delusions is *bad*, and being schizophrenic is *bad*!

It is unnecessary further to belabor the point that the connections between the norm-violating conduct that leads to hospitalization and behavior on esoteric experimental tasks are neither sought nor explicated. Researchers, as well as editors who screen and publish their reports, appear to assume a correspondence between poor performance on an experimental task and the bad, norm-violating conduct that leads schizophrenics' relatives to ask that they be committed to a hospital. The arguments presented here and elsewhere expose this assumption. The idiographic metaphor, turned into the myth of disease, dies hard.

There is something to be admired in Kidd's (1964) unembellished, unabashed use of formal cause explanation. He simply asserts that the inadequacy of the schizophrenic sample on a monocular depth perception task was "due to the inadequate neurological and/or biological functioning [p. 103]" of the subjects in his abnormal group. The blatant idiographic character of this statement could lead even the naive reader to infer that inferior forms of humanity have been turned loose by the Forces of Evil.

9
The Task of Articulating Theory: The Radical Mechanistic Solution

We have discussed many features of the mechanistic world view, the paradigm that guided modern science to its eminent position. Using the machine as the root metaphor of an explanatory system, a theorist builds explanations by developing principles that interrelate units in the universe in terms of the transfer of force between and among events. The general commitment to the mechanistic world view, as expressed by scientists of the nineteenth century, and as reflected in medicine and psychology, has acted circularly to promote the mental disease model for explanation of perplexing, unwanted conduct.

A backward glance at the history of science in the nineteenth century helps to clarify the popularity of the mechanistic world view. The underlying root metaphor—the transmittal of force—had been instrumental in the great scientific and technological achievements of the age. Mechanism altered the direction of biological study and hastened its growth. An up-to-date mechanistic scientist would reject explanations of plant or animal life that employed sterile concepts derived from the formist doctrine of vitalism.

Prior to its being adapted to biology, the success of the mechanistic world view had already been proclaimed for physics and chemistry. In the latter half of the nineteenth century, the "mechanization of biology [Singer, 1959]" promised similar success. The foremost scientists made the mechanistic paradigm into a way of life. For example, the "mechanistic quadrumvirate," Helmholtz, Ludwig, Dubois-Reymond, and Brucke issued a manifesto and swore their famous oath in 1845 "to account for all bodily processes in physio-chemical terms [Fleming, 1964]." Great strides were made in the biological sciences that served medicine, including neurology and its medical counterpart, neuropathology.

It was in this period that the practitioners of biological science—the physicians—took upon themselves the task of explaining and controlling counterexpectational and contranormative conduct. The context in which physicians undertook the diagnosis and treatment of perplexing and unwanted conduct included the apparent resemblance of symptoms of neuropathological disorder to conduct for which no neuropathy could be found.

Hysteria was the overriding concept for classifying conduct the "symptoms" of which resembled neuropathy. In the nineteenth century, the diagnosis of hysteria was likely to be assigned to any woman and to some men who exhibited contranormative conduct in the absence of demonstrable pathology. It was a wastebasket category and was used synonymously with "functional disorders" or "psychogenic illness," expressions still in use in the medical world as a way of excluding organic disorders.

The term *psychopathology* has contributed to the continued use of the mechanistic world view. Even to the Greekless, the sound of the word as well as its visual appearance betokens a scientific conception. The unprefixed term *pathology* was employed as early as the seventeenth century to denote the study of disease. It was not until the middle of the nineteenth century that it was used to denote events other than the causes of somatic sickness. The prefix *psycho* was added to extend the meaning to include "diseases" of the psyche. Although etymologically appropriate, the combining of *psyche* and *pathology* produced an illicit eclecticism. *Pathology* had already been preempted by biological science to communicate about demonstrable disease entities, such as toxins, traumata, parasites, and so on. These entities were continuous with the transfer-of-force metaphor of mechanistic science. *Psyche,* however, was not a category of mechanistic science. It was a term derived from a long forgotten metaphor-to-myth transformation. An abstraction, *psyche* had its home in the world of formism, a metaphor that had no place for causality notions. Thus, from its beginnings, psychopathology was a flawed discipline, mixing the abstractions of formism with the concrete, ponderable objects of the mechanistic universe. A review of the history of medical psychology and psychiatry makes clear that the strain-in-knowing engendered among persons when others engaged in perplexing, counterexpectational conduct was dissolved by the *tour-de-force* of declaring such conduct the product of still-to-be-discovered disease processes. The early models for studying such conduct, now transformed to "illness," was based upon the diagnosis of neurological disorders. Theories of psychopathology mirrored theories of organic pathology.

In the last quarter of the nineteenth century, medical science focused more and more on the sequential causality of internal processes. With the incorporation of unwanted, puzzling conduct into the domain of medicine, the search for sequential causality was extended to abstractions, that is, mind, psyche, consciousness, psychic apparatus, mental machinery, etc.

The present controversy about the ontological status of schizophrenia can be better appreciated if we look back at the historical context that influenced the creation of a new field of endeavor, psychopathology. A prominent strand in the historical texture is "the mechanization of hysteria."

We need not repeat the long history of hysteria. Counterexpectational conduct among women was known to the ancients. The preferred theory placed the causal locus in the positioning of the floating uterus, hence the term *hysteria* (*hysteron* = uterus). From our present perspective, the floating uterus theory was no better nor worse than other theories that failed to take into account the meanings of the perplexing behavior in a human relations context. During most of the nineteenth century, "hysterical" women were not taken seriously by physicians. In fact, it was common to regard hysterical patients as malingerers and dissimulators (Szasz, 1961; Vieth, 1965). For example, the French physician, Falret, in 1866, characterized hysterical women as unlikeable and exceedingly difficult in their domestic relations: "These patients are veritable actresses; they do not know of a greater pleasure than to deceive . . . all those with whom they come in touch. . . . [The] life of the hysteric is one perpetual falsehood [Vieth, 1965]."

When Charcot redefined hysteria as illness (Szasz, 1961), counterexpectational conduct was brought under the purview of mechanistic medicine. The assimilation of "counterfeit illness" to "genuine illness" was facilitated by the surface similarity of the "symptoms" of patients with neuropathological disorders to the odd, perplexing, often outlandish behaviors of patients with no demonstrable neuropathy.

The assimilation of conduct deviations to sickness was accomplished by Charcot. By the 1870s he had established himself as the leading neuropathologist of the century. He had made contributions—through mechanistic biology—to understanding multiple sclerosis, the localization of spinal cord lesions, and other neurological disorders. His biographer (Guillain, 1955) reveals that he turned his attention to hysteria as a result of administrative arrangements at the Salpétrière, where he was assigned to a ward that housed both female hysterics and female epileptics. Charcot's study of hysteria came about as a result of the necessity of working with neurologically unremarkable women patients, some of whom demonstrated conduct which superficially appeared no different from the seizures of epilepsy.

We emphasize the fact that Charcot, and later Freud, Janet, and Prince, among others, approached the subject matter of hysteria from the same mechanistic paradigm that was so successful in diagnosing neuropathology. The odd, unusual, perplexing actions of patients with trauma or disease of the central nervous system was convincingly accounted for as the disruption of the transmittal of energy in identifiable neural pathways. Function and malfunction could be explained in terms of the excitation and inhibition of the flow of impulses through a complex system of nerve fibers.

The history of psychopathology is the history of a noble attempt to apply the mechanistic models of neurological functioning to an understanding of hysteria. The outcome was the mechanization of hysteria. As a parallel to the transmittal of forces over neuronal fibers, the psychopathologists invented psychic apparatus, reinvented mind, and even constructed a gross anatomy of the abstraction "consciousness." The imagery provided by the anatomy and physiology of the nervous system, influenced by concurrent developments in telephone and wireless technology, served as a background for the mechanistic construal of consciousness. Neuropathology provided the metaphors for describing the "mental" components of perplexing, counterexpectational conduct. In one way or another, the anatomy and physiology of the nervous system served as a source of metaphors to account for unwanted conduct some of which looked like the symptoms of neuropathy, and for which no lesion, trauma, or toxin could be located.

It was the mechanization of hysteria that influenced the formulations of theories of abnormal behavior. Later, partly under the influence of Prince—who employed the vague concept *personality* as others might use *mind*—the mechanistic formula helped to establish personality theories that could be applied both to normal and abnormal conduct.

Personality theories were granted more positive status if they contained statements of efficient causality and observable effect. Thus, many theorists interested in explaining misconduct have found it useful to employ the premise, often badly stated, that man is a machine. Freud, for example, whose work developed in the mechanistic ambience, elaborated his theory about misconduct by building on the basic concept of libido. Libido, as a "life energy," could be expended, collected to events, suppressed, and released. Improper distributions of this energy accounted for all counterexpectational behaviors, be they "innocent" slips of the tongue, or outrageous "psychotic" declarations (Freud, 1904/1951). All such behaviors represented a behavioral expenditure of these inborn, instinctual energies.

Consider those behavior scientists who, like Freud, were eager to illuminate the events that took place within the moral enterprise of assigning value-bearing labels (diagnosing). They might have focused on: (1) the causal antecedents to the individual's public, unwanted act; or (2) the conditions surrounding the declaration of negative value upon the act. Historically, the questions raised by the first broad aspect of the moral enterprise—the antecedents of the individual's act—have been regarded as the issues of *personality theory*. To think about antecedents, the personality theorists, including Freud, borrowed heavily from the major mechanistic models. Social psychologists studied the processes by which people judged each other and each other's acts, and from this there developed a body of literature on person perception.

The advantages of joining the social psychological emphasis on person perception to the personality theory approach have been developed by behavior scientists (Bannister, 1977; Landfield, 1977) who have built on George Kelly's personal construct theory. Within this personality theory, the emphases are on the perceiving processes of people as they interact on their world; particularly as they interact in their social world. As we shall see, when behavior scientists take an approach whereby they consider the person in the total judgment context, they see a scene very different from that observed by the mechanistic personality theorist.

MECHANISTIC PERSONALITY THEORIES IN EXPLAINING DEVIANCE

When the personality theory emphasis was the dominant approach in the study of deviant conduct, little attention was paid to the active cognitive processes of the diagnostician—the person who certified that particular conduct was indeed changeworthy. So long as the diagnostician's position in the moral enterprise could be ignored, investigators focused on a onesided, mechanistic explanation of the deviantly behaving person. When the value-declaring actions of a diagnostician became a focus of research, mechanistic models became less and less useful. The following review of the behavior modification movement, built on a radical version of the mechanistic paradigm, reveals the trends described above.

RADICAL MECHANIST EXPLANATIONS OF UNWANTED CONDUCT

Mechanistic Personality Theory and Deviant Behavior

As indicated before, scientists have drawn their metaphors from mechanistic sources. Since the founding of the science of psychology in the nineteenth century, the metaphors were applied to descriptions of the assumed regularities of ongoing, individual behavior. The personality theories that were recruited for use as explanations of unusual and unwanted behavior had been built upon formulae that specified the determinants of repeated, specific behaviors. Concepts like the *stimulus-response bond* and the *generalizing effect of reinforcement* explained the recurring similarities of conduct in the presence of repeated exposures to similar stimuli. In the mechanistic associationistic theory, stimulus situations whose conditions are assumed to be repetitively similar, served as *cues* that logically accounted for instigating the unwanted responses judged to be "characteristics" of a person. Or, on the other hand, investigators might focus on the apparent deviation from repetitive regularity and talk about the breakdown of the somatic or mental machinery implicated in establishing and maintaining repeated responses.

The assumption of repetitiveness of responses has encouraged the search for the antecedents of those behaviors which might be regarded as the "basic symptoms" of conditions such as schizophrenia. For example, a person in a mental hospital has refused to eat. To one who uses a disease model, this refusal would be regarded as a symptom of the patient's mental illness. Alternatively, such a response to food might be seen as being under the control of particular cues in that it previously and regularly had been evoked in the presence of *reinforcements*. One could take a strictly medical perspective, and "treat" the patient by spoon feeding, tube feeding, or administering electric shock therapy. Ayllon and Haughton (1962) chose to apply strict mechanistic principles to describe and bring eating behavior under the exclusive control of food. Nurses were to avoid patients during the meal time. In this way, social reinforcement of noneating, presumably given in the form of attention and sympathy, were removed from the eating situation. Since noneating behaviors were believed to have been reinforced by these social reinforcers, their removal would also lead to the extinction of the unwanted conduct, that is, the behavior that previously had been regarded as a symptom. Using this method, an investigator can lend support to the claim that all behavior, including "symptoms," is strengthened by reinforcement and weakened by removal of reinforcement.

Faulty bonds explain schizophrenia. Whereas Ayllon and Haughton explained the presence of symptoms by referring to the reinforcement of a stimulus-response sequence, other theorists attempted to characterize schizophrenia as a condition in which stimulus-response sequences had been weakened. The concept of *loosened associations* reflects the use of a version of the mechanist position that relies on a concept of disrupted energy exchange systems. Disruptions of energy flow could account for schizophrenia in terms of an inability to maintain regularities of behavior. The normal science would develop the variables that accounted for disrupted energy flow. Perhaps the characteristic anhedonia ascribed to schizophrenia could be related to this disruption. If associations are strengthened by reinforcement, and if reward (a satisfying state) is a reinforcement, then a person who develops a "condition" that affects a "reward system" might be unaffected by rewards that are regarded as standard in our culture. Thus, being unaffected by reinforcing reward, new stimulus-response bonds could not develop and old ones would decay. The observable symptoms could be attributed to loosened associations—a hallmark symptom of schizophrenia.

Additionally, the concept of *overinclusion* suggests that schizophrenia symptoms are somehow a consequence of an "overflowing" of energy. The energy assumed to have been invested in one stimulus-response association would become available to other stimulus-response sequences that include stimuli similar to the originally reinforced stimuli. In that way, the person would give responses inappropriate to the situation and could end up with a diagnosis of schizophrenia.

Application of Strict Mechanism in Hospital Settings

In the early 1960s, psychologists in mental health settings began intensive applications of the mechanistic paradigm. Numerous programs were developed from the basic principle that a behavior will appear regularly in the presence of a stimulus with which it had been associated in a stimulus-behavior-reinforcement sequence. Few writers have expressed the principle as succinctly and as enthusiastically as have Homme, C'de Baca, Cottingham, and Homme (1968):

> When reinforcing events are contingent upon a given behavior, the behavior will increase in strength; when they are not, the behavior will decrease in strength. . . . The great law of life is simple, but this fact ought not to be allowed to obscure another fact: The law is powerful. . . . One can make a pretty good case that, basically, there are only two things that a good contingency manager has to know and do: (a) to reinforce the behavior he wants, and (b) to recognize and reinforce approximations to this behavior [p. 426].

The principle of reinforcement represents one of the integrative, universal laws that psychologists may apply to explain any behavior. A person who responds to a social overture by emitting a string of apparently unrelated words has, at some time in the past, been in a situation in which some type of reinforcement had been contingent upon this behavior. If, on the other hand, the person does not respond at all, a behavior analyst may conclude that reinforcement had never been contingent upon the person's having emitted a socially acceptable verbal response. In the hands of a purist, the reinforcement model contains no place for extending explanation beyond giving statements of contingencies of reinforcement. Thus, the system does not require that a person be described as "mentally ill" or "schizophrenic." Mechanistic behavior analysts do their job by elaborating the reinforcement contingencies related to the unwanted behavior—regardless of the value declared on the behavior.

The reports of numerous investigations attest to the efficacy of altering "psychotic" behaviors through control of reinforcement contingencies. The authors of these reports would not necessarily claim to have effected cures. Instead, they would speak of having altered behaviors. (See, for example, Ayllon & Arzin, 1965; Ayllon & Haughton, 1962; Cotter, 1967; Schaeffer & Martin, 1966.) The application of a behavior modification approach to "psychotic behavior" is best exemplified in the early efforts to apply this straightforward technology. Ayllon (1963) engineered a program to change three aspects of the behavior of a 47-year-old woman who had been classed as a chronic schizophrenic. This woman stole food, hoarded towels in her room, and would wear layer upon layer of clothing.

The food hoarding was particularly problematic. The woman was overweight, and the medical staff had made the judgment that her health was in jeopardy. The woman would not, however, follow the diet prescribed for her. Caretaker staff charted the woman's food stealing, and found that she stole food during two-thirds of her meals. Ayllon prescribed a program defined as *withdrawal of positive reinforcement*. Whenever the woman stole food, her meal was taken from her. In this way, positive reinforcement—the meal—did not follow her stealing behavior. This technology proved very successful. At the end of 14 months, the woman had lost about 70 pounds. (Whether the weight loss came from taking away her meals or from her not consuming the food that she might have stolen is unclear.) At any rate, she also stopped stealing food.

The technique of *stimulus satiation* was used to eliminate the towel hoarding. The success of this technique depends on the principle that an excessive quantity of a reinforcer leads to that reinforcer becoming aversive. The woman was given seven towels daily during the first week of the program, and up to 60 towels daily during the third week. When the patient had 625 towels in her room, she began removing them. The reinforcing quality of the towels was no longer in effect; and, as a result, towel stealing could not be reinforced by the towels.

To eliminate the overdressing, Ayllon recommended a program that required that the patient make the response of stepping on a scale in order to obtain a reinforcement. There is some confusion in the report, however, and one is led to believe that it was not the act of stepping on the scale, but rather someone's judgment that the patient was dressed appropriately that served as the reinforcement. It is reported that if the nurse found that the weight of the woman and her clothing exceeded a preset amount, the positive reinforcement was withheld. The positive reinforcement was the woman's meal, for the weigh-in preceded each meal. If the woman discarded some clothing to meet the weight standard, she was awarded her positive reinforcement. By the tenth week of the application of this technology, the woman was down to about three pounds of clothing.

Other investigators used behavior modification to reduce requests for medications in persons judged to be over requesting (Parrino, George, & Daniels, 1971). Ullman, Forsman, Kenny, McInnis, Unikel, and Zeisset (1965) manipulated the frequency of "sick" and "healthy" verbalizations by regulating reinforcements. Mertins and Fuller (1963) used shaping techniques, conjoined with the reinforcing stimuli of food and praise, to increase the shaving behavior of psychotic patients.

These systematically quantifiable and precise demonstrations of the effects of regulating the exchange of food, meals, and other commodities encouraged further exploration of behaviors that could be brought under control. By 1970, Ulrich, Stachnik, and Mabry (1970), who reviewed developments to that point "with considerable delight," could claim that "an effective, detailed technology for dealing with mental inpatients is now available. It works [p. 81]."

Token economies. The major emphasis, following these early explorations, turned to demonstrating that there could be large-scale applications of the principles of mechanism. The investigators established *token economies* by which the behavior of members of groups of ward inhabitants could be regulated and modified. The reinforcement principle served to guide the implementations of these token economies. Following a demonstration by Ayllon and Azrin (1965), investigators devised programs in which tokens, as a form of currency, were used to reinforce the occurrence of "therapeutically desirable" behaviors. The issued tokens would then be redeemable for a wide variety of privileges and desired items.

Schaeffer and Martin (1966) and Atthowe and Krasner (1968) wrote early reports on programs in which a broad range of behaviors were to be brought under reinforcement contingencies. Social interactions were rated as having been markedly raised by issuing tokens to patients as they engaged each other in social contacts. Shaving, promptly rising from bed, completing assignments on time, and a decrease in general apathy were instigated by the use of tokens.

These early reports were followed by a large number of studies (for example,

Lawson, Greene, Richardson, McClure, & Pandina, 1971; Lloyd & Abel, 1970; Maley, Feldman, & Ruskin, 1973; McReynolds & Coleman, 1972; Winkler, 1970) which were completed to demonstrate the effectiveness of the principles of behavior modification. Indeed, the process has been explored to a point where further progress depends on applications of somewhat sophisticated economic theory. Winkler (1972), observing that patients who had accumulated an excess of tokens were freed from the "iron law of wages," suggested ways for over-coming the tendency to fail to produce. To counteract the possibility of the subjects being freed from the necessity to "work" for the tokens, the behavior regulator might, for example, raise prices, or offer new luxury items, or require that tokens be used within a specified period. Thus, excess capital is not accumu-lated and the laborer is once again shackled to the job. With this elaboration of the principles of the token economy, the behavior modifiers can continue their successful application of the mechanistic paradigm.

Reinforcement of improper behaviors or illness? The data for these programs support the general proposition that the behavior of hospital inmates can be altered by systematic programs of reinforcement. The implications are far-reaching. For example, one may regard these persons as people whose unwanted behavior follows from applications of the same kind of reinforcement processes to which all people are subjected. Their deviant conduct is the effect of this reinforcement process and there is no purpose in evoking the concept of *disease symptoms*.

Furthermore, since these persons will show alterations of behavior following the applications of standard reinforcement technologies, they need not be seen as persons suffering from an anomalous condition that disrupts the workings of the kinds of reinforcement effects to which all persons are subject. If these persons, through reinforcement, can be induced to shave, to eat meals regularly, and to refrain from disruptive outbursts, then there is little reason to assume that these persons suffer from a disorder that renders them impervious to routine reinforce-ments. Further, as Morse (1978) observes, if these people are able to adapt to the complex economic principles which one must master in order to work within the token economies, there is no reason to believe that they cannot use the same kinds of logical principles used by nonschizophrenic persons. In effect, the conceptual contributions stemming from research guided by the strict mechanist position lead to the inference that "schizophrenics" have acquired their unusual habits by the same psychological processes by which all persons adopt their behaviors. On this view, schizophrenics differ not by their function, but by the behaviors they exhibit.

Some puzzles relative to radical mechanist applications. Investigators (Liberman, Teigen, Patterson, & Baker, 1973; Meichenbaum, 1969; Ullman, Foresman, Kenny, McInnis, Unikel, & Zeisset, 1965; Wincze, Leitenberg, & Agras, 1972) have reported the use of behavior modification technology to reduce a person's "sick talk." The *reporting* of beliefs that others regard as unwarranted ("delusions") and *reporting* of imaginings that others do not share ("hallucination"), like other behaviors, have been altered by the use of this technology.

Despite these successes in reducing "sick talk," those who accept responsibility for regulating unwanted behavior are cautious about claiming that the elimination of "sick talk" can be taken as an indication that "sick beliefs" have been eradicated. Explanations couched in the language of radical mechanism have been unfruitful. Those who use the mechanistic paradigm have avoided explaining the interface between judgment, or epistemic behavior, and overt action; that is, between belief and practice. Such avoidance may represent wisdom, considering the problems psychologists confront when they approach the cognition/action sequence. Yet, on an everyday basis, we do observe that our interactions are based on our implicit belief that we are capable of knowing the ways that the other person knows the world. A survey of the literature (Harvey, Ickes, & Kidd, 1976) on how a person knows other people's psychological processes reveals the richness of this daily human endeavor. A person does make a steady stream of hypotheses about how other people perceive events, and much of the observer's social responding is based on these implicit hypotheses. Much of this social interaction is aimed at leading others to "change their minds." Though we do not have a systematic study to validate our expectation, we would predict that few people would believe that one had "changed one's mind" through a process in which one was given four tokens for each ten minutes during which one did not report sensory experiences which others do not share. It is no surprise that psychologists, particularly those using mechanist paradigms, cannot lightly claim that persons who have been reinforced to desist from reporting unwarranted beliefs would no longer show that such beliefs appear to guide their behavior.

Furthermore, it is very difficult to extrapolate, in reverse, the mechanistic principles to explain what caused a person to report such unwarranted beliefs in the first place. It is even more difficult to offer a strict mechanistic explanation of the processes by which a person would develop and maintain such beliefs. One would need to say that the sick talk had been reinforced. This then would require some special definitions of reinforcement; and once such special defining is allowed, reinforcement would become a totally after-the-fact concept. If this ploy is allowed, then the applicability of the reinforcement principle becomes irrefutable. One could interminably claim that a behavior had been caused by reinforcement. The analyst's skill would be directed to locating and describing the pertinent reinforcements. For example, one could say that sick talk had been reinforced by the *attention* of other people. The claim would hold insofar as attention is a reinforcer. But, the fact that sick talk appears, and the fact that "attention" had accompanied the sick talk would be advanced as evidence that attention is a reinforcer. In this circular way, one could continue to make the case that the mechanistic principles of reinforcement account for the acquisition and persistence of unwanted conduct. But without a precise prespecification of reinforcement, the overextension of the concept ultimately demonstrates its ubiquitous, irrefutable, and most important, its *ad hoc* utility. Any concept that achieves this status must be revised.

Mechanism has fallen short in explanations of judgments and beliefs, and in explanations of the interface of epistemic activity and overt conduct. Since mechanistic principles have not offered useful integrations of the events being considered, one must be encouraged to seek out other explanatory systems.

THE EFFECTS OF MECHANISTIC EXPLANATION ON THEORIES ABOUT UNWANTED DEVIANCE

The widespread application of straightforward mechanistic principles has profoundly influenced thought about schizophrenia. As noted before, investigators have demonstrated that the behavior of diagnosed persons is regulated by implementations of programs developed from principles that explain the behavior of all persons. Additionally, the methods of behavior modification require an observer to devise careful records of the target person's conduct. Such records reveal the immense diversity of the patients' behaviors. One must become aware of the highly complex, the highly orderly, the highly agreeable, the highly "logical," and the highly systematic qualities, as well as the unwanted behavior. Careful records show clearly that *most* of the diagnosed person's behavior cannot be called "sick." These considerations provide reasons for abandoning disease explanations of unacceptable conduct.

Another highly significant effect can be identified. When professionals abandon a disease conception, they must consider their reasons for interceding to regulate the behavior of the target person. The issue is forced more strongly if the intercession proves effective. When the person was considered to be *ill,* one could intercede on the grounds of playing a healer's role. One was removing symptoms! If one is removing unwanted behaviors, one must offer a justification for entering a moral enterprise. Such justification is hard to provide. As they strive to justify their own behavior, the behavior modifiers must take into account their own value commitments, which might prompt them to serve the community to uphold conventional moral precepts. (See Mancuso, Eson, & Morrison, 1979.)

The Dilemmas of the Technologist as Moral Entrepreneur

Consider the Ulrich, Stachnik and Mabry (1970) declaration that the behavior modification technology works (p. 81), and the Atthowe and Krasner (1968) report that the first efforts to induce desired behavior had failed because "it soon became clear that almost one-half of the patients were not interested in money or canteen books [p. 39]." In effect, the reinforcement technology works *so long as the subject is "interested" in the reinforcer.* Atthowe and Krasner say that "consequently, for six weeks patients were taken to the canteen and urged or 'cajoled' into buying items which seemed to interest them [p. 39]."

At this point the technologists have become advertising agents for an ongoing economic system. The iron law of wages can be manipulated by creating needs that absorb the excess capital of the workers. The end to be served is to encourage the workers to remain in "gainful employment" so that they may acquire capital to use to purchase these created "needs." The employee's "job" will be to give up unwanted conduct and to acquire wanted behaviors.

As behavior scientists, the investigators should explain the process by which the hospital inmates are brought to place positive value on objects that previously held little positive value. What mechanistic principles explain that process? Is it possible that the process carried a message of coercion? How does "cajoling" effect a person's hierarchical arrangements of judgmental decisions? To avoid such questions, the investigator must move farther and farther from his or her role as scientist, and more and more enact the role of moral entrepreneur.

A thoughtful technologist, additionally, will begin to question the propriety of cajoling an incarcerated person into acquiring needs so that an effective technology can be applied toward altering behavior. Behavior modification experts, since they do control a highly effective technology, must be concerned with who benefits from the application of that technology. The moral issues are unavoidable. Behavior modification technologists cannot escape these considerations by the happy belief that their technology serves so noble an end as the achievement of positively valued "health," and that to achieve "cures" one must often suffer the pains of treatment. They reject these rationalizations when they reject the disease model.

There is a point at which we must examine the moral and ethical issues involved in operant conditioning. How much can we justify in the name of "reshaping" patient behavior, when the very methods we use may themselves be undesirable [Lucero, Vail, & Scherber, 1968, p. 53]?

What of the patient's civil liberties? How can it be ethical to prohibit the use of devices that can result in successful placement of chronic patients in the community? The real deprivation with which we should be concerned—the one most ethically suspect—is the deliberate deprivation of potential benefits to the patient, when the alternative clearly amounts to a life sentence in a mental institution [Miron, 1968, p. 227].

The ethics of operant conditioning are no different from the ethics involved in any other procedure that can be misused. The primary ethical consideration must always be the well-being of the patient and the society from which he comes, and to which he may return [Miron, 1968, p. 228].

The writers from whom we have quoted assume the traditional framework within which one accounts for unwanted behavior by speaking about the intrapersonal conditions of the norm-violating individual. The behavior of the person ("the patient"—even strict mechanists are unable to avoid totally the disease model) requires shaping. Chronic patients need help so that they can return to the community. The well-being of the patient *and* of the society requires that the patient's contingencies of reinforcement be explained. Even a statement as clear-headed as that below, by Ullmann and Krasner (1969), does not lead to the suggestion that there be an investigation of the reinforcement contingencies that affect the behavior modifier's decisions and judgments. The personality tradition forces a focus on the individual's misbehaviors, not on the process by which the individual's conduct is labelled a misbehavior.

> The behavior therapist must make a value judgment whether this behavior should be changed (see Ullmann, 1968). As long as there is no implicit distinction between normal and abnormal behavior itself, the therapist is responsible for the decision to alter the behavior in a way he is not if the behavior is, by definition, "sick." The behavior therapist must therefore decide if the behavior may be ethically subject to modification: Is it in the service of *both* the patient and significant others in his environment for a change to be made? The diagnostic decision may be (1) that the behavior being emitted is not of a nature requiring change, (2) that it would not be in the service of either patient or significant others to change it, or (3) that no behavioral modification program could be devised to change it. In these circumstances, the diagnostic decision is not to undertake treatment [Ullmann & Krasner, 1969, p. 240].

The possible consequences of the exclusive concentration on the reinforcement history of the misbehavior could not be better illustrated than in the passage quoted below. The investigator reporting this study had accepted extensive coercive power in order to help "patients" in the psychiatric hospitals located in Vietnam. The writer of the quoted passage interpreted his professional assignment as a charge to deliver vaunted, modern, U.S. Government-sponsored technology to the people of technology-ravaged Vietnam. Apparently oblivious to any requirement to evaluate his own moral judgment system, he chose to demonstrate the principles of operant conditioning, adding new dimensions to the use of electroconvulsive therapy.

> To all the remaining patients we announced, "People who are too sick to work need treatment. Treatment starts tomorrow—electroconvulsive treatment. It is not painful and is nothing to be afraid of. When you are well enough to work, let us know."
> The next day we gave 120 unmodified electroconvulsive treatments. Although modified ECT was used on some of the patients on the admitting ward, time and drug limitations precluded its use on the chronic wards. Perhaps because of the smaller size and musculature of the Vietnamese people, no symptoms of compression fractures were reported at any time.
> The treatments were continued on a three-times-a-week schedule. Gradually there began to be an evident improvement in the behavior of the patients, the appearance of the ward, and the number of patients volunteering for work. This latter was a result of the ECT's alleviating schizophrenic or depressive thinking and affect with some. With others it was simply a result of their dislike or fear of ECT. In either case our objective of motivating them to work was achieved. . . . Reinforcement which consists of presenting stimuli is called positive reinforcement, whereas reinforcement which consists of terminating stimuli is called negative reinforcement. It can be seen that the ECT (electroconvulsive shock therapy) served as a negative reinforcement for the response of work for those patients who chose to work rather than continue receiving ECT [Cotter, 1967, pp. 24-25].

Krasner (1976), one of the early investigators (Atthowe & Krasner, 1968) of hospital use of behavior modification technology, and an early commentator (Ullmann & Krasner, 1969) on the moral judgments relative to the behavior modification with psychotics, writes as follows on Cotter's work:

> But the issues the Cotter study stimulates are representative of many of the studies identified as behavior modification that are still with us. These issues include the lack of appropriate training

by the planner of the program, a use of aversive and denigrating procedures, ignoring the "rights" of the patients to at least basic subsistence, and most important of all, the "bad" social consequences of the changed behavior [p. 639].

Then Krasner asks the age old question: "Is my value system (or yours) better than Cotter's? By what behavioral decision does my value system (or yours) take precedence over anyone else's? Of course, we are evoking the old dispute of 'who controls the controllers?' [p. 639]"

THE ISSUE OF REFLEXIVITY IN PSYCHOLOGICAL THEORY

A thorough theory of behavior should, like a mirror, be capable of reflecting the behavior of the person who writes the theory. Similarly, if a behavior change expert were to state that reinforcement is "the great law of life," then the law should explain the expert's own behavior. A psychological theory, with its principles, should be reflexive. When Krasner asks a behavior modifier, "Who controls the controllers?" the answer should be, "Whoever has control of the reinforcers."

We propose another question. To highlight the failure of radical mechanism, we would ask, "Why did Krasner ask that specific question?" A strict mechanist, turning the theory back on itself, might reply, "Because he was reinforced for asking that question." To forestall an interminably regressive argument, an outsider to the theory could ask, "What was the reinforcement?" Like all experts who try to work within the society's systems, the behavior modifier is reinforced (if salary, professional esteem, and so forth are reinforcers) for avoiding questions about control of the controller. Surely, if such questions block a person's access to the emoluments available within the mental health world, posing the question might deprive the person of the positively valued goods which society's "tokens" can buy. Indeed, Krasner does write:

We decided that based on our own value systems we would not develop further token economy programs in hospitals. We feel that value decisions, rightly or wrongly, have influenced our behavior as behavior modifiers, and this is true of all who are involved in behavior modification or, in fact, in any professional situation involving assistance to other people [p. 635].

Once scholars make this kind of decision, they limit the extent of their welcome into the mental health bureaucracy. Their access to standard remuneration is diminished. Thus, on the surface, abandoning the position of behavior modifier represents an abandoning of reinforcements. Apparently, then, the controller is able to decide to reject standard reinforcement and follow his or her own value system. The controller controls the controller!

Note that this is precisely what the hospital inmates had tried to do when they would not participate in the behavior modification programs because they had no interest in the tokens and the products that could be purchased with tokens. They, too, had decided. But the behavior modifiers had the power to "cajole" and "urge" the inmates to become interested in the economics of hospital life.

Aside from needing to explain why behavior modifiers are allowed to follow their decisions to express their own values, whereas inmates are not allowed to live out their value orientations, a major theoretical issue deserves attention. How does the mechanistic paradigm explain terms like *decision, interest, value system,* and so forth, particularly in relation to conduct associated with these concepts? Mechanism has proved to be a poor guide to efforts to answer these questions. It is this shortcoming that has highlighted the lack of reflexivity in mechanistic models. The subject of the study is explained by one set of principles, whereas the theorist's behavior is explained by another. In this case, the technology of achieving change of the unwanted behaviors of inmates is cast in terms of energy interchanges, whereas the changes in the behavior of a modifier must be discussed with a different language.

We contend that psychological science should supply concepts that apply equally to the controller and to the subject. One's system of knowings and believings, whether one is the reprimander or the transgressor, functions importantly in the context of efforts to alter unwanted behavior. Psychological science has had its try at counting these structures out of the context. Once "knowings" are figured into the context, we find that the person called a schizophrenic is doing the same thing that the behavior modifier, as a person, is doing. Each is trying to enact a script—a self-defining story—which gives cohesion to experiences in a social world that can confirm or invalidate the authenticity of the script.

SUMMARY

The radical mechanism underlying behavior modification technology comes full circle on itself. All behavior is subject to the same universal laws, says the mechanist. Those behaviors which earn one a diagnosis are not special and need not be seen as symptoms of a disease. They happen to be unwanted behaviors. Those behaviors can be changed by application of the same principles that are applied to changing any human behavior. The technology works, but . . . who controls the controllers?

From a scientist's point of view, another major part of the puzzle remains unanchored. What explains the "behavioral decision" process by which one value system gains precedence over another? The idiographic and mechanistic paradigms in behavioral science, with their emphasis on specifying intrapersonality causality relationships, have not guided explanation of this process. The paradigm that guided Krasner's efforts to modify the behavior of psychotics has little utility in guiding the search for an answer to his question, "Who controls the controllers?"

10

The Task of Articulating Theory: The Contextualist Solution

The contextualist world view takes the presently occurring historical event as its root metaphor. To illustrate the root metaphor of contextualism one would run the least risk of being misunderstood if one spoke only with present participles of verbs. To illustrate the root metaphor of contextualism, reference may be made to incidents in the plot of a drama or of a novel—*persuading* a crowd, *solving* a mystery, *performing* on a musical instrument, or *diagnosing* a person's behaviors as belonging to the syndrome "schizophrenia." To help set off contextualism from idiography and mechanism, we can make use of three stereotypes. The formist is the medieval scholar, trying to uncover the secrets of nature through analysis of abstractions. The mechanist is the laboratory scientist, intent upon constructing an equation that will predict nature's next move. The contextualist is the novelist, who tries—through emplotment—to tell a coherent story about the constantly changing, renewing world of people and their institutions.

Contextualism at first appears chaotic to those who have been schooled to use the idiographic or mechanist world views. The categories of discussion in mechanism, for example, are integrative. Mechanistic laws and principles ascribe order and regularity to the objects of the universe, and truth statements imply that the categorical statements (statements of laws and principles) shall be repetitively reaffirmed. Laws describe universal relationships, and meanings of events are expected to remain stable. Quite different are the irreducible categorical statements of contextualism: *change* and *novelty*. Events change constantly, for the very integration of the conditions of an event will alter the context of a future event that appears to have a similarity to a preceding event. The reading of *King Lear*, for example, exemplifies the interactive effects of changing conditions on the perception of the characters. It is not until the last lines are read that the earlier scenes become fully meaningful.

Piaget's theories of psychological functioning illustrate the use of a contextualist paradigm in behavioral science. Piaget (1952) constructed category statements that attempted to define the epistemic activity of the behaving person. These category statements embody a conception of persistent change. In describing a psychological event, Piaget expounded a basic principle that any incorporation of the stimulus situation into a person's epistemic structures implies adjustments (accomodations). These adjustments alter the conditions that enter the context of seemingly similar, future behavioral events, in that the same person's knowings of the events have changed. In that way, the "same" environmental information will take on meanings that vary from the meanings assigned to events on previous occasions. Thus the world, as experienced by the person, changes with each change of a person's epistemic sortings.

It is important to note that Piaget's theories, like other behavior theories that emphasize cognitive processes, present a system for discussing events in which persons make judgments. How judgments are made is the problem that needs to be examined to explain the emergence of the concept of schizophrenia. The diagnosis of schizophrenia is a judgmental event, and the event may be explained through treating it within a contextualist theory, for example, the theory of Piaget (1932, 1952) or of George Kelly (1955). The declaration of a judgment, making a diagnosis ("the inappropriately behaving person suffers from the disease"), requires analysis as a historical event. This means that the behavior analyst must take into account the texture of the "judging" situation. Thus, the epistemic system of the diagnostician must be examined no less than the epistemic system of the person being judged.

In attaching the label schizophrenia to the thousands of persons included as subjects in the hundreds of articles in our review, diagnosticians engaged in a judgmental enterprise. If a behavior scientist were to attempt to explain actions that are obviously *moral* judgment events, the acts of both the reprimander and the transgressor would hold equal interest. But in psychiatric diagnosis, where the moral quality of the judgment is tacit, the scientist, operating within the formist-mechanistic eclecticism, focuses on the putative patient as an object rather than as an involved, problem-solving person. The discussion in Chapter 5 directed attention to the diagnostician's work of judging the appropriateness, propriety, and convincingness of a person's role enactments. In so doing, the diagnostician tries to integrate accumulated information into a *cohesive* and *consistent* structure. Our review demonstrates that the illness metaphor provides neither cohesiveness nor consistency to the act of diagnosis, although the use of the illness metaphor does serve to integrate observations and judgments into a traditional belief-value structure. It is a constant temptation for the diagnostician to ignore the fact that the putative patient, like the diagnostician, makes judgments and strives for coherence, consistency, and integration. Those who review the judgments and conduct of the prepatient might conclude that the prepatient also uses metaphors that are incoherent and inconsistent, rather than the metaphors that unite and clarify meaning. It is no longer justifiable, however, to employ one psychological theory (disease) to explain the conduct of one of the participants in the diagnostic interaction and another (inductive logic) to explain the other participant. If the conduct of the diagnostician is illuminated through the use of the concepts that define judgmental processes, the conduct of the target of the diagnosis must be constructed out of the same conceptual materials. It is not that contextualism has been totally absent from explanations of unwanted conduct. Analysis shows that this world view has been present, if, at times, inadvertently.

SOCIOCULTURAL EXPECTATIONS IN THE CONTEXT OF THE MORAL ENTERPRISE

It is instructive to consider first some historical instances in which unwanted behaviors became transformed into "signs" that allowed a person to be classified as an occupant of a special status. In the early part of the twentieth century, for example, a literate and vocal minority introduced socialist doctrines to American wage earners. Rational debate might have countered their claims. As an ancillary to dialectic, there emerged a more subtle, and perhaps much more effective, means of blunting enthusiasm for socialistic conceptions. Over several decades, significant power groups created the highly negatively valued role of "red" or "bolshevik." Persons who engaged in the unwanted behavior of advocating that the government of the United States take on a socialistic orientation were regarded as candidates to be labeled with this negatively valued role-ascription. A "red" not only advocated governmental socialism, but also advocated violence rather than electoral proceedings, and would be categorized as godless (and, therefore, opposed to all traditional morality), disloyal, unpatriotic, and so forth. On occasion, a helpful mental health worker could find evidence that a "red" had undergone a childhood marked by disturbed parent-child relationships (Lindner, 1954). Aside from enlisting this kind of academic help, the creators of the role could arrange dramatic court trials and deportation proceedings, all of which aided in defining the role as one that could be best filled by alien creatures who spoke English with the heavy accents of Southern or Eastern Europe. Over the years, the label "red" took on the semantic freight of *unwanted conduct* in much the same manner as did the label "schizophrenic." Even a barely literate American mother of Eastern European origins could successfully declare negative valuations on her children's unwanted acts by addressing her children with the label "bolsheviki."

Consider a more current role. The role "unmarried mother" has until recently been as clearly defined as the role assigned to her "bastard." We recognize immediately that both these roles—unmarried mother and bastard—are very fluid. Even the government of Mussolini's Italy appreciated the necessity of legally proscribing the public identification of those whose parents had engaged in illicit sexual activity. Legislative changes currently contribute to the rapid alteration of the "unmarried mother" role. Many unmarried women have taken advantage of legislation allowing them to adopt children. Governmental bodies, through programs of aid for dependent children, now support hundreds of thousands of unmarried mothers. Young women of middle-class origin now frequently elect to rear their own out-of-wedlock children, while celebrities of the entertainment world openly declare their parentage of children whose identity they once would have kept carefully hidden. Clearly, the role "unmarried mother" is a role in rapid transition.

Mental health workers of the recent past have helped shape the role that was assigned to those who had engaged in illicit sexual behavior. In light of the obvious transitoriness of the role, it is interesting to speculate on today's public reaction to the following passage:

> Unmarried motherhood in our culture almost always represents a distorted or unrealistic way out of inner difficulties. It is thus comparable to a neurotic symptom on the one hand or to impulsive delinquent behavior on the other. The adolescent girl who has sexual relations with men or boys is lacking in a capacity to protect herself. Her reality sense is not sufficient to cope with her biological drives or with her conflicts centering around her struggle for emancipation. Wishes, conflicts, or fantasies are acted out and by accident or design the girl may become pregnant.
>
> Obviously, the ego may be weak and the reality sense inadequate for a great variety of reasons. From what has been said about adolescence it does not seem surprising that mother-hood should occur as a not uncommon symptom. . . . Our adolescent unmarried mothers are usually bewildered, struggling girls who have never achieved an inner harmony. Constitutional factors and even more significant factors in the girl's family life determine whether her ego will be free enough from neurotic conflict so that she will not hazard her future in a distorted effort to solve her conflicts [Clothier, 1955, p. 640].

The language of Clothier's statement grants no status to the observation that the "unmarried mother" is a role in transition. In keeping with disease models, she declared that motherhood out-of-wedlock is a symptom of disease.

Another example of role definition in relation to unwanted behaviors is to be found in studies of witchcraft. Recent discussions (Robbins, 1959; Szasz, 1970) describe the sixteenth-century development of the role of "witch." As a part of the general movement to counteract the protest against Roman Catholic hege-mony, significant power groups encouraged the formulation and promulgation of the "witch" role. Persons involved in the development of nonorthodox knowl-edge threatened the then current theology. Such unwanted behavior had to be discouraged. By identifying the search for new knowledge as one of the attributes of wizardry, any person who engaged in such unwanted behavior could be overtly or covertly identified as a witch. Just as the philosophers and savants of the twentieth century could lend their expertise to defining the roles of "unmar-ried mother" or "red," the intelligentsia of the sixteenth century lent their expertise to defining the role of "witch." Witches had abandoned God (and the conventional moral proprieties prescribed by God). They met in secret conclaves, plotting the rise of an antichrist, and thus represented the "special danger" of their time. When they gathered at the Witch's Sabbath, they exchanged arcane knowledge which, it was declared, might be useful in destroying the established order.

The validity of the role definition received affirmation from the highest places. No less an authority than King James VI of Scotland personally took evidence that his righteous self had earned the enmity of the devil and a band of the demon's earthly allies. Citizens of seventeenth-century Scotland could hardly deny the ontological base of the role "witch." After all, their king, who was to become James I of England and the supporter of a noted translation of the Bible, had attended the trial of those accused of collusion with Satan. He had approved the death sentence of 29 witches found guilty of plotting his death. Furthermore, he had written a learned treatise on the subject of witchcraft.

Few modern students of deviant behavior fail to recognize that King James's subjects accepted an unscientific epistemological basis for defining the witch role. We are asked to believe that our current, more scientific approach to these matters provides a better explanation of the puzzling conduct that was regarded as a sign of witchery. Our mental illness formulations, in fact, promise to explain the almost incredible instances wherein individuals willingly assigned the role of witch to themselves. Expert psychological testimony asserts that these persons were "obviously" occupants of the other expertly defined status "mentally ill person."

> Further impetus to these persecutions was undoubtedly given by many of the suspects themselves, who, although obviously ill by our present standards, participated so actively in the beliefs of the time that they often freely "confessed" their transactions with the devil, almost gleefully pointed out the "marks" he had left on their bodies, and claimed great powers as a result of their evildoing. Others suffering from severe depressions, elaborated on their terrible sins and admitted themselves to be beyond redemption. . . . (Even today many psychotics are convinced of their hopeless guilt and damnation.) [Coleman, 1972, p. 33]

Advocates of the more recent medical model, then, explain events in which certain persons allowed others and themselves to be classified as occupants of a particular status on the basis of their having engaged in unwanted behaviors. Persons who "claimed great powers as a result of their evil doings"—that is, persons who claimed that they had achieved the kinds of knowledge they ought not have achieved—were labeled witches. Modern mental health practitioners prefer that they be labeled *mentally ill*.

At the time when the role of witch attained its greatest support, the label "witch" effectively served as a diagnostic category for those persons who wandered into the folly of seeking knowledge that derived from "arcane sciences." Just as modern role-defining processes create the possibilities of ascribing the role of "red" to a candidate for the presidency, sixteenth-century role-defining processes might suggest the possibility of ascribing the role of witch to intellectuals—Galileo, DaVinci, Cervantes. When the entrenched power structure lost its struggle to control the potential reformers, the role of witch lost its utility. A modern scholar has no difficulty in recognizing the rootless structure of the witch role.

One additional example of a role in transition will aid in directing our essay: The role's occupant is a man, aged about 32 years. He usually wears an open leather vest over his hairy chest, allowing his large paunch to be partially exposed to view. On one Sunday afternoon he and an associate have removed all of their clothing and are lounging on the grassy slope alongside a major interstate highway. Several other clothed friends accompany them. Occasionally the two naked men stand close to the highway to shout and wave their beer cans at the occupants of passing autos. Toward the middle of the sunny afternoon, a State Police patrol car pulls alongside the impromptu picnic; and the police, using surprisingly mild language, urge the young men to dress and leave the roadside. The members of the group gleefully coach the two nudes as they slip into their heavy denim trousers, and following a hearty, obscenity-laden farewell, they mount their motorcycles and roar off toward their next adventure.

Blatant public nudity, in other circumstances, has led to taking people to professional mental health workers. There, after evoking and reviewing other aspects of the nude's belief system, the worker may declare that the culprit should be diagnosed and incarcerated. In the case of the young men described above, an entirely different role definition surrounds the unwanted behavior. These young men are classed as members of a "motorcycle gang." They are known to the police and to many of the citizens of a large metropolitan area. The newspapers frequently print accounts of their strange activities, particularly when the men become publicly violent toward each other and the women with whom they share their communal living arrangements. Their outlandish Sunday afternoon nudity occurs in a context that includes the policemen's understanding of the role "motorcycle gang member." These conceptions would not have been available to a policeman in 1958, and the social response could have been very different at that time.

In another social context, someone could be empowered to interview these young men and then pass the judgment that their behavior is based on an outlandish and nonconfirmable belief system. Their antiauthority views could be declared "delusions of persecution." The extravagant machismo life style encouraged by their belief system could be interpreted as a "danger to self and community."

Within the context of current social beliefs, arising in part from the unsettling events of the late 1960s and early 1970s, the behavior of these young men does not arouse the public reaction that would have been generated in another era. Today's power agents would find it difficult to assign these young men to the readily available role category, *mentally ill*. (For convenience, however, a judge might remand the young men to a county jail, pending psychiatric examination.) The police are not urged to take strong action, because the life style—the conduct—of these young men is now incorporated into a broader stream of deplorable, but tolerable behavior. That conduct is seen as a part of the role occupied by members of a motorcycle gang.

The "red," the unmarried mother role, the witch role, and the motorcycle gang member role are examples of historical processes. At given periods, the power agents in a society respond to the presence of unwanted behavior by constructing a negatively valued category to which practitioners of unwanted conduct may be assigned. The public demonstration of the unwanted behavior then assures that a person is assigned to the negatively valued status, one such status being "mentally ill" person. (This proposition is elaborated in Chapter 11.)

It follows that the declaration of negative value becomes attenuated when the unwanted behaviors are no longer matters of concern to those who hold significant power in a society. When previously unorthodox knowledge becomes acceptable to those who hold power, the creators of such knowledge need not fear the accusation of witchcraft. When contraception and abortion are economically and technically available and given moral and legal sanction, psychoanalytic conferences about the flawed psychosexual development of unmarried mothers are futile. When a society recognizes its inability to incorporate all its educated youth into the conventional job market, it ceases to declare a negative value on youthful extravagant personal expression and instead allows the development of some neutrally valued "outsider" role definitions.

But organized societies need to respond to one aspect of unwanted behavior that threatens the core of all knowledge and all truth. Madmen disrupt not only because they operate from beliefs and cognitions which others do not share; they also simultaneously disrupt by showing that they reject widely shared beliefs about the basis of knowledge and truth. Brandt (1975) discusses this matter in everyday language:

> Sometimes we do live with our crazies. Sociologists have shown that a great deal of crazy behavior goes undetected: Where it is detected it is often ignored. But generally we refer behavior that violates our sense of reality to our mental health system, whose specific task is to enforce our sense of reality, the complex reality of white, middle-class America.
>   . . . No evidence of an absolute reality exists. Even the physicists talk about probable realities, of "things" tending toward reality, of reality as a potential, not as an actual. All realities are relative to the time and the culture which produced them. Within this broad, fragmented social structure where the most diverse things are "real," the mental health system enforces one symbolic universe, one sense of reality, based on one cultural tradition and one set of values [pp. 26-27].

Reviews of the schizophrenia research, which is carried on in the atmosphere of traditional mechanistic science, do not treat the issue raised by Brandt. Few studies have directly addressed the question of how people react to those who seriously disconfirm cherished realities by enacting behaviors from a "reality" that is not readily validated. We predict that societies, particularly those that stress realist epistemologies in their educational systems, will persist in maintaining a right to relegate those who are "out of contact with reality" to a special role. It is very difficult to envision an organized society that will work to promote a world view that incorporates a dispersive position with regard to the basic laws of the cosmology. It is even more difficult to envision full social support of a theory of behavior that allows for multiple realities and for wholehearted constructive alternativism.

SOME ELEMENTS OF A CONTEXTUALIST THEORY OF BEHAVIOR

Diacritical Dimensions as Basic Units in the Theory

To adopt a contextualist paradigm, one must first repudiate the view implied in mechanistic stimulus-response theories that "whole responses" or icons of whole responses are "stored" within a person, where they remain until called forth by appropriately bonded stimuli. In its place, one adopts the view that re-cognitions, that is the repetitions of responses, are to be conceptualized as fresh, personalized restructurings of events. Neisser expresses this perspective as follows:

> What seems familiar is not the stimulus object, after all, but the perceived object. Perhaps we experience familiarity *to the extent that the present act of visual synthesis is identical to an earlier one.* Admittedly this is not an easily testable hypothesis, but it does have important consequences for the general interpretation of memory. . . . It also suggests a way of understanding a number of phenomena; how familiarity-recognition can occur with an actually incorrect identification, or identification without recognition; why recognition depends on context, and yet may also transcend it; why we generally recognize our own images and hallucinations as familiar, but need not.
>
> It is well known that tests of recognition do not always yield perfect scores. Their difficulty depends on the alternatives which are presented to the subject; when these are very similar to the item shown earlier, errors often result. On the present interpretation, it is not the absolute similarity among items which is critical, but their similarity along dimensions used by the subject in the two acts of synthesis involved. A storekeeper will be taken in by a counterfeit bill if his present perception does not bring out those details which distinguish it from the real thing. But, no matter how carefully he looks now, it will still deceive him if these details were never elaborated in his earlier perceptions of genuine bills [Neisser, 1967, pp. 98-99].

Within this conception, consistency need not be described as a matter of reenactment of a behavior which is "an engram" of the stimulus situation first contiguously associated with that stimulus. Events, to perceivers, are designated through their location along a person's fixed number of dimensions of variations—along the available diacritical dimensions or constructs. Stimulus events attain "meaning" only in reference to some parameters of a person's given dimensions. To the perceiver, two recurring stimulus events are regarded as similar only in that the epistemic sorting leads to these events being represented at common locations along a particular set of common dimensions. The dimensions—alternatively called constructs in some discussions (Bannister, 1977; Bieri, Atkins, Briar, Leaman, Miller, & Tripodi, 1966; Kelly, 1955; Landfield, 1977; Mancuso, 1970; Sarbin, Taft, & Bailey, 1960)—assumed to underlie a person's behavior are personal and idiosyncratic, though sound evidence validates a principle that describes cultural sharing of constructs. When two persons do not share the same construing system and this fact becomes apparent in their interaction, disequilibrium will result. The context will then contain evidences of movement toward restoring balance. At such points, various reprimands may occur, among which is the technique of dismissing the viewpoint of one of the participants by ascribing his or her belief to craziness.

Motivation as Maintaining Optimum Strain-in-Knowing

The constructivist perspective depends on a principle that persons strive for optimal degrees of strain or arousal; that is, persons strive to avoid unfamiliarity and the inability to integrate incoming information. For example, as people judge other persons—as well as themselves—they attempt to hold those persons fixedly located within their system of person-perceiving dimensions. People want to know the people with whom they interact. Failure to know an event or a person is associated with strain.

The strain-in-knowing concept provides the motivational propositions for a contextualist theory of unwanted deviant conduct (Sarbin, 1962, 1968a, 1969b). As such, it relates to a series of concepts that describe all instigation to action in terms of a person's efforts to maintain a balance between epistemic structure and the sensory input that continuously arrives from the distal and proximal ecologies. Kelly (1955), when he stated his fundamental postulate, put the concept of *invalidation* at the foundation of his theory. For Kelly, all of a person's psychological actions are channelized toward building and maintaining a construct system that allows for continuously successful anticipation of events. Piaget likewise built his theory of cognitive development with the concept of equilibrium at its center.

> If this fundamental interaction between internal and external is taken into account, all behavior is an *assimilation* of reality to prior schemata (schemata which, in varying degrees are due to heredity) and all behavior is at the same time an accommodation of these schemata to the actual situation. The result is that developmental theory necessarily calls upon the concept of equilibrium between internal and external factors or, speaking more generally, between assimilation and accommodation [Piaget, 1968, p. 103].

Festinger's (1957) theory of cognitive dissonance is another variation of this general disequilibrium theory of motivation. Theoretically, dissonance is treated as a negative state of tension that motivates a person to change one or both competing beliefs at those times when two such epistemic structures are activated by sensory input.

As with any psychological concept, the general concept of cognitive imbalance has been exposed to, but nonetheless has survived, severe scrutiny (Chapanis & Chapanis, 1964). The continuing vitality of the concept is expressed by Flavell (1977), who has elaborated on Piaget's disequilibrium model, calling attention to events which "have the capacity to elicit the child's cognitive interest and activity only by virtue of their *relation* to his cognitive system [pp. 20-21]." These interest-arousing events, being "partly but not fully assimilable to his existing cognitive schemes [p. 21]," are the events which promote information-seeking activity which in turn leads to a resolution of the moderate discrepancy between input and cognition. Such resolution, in most cases, leads to further cognitive growth.

Zanna and Cooper (1976) tie the concept of *arousal* to the concept of imbalance between schemata and input. These investigators have conducted and interrelated studies that demonstrate that dissonance may be associated with motivational states having physiological correlates. Similarly, Mancuso (1977) draws together evidence that physiological arousal indicators may be measured in young infants who are shown moderately discrepant visual stimuli.

The concept of arousal, which is seen to be associated with discrepancy, is a key notion in any contextualist motivation position. As Sarbin (1962, 1969b) has noted, arousal alters internal conditions so that arousal-produced stimuli are an important source of the sensory input from a person's proximal ecology. The sensory input from these stimuli must be instantiated, just as any other stimuli must be incorporated into existing cognitive systems. These stimuli, too, require explanation by the cognizing person.

Sarbin (1969b), in another place, brought together the concepts that specify our motivation position.

> Human beings seek out optimal ranges of tension, strain, and activation, the level of optimality varying with ongoing activities. When inputs are not readily instantiated, the person engages in increased cognitive activity of two sorts: (a) searching the ecology for additional inputs that have cue properties, and (b) reviewing or reciting a catalog of concepts or premises against which to match non-instantiable input. This is the condition of cognitive strain. Note that cognitive strain may be of such intensity as to spill over. . . . [when this happens,] the somatic world is increased in complexity [pp. 194-5].

Some features of this contextualist position on motivation are specifically noted. First, cognitive strain, in itself is seen to be "energizing." Energies are not imported from sources external to the process of cognition. Second, strain derives from any incongruity between any stimulus input and the cognitive organizations that would instantiate that input. The model does not depend on the input of universally arousing stimuli. Nor is it necessary to posit that only previously arousing stimuli will again evoke arousal. It follows, then, that a stimulus event is arousing relative to the context in which the stimulus occurs, and that the person's epistemic systems are a salient strand of that context.

Constructs as the Stable Features of a Personality

The concept of cognitive strain henceforth will represent the core motivational concept in the following attempt to articulate the "symptoms of schizophrenia" to a contextualist theory.

Although we use cognitive strain as a general term, the reader is cautioned against equating "cognitive" with "mental." Our position is that knowing is an action, a sometimes silent, covert way of locating self and others in multiplex ecologies. To avoid the tendency to reify, we shall use synonyms, such as, "strain-in-knowing," "epistemic strain," etc. Those behaviors that have been given the status of symptoms can be understood in the context of a social psychology of knowing. The basis of an understanding of how people know each other is to be found in the extensive literature on implicit personality theory and person perception (Sarbin, Taft, & Bailey, 1960; Rosenberg, 1977; Rosenberg & Sedlak, 1972; Schneider, 1973; Warr & Knapper, 1968; Wegner & Vallacher,

1978). Among the principles given empirical support in this corpus of research and analysis are the following: (1) People judge other persons in terms of bipolar scales such as *warm-cold, strong-weak, good-bad*, and so forth. (2) Persons acting as judges of other persons follow an assumption that constructs are related to each other in hierarchial fashion. *Good-bad*, for example, is implied by the construct *beautiful-ugly*. (3) Persons judge others as if the polarities of particular constructs logically align with each other. *Good*, for example, takes the same valence as *beautiful*. This list of person-perception principles could be extended. At this point, the list is adequate to support an argument that approaches to general behavior theory are available and they fit comfortably into a contextualist position, by stressing personal epistemic systems as an inseparable aspect of every event.

From these principles and premises, behavior consistency may be conceptualized as re-cognition—a resynthesizing that accompanies the continuous flow of incoming information. This system of explanation emphasizes a person's continuous efforts to attain integrity and coherence in construing, that is, to avoid the strain-in-knowing that accompanies surprise and novelty. This system of explanation opens up the proposition that a person may transform stimuli while striving for integrity and coherence. By a reorganization of their belief-value systems, persons instantiate themselves or others in terms somewhat different from those used in previous instances. The target person is transformed by such reconstruction. Epistemic transformations are regular, everyday actions: To accept the fact that people engage in such epistemic actions carries no warrant that they be identified as "abnormal" or "ill." Every person seeks to avoid nonoptimal cognitive strain, and any variety of cognitive organization can be employed to achieve one's goals.

Not only does this model allow us to explore other means of breaking out of the mechanistic explanations of unusual behavior; it also allows, perhaps more importantly, effective explanations of behavior based on a person's efforts to answer the recurring question, "Who am I (in relation to you)?" The constructivist approach, unlike the idiographic or mechanistic, encourages the examination of such human actions as role creation and role enactment. A theorist can speak of a society inventing constructs, amalgams of which define invented roles. One can speak of social transmission of constructs to individuals, and the means by which individuals learn the constructs applicable to transmitted roles. (A fuller account of a contextual theory of deviant conduct is the task of Chapter 11.)

Most importantly, by describing how persons learn *constructs and their use*, rather than how they acquire *responses*, we can discuss how a person creatively invents new roles (see Kelly, 1955). With a contextualist theory that includes epistemic actions, one can speak of skill in reassembling role descriptions, and of the usefulness of this skill in social interactions where the participants are required to "imagine" the roles the other person can assume or enact. We can address the question of how a person learns the role of a "crazy." Or we can look into the structure of the epistemic actions of a mental health worker who makes the determination that a person is convincingly enacting the role of "schizophrenic."

In effect, then, theorists explaining unwanted behavior need not be restricted to using a mechanistic theory of behavior, nor an idiographic theory of abstract forms. Constructivism has had an immense impact in areas that once appeared to be the exclusive province of mechanism. In a field which once provided schizophrenia investigators with models for studying "loosened associations"—the field of verbal learning—scholars have openly declared the inutility of mechanistic models, and now advocate a turn to constructivist (Cofer, 1973) and contextualist positions (Jenkins, 1974). We repeat this advocacy relative to explanations of deviant conduct: Unwanted behavior is best explained when investigators and scholars take into account both participants in the diagnostic process, complete with their belief-value systems. Such an account may be phrased effectively in language that speaks of representations developed from the construct systems of the participants in this role-defining transaction. This language of contextualism is found in the ambience of social psychology.

CONTEXTUALIST TRENDS IN SCHIZOPHRENIA RESEARCH

The review of the core sample of schizophrenia research reveals that some researchers are actively exploring the contextualist paradigm as they find that their puzzles are not amenable to mechanistic solutions. Questions are not yet being phrased fully from within contextualist models, but it is apparent that a number of investigators are aware that they must deal with related elements as they study other elements within particular contexts, and that apparently similar elements are not similar if their embedding context has changed. As one would expect, this realization is being more fully developed in treatments of topics related to language. For example, investigators are no longer treating words as stimuli which must be organized in a universally similar way. Some of the current work on cognitive processing takes into full consideration the idiosyncratic organizations that can be imposed on stimulus words. Work on attention and arousal functioning also has shown that investigators are aware of the utility of treating arousal as a context-embedded element. We review some context-sensitive studies of attention and of cognitive processes to illustrate the trend in theory articulation.

Attention Research

An earlier section of this chapter contains a discussion of arousal. The reference to Flavell's (1977) moderate discrepancy hypothesis related "partly, but not fully assimilable [p. 21]" events to infant interest and attention. Ginsberg and Opper (1969) have written a clear statement on this relationship between discrepancy, arousal, and attention.

. . . But the infant does not simply look at more and more things. His visual preferences become selective. The infant's attention is directed at events which are *moderately* novel. . . . This motivation principle may appear deceptively simple and trite. In reality, however, it represents a point of view which is radically different from previous (and some current) theories and is only now receiving the attention it deserves. . . . It is not the object *per se* that attracts attention; instead curiosity is a function of the *relation* between the new object and the individual's previous experience. . . . In sum, the novelty principle asserts that what determines curiosity is not the physical nature of the object, but rather the degree to which the object is discrepant from what the individual is familiar with, which, of course, depends entirely on the individual's experience [p. 39].

We find, then, that the association between cognitive processes, attention, and motivation has been well worked into theories in developmental psychology (see also Mancuso, 1977). Additionally, the study of attention provides one unifying theme to the constant effort to build a solid theory of behavior. Terminology changes. Like the tantalizing and exhilarating themes of a symphony, the conception of attention often takes vaguely recognizable forms and at times hides within the ongoing discussion of motivation. In a general sense, the concept of attention describes how a person's psychological processes are directed and elaborated. Different technologies have been applied to the study of attention. Some investigators have attempted to define attention physiologically (Hillyard, Hink, Schwent, & Picton, 1973; Kinsbourne, 1973). Psychologists who have chosen to take an information-processing approach to behavior explanation (Garner, 1974; Moray, 1970) have extensively treated attention. In studies of infants, investigators have been particularly resourceful in exploring means of defining attention, using techniques like receptor orientation (Lewis, Kagan, & Kalafat, 1966), and changes in cardiac response (Berg, 1972).

An examination of the schizophrenia model is facilitated by reviewing the efforts of scientists to treat attention contextually. A reading of Lewis's review (1971), for example, shows how schizophrenia researchers failed to use a sophisticated definition of attention. The schizophrenia investigators had for a long time missed the crucial core of the moderate novelty hypothesis—that is, that the attentional process must be related to the cognitive skills and structures the subjects have available to guide their search procedures. Had this crucial consideration been taken into account, the investigators might not have focused exclusively on the form or the mechanics of the schizophrenics' information-processing systems. Instead, they might have given more attention to the epistemic systems which the schizophrenics have available to guide their information processing.

In a manner that is somewhat perverse, considering the usual orientations in the discipline of psychology, the matter of interpretation of stimuli had been most closely considered by those investigators who focus on the physiological features of the attentional activity of schizophrenics (Ax, Bamford, Beckett, Fretz, & Gottlieb, 1970; Bernstein, 1970; Magaro, 1973; Thayer & Silber, 1971). Magaro (1973) in drawing conclusions from his vast study of schizophrenia, presents this interpretation of his results:

Considering the laboratory as the independent variable leads to the prediction that the long-term hospitalized stimulus-deprived patient would exhibit a higher basal level than all other comparable groups. This is what occurred in the present study. The only significant resting basal level finding was that chronics were higher than acutes. . . . [The findings of this study are interpreted] not in terms of schizophrenia but in terms of novelty of the experimental situation for individuals grouped by length of time in a stimulus deprivation condition [p. 278].

Similarly, Thayer and Silber (1971) draw the conclusion:

. . . the results are surprisingly consistent in showing that there is a basic association between psychophysiological responding and tonic arousal level: The higher the individual's basal arousal, the greater, faster and more enduring is his responding, and this would appear independent of psychiatric status when tonic level is controlled. Further, at least some of the variation appears, irrespective of tonic level, to be related to the interpretation made by S of the situation [p. 169].

Bernstein's (1970) treatment of his results hews more closely to the traditional disease line for schizophrenia; but he has, nevertheless, taken the moderate novelty principle into account. He notes Sokolov's (1963) position that "OR (orienting response) habituation depends on a restructuring of the internalized model at every point of mismatch until the model again becomes redundant with current input [p. 154]." But instead of bringing into focus his "schizophrenic" subjects' epistemic models, Bernstein rushes to the mechanistically based conclusion that, "Chronic schizophrenics as a group, therefore, may absorb information from their environment quickly, perhaps sacrificing detail for speed [p. 154]."

The investigator who studies attention, whether "schizophrenic" attention or "normal" attention, must consider the beliefs and values that a person brings to a situation, the novelty of the situation relative to the subject's epistemic structures, and the range of interpretations the subject can make. Attention is not to be regarded as an entity that has a span; nor is it useful to think of attention as an extra energic variable brought into play by stimuli that have universal attention-getting status.

Schneider's (1976) conclusion, "there is no evidence from this study that the mechanisms of selective attention are not intact in delusional schizophrenics [p. 172]," follows from a careful study with a technique known as shadowing. Persons are required to listen to verbal material being transmitted through headphones. They are instructed to repeat verbatim the material arriving at the right ear. At the same time, distracting material is transmitted into the left ear. The person is instructed to ignore that material. Schneider used three types of distraction material. Messages to the left ear dealt with (1) material from a physics textbook, (2) discussion of the character of the Veteran's Administration hospital in which the members of the patient sample resided, or (3) material related to the topic of the delusions which the schizophrenic sample reported. In this way, the information in one of the distractor message channels was somewhat relevant to the patients, but not to the nonpatients. Additionally the material related to delusions would be more relevant than the material on the hospital or the material from the physics textbook.

Schneider took measures by counting errors made during the shadowing process. Errors would occur whenever a person missed a word that was given in the target channel or whenever a person spoke a word that was not in the relevant message. The final outcome of Schneider's analyses can be simply stated. The schizophrenic sample made more errors than did the comparison *only* when the distractor material related to the person's delusional (read: personally meaningful) material. The nonschizophrenic persons, incidentally, did not show an effect due to the delusion-related materials. Like so many other studies of hospitalized persons, Schneider's study can be criticized for ignoring the possible intrusion of hidden variables. In any case, the investigation can be treated as a study of the effects of moderate discrepancy. Schneider showed that when material has some relevance to the epistemic system of the person, that material is difficult to ignore. To fully test this hypothesis, an investigator would need to provide the nonschizophrenic persons with equally relevant distractors. Nevertheless, the results are compatible with the moderate discrepancy hypothesis. Most important, the work suggests that the attention-related processes of "schizophrenics" cannot be differentiated from those of ordinary persons.

Russell and Knight (1977) illustrate the value of a contextualist approach in a particularly special way; and they, too, arrive at a conclusion similar to that developed by Schneider (1976):

> Our results do not support the claim that the mechanisms and operations involved in the extraction of purely perceptual information from visual displays is a region of basic deficit in process schizophrenics. . . . Together [with other cited results] they would appear to severely undermine the theories that postulate a primary perceptual deficit in schizophrenia [p. 25].

In the first place, Russell and Knight place the matter of attention totally within an information processing system. Though their studies deal with issues that formerly would have been discussed as attentional deficit in schizophrenia, they do not once use the term *attention*. Aware of the active nature of knowing, they discuss *search* of the information field. Further, Russell and Knight do not assume that a measure on a single task will produce a measure of a cognitive deficit. Instead, they persistently analyzed the participant's patterns of responses. For example, schizophrenic samples and the control samples were required to conduct a search of a stimulus array to find a specified target stimulus that was included in the display. The task was made more complex by increasing the similarity between the target stimulus and the surrounding stimuli. For example, subjects were required to search for a letter X embedded in round-shaped letters, such as O, C, and G. The task was then complicated by requiring that the search be conducted for an S surrounded by straight-line letters, such as K, V, and N. The main focus of these studies was the comparison of performances in terms of rates of increase in response times as the tasks were made more complex. Schizophrenic subjects consistently used more time to complete the search. They did not, however, make more errors of various types. And, more importantly, the rate of increase in time to complete tasks was, essentially, the same for the schizophrenic and the control groups. One would expect that an attentional deficit would be revealed by a magnified effect in performing the more complex tasks, where the processing of initial input would require more time and more complex manipulation of input data. Such an effect was seen under only one of the special complicating conditions. Russell and Knight summarize as follows: "Schizophrenics and controls were affected in the same way and, with the exception already noted, to very much the same degree by these manipulations [pp. 24-25]."

Reports such as the foregoing provide the contrary findings necessary for a paradigm revolution. Such studies lay to rest the attention deficit, one of those hypotheses regularly resuscitated to make credible the assumed psychological fault that "causes" outlandish, unwanted behavior. In addition, such studies demonstrate the futility of attempting to treat attention as a fixed entity whose function can be assessed independent of the entire epistemic action. Following the lead of these investigators, the next generation of scientists can discontinue the search for the basic flaw of schizophrenia and instead direct their energies to the study of the entire interbehavioral context in which some persons are assigned the diagnosis of schizophrenia.

Contextualist Approaches and the Cognitive Deficit Hypothesis

In the last decade, experimental psychologists have radically transformed the understanding of memory and knowing. The studies of these processes best reflect the ways in which the contextualist paradigms have transformed an area of the psychological sciences. At one time, memory and categorizing behavior were treated as quite separate functions, and efforts were directed toward establishing mechanistic principles to explain these functions. Current theory unites the memory and categorizing concepts. Memory performance is now regarded as a positive function of the cognitive elaboration that is performed on to-be-remembered material. Posner (1973) aptly expresses the contextualist position:

> . . . A classification system imposed upon materials at input limits the ways in which the material can be used at retrieval. If subjects are allowed to use *their input categories*, recall can be relatively effortless and effective. Otherwise, recall is slow and less accurate. The organization of information during learning has consequences for the ease with which it can be used later [p. 33; italics added].

When these propositions are introduced into the effort to establish the nature of cognitive deficit in schizophrenia, a simple conclusion may follow. We advance the proposition that some—perhaps only a few—"schizophrenics" do not use the same organizational categories used by most people. They are handicapped when experimenters plan studies of cognitive process and include material that can best be organized by categories that most people will use. Following Posner's proposition, their recall of the material would be slow and less accurate. In the end, if experimenters are willing to accept slower functioning as an indication of cognitive deficit, then, of course, they will find evidence for cognitive deficit in schizophrenia. From the perspective outlined here, however, they would be claiming that an atypical, even original, category system represents a cognitive deficit.

Koh and Peterson (1978) report a very useful study that relates to the issues raised here. These investigators worked out a procedure by which they experimentally induced participants to impose category systems of different levels of complexity onto different terms presented to them. For example, the lowest level of encoding strategy involved having subjects report on whether or not a term contained particular letters. Koh and Peterson referred to this as categorization by phoneme. The highest level of categorization was induced by having subjects indicate whether or not a term could fit meaningfully in sentences containing a blank space—a semantic strategy. The study raises the question: Is the recall function of schizophrenics affected, as is the recall of normals, by variations in "level of processing?"

In one variation of the procedure, people were shown the word *weight,* and then asked, "Does the word rhyme with *crate?*" In a second variation of the procedure, subjects were asked to provide the term to fit into a particular category. For example, they were asked, "Write a word that is a member of the following category, *animal.*" Also, on this variation, participants were forewarned that they would be asked to recall material from the task. In this way, participants were induced to assign the terms to some aspect of a category system, prior to the recall exercise.

The analysis of the data produced by the participants' responses showed that for the most part the schizophrenics were quite similar to the nonschizophrenics, particularly in the first variation of the categorizing procedure. As in all the schizophrenia research, the small differences that appeared can be explained by reference to a variety of factors. For example, Koh and Peterson point out that though the procedure does induce processing by category, "the experimenters may not have gained full control over the subjects' encoding operations in the [self-generating] condition, and thereby the schizophrenics in the present study may have been less alert and active in these extra operations [p. 311]." The nonschizophrenics might have been able, for example, to refer demonstrated facility on the task to personal self esteem, and thus their arousal level, owing to possible showing of poor performance, may have contributed to heightened attention. The schizophrenic sample, having already been convinced of their stigmatization, would not be likely to invest their performance with any aspect of self-status maintenance.

The findings and conclusions developed by Koh and Peterson are a significant reflection of what has happened to the study of cognitive deficit as a result of assuming the tenets of a contextualist approach. As such, their work extends that of other researchers (Knight, Sherer, Putchat, & Carter, 1978; Koh, Kayton, &

Peterson, 1976; Koh, Szoc, & Peterson, 1977; Larsen & Fromholt, 1976; Neufeld, 1977; Schneider, 1976). The general conclusion of all this work can be safely summarized as follows: When the material to be sorted is presented in ways that take into account and correct for the content of the participants' cognitive organizational systems, there are no significant differences between the functioning of those called schizophrenic and those not called schizophrenic.

Another study, reported by Larsen and Fromholt (1976) further illustrates this contra-paradigm statement. They too investigated the possibility that schizophrenics show a cognitive deficit that interferes with recall. Larsen and Fromholt, in effect, forced the participants to develop and to use equivalent categorizing schemes.

Subjects were to recall words from a 25-word list which they had studied and then tried to recall. They were not instructed, however, simply to memorize or to learn the 25-word list. They were asked, instead, to sort repeatedly the words into sets of words, on the basis of categories into which the terms would fit. When the subject was able to complete two consecutive sortings such that the sets were identical and contained the same terms, the participant discontinued the sorting.

Larsen and Fromholt implemented this procedure on the basis of the assumption that through this sorting, each participant would have achieved a stable structural organization of the 25 terms. Thus, since recall depends on level and adequacy of structure imposed on to-be-recalled material, all participants would be equally prepared to recall the material.

By using this carefully developed contextualist strategy, Larsen and Fromholt showed that the schizophrenic sample did not differ from the nonschizophrenic sample when they reported their recalled words. The schizophrenic sample, like the normal sample, recalled an average of about 18 words. The two samples did differ in their skill in achieving stable categories. While 92 percent of the normal sample was able to achieve a stable sorting within a 10-trial limit, only 71 percent of the schizophrenics did so. The schizophrenic participants, on the average, achieved a stable organization in six trials, whereas the normals achieved a stable sorting in about three trials.

Larsen and Fromholt concluded as follows:

> These results fail to support the assumption that deficient retrieval operations contribute significantly to the well-documented schizophrenic recall deficit, whereas they are consistent with the hypothesis of a mnemonic organization deficiency in schizophrenia. At the same time, the study suggests that such a deficiency may be effectively counteracted by means of a suitable acquisition method [p. 64].

Following the general orientation established in this essay, one may regard the "effective counteracting" as a matter of inducing the hospitalized subjects to organize input in ways compatible with the organizations used by the experimenter and by other participants in the study. Further, the procedure forces schizophrenics to search out and use organization schemata that usefully integrate the material. In other words, Larsen and Fromholt's procedure presses the participants into using a metacognitive strategy. It is likely that some of the persons whose conduct leads to the diagnosis schizophrenia do not use the same metacognitive strategies that most of us find useful in organizing the immense quantity of input that continuously excites our sensory organs.

These are but two of the recent studies that show the parallelism of the cognitive functioning of schizophrenics and nonschizophrenics. Such parallelism is shown, however, only when there are operations to equalize the content of the participant's epistemic organizational system. Similar results were achieved under similar conditions in a study reported by Koh, Kayton, and Peterson (1976), who also insured that subjects had imposed some kind of structure on the input. They had subjects sort terms in the category *pleasant-unpleasant*. The recall performance of the schizophrenics equalled that of the normals.

One study (Russell & Beekhuis, 1976) complicates this trend. They concluded that schizophrenics show a recall deficit despite their ability to develop and use a subjective categorization system that matches that of normals. Unlike Koh and Peterson (1978), Russell and Beekhuis had no indication that all the subjects had in fact achieved an organization of the test materials which they could use consistently. In effect, then, their procedures provide no way to assess whether or not schizophrenics show a recall deficit despite achieving a stable organization. Their study does not provide a logical contradiction of the overall points, which are: diagnosed schizophrenics might show low skill in using the metacognitive strategy of developing and imposing a stable organization, but when induced to do so, they do not show the deficit in recall that is associated with failure to organize input.

The trends in this series of studies are clear. It is illegitimate to attribute cognitive deficit to schizophrenics without clearly accounting for the contextual conditions in which the presumed deficit is demonstrated. The cognitive organizational system a person brings to a task represents a salient aspect of the context. Because one's epistemic system is simple or idiosyncratic is no justification for making the value judgment that such systems are deficient, the products of diseased minds. There is no universal quality that must be embedded in a person's cognitive organizational schemes. When the diagnostician makes value pronouncements relative to the quality of cognizing systems—"thought disorder," "cognitive deficit," "schizophrenic distortion"—we witness a social interactive process, not the work of a scientific, value-free, objective, impartial arbiter of something that is carelessly called reality.

PSYCHIATRIC TRENDS TOWARD CONTEXTUALISM

Although medically trained psychiatrists have relied heavily on disease models, there have been noteworthy efforts (Jaspers, 1913; Shands, 1970) to develop complete contextualist approaches to the practice of psychiatry. For example, Boisen (1936), while working as a chaplain at the Elgin (Illinois) State Hospital, interpreted psychosis as the creative effort of a person to come to grips with existential and cosmological problems. In examining the biographies of religious leaders and mental hospital inmates, he noted that during crisis situations, the person would engage in behavior that modern diagnosticians would label psychosis. The sequence *crisis—"psychosis"—resolution* was applicable to conduct whether or not it was declared psychotic by professionals. Laing (1967) has elaborated a similar theory. He recognizes that the term "schizophrenia" conceals more than it reveals: "We have to decide whether to use old terms in a new way, or abandon them to the dustbin of history. There is no 'condition' of 'schizophrenia,' but the label is a social fact and the social fact is a *political event* [p. 83]."

A promising beginning for an establishment-supported contextualist account of contranormative conduct was the double bind hypothesis of Bateson, Jackson, Haley, and Weakland (1956). Uncritical of the ambiguities inherent in the diagnostic language, they continued to employ schizophrenia as a way of categorizing people. The "double bind" was a contextualist notion. It was a way of describing family interactions in which the target person was placed in a "no win" situation. The ultimate response of the target person to prolonged conflict was atypical, odd, bizarre actions, that is, actions that placed the family in a condition of strain. The subjects of their first investigations were diagnosed schizophrenics—hence the maintenance of the diagnostic category. Additionally, this work has been supported principally by grants from the National Institute of Mental Health, a bureaucratic organization committed to the medical model. The important feature of their contribution, however, was the proposition that the unwanted conduct was the product of an intricate interweaving of contrary communications. These investigators tried to avoid the principles of the mechanistic disease model and the idiographic badness model, and saw "schizophrenia" (undefined) as a special type of adjustment of one person to a set of conditions imposed by other persons.

A mountain of research papers and congress reports have accumulated in an effort to show that family patterns of communication contribute to the development of the conditions that are labelled schizophrenia. A great deal has been learned about family interactions in the course of studying the families of schizophrenics. This work, summarized in five chapters of a recent handbook (Wynne, Cromwell, & Matthysse, 1978), reflects the use of contextual ideas among which appear occasional encroachments of an idiographic metaphysics. It is not unlikely that family communication studies supported, say, by a granting agency committed to educational reforms, might have begun from a more defensible independent variable, say, "stupidity," making unnecessary the anchoring of the contextual variables in a theory of badness.

Those investigators and therapists who have elected to explore the intricacies of family communication contexts are often confronted by the contradiction inherent in working from the illicit eclecticism that unsuccessfully mixes the categories of deviant communicational contexts. At a conference of experts in family communication, Carl Whitaker, a leader in the field of family therapy, in an informal discussion, remarked, "Instead of assuming that there aren't any schizophrenics it's very much simpler if we assume that we're all schizophrenics. . . . The only trouble is that most of us haven't got guts enough to be schizophrenic except in the middle of the night when we're sound asleep, and we try to forget it by morning [Berger, 1978, p. 82]."

The efforts of these contextualist-oriented psychiatric practitioners have made little headway within the profession. We would conclude that the profession of psychiatry is not in the position to implement the full implications of the message generated by the thought from which these theories spring. It is true that there has been a flirtation with community psychiatry and social psychiatry. The failure to bring this overture to full consummation, however, can easily be traced to psychiatry's continued reliance on mechanistic principles. Setting up community clinics to treat target persons as the effects of specific causes does little to rearrange the intricate context in which develop those persons who ultimately become the subjects of the psychiatrist's diagnostic practices.

REPRISE

The foregoing paragraphs support the argument that efforts to understand unwanted conduct have, in the past, focused mainly upon idiographic "flawed minds" or upon mechanically connected intrapersonal antecedents, concommitantly neglecting social processes by which people assign a negative evaluation to an act, and also ignoring issues of role definition and role assignment. The neglect of social processes helps maintain the position that unwanted behaviors are problems of the *individual* and are to be explained in terms of how those behaviors are mechanically "caused" within the individual. At the same time, the "mentally ill person" can be regarded as an identifiable role (Nunnally, 1961) to which persons are assigned by others—professionals or amateurs. Can we generalize from the history of the role of witch to the role "schizophrenic?" The data of our analysis, together with a respect for historical processes, lead us to predict that schizophrenia, like witchcraft, will disappear when societies repudiate the practice of sequestering or regarding as "sick" those who persist in residual deviance.

Equally important, the role of "schizophrenia" cannot be sustained when behavior scientists move fully into practicing a contextualist science that accounts for both the epistemic or judgmental processes of the diagnostician and those who become the targets of the diagnosis. At this point there is sufficient work from the normal science of psychology to show that contextualist approaches are the most useful in explaining these judgmental processes. Furthermore, a strong chain of contextually-based reports demonstrate that the psychological processes of those diagnosed as schizophrenic cannot be differentiated from the processes of those who do not bear the diagnosis. Meanings are developed and are applied in contexts; they vary immensely, depending on the contexts in which they are developed and applied. Each individual who strives for meaning and for the resolution of cognitive strain brings his or her own personalized epistemic system into the context. One person might communicate a categorization of an event by performing an unusual body movement. Another person enacting the role of diagnostician might communicate a categorization of an event by assigning the term *schizophrenic*. Each demonstrates participation in a contextually embedded psychological process, and each has derived a strain-reducing meaning for the event that came into attention. Further, the ultimate outcomes of these epistemic actions are embedded in a larger social context. The diagnostician's categorization may lead to radical transformations of the first person's epistemic actions: the person is now a patient.

11

A Contextual Model for Unwanted Conduct: The Transvaluation of Social Identity

Having demonstrated the lack of utility of the schizophrenia model, it is now time to suggest an alternate way of looking at unwanted conduct. We have made the point repeatedly that the concept of schizophrenia, like its predecessor, dementia praecox, was invented to communicate about certain classes of non-conforming, unacceptable conduct. Schizophrenia is but one in a long line of conceptions whose primary purpose was to identify persons whose conduct was contranormative. It was but one way that a society could go in its endless search for solutions to the problem of unwanted conduct.

The findings and arguments in earlier chapters compel us to examine unwanted conduct from a perspective formed by the basic observation: human conduct occurs in social contexts and these contexts include systems of norms (standards, codes of propriety, role expectations, moral rules). To say that a person violates a norm is to say that he or she has engaged in some overt act and that the act has been judged by another person or persons as inappropriate, improper, immoral, silly, bizarre, dangerous, foolhardy, stupid, and so on. In short, an adequate theory of human conduct must begin at the intersection of action and valuation. Human beings are constantly assigning value to the acts of others and themselves, the values deriving from normative systems. And we can ignore this universal characteristic only at the expense of an incomplete account of the human condition.

Contained in these introductory remarks are the basic categories for a theory of conduct that can illuminate the problems for which the schizophrenia disease concept was invented: action, social structure, and valuation. It is important that a theory of conduct contain categories that help account for both normative and contranormative conduct. A theory that makes use of one set of categories for unwanted conduct and another set of categories for acceptable conduct—in to-day's critical climate—can expect to be rejected on logic-of-science grounds. We have demonstrated that the feebleness of the schizophrenia model as a heuristic base for a science of unwanted conduct is a function of the imposition of a formist category: *badness*. Hence one set of categories is invented to account for essentially bad (unwanted) conduct, another set for good conduct; that is, the conduct of "normal" persons.

A caution for the reader: Our analysis of the mythic properties of the schizo-phrenia story must not be interpreted as a mere change in labels. To be sure, a new metaphor has a heuristic effect—note the scientific productivity and the use of the diagnosis in forensic settings when the twentieth-century term "schizo-phrenia" displaced the nineteenth-century "dementia praecox." In the 1920s and 1930s, Adolph Meyer introduced parergasia, a concept that reflected a more contextual approach to deviant conduct. The profession was not yet ready for the new vocabulary and its implications for theory and practice, and it disappeared from textbooks and journals. Rather than provide a new vocabulary, it has been our intention to demonstrate that no entity exists that corresponds to the ambig-uous criteria for schizophrenia. When our critics ask, If not schizophrenia, what do you call it? We reply: There is no "it" to be labelled with a diagnostic term. We hasten to add that all of us exhibit behavior at one time or another that others might call crazy (Morse, 1978), but such behavior can be understood only in a context that includes the person who utters the valuational term.

In the succeeding paragraphs, we shall make the case that the degradation of social identity is a feature of the context that influences the labelling, isolation, and sequestering of certain persons for voluntary or coercive control. Degrada-tion is a form of transvaluation. Unlike the traditional psychopathologists who begin their examination of a "mental patient" after the person has been subjected to the degradation of social isolation, sequestering, diagnosing, drugging, and hospitalization, we begin our work with an analysis of the conditions that foster the downward transvaluation of a person.

THE DIMENSIONS OF THE TRANSVALUATION MODEL

The metaphor of choice is the transvaluation of social identity. The construction of the metaphor was helped along by employing conceptions derived from mod-ern role theory (Goffman, 1961; Mead, 1934; Sarbin, 1943, 1956; Sarbin and Allen, 1968). The basic postulate of the theory is that action and valuation of action occur in the context of social organization. The poetic abstraction "man alone" or "woman alone" has no useful place in an account of human conduct.

A basic postulate in the theory is that human beings constantly strive to locate themselves in their environments. Successful locating of self forestalls epistemic strain. Failure raises strain. In order to make proper choices from their role repertoires, persons must locate themselves with regard to the world of occurrences. This world may be differentiated into a number of ecologies, among them the social ecology or role system, the normative ecology, the self-maintenance ecology, and the transcendental ecology. At this point, our concern is with placement in the social ecology. Constantly confronted with the necessity of locating the self in the role system, a person's misplacement may lead to embarrassing, perilous, or even fatal consequences.

To locate oneself in the role system, a person makes use of an inferential process: on the basis of available cues and knowledge of the role system, the individual infers the role of other(s) and concurrently of self. The process can be described as the efforts of an individual to find answers to the question *Who am I?* Ordinarily the answer is constructed from considering at the same time the reflexive question: *Who are you?* Finding one's place in the role system is a reciprocal event—answers to the question *Who am I?* are determined by the answers to the question *Who are you?* and vice versa. The totality of such answers defines a person's social identity.

Who am I? questions stimulate answers drawn from categories of the role system, such as name, age, sex, occupation, nationality, membership, religious affiliation, marital status, ethnicity, political party affiliation, and so on. It is important to note that role categories imply context-embedded relationships—there can be no role of lawyer without the complementary role of client; no role of mother without the role of child, no role of Chicano without the role of Anglo. Further, the social systems in which the person operates are strands in the same context that embeds the role relationships.

Role relationships being the definers of one's social identity, planned or unplanned changes in role relationships change the answers to the *who am I* and *who are you* questions and the simultaneous inferences about social identity. Changes in social identity are the rule, occurring with changes in the roles of complementary others; for example, one's location in social space is different when one interacts with an adult or with a child, with a nurse or with a physician, with a victim or with a victimizer. To understand the conduct of a participant in a culture requires a set of dimensions that makes it possible to determine the relative contribution of *particular roles* to one's social identity; further, these dimensions should facilitate recognition of the effects of upgrading or downgrading one's placement in the role system. For this purpose, we use a three-dimensional model that provides the means for assessing the total value of a person's social identity at any point in time (Sarbin, 1968a). The three dimensions are (a) the status dimension, (b) the involvement dimension, and (c) the value dimension. The appropriateness of this model to account for the act of declaring value on role performances will become apparent in the following paragraphs. The better to describe the model, the reader can imagine a three-dimensional space: the status dimension is a scale on the horizontal, the value dimension is a scale on the vertical, and the involvement dimension is a scale on the front-to-rear. Because the dimensions are not independent, the cube would

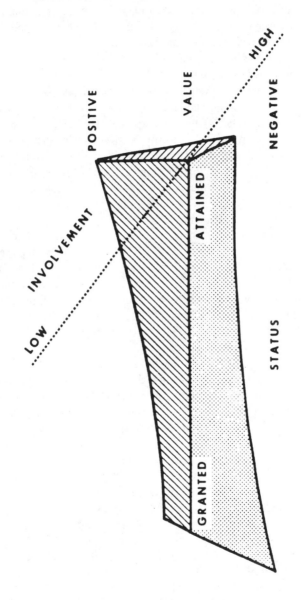

Fig. 1. The three dimensional model of social identity: status, value, and involvement.

not be the most appropriate model. A wedge, triangular at the non-cutting edge, would be an approximate representation (see Figure 1). (See Sarbin and Scheibe, 1970.)

Status and Role

"Status" is used in the sociological sense. It is the unit of social structure. Position is a synonym. The relationship between role and status may be constructed as follows: A status or position is an abstraction or set of beliefs defined by the expectations held by members of a social group; role is a set of public behaviors enacted by an individual to validate his or her occupancy of a particular status. Another way of differentiating these related concepts is to regard status as an epistemic notion, a set of expectations as perceived by persons, and to regard role as a unit of conduct, characterized by performances. This set of definitions leans on Linton's (1936) classification of statuses (and their corresponding roles) as *ascribed* or *achieved*. For conceptual analysis, Linton separated statuses defined primarily by biological characteristics, such as age, sex, and kinship, which he called *ascribed*, from those characterized by attainment or option, which he called *achieved*. Examples of ascribed statuses are mother, son, adult, child, uncle, male, Jew, American, and person; of achieved statuses, medicine man, student, ballet dancer, and voter. This two-valued classification is too limiting. Numerous instances show the contribution of both ascriptive and achievement factors. To be a candidate for the achieved status of President, for example, requires that one occupy certain ascribed statuses in regard to age, sex, and nativity. In the social identity model, the status dimension is not represented as two orthogonal axes. The status dimension is represented as one two-poled dimension. The underlying conception is the degree of choice prior to entry into any particular status. At one end point of the dimension are statuses granted to the individual simply in virtue of membership in a society, for example, *person*. Sex roles, age roles, kinship roles, and nationality are in the same region of the dimension. The other end point is defined by statuses with high degrees of choice, such as member of the Chamber of Commerce or secretary of the hospital auxiliary. Several paths lead to filling a position at the choice end, among them election, nomination, training, revelation, and achievement. There are some statuses in the middle of the dimension where ascriptive and achievement features are evident. Kindergarten teacher, for example, is an achieved role. However, the fact that the teacher is expected to serve as a mother surrogate suggests ascription.

Statuses that are heavily ascribed are further defined as less differentiated. The skills required to make good the occupancy of statuses at the ascribed end are nonspecific. Such statuses are assigned to large numbers of members in a society. Thus every adult member in principle is granted the minimal status of cultural participant or person; that is, all adults are expected to conform to certain propriety norms that have priority over specific expectations attached to any attained or choice status. Among these propriety norms are communication rules, modesty codes, rules for controlling ingroup aggression, and rules governing property.

Statuses at the achieved end may be additionally defined as optional and highly differentiated, their requirements applying to a few potential candidates. Examples would be a Nobel Prize winner, a tennis champion, and the chairman of the Joint Chiefs of Staff. The dimension is highly correlated with legitimate power. In addition to the bare minimum of rights granted in virtue of an individual's holding the ascribed status of person, individuals acquire grants of legitimate power according to the location of their statuses toward the achievement or choice end of the dimension. In general, then, one's social identity may include several validated statuses located at different points on the status dimension, some carrying explicit grants of power, others little or none. In some contexts, one's social identity may not include validated statuses that carry any grants of power, thus putting the person at a disadvantage in strategic interactions with persons who hold power. The utility of this formulation in influencing deviant conduct is almost universally recognized by family therapists (Berger, 1978).

Involvement

Involvement is the action component of the model. This dimension reflects the degree of freedom to become involved or disinvolved in a role. It is recognized in two ways: (1) the amount of *time* given to the occupancy of certain statuses, and (2) the degree of *organismic energy* expended in the role enactment. An individual whose identity includes a status at the achievement end of the continuum has the freedom to be highly involved in the role enactment at one time and not involved at other times. In short, the possibility exists for variation in time and effort expended in enacting attained roles. A professor is highly involved in the role when he or she is in the lecture hall, in the library, or reading student reports. Professors are relatively uninvolved in the professor role, when attending a concert, selecting a wardrobe, or repairing a broken lock. At the ascribed or granted end, involvement is typically high. One has little freedom to become disinvolved. To be cast in the role of adult male, for example, means occupying the status nearly all the time. Peterson (1972) has shown with dramatic clarity that to be cast in the role of governess in Victorian England demanded high involvement, and the typical governess had no choice to become disinvolved and choose an alternate career. To be assigned exclusively to the extreme granted role of person, or its negatively valued counterpart, nonperson, similarly means being in role all the time. To use a current theatrical metaphor, the actor in the ascribed role is "on" all the time. Common examples of roles that are highly involving and without choice for disinvolvement are prisoners in maximum security institutions, committed inmates of state mental hospitals, inmates of concentration camps, the pauperized poor in urban ghettos, young children in authoritarian households, and novices in religious orders. The social identity of a member of these classes of persons includes few, if any, achieved roles in which enactment would be intermittent. Legitimate opportunities for obtaining multiple perspectives, or role distance, in Goffman's (1961) terms, are absent when one's identity is composed exclusively of a small number of granted roles.

Valuations

Into this model one may introduce a vocabulary that helps define the variations in assigning value to the conduct of others. Two qualitatively different types of valuation are easily identified: esteem and respect. Esteem (the root is also seen in *estimate*) is value assigned for performance of roles in the achieved (choice) region of the status dimension. The awarding of tokens of esteem, prizes, emoluments, praise, gold stars, honorific titles, symbols of power, and authority follow upon the enactment of proper, appropriate, and convincing role performances.

Respect calls out a different set of responses. Respect is first assigned to the status or office, not to the person enacting the corresponding role. In many societies, a grant of respect is assigned to motherhood. In some social orders, *machismo* carries a grant of respect. Being regarded as a person—a member of a particular social group—means being assigned some minimal recognition that one is respected.

In the same way that it takes a public performance to initiate esteem valuations for achieved roles, for example, the activities of a piano virtuoso, it takes a public performance to initiate valuations of *disrespect* for ascribed roles, for example, those of parent, son, or person. The conditions for assigning disrespect vary from context to context. For example, under most circumstances, the granted status of person includes expectations that reciprocity rules will be followed in face-to-face discourse. Silence, a violation of reciprocity, is expected or allowed in some contexts and not others. Participants in certain religious orders follow special rules for discourse, rules that expect silence. Unless a supporting context can be found, when reciprocity rules are violated, the audience is placed in a condition of strain. One way of resolving the strain is to declare the silent one a nonperson. (The term nonperson is not a part of any diagnostic system. Therefore, labels such as *catatonia, mutism* and *schizophrenia* are employed.) It is important to note that the disrespect valuation inherent in identifying an individual as a nonperson can be effectively applied only by someone who has legitimate or coercive power.

The model's utility in helping us understand human conduct becomes apparent when we consider the value dimension in more detail. At the same time that the public role enactments provide the basis for locating an individual's identity on the status dimension, they provide the basis for observers to make declarations of value. The relevant audiences that assign value to role enactments present an acute problem. Standards of judgment vary for different sectors. Family members are more concerned with assigning value to the enactment of family (ascribed) roles, employers with assigning value to performance on the job, drama critics with assigning value to the stage performances of actors, juries with assigning value to the actions of defendants, and so on.

As the vertical scale in our three-dimensional model, the value dimension has a neutral point and positive and negative end points. As described earlier, the region from the neutral point to the positive end point is the region of esteem—applicable to the valuation of choice, achieved roles; the region from the neutral point to the negative end point is the region of disrespect.

Role Dependent Value Variations

From this exposition, it is clear that public performances are always subject to value declarations by significant others. On the positive side, performances can lead to the maintenance of respectability for the granted components of roles and to commendations or promotions for the achieved components. On the negative side, performances in heavily ascribed statuses can lead to the loss of respect, the ultimate derogation being assigned the disrespected status of nonperson; performances in achieved statuses can lead to demotion and reduction in esteem.

When considering the nonperformance of roles heavily weighted with achievement criteria, valuations tend to be more neutral than those declared on the nonperformance of granted roles. Being fired from a job, being dropped from an athletic team, or flunking a course would be examples of demotion: the person's conduct before the demotion would ordinarily not perturb or outrage a community. Demotion is explained in rule-following language: lack of skill, lack of seniority, lack of preparation, and so on. The quality of valuations declared on performances of primarily achieved roles vary from positive to neutral, from high esteem to little or no esteem. Further, the granting of esteem does not vary with the differential power of the judge as in the case of the granting of disrespect. Theater goers in the cheap gallery seats can applaud as heartily as those in the expensive boxes.

Let us consider further role enactments aimed at validating statuses that are heavily ascribed or granted. Little or no positive value is declared for the enactment of granted roles. An individual is not praised for participation in a culture as a male, an adult, a father, an American, a person. We are *expected* to enact such roles without incentive motivation. The status carries with it a grant of respect that is subject to being cancelled when the status occupant publicly fails to enact appropriate role behavior. The *nonperformance* of granted roles, however, calls out intense negative valuations. For example, in place of respect for *being* a man, the male loses respect when he fails to perform according to the local expectations for masculine sexuality. Other things being equal, a woman is respected for *being* a mother, for occupying the position of mother. If she *fails* to show interest in the care and welfare of her children, she is subject to valuations of disrespect. The same analysis applies to individuals who fail to act according to age standards, kinship norms, or national identity norms. The status of *person*—the very endpoint of the status dimension—carries with it silent expectations that the status occupant will engage in role behavior to meet minimal expectations. We have already mentioned that these expectations may be regarded as *propriety norms* for dealing with age- and sex-graded behavior, kinship, and reciprocal social interaction (communication), modesty, property, and ingroup aggression. When those who value the norms of propriety perceive violations of these role requirements, no form of transvaluation is available for the individual holding the minimal granted position other than the declaration of nonperson.

SOCIAL RESPONSE TO NONPERSON STATUS

If the label of disrespect is applied by an individual or group empowered to apply such labels, the society goes to work to treat the individual as a nonperson. A term widely used to represent nonperson is *brute*, sometimes rendered as *beast*, *animal*, or *low-grade human* (Platt & Diamond, 1965). Such labels are not a part of our scientific and professional lexicon because we have coined special euphemisms which *only for a short time* attenuate the strong negative valuational component—for example, the hard-to-reach, the disadvantaged, slum dwellers, clients, wards, charity cases, paupers, the socially ill, welfare recipients, the masses, the unemployed, problem-families, damaged human material, immigrants, aliens, and so on. The euphemistic component fails to conceal the underlying reference of the label, that of nonperson. The labelled individual is likely to be perceived as without grade on the status dimension and without respect valuation.

The pejorative labels provide a means of codifying answers to the *who are you* question *and to designate a degraded social identity*. The pejorative label, for example, *schizophrenic*, is assigned by mental health workers. The label serves the same function as visible stigmata of degradation. In some totalistic settings, where there may be ambiguity in identifying a member of the degraded class, those in power legislate that appropriate emblems or identifying marks be worn. Special clothing in prisons and hospitals, tattooed serial numbers, and insignia are common examples. The Star of David had to be worn by Jews in Nazi Germany. In England an act was passed in 1697 directing any person on relief to wear a pauper's badge. In this way, the degraded poor could be publicly identified as different from the respectable poor. Stigmata of degradation serve the purpose of identifying nonpersons. Even branding has been used to designate such declared nonpersons as harlots, heretics, and slaves. In modern times, nonvisible stigmata in the form of diagnostic labels have been employed—mental patients, psychotics, schizophrenics, lunatics, etc.

Note that societies do not concern themselves with stigmatizing people who are unsuccessful in achieved roles. Loss of esteem occurs in a public context, and is explained according to prevailing beliefs about entering and exiting from achieved roles. The loss of esteem for nonperformance of an achieved role is seldom taken as a starting point for elaborating a causal theory. When a champion loses the title, an industrial executive is demoted, or a politician defeated, explanations are drawn from rule-following models. Failure is attributed to lack of practice, ageing, superior competition, economic considerations, etc. Just as the *acquisition* of an achieved status is explained through the application of rule-following models, so the loss of status is accounted for in the same way. To repeat: esteem is granted for appropriate performance of achieved roles. Respect is granted, not necessarily on public performances, but on the expectation that the status occupant observes the salient propriety norms. Disrespect is assigned to the person who publicly fails to meet propriety norms. The occasion for assigning disrespect—the nonperformance of granted roles—encourages explanations of a causal kind, such as defective gene pools, humoral displacements, depravity, constitutional psychopathic inferiority, unconscious conflicts, toxins, psychic forces, psychosexual complexes, etc. The proper occupancy of ascribed statuses is fundamental to the maintenance of a collectivity—they are the givens. Behavior scientists have not invoked rule-following models to account for either enactment or nonenactment. Instead, mechanistic and formistic principles presumably located in the body, the germ plasm, or the psyche are sought.

To degrade an individual's identity, one may deprive the person of opportunities for the enactment of choice (achieved) roles. This can be implemented by placing the person in a totalistic setting such as a prison, concentration camp, or other cultural unit with very limited provisions for enacting achieved roles and concomitantly no provision for becoming disinvolved from the requirements of ascribed roles. In this way, people in such settings are left only with roles heavily weighted with ascribed characteristics, with no freedom for disinvolvement. People in such statuses cannot escape the strain of being continuously involved in a limited number of granted roles. They are constantly at risk lest a failure to perform will lead to degradation or disrespect. Totalistic institutional arrangements are not the only situations where degradation may occur. Some family and other primary group arrangements fit many of the criteria for total institutions (Goffman, 1961).

These arrangements create the conditions for strain. If no opportunities exist for acquiring esteem valuations, and if the opportunity is everpresent for failure in ascribed roles, then conditions for strain-in-knowing (briefly discussed in the previous chapter) arise. One is activated to develop a way of knowing one's location in the social matrix. At times this strain reaches high levels of intensity; and, with constant invalidation of the effort to enact suitable roles, the strain might persist for extended periods of time. The efforts to achieve personal identity may become desperate.

UNACCEPTABLE RESOLUTIONS OF EPISTEMIC STRAIN

It is a legitimate question whether the payoffs are commensurate with the high degree of strain imposed on the individual. It is no wonder that from the point of view of the dominant normative system, indices of social pathology are highest among populations that hold only granted status. If, let us say, people are unemployable and have no other vehicles for achieving a positively valued identity, they have few chances of displaying conduct that may be esteemed by themselves or others. If the dominant system places a negative valuation on being unemployable, then we have a situation that shares features of institutions usually cited as totalistic: maximum security prisons, locked wards of mental hospitals, thought-control camps. These more obviously totalistic social organizations lead to degradation *in extremis*, to the identity of a nonperson.

The differences in degree between these more obviously totalistic settings and the settings that provide potential candidates for contemporary mental health services are reflected in the fact that the relevant social structures are not completely totalistic. These potential candidates for valuation by agents of the social order acquire beliefs during their early socialization experiences that someday they may perform roles-by-choice and thus attain esteem. First, in the bosom of the family, then in the early years of school, then through the mass media, children are led to believe that they have a chance to occupy statuses that include achieved as well as granted components. Such a system of beliefs might be elided into the following shorthand premise: *In addition to being a person, male, an Italian-American, etc., I am a worthy and esteemed member of society.* Relevant and significant others in the social ecology, however, may withhold confirming positive valuations because the individual is not perceived as occupying achieved statuses. A contrary premise is formed: *I am not a worthy and esteemed member of society.* Such paired contradictory premises are the conditions of epistemic strain, a state of affairs for which *problem* is a more apt metaphor than *sickness.*

The concept of epistemic strain and counterpart concepts developed in the psychological literature, as described in Chapter 10, provide the motivation statement in the transvaluation model. Under conditions of epistemic strain, that is, when a person has a problem, individuals are mobilized to restore a contextual equilibrium. They must act.

In the resolution of epistemic strain associated with status problems, persons may engage in conduct subject to the valuational activities of significant others. When the strain-in-knowing occurs in connection with solving social identity problems connected with ascribed roles, the target person finds himself or herself with limited opportunities for resolution. The cognitive networks for defining social situations available to degraded individuals are, by definition, limited; and so is the range of possible actions. The social networks of individuals esteemed for their performance of roles-by-choice provide many resources for resolving strain and reconciling contrary premises. The people reared in marginal circumstances in our society are the very people who are least equipped to achieve satisfying resolutions to the status-induced epistemic strain that was, in the first place, created by their having been restricted to highly involving assigned statuses. Members of the marginal classes, which supply the hospitals with a steady flow of clients, thus are most susceptible to status-induced problems and are least able to develop acceptable solutions.

The person faced with status-induced problems may choose from three broad strategies for resolving epistemic strain occasioned by the contradictory premises (a) *I am a person,* and (b) *I am not a person.* The individual can engage in instrumental acts to validate the first premise. The objective of such actions is to change the person's status, valuation, and opportunities for disinvolvement. If the acts place the significant (and usually more powerful) others at risk, the person is likely to be declared unfit, crazy, or dangerous (Sarbin, 1967a). Rather than risk increased degradation, the individual can employ a strategy to validate the second premise by engaging in acts to justify being in a nonperson status. The individual can perform in ways that are not governed by the rules of personhood. Dostoevski's *Underground Man* regarded himself as a fly, a cipher, a nothing. The third strategy involves modulated action through the exercise of skill in imagining. One can validate the first premise through symbolic means, by constructing a pseudocommunity (Cameron, 1948) in which one can perform roles that provide esteem. Don Quixote and Walter Mitty are exemplars of this form of action—Don Quixote acting out his imaginings in the world of other people, Walter Mitty in the private world of fantasy.

Designations as disrespect and lack of esteem are used as a first step toward controlling the conduct of degraded persons. A society manages to employ a variety of instrumental and ritual actions to control or contain conduct: execution, banishment, sequestering, incarceration, flogging, reprimanding, shaming, and branding. The tradition that has supported schizophrenia as diagnosis is one of many traditions arising from society's needs to control its nonconforming members. That schizophrenia has become a euphemism for unwanted and unwelcome conduct cannot be gainsaid.

CONCLUSION

Our objective in sketching the social identity model is only to illustrate that it is possible to look at unwanted conduct without recourse to the mystification of medical diagnosis. The model recognizes explicitly that assignment of value— positive or negative—for certain acts is a moral enterprise. In a democracy, such an enterprise belongs to the people and those to whom magisterial functions have been delegated by the people. To assign this task to physicians and their surrogates is to give power to a select group who have demonstrated no special competence as moralists.

Schizophrenia is a moral verdict masquerading as a medical diagnosis. We propose an unmasking. The recognition that the schizophrenia model persists because of its mythic quality should hasten the construction of new metaphors to communicate about unwanted conduct. This chapter proposes one such metaphor: the unwanted conduct that is taken to be symptomatic of schizophrenia flows from the degradation of social identity, a social process dependent on identifiable contexts. No bit of behavior per se is unwanted. Only in some contexts and not in others is an action subject to valuations that may have immediate and remote effects on answering the all-important human question: *Who am I?*

Epilogue:
In Search of the Unicorn

We have come to the end of our journey. Among other things, we have tried to establish that the schizophrenia model of unwanted conduct lacks credibility. The analysis directs us ineluctably to the conclusion that schizophrenia is a myth. To demonstrate the mythic character of a concept is not to make light of the events presumably illuminated by that concept. The woman who reports that her husband forces her to enact the role of prostitute is not a myth.

Because they have utility, myths must be taken seriously. The student of myths is enjoined to ask detailed questions about their utility. The prime question is: Whose interests are served by the individual or collective actions guided by a particular myth? It is not long since the myth of Aryan superiority provided the justification for unspeakable horrors, and the myth of the Manifest Destiny of the Anglo-Saxon peoples chartered American expansionist political and economic activities. The myth of schizophrenia has multiple utilities, as we have shown throughout our analysis and especially in Chapters 8, 9, and 10. These utilities center on the social control of persons whose conduct sometimes offends the moral proprieties of others. A major spin-off utility is the financial support granted to huge medical, pharmaceutical, and bureaucratic establishments.

Until exploded, a myth generates actions designed to strengthen the beliefs and actions that give it force. Scientists develop tools and technologies to locate the supposed empirical basis of the myth. Seventeenth-century scientists sought to identify phlogiston, the mythic substance regarded as a necessary constituent of combustible bodies and surrendered in the process of burning. Eighteenth-century scientists, influenced by Mesmer's application of the myth of animal magnetism, constructed theories and methods to identify the properties of purported "action-at-a-distance." Nineteenth-century physicists directed their efforts to discovering the characteristics of a mythic medium, ether, presumably filling all space and making possible the motions of light, heat, and electricity.

These examples of myths from the history of science are instructive. They give force to the metaphor-to-myth transformation as a common occurrence in the development of scientific (and lay) efforts to solve puzzles.

When people (scientists or laymen) encounter events for which they have no ready-made linguistic form—events that induce epistemic strain—they make use of a metaphor from another universe of discourse. They select a term that captures similarity but at the same time contains the connotation of difference. Under specifiable conditions (Chun & Sarbin, 1970) a metaphor may be literalized. Such reification may expand to become a myth. Phlogiston, animal magnetism, and ether were once lively metaphors.

One strategy for exposing a myth is to show its metaphoric foundation and to demonstrate that its literalization was illegitimate. To make use of a metaphoric marker and say, "It is *as if* the thinking, feeling, and acting of a person are split off from each other" does not have the same implications as saying, "He has a split mind," especially when rendered through the use of esoteric Greek word forms as in "He is suffering from schizophrenia."

The usual procedure for dissolving a myth is given a reverse twist in Salzinger's book *Schizophrenia: Behavioral Aspects* (1973). Salzinger begins by noting that a common characteristic is shared by both schizophrenia and the unicorn, that creature so commonly known to be a denizen of fabulous forests: They are both difficult to pin down.

> Imagine that you are given the following task: you are to describe the unicorn, explain where it comes from, and specify how to capture it. If you know anything about unicorns you will immediately go to the library and start looking under Mythology. There you will find descriptions of a fabulous animal with one horn, and, in the more expensive books, you will discover colored illustrations. The pictures and verbal descriptions will show that the unicorn comes in assorted colors and sizes, and that it has a single horn in the middle of its forehead. If you stop at that point, you will arrive at a satisfactory description, but if you delve further you will find that the unicorn cannot be captured except by a virgin, and even then rarely. What's more, the essential conditions are not very well specified. . . .
>
>   How does this relate to schizophrenia? Let me state the relation in as simple and straight-forward a way as I can: *schizophrenia is a unicorn.* In neither case do we have definitive information about the cause for its appearance. In both cases a voluminous literature is available, and in both cases various authors have written about the phenomenon lacking the knowledge of what others proposed. Schizophrenia, like the unicorn, is described in various ways by various people. And its elimination, like the capture of the unicorn, appears to require some special conditions, not all of which have been specified. Finally, whether or not these conditions exist, belief in their existence has had significant consequences [Salzinger, 1973, pp. 1-2; italics added].

At this point, the reader of Salzinger's book would expect a conclusion of the form: since the unicorn is a mythical beast, and "schizophrenia is a unicorn," therefore schizophrenia is a mythical entity. Surprisingly, the author goes on to say:

> The implication of all this is that the subject of schizophrenia requires special treatment. The many uncertainties about it demand that we devote a good deal of space to the methods that

produced the descriptions in conflict, that we do not pretend to be able to describe *this disorder* simply, and that, at least in the areas of greatest dispute, we avoid drawing definitive conclusions. Furthermore, it implies that no formal and complete definition of schizophrenia is available . . . [p. 2; italics added].

The remainder of Salzinger's book attempts to analyze current research and theory. In the epilogue, some 145 pages later, Salzinger concludes his analysis:

Research has yielded significant consistencies about the *behavior of the schizophrenic* with respect to the importance of the concept of reinforcement contingency. In every chapter we have shown that *deficits attributed to schizophrenia* can be modified by the proper administration of reinforcement over surprisingly short periods of time. The implication is obvious. Behavior theory should be more widely applied *to schizophrenics*, whether the cause is biological or social . . . [p. 145, italics added].

If we take Salzinger's pithy premise, "schizophrenia is a unicorn," and place it adjacent to a distillation of the latter quotations, we would have the materials for an interesting exercise in logic. Since schizophrenia and unicorns are defined as identical ("schizophrenia is a unicorn") and schizophrenia is regarded as a credible entity ("this disorder," "behavior of the schizophrenic"), then the unicorn must be a credible entity.

To be sure, Salzinger did not intend this conclusion, although it does follow from his statements. Yet there is a lesson here. We can breathe life into mythical inventions and convince ourselves of their credibility.

To conclude our book, we, too, use the figure of the unicorn. We hold that the unicorn is a mythical beast. Defined in this way, the unicorn is an apt metaphor for schizophrenia. Both schizophrenia and the unicorn share membership in the class *mythic entities*.

The reader is urged to dwell on this conclusion while reading Rilke's (1949) sonnet on the unicorn.

This is the creature that has never been.
They never knew it, and yet, nonetheless,
they loved the way it moved, its suppleness,
its neck, its very gaze, mild and serene.
Not there, because they loved it, it behaved
as though it were. They always left some space.
And in the clear unpeopled space they saved
it lightly reared its head, with scarce a trace
of not being there. They fed it, not with corn,
but only with the possibility
of being. And that was able to confer
such strength, its brow put forth a horn. One horn.
Whitely it stole up to a maid, to *be*
within the silver mirror and in her [p. 95].

Notes

CHAPTER 2

[1]Throughout this work we will use the terms *schizophrenia* and *schizophrenic* as they repeatedly are used by most scholars who study the unwanted and perplexing behavior that—under some conditions—allows persons to be treated as if they were suffering from a disease. The disease model which has been used to explain this behavior has served as the frame for these events; and people speak of *schizophrenia* when they refer to the enactment of certain kinds of conduct, or of *a schizophrenic* when they refer to a person who enacts such conduct. Since our discourse constantly considers the work of active scholars who have adopted this usage, we cannot efficiently alter terminology throughout this work. At times the term *schizophrenia* stands unqualified. At times we will enclose the terms *schizophrenia* or *schizophrenic* in quotation marks. At other times we will use the phrases "behavior which carns the label schizophrenia," or "persons who have been classed as schizophrenic." These usages will serve as reminders that we do not accept schizophrenia as a known or knowable entity. The aim of this whole work, obviously, is to demonstrate the appropriateness of our view.

CHAPTER 6

[1]A preliminary version of this chapter was delivered to the Fifth Annual meeting of the American Association for the Abolition of Involuntary Mental Hospitalization, April 14, 1975, New York, New York.

CHAPTER 8

[1]The terms *formism*, *mechanism*, and *contextualism* derive from Pepper's 1942) estimable treatise on metaphysical and epistemological systems. The terminology will be clarified at points where it is useful to elaborate Pepper's ideas. Initially we use Pepper's term *formism* rather than the term *idiography*, but as we proceed we will adopt a usage recommended by White (1972). White substitutes the term *idiography* for the term *formism*, on the grounds that the term is more self-explanatory. Not only do we agree, but we also note that the use of the term *idiographic* by Allport (1961), widely known among psychologists, amply reflects the application of a formist approach to personality explanation.

References

Abrams, R., Taylor, M.A., & Gaztanaga, P. Manic depressive illness and paranoid schizophrenia. *Archives of General Psychiatry,* 1974, **31,** 640-642.

Agnew, J. & Bannister, D. Psychiatric diagnosis as a pseudospecialist language. *British Journal of Medical Psychology,* 1973, **46,** 69-73.

Allen, D.W., & Alston, E.F. Letters to the editor. *San Francisco Examiner and Chronicle,* November 4, 1974, p. 40.

Allport, G.W. *Pattern and growth in personality.* New York: Holt, Rinehart, and Winston, 1961.

American Psychiatric Association. *Diagnostic and statistical manual: Mental disorders* (DSM-I). Washington, D.C.: American Psychiatric Association, 1952.

American Psychiatric Association. *Diagnostic and statistical manual of mental disorders.* (2nd ed.) (DSM-II). Washington, D.C.: American Psychiatric Association, 1968.

American Psychiatric Association Task Force on Nomenclature and Statistics. *DSM-III Draft: Diagnostic and statistical manual of mental disorders.* Washington, D.C.: American Psychiatric Association, 1978.

American Psychiatric Association: Task Force on Nomenclature and Statistics. *Micro-D: Revisions in the diagnostic criteria of the DSM-III 1/15/78 draft.* Washington, D.C.: American Psychiatric Association, 1979.

Ames, R. Physical maturing among boys as related to adult social behaviors. *California Journal of Educational Research,* 1957, **8,** 69-75.

Anderson, M.L. The use of IQ tests in blaming the victims: Predicting incompetence rather than generating intelligence. *San Jose Studies,* 1978, **4,** 72-96.

Angrist, S., Lefton, M., Dinitz, S., & Pasamanick, B. *Women after treatment: A study of former mental patients and their normal neighbors.* New York: Appleton-Century-Crofts, 1968.

Arey, L.B. The indirect representation of sexual stimuli by schizophrenic and normal subjects. *Journal of Abnormal and Social Psychology,* 1960, **61,** 424-431.

Arieti, S. Special logic of schizophrenic and other types of autistic thought. *Psychiatry,* 1948, **11,** 325-338.

Asarnow, R.F. & MacCrimmon, D.J. Residual performance deficit in clinically remitted schizophrenics: A marker of schizophrenia. *Journal of Abnormal Psychology,* 1978, **87,** 597-608.

Atkinson, R.L. & Robinson, N.M. Paired-associate learning by schizophrenic and normal subjects under conditions of personal and impersonal reward and punishment. *Journal of Abnormal and Social Psychology,* 1961, **62,** 322-326.

Atthowe, J.M. & Krasner, L. Preliminary report on the application of contingency reinforcement procedures (token economy) on a "chronic" psychiatric ward. *Journal of Abnormal Psychology,* 1968, **73,** 37-43.

Ax, A., Bamford, J., Beckett, P., Fretz, N., & Gottlieb, G. Autonomic conditioning in chronic schizophrenia. *Journal of Abnormal Psychology,* 1970, **76**, 140-154.

Ayllon, T. Intensive treatment of psychotic behavior by stimulus satiation and food reinforcement. *Behavior Therapy and Research,* 1963, **1**, 53-61.

Ayllon, T. & Azrin, N.H. The measurement and reinforcement of behavior of psychotics. *Journal of Experimental Analysis of Behavior,* 1965, **8**, 357-383.

Ayllon, T. & Haughton, E. Control of the behavior of schizophrenic patients by food. *Journal of Experimental Analysis of Behavior,* 1962, **5**, 343-352.

Bannister, D. The logical requirements of research into schizophrenia. *British Journal of Psychiatry,* 1968, **114**, 181-188.

Bannister, D. (Ed.). *New perspectives in personal construct theory.* New York: Academic Press, 1977.

Bartko, J.J., Strauss, J.S., & Carpenter, W.T. An approach to the diagnosis and understanding of schizophrenia. Part II. Expanded perspectives for describing and comparing schizophrenic patients. *Schizophrenia Bulletin,* 1974, **1**, 50-60.

Bateson, G., Jackson, D.D., Haley, J., & Weakland, J.H. Toward a theory of schizophrenia. *Behavioral Science,* 1956, **1**, 251-264.

Baxter, J.C. & Becker, J. Anxiety and avoidance behavior in schizophrenics in response to parental figures. *Journal of Abnormal and Social Psychology,* 1962, **64**, 432-437.

Baxter, J.C., Becker, J., & Hooks, W. Defensive styles in the families of schizophrenics and controls. *Journal of Abnormal and Social Psychology,* 1963, **66**, 512-518.

Bazelon, D. The perils of wizardry. *American Journal of Psychiatry,* 1974, **131**, 1317-1322.

Becker, H.S. *Outsiders.* New York: Free Press of Glencoe, 1963.

Becker, J. & Finkel, P. Predictability and anxiety in speech by parents of female schizophrenics. *Journal of Abnormal Psychology,* 1969, **74**, 517-523.

Begelman, D.A. Schizophrenia versus organic impairment in abstractability. *British Journal of Psychiatry,* 1966, **112**, 783-788.

Bellak, L. Tracing the origins of schizophrenia. *Psychiatry and Social Science Review,* 1970, **4**, 14-17.

Berg, W.K. Habituation and dishabituation of cardiac responses in 4-month-old infants. *Journal of Experimental Child Psychology,* 1972, **14**, 92-107.

Berger, M.M. (Ed.). *Beyond the double bind.* New York: Brunner/Mazel, 1978.

Bernstein, A. Phasic electrodermal orienting response in chronic schizophrenics. II. Response to auditory signals of varying intensity. *Journal of Abnormal Psychology,* 1970, **75**, 146-156.

Bieri, J., Atkins, A.L., Briar, S., Leaman, R.L., Miller, H., & Tripodi, T. *Clinical and social judgment.* New York: Wiley, 1966.

Blatt, S.J. & Wild, C.M. *Schizophrenia: A developmental analysis.* New York: Academic Press, 1976.

Bleuler, E. *Dementia praecox, or the group of schizophrenias.* Translated by J. Zitkin. New York: International Universities Press, 1950. (First published in German, 1911.)

Bleuler, M. A 23-year longitudinal study of 208 schizophrenics and impressions in regard to the nature of schizophrenia. In D. Rosenthal and S. Kety (Eds.), *The transmission of schizophrenia,* New York, Pergamon Press, 1968. Pp. 3-12.

Blum, J.D. On changes in psychiatric diagnosis over time. *American Psychologist,* 1978, **33**, 1017-1031.

Blumenthal, R., Meltzoff, J., & Rosenberg, S. Some determinants of persistence in chronic schizophrenic subjects. *Journal of Abnormal Psychology,* 1965, **70**, 246-250.

Boardman, W.K., Goldstone, S., Reiner, M.L., & Fathauer, W.F. Anchor effects, spatial judgments, and schizophrenia. *Journal of Abnormal and Social Psychology,* 1962, **65**, 273-276.

Boisen, A.T. *Exploration of the inner world.* New York: Harper, 1936.

Boland, T. & Chapman, L. Conflicting predictions from Broen's and Chapman's theories of schizophrenic thought disorder. *Journal of Abnormal Psychology,* 1971, **78**, 52-58.

Braatz, G. Preference intransitivity as an indicator of cognitive slippage in schizophrenia. *Journal of Abnormal Psychology,* 1970, **75**, 1-6.

Braginsky, B.M. & Braginsky, D.D. *Hansels and Gretels*. New York: Holt, Rinehart, & Winston, 1971.

Braginsky, B.M. & Braginsky, D.D. *Mainstream psychology: A critique*. New York: Holt, Rinehart & Winston, 1974.

Braginsky, B.M., Braginsky, D.D., & Ring, K. *Methods of madness: The mental hospital as a last resort*. New York: Holt, Rinehart & Winston, 1969.

Brandt, A. *Reality police: The experience of insanity in America*. New York: William Morrow, 1975.

Broadbent, D.E. *Decision and stress*. New York: Academic Press, 1971.

Broekema, V. & Rosenbaum, G. Cutaneous sensitivity in schizophrenics and normals under two levels of proprioceptive arousal. *Journal of Abnormal Psychology*, 1975, **84**, 30-35.

Broen, W.E. Limiting the flood of stimulation: A protective deficit in chronic schizophrenics. In R. Soslo (Ed.), *Contemporary issues in cognitive psychology: The Loyola symposium*. New York: Wiley, 1973. PP. 191-211.

Broen, W.E. & Nakamura, C. Reduced range of sensory sensitivity in chronic nonparanoid schizophrenics, *Journal of Abnormal Psychology*, 1972, **79** (1), 106-111.

Broen, W.E. & Storms, L.H. Lawful disorganization: The process underlying a schizophrenic syndrome. *Psychological Review*, 1966, **73**, 265-279.

Bromet, E. & Harrow, M. Behavioral overinclusion as a prognostic index in schizophrenic disorders. *Journal of Abnormal Psychology*, 1973, **82**, 345-349.

Brown, R. Schizophrenia, language and reality. *American Psychologist*, 1973, **28**, 395-403.

Brown, R. & Berko, J. Word association and the acquisition of grammar. *Child Development*, 1960, **31**, 1-14.

Bruner, J.S., Goodnow, J.J., & Austin, G.A. *A study of thinking*. New York: Wiley, 1956.

Burrow, T. *The social basis of consciousness*. New York: Harcourt Brace, 1927.

Burstein, A.G. Some verbal aspects of primary process thought in schizophrenia. *Journal of Abnormal and Social Psychology*, 1961, **62**, 155-157.

Buss, A. & Lang, P.J. Psychological deficit in schizophrenia: I. Affect, reinforcement, and concept attainment. *Journal of Abnormal and Social Psychology*, 1965, **70**, 2-24.

Calhoun, J. Effects of performance payoff and cues on recall by hospitalized schizophrenics. *Journal of Abnormal Psychology*, 1970, **76**, 485-491.

Cameron, N. *The psychology of behavior disorders*. Boston: Houghton-Mifflin, 1948.

Campion, E. & Tucker, G. A note on twin studies, schizophrenia, and neurological impairment. *Archives of General Psychiatry*, 1973, **29**, 460-464.

Campbell, D. *The puritan in Holland, England, and America*. Vol. II. New York: Harper, 1892.

Cancro, R. & Sugerman, A.A. Psychological differentiation and process-reactive schizophrenia. *Journal of Abnormal Psychology*, 1969, **74**, 415-419.

Carlsson, A. Antipsychotic drugs, neurotransmitters, and schizophrenia. *American Journal of Psychiatry*, 1978, **135**, 164-173.

Carpenter, M.D. Sensitivity to syntactic structure: Good versus poor premorbid schizophrenics. *Journal of Abnormal Psychology*, 1976, **85**, 41-50.

Cartwright, R. Sleep fantasy in normal and schizophrenic persons. *Journal of Abnormal Psychology*, 1972, **80**, 275-279.

Cash, T., Neale, J., & Cromwell, R. Span of apprehension in acute schizophrenics: Full-report technique. *Journal of Abnormal Psychology*, 1972, **79**, 322-326.

Cavanaugh, D.K., Cohen, W., & Lang, P.J. The effect of "social censure" and "social approval" on the psychomotor performance of schizophrenics. *Journal of Abnormal and Social Psychology*, 1960, **60**, 213-218.

Cazzullo, C.L., Smeraldi, E., & Penato, G. The leucocyte antigenic system HL-A as a possible genetic marker for schizophrenia. *British Journal of Psychiatry*, 1974, **125**, 25-27.

Cegalis, J.A., Leen, D., & Solomon, E.J. Attention in schizophrenia: An analysis of selectivity in the functional visual field. *Journal of Abnormal Psychology*, 1977, **86**, 470-482.

Chapanis, N.P. & Chapanis, A. Cognitive dissonance: Five years later. *Psychological Bulletin*, 1964, **61**, 1-22.

Chapman, L.J. Confusion of figurative and literal usages of words by schizophrenics and brain damaged patients. *Journal of Abnormal and Social Psychology*, 1960, **60**, 412-416.

Chapman, L.J. A reinterpretation of some pathological disturbances in conceptual breadth. *Journal of Abnormal and Social Psychology*, 1961, **62**, 514-519.

Chapman, L.J. & Baxter, J.C. The process-reactive distinction and patients' subculture. *Journal of Nervous and Mental Disease*, 1963, **136**, 352-359.

Chapman, L.J., Cameron, R., Cocke, J.G., & Pritchett, T. Effects of phenothazine withdrawal on proverb interpretation by chronic schizophrenics. *Journal of Abnormal Psychology*, 1975, **84**, 24-29.

Chapman, L.J. & Chapman, J.P. *Disordered thought in schizophrenia*. Englewood Cliffs, N.J.: Prentice-Hall, 1973. (a)

Chapman, L.J. & Chapman, J.P. Problems in the measurement of cognitive deficit. *Psychological Bulletin*, 1973, **79**, 380-385. (b)

Chapman, L.J. & Chapman, J.P. Schizophrenic cognitive deficit as a function of scoring standards. *Journal of Abnormal Psychology*, 1975, **84**, 114-121.

Chapman, L.J., Chapman, J.P., & Daut, R.L. Schizophrenic response to affectivity in word definition. *Journal of Abnormal Psychology*, 1974, **83**, 616-622.

Chapman, L.J., Chapman, J.P., & Daut, R.L. Schizophrenic inability to disattend from strong aspects of meaning. *Journal of Abnormal Psychology*, 1976, **85**, 35-40.

Chapman, L.J., Chapman, J.P., & Miller, G.A. A theory of verbal behavior in schizophrenia. In B.A. Maher (Ed.), *Progress in experimental personality research*. Vol. 1. New York: Academic Press, 1964. Pp. 49-77.

Chapman, L.J., Day, D., & Burstein, A. The process-reactive distinction and prognosis in schizophrenia. *Journal of Nervous and Mental Disease*, 1961, **133**, 383-391.

Chapman, L.J. & Taylor, J.A. The breadth of deviate concepts used by schizophrenics. *Journal of Abnormal and Social Psychology*, 1957, **54**, 118-123.

Cheek, F.E. A serendipitous finding: Sex roles and schizophrenia. *Journal of Abnormal and Social Psychology*, 1964, **69**, 392-400.

Chun, K. & Sarbin, T.R. An empirical demonstration of the metaphor to myth transformation. *Philosophical Psychology*, 1970, **4**, 16-21.

Cicchetti, D.V. Reported family dynamics and psychopathology. I. The reactions of schizophrenics and normals to parental dialogues. *Journal of Abnormal Psychology*, 1967, **72**, 282-289.

Cicchetti, D.V., Klein, E.B., Fontana, A.F., & Spohn, H.E. A test of the censure-deficit model in schizophrenia, employing the Rodnick-Garmezy visual-discrimination task. *Journal of Abnormal Psychology*, 1967, **72**, 326-334.

Clothier, F. The unmarried mother of school age as seen by a psychiatrist. *Mental Hygiene*, 1955, **39**, 631-646.

Cocozza, J.J. & Steadman, H.J. The failure of psychiatric predictions of dangerousness: Clear and convincing evidence. *Rutgers Law Review*, 1976, **29**, 1084-1101.

Cofer, C. Constructive processes in memory. *American Scientist*, 1973, **61**, 537-543.

Cohen, B.D. & Cahmi, J. Schizophrenic performance in a word communication task. *Journal of Abnormal Psychology*, 1967, **72**, 240-246.

Cohen, B., Nachmani, G. & Rosenberg, S. Referent communication disturbances in acute schizophrenia. *Journal of Abnormal Psychology*, 1974, **83**, 1-13.

Coleman, J.C. *Abnormal psychology and modern life*. Fair Lawn, New Jersey: Scott, Foresman, 1972.

Coleman, J.S. et al. *Equality of educational opportunity*. Washington, D.C.: U.S. Government Printing Office, 1966.

Cotter, L.H. Operant conditioning in a Vietnamese mental hospital. *American Journal of Psychiatry*, 1967, **124**, 23-28.

Cox, G., Costanzo, P., & Coie, J. A survey instrument for the assessment of popular conceptions of mental illness. *Journal of Consulting and Clinical Psychology*, 1976, **44**, 901-909.

Craik, F.J.M. & Lockhart, R.S. Levels of processing: A framework for memory search. *Journal of Verbal Learning and Verbal Behavior*, 1972, **11**, 671-684.

Cromwell, R.L. Concluding remarks. In L.C. Wynne, R.L. Cromewell, & S. Matthysse (Eds.), *The nature of schizophrenia*. New York: Wiley, 1978. Pp. 76-83.

Crumpton, E. Persistence of maladaptive responses in schizophrenia. *Journal of Abnormal and Social Psychology*, 1963, **66**, 615-618.

Dain, N. *Concepts of insanity in the United States*. New Brunswick, N.J.: Rutgers University Press, 1964.

Davies-Osterkamp, S., Rist, F., & Bangert, A. Selective attention, breadth of attention, and shifting attention in chronic nonparanoid schizophrenics. *Journal of Abnormal Psychology*, 1977, **86**, 461-469.

Davis, G.C., Bunney, W.E., DeFraites, E.G., Kleinman, J.E., Van Kanmen, D.P., Post, R.M., & Wyatt, D.N. Intravenous naloxone administration in schizophrenia and affective illness. *Science*, 1977, **197**, 74-76.

Davis, J.M. The efficacy of tranquilizing and anti-depressant drugs. *Archives of General Psychiatry*, 1965, **13**, 552-572.

Davis, W. & DeWolfe, A. Premorbid adjustment and affective expression in schizophrenia. *Journal of Abnormal Psychology*, 1971, **78**, 198-201.

Davison, G.S. & Neale, J.M. The effects of signal-noise similarity on visual information processing of schizophrenics. *Journal of Abnormal Psychology*, 1974, **83**, 683-686.

DeMille, R. & Licht, L. Failure of an alternation learning test to discriminate between lobotomized and unlobotomized schizophrenics. *Journal of Abnormal Psychology*, 1966, **71**, 60-64.

DePorte, M.V. *Nightmares and hobbyhorses*. San Marino, California: The Huntington Library, 1974.

Depue, R.A. & Woodburn, L. Disappearance of paranoid symptoms with chronicity. *Journal of Abnormal Psychology*, 1975, **84**, 84-86.

Dershowitz, A.M. The law of dangerousness: Some fictions about predictions. *Journal of Legal Education*, 1970, **23**, 24-47.

Dershowitz, A.M. Preventive confinement: A suggested framework for constitutional analysis. *Texas Law Review*, 1973, **51**, 1277-1324.

DeWolfe, A.S. The effect of affective tone on the verbal behavior process and reactive schizophrenics. *Journal of Abnormal and Social Psychology*, 1962, **64**, 450-455.

Diggory, J.C. & Loeb, A. Motivation of chronic schizophrenics by information about their abilities in a group situation. *Journal of Abnormal and Social Psychology*, 1962, **65**, 48-52.

Dohrenwend, B.P. & Chin-Shong, E. Social status and attitudes toward psychological disorder: The problem of tolerance of deviance. *American Sociological Review*, 1967, **32**, 417-433.

Dohrenwend, B.S. & Dohrenwend, B.P. Field studies of social factors in relation to three types of psychological disorder. *Journal of Abnormal Psychology*, 1967, **72**, 369-378.

Dokecki, P.R., Polidoro, L.A., & Cromwell, R.L. Commonality and stability of word association responses in good and poor premorbid schizophrenics. *Journal of Abnormal Psychology*, 1965, **70**, 312-316.

Donovan, M.J. & Webb, W.W. Meaning dimensions and male-female voice perception in schizophrenics with good and poor premorbid adjustment. *Journal of Abnormal Psychology*, 1965, **70**, 426-431.

Dorfman, D.D. The Cyril Burt question: New findings. *Science*, 1978, **201**, 1177-1186.

Draguns, J.G. Responses to cognitive and perceptual ambiguity in chronic and acute schizophrenics. *Journal of Abnormal and Social Psychology*, 1963, **66**, 24-30.

Drennen, W., Gallman, W., & Sausser, G. Verbal operant conditioning of hospitalized psychiatric patients. *Journal of Abnormal Psychology*, 1969, **74**, 454-458.

Ellinwood, E.H., Sudilovsky, A., & Nelson, L. Behavioral analysis of chronic amphetamine intoxication. *Biological Psychology*, 1972, **4**, 215-230.

Ellman, G.L., Jones, R.T., & Rychert, R.C. Mauve spot and schizophrenia. *American Journal of Psychiatry*, 1968, **125**, 849-851.

Endicott, J. & Spitzer, R.L. Use of the research diagnostic criteria and the schedule for affective disorders and schizophrenia to study affective disorders. *American Journal of Psychiatry*, 1979, **136**, 52-56.

Farina, A. Patterns of role dominance and conflict in parents of schizophrenic patients. *Journal of Abnormal and Social Psychology*, 1960, **61**, 31-38.

Farina, A. & Holzberg, J.D. Attitudes and behaviors of fathers and mothers of male schizophrenic patients. *Journal of Abnormal Psychology*, 1967, **72**, 381-387.

Farina, A. & Holzberg, J.D. Interaction patterns of parents and hospitalized sons diagnosed as schizophrenic or nonschizophrenic. *Journal of Abnormal Psychology*, 1968, **73**, 114-118.

Farina, A., Holzberg, J.D., & Dies, R.R. The influence of the parents and verbal reinforcement on the performance of schizophrenic patients. *Journal of Abnormal Psychology*, 1969, **74**, 9-15.

Farnsworth, D. *The Farnsworth-Munsell 100 hue test for examination of color discrimination: Manual*. Baltimore: Munsell Color Co., 1957.

Feffer, M.H. The influence of affective factors on conceptualization in schizophrenia. *Journal of Abnormal and Social Psychology*, 1961, **63**, 588-596.

Fenz, W. & Velner, G. Physiological concomitants of behavioral indexes in schizophrenia. *Journal of Abnormal Psychology*, 1970, **76**, 27-35.

Festinger, L. *A theory of cognitive dissonance*. Stanford, California: Stanford University Press, 1957.

Fitzgibbons, D.J. & Shearn, C.R. Scale for the measurement of attitudes about schizophrenia. *Journal of Consulting and Clinical Psychology*, 1972, **38**, 288-295.

Flavell, J.H. Abstract thinking and social behavior in schizophrenia. *Journal of Abnormal and Social Psychology*, 1956, **52**, 208-211.

Flavell, J.H. *Cognitive development*. Englewood Cliffs, N.J.: Prentice-Hall, 1977.

Fleming, D. (Ed.), Loeb, J. *The mechanistic conception of life*. Cambridge, Harvard, 1964 (originally published 1912).

Fontana, A.F., Klein, E.B., & Cicchetti, D.V. Censure sensitivity in schizophrenia. *Journal of Abnormal Psychology*, 1967, **72**, 294-302.

Fox, R. Rate of binocular rivalry alternation in psychotic and nonpsychotic patients. *Journal of Abnormal Psychology*, 1965, **70**, 34-37.

Freeman, H.W. & Simmons, D.G. *The mental patient comes home*. New York: Wiley, 1963.

Freud, S. *Psychopathology of everyday life*. New York: New American Library, 1951. (First published in German, 1901.)

Freud, S. *An outline of psychoanalysis*, New York: W.W. Norton, 1949. (First published in German, 1940).

Friedhoff, A.J. & Van Winkle, E. The characteristics of an amine found in the urine of schizophrenic patients. *Journal of Nervous and Mental Diseases*, 1962, **135**, 550-555.

Fulker, D.W. A biometrical genetic approach to intelligence and schizophrenia. *Social Biology*, 1974, **20**, 266-275.

Fuller, G.D. & Kates, S.L. Word association repertoires of schizophrenics and normals. *Journal of Consulting and Clinical Psychology*, 1969, **33**, 497-500.

Garfinkel, H. Conditions of successful degradation ceremonies. *American Journal of Sociology*, 1956, **61**, 420-424.

Garmezy, N., Clarke, A.R., & Stockner, C. Child rearing attitudes of mothers and fathers as reported by schizophrenic and normal patients. *Journal of Abnormal and Social Psychology*, 1961, **63**, 176-182.

Garner, W.R. *The processing of information and structure*. Hillsdale, N.J.: Erlbaum Associates, 1974.

Gelburd, S. & Anker, J. Humans as reinforcing stimuli in schizophrenic performance. *Journal of Abnormal Psychology*, 1970, **75**, 195-198.

Ginsburg, H. & Opper, S. *Piaget's theory of intellectual development*. Englewood Cliffs, N.J.: Prentice-Hall, 1969.

Gladis, M. Age differences in repeated learning tasks in schizophrenic subjects. *Journal of Abnormal and Social Psychology*, 1964, **68**, 437-441.

Gladis, M. & Wischner, G.J. Schizophrenic and normal response patterns to "aversive" and "neutral" associations in two paired-associate paradigms. *Journal of Abnormal and Social Psychology*, 1962, **64**, 249-256.

Goffman, E. *Asylums*. Garden City, N.Y.: Doubleday, 1961.

Goldman, A.R. Differential effects of social reward and punishment on dependent and dependency-anxious schizophrenics. *Journal of Abnormal Psychology*, 1965, **70**, 412-418.

Goldstein, K. & Scheerer, M. Abstract and concrete behavior: An experimental study with special tests. *Psychological Monographs*, 1941, **53** (2).

Goldstein, M.J. & Acker, C.W. Psychophysiological reactions to films by chronic schizophrenics. II. *Journal of Abnormal Psychology*, 1967, **72**, 23-29.

Goldstein, M.J., Acker, C.W., Crockett, J.T., & Riddle, J.J. Psychophysiological reactions to films by chronic schizophrenics. I. Effects of drug status. *Journal of Abnormal Psychology*, 1966, **71**, 335-344.

Goodman, I.Z. Influence of parental figures on schizophrenic patients. *Journal of Abnormal Psychology*, 1968, **73**, 503-512.

Goodstein, L.D., Guertin, W.H., & Blackburn, H.L. Effects of social motivational variables on choice reaction time of schizophrenics. *Journal of Abnormal and Social Psychology*, 1961, **62**, 24-27.

Gorham, D.R. A proverbs test for clinical and experimental use. *Psychological Reports*, 1956, **2** (Monograph Supplement No. 1).

Gosling, R., Kerry, R.J., Orme, J.E., & Owen, G. Creatine phosphokinase activity in newly admitted psychiatric patients. *British Journal of Psychiatry*, 1972, **121**, 351-355.

Gottesman, J.J. Schizophrenia and genetics: Where are we? Are you sure? In L.C. Wynne, R.L. Cromwell, S. Matthysse (Eds.), *The nature of schizophrenia*. New York: Wiley, 1978. Pp. 59-69.

Gottesman, J.J. & Shields, J. *Schizophrenia and genetics*. New York: Academic Press, 1972.

Gottesman, L. Forced-choice word associations in schizophrenia. *Journal of Abnormal and Social Psychology*, 1964, **69**, 673-675.

Gottesman, L. & Chapman, L.J. Syllogistic reasoning errors in schizophrenia. *Journal of Consulting Psychology*, 1960, **24**, 250-255.

Green, P. Defective interhemispheric transfer in schizophrenia. *Journal of Abnormal Psychology*, 1978, **87**, 472-480.

Guilford, J.P. The structure of intellect. *Psychological Bulletin*, 1956, **53**, 267-293.

Guillain, G. *JM. Charcot, 1825-1893: His life, his work*. Translated by P. Bailey. New York: Hoeber, 1959. (First published in French, 1955.)

Gur, R.E. Left hemisphere dysfunction and left hemisphere overactivation in schizophrenia. *Journal of Abnormal Psychology*, 1978, **87**, 226-238.

Ham, M.W., Spanos, N.P., & Barber, T.X. Suggestibility in hospitalized schizophrenics. *Journal of Abnormal Psychology*, 1976, **85**, 550-557.

Hamlin, R.M., Haywood, H.C., & Folsom, A.T. Effect of enriched input on schizophrenic abstraction. *Journal of Abnormal Psychology*, 1965, **70**, 403-404.

Hamlin, R.M. & Ward, W.W. Schizophrenic intelligence, symptoms, and release from the hospital. *Journal of Abnormal Psychology*, 1973, **81**, 11-16.

Hamsher, K.S. & Arnold, K.O. A test of Chapman's theory of schizophrenic thought disorder. *Journal of Abnormal Psychology*, 1976, **85**, 296-306.

Harford, T. & Solomon, L. Effects of a "reformed sinner" and a "lapsed saint" strategy upon trust formation in paranoid and nonparanoid schizophrenic patients. *Journal of Abnormal Psychology*, 1969, **74**, 498-504.

Harrow, M., Himmelhoch, J., Tucker, G., Hersh, J., & Quinlan, D. Overinclusive thinking in acute schizophrenic patients. *Journal of Abnormal Psychology*, 1972, **79**, 161-168.

Harrow, M., Tucker, G.J., Himmelhoch, J., & Putnam, N. Schizophrenic thought disorders after the acute phase. *American Journal of Psychiatry*, 1972, **128**, 824-829.

Harway, N.I. & Salzman, L.F. Size constancy in psychopathology. *Journal of Abnormal and Social Psychology*, 1964, **69**, 606-613.

Harvey, J.H., Ickes, W.J., & Kidd, R.F. (Eds.) *New directions in attribution research*. Hillsdale, N.J.: Lawrence Erlbaum Associates, 1976.

Haywood, H.C. & Moelis, I. Effect of symptom change on intellectual function in schizophrenia. *Journal of Abnormal and Social Psychology*, 1963, **67**, 76-78.

Heath, R.J., Martens, M.D., Leach, B.E., Cohen, M., & Feigley, C. Effect of behavior in humans with the administration of taraxein. *American Journal of Psychiatry*, 1957, **114**, 14-24.

Heffner, P.A., Strauss, M.E., & Grisell, J. Rehospitalization of schizophrenics as a function of intelligence. *Journal of Abnormal Psychology*, 1975, **84**, 735-736.

Heilbrun, A.B. & Heilbrun, K.S. Content analysis of delusions in reactive and process schizophrenics. *Journal of Abnormal Psychology*, 1977, **86**, 597-608.

Helzer, J.E., Clayton, P.J., Pambakian, R., Reich, T., Woodruff, R.A., & Reveley, M.A. Reliability of psychiatric diagnosis. II. The test/retest reliability of diagnostic classification. *Archives of General Psychiatry*, 1977, **34**, 129-141.

Herron, W.G. The process-reactive classifications of schizophrenia. *Psychological Bulletin*, 1962, **59**, 329-343.

Heston, L.L. The genetics of schizophrenic and schizoid disease. *Science*, 1970, **167**, 249-256.

Hewitt, D. Some familial correlations in height, weight, and skeletal maturity. *Annals of Human Genetics*, 1957, **22**, 26-35.

Higgins, J. & Mednick, S. Reminiscence and stage of illness in schizophrenia. *Journal of Abnormal and Social Psychology*, 1963, **66**, 314-317.

Higgins, J., Mednick, S.A., & Phillip, F.J. Associative disturbance as a function of chronicity in schizophrenia. *Journal of Abnormal Psychology*, 1965, **70**, 451-452.

Hillyard, S.A., Hink, R.F., Schwent, V.L., & Picton, T.W. Electrical signs of selective attention in the human brain. *Science*, 1973, **182**, 177-180.

Hirsch, C.L. & DeWolfe, A.S. Associative interference and premorbid adjustment in schizophrenia. *Journal of Abnormal Psychology*, 1977, **86**, 589-596.

Hirt, M., Cuttler, M., & Genshaft, J. Information processing by schizophrenics when task complexity increases. *Journal of Abnormal Psychology*, 1977, **86**, 256-260.

Hoffer, A. & Mahon, M. The presence of unidentified substances in the urine of psychiatric patients. *Journal of Neuropsychiatry*, 1961, **2**, 331-362.

Hoffer, A. & Osmond, H. Malvaria: A new psychiatric disease. *Acta Psychiatrica Scandinavia*, 1963, **39**, 335-366.

Hole, C. *Witchcraft in England*. London: B.T. Botsford, Ltd., 1945.

Hollingshead, A.B. & Redlich, F.C. *Social class and mental illness: A community study*. New York: Wiley, 1958.

Homme, L., C'de Baca, P., Cottingham, L., & Homme, A. What behavior engineering is. *Psychological Record*, 1968, **18**, 425-434.

Horst, P., Wallin, P., & Guttman, L. *The prediction of personal adjustment*. New York: Social Science Research Council, 1941.

Hunt, W., Wittson, C., & Hunt, E.A. A theoretical and practical analysis of the diagnostic process. In P.H. Hoch and J. Zubin (Eds.), *Current problems in psychiatric diagnosis*. New York: Grune & Stratton, 1953, Pp. 53-65.

Hyman, R. & Frost, N. Gradients and schema in pattern recognition. In P.M.A. Rabbitt (Ed.), *Attention and performance V*. New York: Academic Press, 1975. Pp. 631-654.

Inhelder, B. & Piaget, J. *The early growth of logic in the child*. New York: Norton, 1969.

Iversen, S.D. & Iversen, L.L. *Behavioral pharmacology*. New York: Oxford University Press, 1975.

Jackson, D. (Ed.). *The etiology of schizophrenia*. New York: Basic Books, 1960.

Janet, P. *The mental state of hystericals: A study of mental stigmata and mental accidents*. London and New York: Putnam, 1911.

Jaspers, K. *General psychopathology*. Translated by J. Hoenig and M.W. Hamilton. Chicago: University of Chicago Press, 1963. (First published in German, 1913.)

Jaynes, J. *The origin of consciousness in the breakdown of the bicameral mind*. Boston: Houghton-Mifflin, 1976.

Jenkins, J.J. Remember that old theory of memory? Well, forget it. *American Psychologist*, 1974, **29**, 785-795.

Jones, M.C. The later careers of boys who were early- or late-maturing. *Child Development*, 1957, **28**, 113-128.

Jones, M.C. A study of socialization patterns at the high school level. *Journal of Genetic Psychology*, 1958, **40**, 87-111.

Jones, M.C. & Bayley, N. Physical maturing among boys as related to behavior. *Journal of Educational Psychology*, 1950, **41**, 129-148.

Jourard, S. *Self-disclosure: An experimental analysis of the transparent self.* New York: Wiley, 1971.

Kamin, L.F. *The science and politics of IQ.* New York: Halsted Press, 1974.

Kane, E., Nutter, R.W., & Wekowicz, J.E. Response to cutaneous pain in mental hospital patients. *Journal of Abnormal Psychology*, 1971, **77**, 52-60.

Kantor, J.R. *The scientific evolution of psychology.* Vol. 2. Chicago: The Principia Press, 1969.

Kantorowitz, D.A. & Cohen, B.D. Referrent communication in chronic schizophrenia. *Journal of Abnormal Psychology*, 1977, **86**, 1-9.

Karras, A. The effects of reinforcement and arousal on the psychomotor performance of chronic schizophrenics. *Journal of Abnormal and Social Psychology*, 1962, **65**, 104-111.

Kasanin, J.S. The disturbance of conceptual thinking in schizophrenia. In J.S. Kasanin (Ed.), *Language and thought in schizophrenia.* New York: W.W. Norton, 1964. Pp. 41-49.

Kelly, G.A. *The psychology of personal constructs.* New York: W.W. Norton, 1955.

Kendler, H.H. & Kendler, T.S. Vertical and horizontal processes in problem solving. *Psychological Review*, 1962, **69**, 1-16.

Kendler, H.H. & Kendler, T.S. Reversal-shift behavior: Some basic issues. *Psychological Bulletin*, 1969, **72**, 229-232.

Kesey, K. *One flew over the cuckoo's nest.* New York: Signet Books, 1962.

Kety, S.S. Biochemical theories of schizophrenia. A two-part review of current theories and of the evidence used to support them. *Science*, 1959, **129**, 1528-1532, 1590-1596.

Kety, S.S. Recent biochemical theories of schizophrenia. In D. Jackson (Ed.), *The etiology of schizophrenia.* New York: Basic Books, 1960. Pp. 120-145.

Kety, S.S. Biochemical hypotheses and studies. In L. Bellak and L. Loeb (Eds.), *Schizophrenic syndrome.* New York: Grune and Stratton, 1969. Pp. 155-171.

Kety, S.S. From rationalization to reason. *American Journal of Psychiatry*, 1974, **131**, 957-962.

Kety, S.S., Rosenthal, D., Wender, P.H., & Schulsinger, F. The types and prevalence of mental illness in the biological and adoptive families of adoptive schizophrenics. In D. Rosenthal and S.S. Kety (Eds.), *The transmission of schizophrenia.* New York: Pergamon Press, 1968. Pp. 345-362.

Kety, S.S., Rosenthal, D., Wender, P.H., Shulsinger, F., & Jacobsen, B. Mental illness in the biological and adoptive families of adopted individuals who have become schizophrenic: A preliminary report based upon psychiatric interviews. In R. Fieve, D. Rosenthal, and H. Brill (Eds.), *Genetic research in psychiatry.* Baltimore: Johns Hopkins Press, 1975. Pp. 147-165.

Kety, S.S., Rosenthal, D., Wender, P.H. & Shulsinger, F. Studies based on a total sample of adopted individuals and their relatives. *Schizophrenia Bulletin*, 1976, **2**, 413-428.

Kidd, A.H. Monocular distance perception in schizophrenics. *Journal of Abnormal and Social Psychology*, 1964, **68**, 100-103.

Kidd, K.K. & Cavalli-Sforza, L. An analysis of the genetics of schizophrenia. *Social Biology*, 1974, **20**, 254-265.

Kiesler, C.A. & Pallak, M.S. Arousal properties of dissonance manipulations. *Psychological Bulletin*, 1976, **83**, 1014-1025.

Keith, S.J., Gunderson, J.G., Reifman, A., Buchsbaum, S. & Mosher, L.R. Special report: Schizophrenia 1976. *Schizophrenia Bulletin*, 1976, **2**, 509-565.

King, G.F., Armitage, S.G., & Tilton, J.R. A therapeutic approach to schizophrenics of extreme pathology: An operant-interpersonal method. *Journal of Abnormal and Social Psychology*, 1960, **61**, 276-286.

Kinsbourne, M. The control of attention by interaction between the cerebral hemispheres. In S. Kornblum (Ed.), *Attention and performance: IV.* New York: Academic Press, 1973. Pp. 239-256.

Kittrie, N.N. *The right to be different.* Baltimore: Johns Hopkins Press, 1971.

Klein, E.B., Cicchetti, D., & Spohn, H. A test of the censure-deficit model and its relationship to premorbidity in the performance of schizophrenics. *Journal of Abnormal Psychology*, 1967, **72**, 174-181.

Klein, E.B. & Spohn, H.E. Further comments on characteristics of untestable chronic schizophrenics. *Journal of Abnormal and Social Psychology*, 1964, **68**, 355-358.

Klein, D.F. & Davis, J.M. *Diagnosis and drug treatment of psychiatric disorder.* Baltimore: Williams and Wilkins, 1969.

Knight, R., Sherer, M., Putchat, C., & Carter, G. A picture integration task for measuring iconic memory in schizophrenics. *Journal of Abnormal Psychology*, 1978, **87**, 314-321.

Knight, R., Sherer, M., & Shapiro, J. Iconic imagery in overinclusive and nonoverinclusive schizophrenics. *Journal of Abnormal Psychology*, 1977, **86**, 242-255.

Koh, S.D., Kayton, L., & Peterson, R.A. Affective encoding and consequent remembering in schizophrenic young adults. *Journal of Abnormal Psychology*, 1976, **85**, 156-166.

Koh, S.D. & Peterson, R.A. Encoding orientation and the remembering of schizophrenic young adults. *Journal of Abnormal Psychology*, 1978, **87**, 303-313.

Koh, S.D., Szoc, R., & Peterson, R.A. Short-term memory scanning in schizophrenic young adults. *Journal of Abnormal Psychology*, 1977, **86**, 451-460.

Kolb, L.C. *Noyes' modern clinical psychiatry.* Philadelphia: Saunders, 1977.

Kopfstein, J. & Neale, J. A multivariate study of attention dysfunction in schizophrenia. *Journal of Abnormal Psychology*, 1972, **80**, 294-298.

Korboot, P.J. & Damiani, N. Auditory processing speed and signal detection in schizophrenia. *Journal of Abnormal Psychology*, 1976, **85**, 287-295.

Kraepelin, E. *Lehrbuch der psychiatrie.* (5th ed.) Leipzing: Barth, 1896.

Krasner, L. Behavior modification: Ethical issues and future trends. In H. Leitenberg (Ed.), *Handbook of behavior modification and behavior therapy.* Englewood Cliffs, N.J.: Prentice-Hall, 1976, 627-649.

Krasner, L. & Ullmann, L.P. *Research in behavior modification.* New York: Holt, Rinehart & Winston, 1965.

Kreitman, N. & Smythies, J.R. Schizophrenia: Genetic and psychosocial factors. In J.R. Smythies (Ed.), *Biological psychiatry.* London: Heinemann, 1967. Pp. 1-24.

Kringlen, E. *Heredity and environment in functional psychoses.* London: Heinemann, 1967.

Kristofferson, M.W. Shifting attention between modalities: A comparison of schizophrenics and normals. *Journal of Abnormal Psychology*, 1967, **72**, 395-401.

Kubie, L.S. The myths of Thomas Szasz. *Bulletin of the Menninger Clinic*, 1974, **38**, 497-502.

Kugelmass, S. & Fondeur, M.R. Zaslow's test of concept formation: Reliability and validity. *Journal of Consulting Psychology*, 1955, **19**, 227-229.

Kuethe, J.L. Social schemas. *Journal of Abnormal and Social Psychology*, 1962, **64**, 31-38.

Kuhn, T. *The structure of scientific revolution.* Chicago: University of Chicago Press, 1970.

Lachman, R., Lachman, J.L., & Butterfield, E.C. (Eds.). *Cognitive psychology and information processing.* Hillsdale, N.J.: Lawrence Erlbaum Associates, 1979.

Laing, R.D. *The politics of experience.* New York: Ballantine Books, 1967.

Landfield, A. (Ed.). *Nebraska Symposium on motivation 1976.* Lincoln, Nebraska: University of Nebraska Press, 1977.

Lane, E.A. & Albee, G.W. Childhood intellectual development of adult schizophrenics. *Journal of Abnormal and Social Psychology*, 1963, **67**, 186-189.

Lane, E.A. & Albee, G.W. Associative interference in the verbal learning performance of schizophrenics and normals. *Journal of Abnormal and Social Psychology*, 1964, **68**, 221-226.

Lane, E.A. & Albee, G.W. On childhood intellectual decline of adult schizophrenics: A reassessment of an earlier study. *Journal of Abnormal Psychology*, 1968, **73**, 174-177.

Lane, R.C. & Singer, J.L. Familial attitudes in paranoid schizophrenics and normals from two socioeconomic classes. *Journal of Abnormal and Social Psychology*, 1959, **59**, 328-339.

Lang, P.J. & Buss, A. Psychological deficit in schizophrenia. II. Intereference and activation. *Journal of Abnormal Psychology*, 1965, **70**, 77-106.

Langer, E.J. & Abelson, R.P. A patient by any other name . . .: Clinician group difference in labelling bias. *Journal of Consulting and Clinical Psychology*, 1974, **42**, 4-9.

Langer, J., Stein, K., & Rosenberg, B.G. Cognitive interference by nonverbal symbols in schizophrenics. *Journal of Abnormal Psychology*, 1969, **74**, 474-476.

Larsen, S.F. & Fromholt, P. Mnemonic organization and free recall in schizophrenia. *Journal of*

Abnormal Psychology, 1976, **85**, 61-65.

LaRusso, L. Sensitivity of paranoid patients to nonverbal cues. *Journal of Abnormal Psychology*, 1978, **87**, 463-471.

Lawson, J.A., McGhie, A., & Chapman, J. Distractability in schizophrenia and organic cerebral disease. *British Journal of Psychiatry*, 1967, **113**, 527-535.

Lawson, R.B., Greene, R.T., Richardson, J.S., McClure, G., & Pandina, R.J. Token economics program in a maximum security correctional hospital. *Journal of Nervous and Mental Disease*, 1971, **152**, 199-205.

Lemert, E.M. Paranoia and the dynamics of exclusion. *Sociometry*, 1962, **25**, 2-25.

Lerner, M.J. Responsiveness of chronic schizophrenics to the social behavior of others in a meaningful task situation. *Journal of Abnormal and Social Psychology*, 1963, **67**, 295-299.

Lerner, M.J. & Fairweather, G.W. Social behavior of chronic schizophrenics in supervised and unsupervised work groups. *Journal of Abnormal and Social Psychology*, 1963, **67**, 219-225.

Leventhal, D.W., McGaughran, L.S., & Moran, L.J. Multivariate analysis of the conceptual behavior of schizophrenic and brain-damaged patients. *Journal of Abnormal and Social Psychology*, 1959, **58**, 84-90.

Levine, F. & Whitney, N. Absolute auditory threshold and threshold or unpleasantness of chronic schizophrenic patients and normal controls. *Journal of Abnormal Psychology*, 1970, **75**, 74-77.

Lévi-Strauss, C. *Structural anthropology*, Translated by C. Jacobson & B.G. Schoepf. New York: Basic Books, 1963.

Levy, S.M. Schizophrenic symptomatology: Reaction or strategy? A study of contextual antecedents. *Journal of Abnormal Psychology*, 1976, **85**, 435-445.

Lewisohn, P.M. & Riggs, A. The effect of content upon the thinking of acute and chronic schizophrenics. *Journal of Abnormal and Social Psychology*, 1962, **65**, 206-207.

Lewis, M. Individual differences in the measurement of early cognitive growth. In J. Hellmuth (Ed.), *Exceptional infant: Studies in abnormalities*. New York: Brunner/Mazel, 1971. Pp. 172-210.

Lewis, M., Kagan, M., & Kalafat, J. Patterns of fixation in infants. *Child Development*, 1966, **37**, 332-341.

Liberman, R.P., Teigen, J., Patterson, R., & Baker, V. Reducing delusional speech in chronic paranoid schizophrenics. *Journal of Applied Behavior Analysis*, 1973, **6**, 57-64.

Lindner, R. *The fifty minute hour: A collection of true psychoanalytic tales.* New York: Bantam, 1954.

Linton, R. *The study of man.* New York: Appleton-Century, 1936.

Little, J.C. A double-blind controlled comparison of the effects of chlorpromazine, barbiturate and a placebo in one hundred and forty-two chronic psychotic patients. *Journal of Mental Science*, 1958, **104**, 334-349.

Lloyd, K.E. & Abel, L. Performance on a token economy psychiatric ward: A two year summary. *Behavior Research and Therapy*, 1970, **8**, 1-9.

Lorr, M., & Klett, C.J. *Inpatient multidimensional psychiatric scale.* Palo Alto, Calif., Consulting Psychologists Press, 1967.

Lucero, R.J., Vail, D.J., & Scherber, J. Regulating operant-conditioning programs. *Hospital and Community Psychiatry*, 1968, **19**, 53-54.

Luchins, D. The dopamine hypothesis of schizophrenia: A critical analysis. *Neuropsychobiology*, 1975, **1**, 365-378.

Lukes, S. *Individualism.* New York: Harper & Row, 1973.

Magaro, P.A. Perceptual discrimination performance of schizophrenics as a function of censure, social class, and premorbid adjustment. *Journal of Abnormal Psychology*, 1967, **72**, 415-420.

Magaro, P.A. Size estimation in schizophrenia as a function of censure, diagnosis, premorbid adjustment, and chronicity. *Journal of Abnormal Psychology*, 1969, **74**, 306-313.

Magaro, P.A. Form discrimination performance of schizophrenics as a function of social censure, premorbid adjustment, chronicity, and diagnosis. *Journal of Abnormal Psychology*, 1972, **80**, 58-66.

Magaro, P.A. Skin conductance basal level and reactivity in schizophrenia as a function of chronicity, premorbid adjustment, diagnosis, and medication. *Journal of Abnormal Psychology*, 1973, **81**, 270-281.

Magaro, P.A., Gripp, R., McDowell, D.J., Miller, J.W. *The mental health industry: A cultural phenomenon.* New York: Wiley, 1978.

Magaro, P.A. & Vojtisek, J. Embedded figures performance of schizophrenics as a function of chronicity, premorbid adjustment, diagnosis, and medication. *Journal of Abnormal Psychology*, 1971, **77**, 184-191.

Maley, R.F., Feldman, G.L., & Ruskin, R.S. Evaluation of patient improvement in a token economy treatment program. *Journal of Abnormal Psychology*, 1973, **82**, 141-144.

Mancuso, J.C. (Ed., *Readings for a cognitive theory of personality*. New York: Holt, Rinehart & Winston, 1970.

Mancuso, J.C. Current motivational models in the elaboration of personal construct theory. In A.W. Landfield (Ed.), *Nebraska symposium on motivation: 1976*. Lincoln, Nebraska: University of Nebraska Press, 1977. Pp. 43-97.

Mancuso, J.C. The mental illness metaphor as an inducement to rejection. Plenary address at *The Community Imperative*, Washington, D.C., 1978.

Mancuso, J.C. & Dreisinger, M. A view of the historical and current development of the concept of intelligence. *Psychology in the Schools*, 1969, **6**, 137-151.

Mancuso, J.C., Eson, M.E., & Morrison, J.K. Psychology in the morals marketplace: Role dilemma for community psychologists. In J.K. Morrison (Ed.), *A consumer approach to community psychology*. Chicago: Nelson Hall, 1979. Pp. 261-294.

Mancuso, J.C. & Sarbin, T.R. A paradigmatic analysis of psychological issues at the interface of jurisprudence and moral conduct. In T. Lickona (Ed.), *Moral development and behavior*. New York: Holt, Rinehart & Winston, 1976. Pp. 326-341.

Manis, M., Houts, P.S., & Blake, J.B. Beliefs about mental illness as a function of psychiatric status and psychiatric hospitalization. *Journal of Abnormal and Social Psychology*, 1963, **67**, 226-233.

Mannheim, K. *Ideology and utopia*. New York: Harcourt, 1936.

Marks, J., Stauffacher, J.C., & Lyle, C. Predicting outcome in schizophrenia. *Journal of Abnormal and Social Psychology*, 1963, **66**, 117-127.

Martin, W.A., Garey, R.E., & Heath, R.G. Cerebrospinal fluid creatine kinase in acutely psychotic patients. *Journal of Neurology, Neurosurgery, and Psychiatry*, 1972, **35**, 726-729.

McCreary, C. Comparison of measures of social competency in schizophrenics and the relation of social competency in socioeconomic factors. *Journal of Abnormal Psychology*, 1974, **83**, 124-129.

McGaughran, L.S. & Moran, L.J. Differences between schizophrenic and brain-damaged groups in conceptual aspects of object sorting. *Journal of Abnormal and Social Psychology*, 1957, **54**, 44-49.

McGhie, A. & Chapman, J. Disorders of attention and perception in early schizophrenia. *British Journal of Medical Psychology*, 1961, **34**, 103-116.

McKinnon, T. & Singer, G. Schizophrenia and the scanning cognitive control: A reevaluation. *Journal of Abnormal Psychology*, 1969, **74**, 242-248.

McReynolds, W.T. & Coleman, J. Token economy: Patient and staff changes. *Behavior Research and Therapy*, 1972, **10**, 29-34.

Mead, G.H. *Mind, self, and society*. Chicago: Chicago University Press, 1934.

Mednick, S.A. A learning theory approach to research in schizophrenia. *Psychological Bulletin*, 1958, **55**, 316-327.

Meehl, P. *Clinical versus statistical prediction*. Minneapolis: University of Minnesota Press, 1954.

Meehl, P. Schizotaxia, schizotype, and schizophrenia. *American Psychologist*, 1962, **17**, 827-838.

Meehl, P.E. & Rosen, A. Antecedent probability and the efficacy of psychometric signs, patterns, or cutting scores. Psychological Bulletin, 1955, **52**, 194-216.

Mehlman, B. The reliability of psychiatric diagnosis. *Journal of Abnormal and Social Psychology*, 1952, **47**, 577-578.

Meichenbaum, D.H. The effects of instruction and reinforcement on thinking and language behavior in schizophrenics. *Behavior Research and Therapy*, 1969, **7**, 101-114.

Meichenbaum, D.H. Effects of social reinforcement on the level of abstraction in schizophrenics. *Journal of Abnormal Psychology*, 1966, **71**, 354-362.

Meltzer, H.Y. Creatine kinase and adolase in serum: Abnormality common to acute psychoses. *Science*, 1968, **159**, 1368-1370.

Meltzer, H.Y. Muscle enzyme release in acute psychoses. *Archives of General Psychiatry*, 1969, **21**, 102-112.

Meltzer, H.Y. Creatine phosphokinase activity and clinical symptomology. *Archives of General Psychiatry*, 1973, **29**, 589-593.

Meltzer, H.Y. Neuromuscular dysfunction in schizophrenia. *Schizophrenia Bulletin*, 1976, **2**, 106-146.

Meltzer, H.Y., Grinspoon, L., & Shader, R.I. Serum creatine phosphokinase and aldolase activity in acute schizophrenic patients and their relatives. *Comprehensive Psychiatry*, 1970, **11**, 552-558.

Mertins, G.C. & Fuller, G.B. Conditioning of motor behavior in regressed psychotics. I. An objective measure of personal habit training with "regressed" psychotics. *Journal of Clinical Psychology*, 1963, **19**, 333-337.

Miller, D. & Schwartz, M. County lunacy commission hearings: Some observations of commitments to a state hospital. *Social Problems*, 1966, **14**, 26-35.

Miller, G.A. & Selfridge, J.A. Verbal context and the recall of meaningful material. *American Journal of Psychology*, 1950, **63**, 176-185.

Millon, T. & Millon, R. *Abnormal behavior and personality: A biosocial learning approach*. Philadelphia: Saunders. 1974.

Miron, N.B. Issues and implications of operant conditioning. *Hospital and Community Psychiatry*, 1968, **19**, 226-228.

Mitchell, K.M. An analysis of the schizophrenic mother concept by means of the Thematic Apperception Test. *Journal of Abnormal Psychology*, 1968, **73**, 571-574.

Monahan, J. The prediction and prevention of violence. In *Proceedings of the Pacific Northwest Conference on Violence and Criminal Justice*, 1973.

Moran, L.J., Gorham, D.R., & Holtzman, W.H. Vocabulary knowledge and usage of schizophrenic subjects: A six year follow-up. *Journal of Abnormal and Social Psychology*, 1960, **61**, 246-254.

Moray, N. *Attention: Selective processes in vision and hearing*. New York: Academic Press, 1970.

More, D.M. Developmental concordance and discordance during puberty and early adolescence. *Monographs of the Society for Research in Child Development*, 1953, **18** (Whole No. 1).

Moriarty, D. & Kates, S.L. Concept attainment of schizophrenics on materials involving social approval and disapproval. *Journal of Abnormal and Social Psychology*, 1962, **65**, 355-364.

Morse, S.J. Crazy behavior, morals, and science: An analysis of mental health law. *Southern California Law Review*, 1978, **51**, 527-654.

Mosher, L.R. The center for studies of schizophrenia. *Schizophrenia Bulletin*, 1969, 4-6.

Mosher, L.R. & Feinsilver, D. *Special report on schizophrenia*. U.S. Department of Health, Education, and Welfare: Public Health Service; Health Services and Mental Health Administration; National Institute of Mental Health, April, 1970.

Nasrallah, H., Donnelly, E.F., Bigelow, L.B., Rivera-Calimlim, L., Rogol, A., Plotkin, N., Rauscher, F.P., Wyatt, R.J., & Gillin, J.C. Inhibition of dopamine synthesis in chronic schizophrenia. *Archives of General Psychiatry*, 1977, **34**, 649-655.

Nathanson, I.A. A semantic differential analysis of parent-son relationships in schizophrenia. *Journal of Abnormal Psychology*, 1967, **72**, 277-281.

Neale, J., McIntyre, C., Fox, R., & Cromwell, R. Span of apprehension in acute schizophrenics. *Journal of Abnormal Psychology*, 1969, **74**, 593-596.

Neisser, U. *Cognition and reality*. San Francisco: W.H. Freeman, 1976.

Neisser, U. *Cognitive psychology*. New York: Appleton-Century-Crofts, 1967.

Nemeth, C. A critical analysis of research using the prisoner's dilemma paradigm for the study of bargaining. In L. Berkowitz (Ed.), *Advances in experimental social psychology*. (Vol. 6) New York: Academic Press, 1972. Pp. 203-234.

Neufeld, R.W.J. Components of processing deficit among paranoid and nonparanoid schizophrenics. *Journal of Abnormal Psychology*, 1977, **86**, 60-64.

Nolan, J.D. Effects of overtraining on reversal and extra-dimensional shifts in schizophrenics. *Journal of Abnormal Psychology*, 1970, **75**, 323-328.

Nolan, J.D. A within-subjects analysis of discrimination shift behavior in schizophrenics. *Journal of Abnormal Psychology*, 1974, **83**, 497-511.

Nolan, J.D. & Anderson, D. Effect of excessive overtraining and aversive feedback on reversal and extradimensional shifts in schizophrenics. *Journal of Abnormal Psychology*, 1973, **81**, 27-35.

Nunnally, J. *Popular conceptions of mental health*. New York: Holt, Rinehart and Winston, 1961.

Nuttall, R.L., & Solomon, L.F. Prognosis in schizophrenia: The role of premorbid, social class and demographic factors. Unpublished paper, Boston College, 1965.

O'Keefe, G. & DeWolfe, A. Reversal shift in process and reactive schizophrenic, brain-damaged, and control group patients. *Journal of Abnormal Psychology*, 1973, **82**, 390-398.

Olson, D.R. Language and thought: Aspects of a cognitive theory of semantics. *Psychological Review*, 1970, **77**, 257-273.

Olson, D.R. From utterance to text: The bias of language in speech and writing. *Harvard Educational Review*, 1977, **47**, 257-281.

Oltmanns, T.F. Selective attention in schizophrenic and manic psychoses: The effect of distraction on information processing. *Journal of Abnormal Psychology*, 1978, **87**, 212-225.

Oltmanns, T.F. & Neale, J.M. Schizophrenic performance when distractors are present: Attentional deficit or differential task difficulty. *Journal of Abnormal Psychology*, 1975, **84**, 205-209.

Orne, M.T. On the social psychology of the psychological experiment: With particular reference to demand characteristics and their implications. *American Psychologist*, 1962, **17**, 776-783.

Osgood, C.E., Suci, G.J., & Tannenbaum, P.H. *The measurement of meaning*. Urbana, Illinois: University of Illinois Press, 1957.

Parrino, J.J., George, L., & Daniels, A.C. Token control of pill-taking behavior in a psychiatric ward. *Journal of Behavior Therapy and Experimental Psychiatry*, 1971, **2**, 181-185.

Paterson, T.T. *Management theory*. London: Business Publications, Ltd., 1966.

Paul, G.L. Chronic mental patient: Current status-future directions. *Psychological Bulletin*, 1969, **71**, 81-94.

Pavlov, J. Attempt at a psychological explanation of compulsive neurosis and paranoia. In Y. Popov and L. Rokhlin (Eds.), *I.P. Pavlov, Psychopathology and Psychiatry*. Moscow: Foreign Languages, Publishing House, no date. (First published in Russian, 1933).

Pavlov, J.P. *Lectures on conditioned reflexes*. New York: International, 1927.

Payne, R.W. An object classification test as a measure of overinclusive thinking in schizophrenic patients. *British Journal of Social and Clinical Psychology*, 1962, **1**, 213-221.

Payne, R.W. & Caird, W.K. Reaction time, distractability, and overinclusive thinking in psychotics. *Journal of Abnormal Psychology*, 1967, **72**, 112-121.

Payne, R.W., Caird, W.K., & Laverty, S.G. Overinclusive thinking and delusions in schizophrenic patients. *Journal of Abnormal and Social Psychology*, 1964, **68**, 562-566.

Payne, R.W. & Friedlander, D. A short battery of simple tests for measuring overinclusive thinking. *Journal of Mental Science*, 1962, **108**, 362-367.

Payne, R., Hochberg, A., & Hawks, D. Dichotic stimulation as a method of assessing disorder of attention in overinclusive schizophrenic patients. *Journal of Abnormal Psychology*, 1970, **76**, 185-193.

Payne, R.W., Matussek, P., & George, E.I. An experimental study of schizophrenic thought disorder, *British Journal of Psychiatry*, 1959, **105**, 627-652.

Peastrel, A.L. Studies in efficiency: Semantic generalization in schizophrenia. *Journal of Abnormal and Social Psychology*, 1964, **69**, 444-449.

Pepper, S.C. *World hypotheses*. Berkeley: University of California Press, 1942.

Perucci, R. *Circle of madness*. Englewood Cliffs, N.J.: Prentice-Hall, 1974.

Peterson, M.J. The role of the governess in Victorian England. In M. Vicinus (Ed.), *Suffer and be still*. Bloomington, Indiana: Indiana University Press, 1972. Pp. 3-19.

Phillips, L. Case history data prognosis in schizophrenia. *Journal of Nervous and Mental Disease*, 1953, **117**, 515-525.

Phillips, L., Boverman, J.K., & Zigler, E. Social competence and psychiatric diagnosis. *Journal of Abnormal Psychology*, 1966, **71**, 209-214.

Phillips, L., Boverman, J.K., & Zigler, E. Sphere dominance, role orientation, and diagnosis. *Journal of Abnormal Psychology*, 1968, **73**, 306-312.

Piaget, J. *The moral judgment of the child*. London: Kegan Paul, 1932.

Piaget, J. *The origins of intelligence in children*. New York: International Universities Press, 1952.

Piaget, J. *Six psychological studies*. New York: Vintage Books, 1968.

Platt, A.M. & Diamond, B.L. The origins and development of the "Wild Beast" concept of mental illness and its relation to theories of criminal responsibility. *Journal of the History of the Behavioral Sciences*, 1965, **1**, 355-367.

Pollin, W. & Stabeneu, J.R. Biological, psychological, and historical differences in a series of MZ twins discordant for schizophrenia. In D. Rosenthal and S.S. Kety (Eds.), *The transmission of schizophrenia*. New York: Pergamon Press, 1968. Pp. 317-332.

Posner, M.I. *Cognition: An introduction*. Glenview, Illinois: Scott, Foresman, 1973.

Posner, M.I. & Keele, S.W. On the genesis of abstract ideas. *Journal of Experimental Psychology*, 1970, **83**, 304-308.

Price, R.H. Analysis of task requirements in schizophrenic concept-identification performance. *Journal of Abnormal Psychology*, 1968, **73**, 285.

Price, R.H. & Denner, B. (Eds.). *The making of a mental patient*. New York: Holt, Rinehart & Winston, 1973.

Professional Staff of the U.S.-U.K. Cross-National Project. The diagnosis and psychopathology of schizophrenia in New York and London. *Schizophrenia Bulletin*, 1974, **11**, 80-102.

Rabkin, J.G. Public attitudes toward mental illness: A review of the literature. *Schizophrenia Bulletin*, 1974, **10**, 9-33.

Rabkin, J.G. Opinions about mental illness: A review of the literature. *Psychological Bulletin*, 1972, **77**, 153-171.

Randrup, A. & Munkvad, I. Biochemical, anatomical and psychological investigations of stereotyped behavior induced by amphetamines. In E. Costa and S. Garrantini (Eds.), *Amphetamines and related compounds*. New York: Raven Press, 1970. Pp. 595-713.

Raulin, M.L. & Chapman, L.J. Schizophrenic recall and contextual constraint. *Journal of Abnormal Psychology*, 1976, **85**, 151-155.

Resnick, L.B. (Ed.). *The nature of intelligence*. Hillsdale, New Jersey: Lawrence Erlbaum Associates, 1976.

Rice, G. Disordered language as related to autonomic responsivity and the process-reactive distinction. *Journal of Abnormal Psychology*, 1970, **76**, 50-54.

Richter, D. The impact of biochemistry on the problem of schizophrenia. In D. Kemali, G. Bartholini, and D. Richter (Eds.), *Schizophrenia today*. New York: Pergamon Press, 1975. Pp. 71-83.

Riegel, K.F. (Ed.). *Intelligence: Alternative views of a paradigm*. Basel: S. Karger, 1973.

Ries, H.A. & Johnson, M.H. Commonality of word associations and good and poor premorbid schizophrenia. *Journal of Abnormal Psychology*, 1967, **72**, 487-488.

Rilke, R.M. *Sonnets to Orpheus*. Translated by J.B. Leishman. London: Hogarth Press, 1949.

Ritzler, B.A. Proprioception and schizophrenia: A replication study with nonschizophrenic patient controls. *Journal of Abnormal Psychology*, 1977, **86**, 501-509.

Ritzler, B.A. & Smith, M. The problem of diagnostic criteria in the study of the paranoid subclassification of schizophrenia. *Schizophrenia Bulletin*, 1976, **2**, 209-217.

Robbins, R.H. *The encyclopedia of witchcraft and demonology*. New York: Crown, 1959.

Rock, J. *Orientation and Form*. New York: Academic Press, 1973.

Rodnick, E.H. & Garmezy, N. An experimental approach to the study of motivation in schizophrenia. In M.R. Jones (Ed.), *Nebraska symposium on motivation: 1957*. Lincoln: University of Nebraska Press, 1957. Pp. 109-184.

Rommetveit, R. *On message structure*. New York: Wiley, 1974.

Rosen, B., Engelhardt, D., Freedman, N., Margolis, R., Rudorfer, L., & Paley, H. Prediction of psychiatric hospitalization. II. The hospitalization proneness scale: A cross-validation. *Journal of Abnormal Psychology*, 1972, **80**, 271-274.

Rosenberg, S. New approaches to the analysis of personal constructs in person perception. In A.W. Landfield (Ed.), *Nebraska symposium on motivation: 1976*. Nebraska: University of Nebraska Press, 1977, 179-242.

Rosenberg, S. & Cohen, B.D. Referential processes of speakers and listeners. *Psychological Review*, 1966, **73**, 208-231.

Rosenberg, S. & Sedlak, A. Structural representations of implicit personality theory. In L. Berkowitz (Ed.), *Advances in experimental social psychology*. Vol. 6. New York: Academic Press, 1972. Pp. 235-297.

Rosenhan, D. On being sane in insane places. *Science*, 1973, **179**, 250-258.

Rosenthal, D. *Genetic theory and abnormal behavior*. New York: McGraw-Hill, 1970.

Rosenthal, D. Problem of sampling and diagnosis in the major twin studies of schizophrenia. *Journal of Psychiatric Research*, 1962, **1**, 116-134.

Rosenthal, D. & Kety, S.S. (Eds.) *The transmission of schizophrenia*. Oxford: Pergamon Press, 1968.

Rotenberg, M. The Protestant ethic against the spirit of psychiatry. *British Journal of Sociology*, 1975, **26**, 52-65.

Rothman, D.J. *The discovery of asylum*. Boston: Little, Brown, 1971.

Royer, F. & Friedman, S. Scanning time of schizophrenics and normals for visual designs. *Journal of Abnormal Psychology*, 1973, **82**, 212-219.

Rubens, R.L. & Lapidus, L.B. Schizophrenic patterns of arousal and stimulus barrier functioning. *Journal of Abnormal Psychology*, 1978, **87**, 199-211.

Russell, P.N. & Beekhuis, M.E. Organization in memory: A comparison of psychotics and normals. *Journal of Abnormal Psychology*, 1976, **85**, 527-534.

Russell, P.N. & Knight, R.G. Performance of process schizophrenics on tasks involving visual search. *Journal of Abnormal Psychology*, 1977, **86**, 16-26.

Ryle, G. *The concept of mind*. Oxford: Hutchinson's Library, 1948.

Salzinger, K. *Schizophrenia: Behavioral aspects*. New York: Wiley, 1973.

Salzinger, K. & Pisoni, S. Reinforcement of affect responses of schizophrenics during the clinical interview. *Journal of Abnormal and Social Psychology*, 1958, **57**, 84-90.

Salzinger, K. & Pisoni, S. Some parameters in the conditioning of verbal affect responses in schizophrenic subjects. *Journal of Abnormal and Social Psychology*, 1961, **63**, 511-516.

Sampson, E.E. Psychology and the American ideal. *Journal of Personality and Social Psychology*, 1977, **35**, 767-782.

Santayana, G. *The genteel tradition*, (ed.) D.L. Wilson. Cambridge: Harvard University Press, 1967.

Sarbin, T.R. The concept of role taking. *Sociometry*, 1943, **6**, 273-284.

Sarbin, T.R. The logic of prediction in psychology. *Psychological Review*, 1944, **51**, 210-228.

Sarbin, T.R. Role theory. In G. Lindzey (Ed.), *Handbook of Social Psychology*. Cambridge: Addison Wesley, 1954. Pp. 235-236.

Sarbin, T.R. A new model of the behavior disorders. *Tijdschzift voor Psychologie*, 1962. **10**, 325-341.

Sarbin, T.R. Anxiety: The reification of a metaphor. *Archives of General Psychiatry*, 1964, **10**, 630-638.

Sarbin T.R. On the futility of the proposition that some people be labelled "mentally ill." *Journal of Consulting Psychology*, 1967, **31**, 447-453.(a)

Sarbin, T.R. The dangerous individual: An outcome of social identity transformation. *British Journal of Criminology*, 1967, **7**, 285-295.(b)

Sarbin, T.R. The transformation of social identity: A new metaphor for the helping professions. In L. Roberts, N. Greenfield, and M. Miller (Eds.), *Comprehensive mental health: The challenge of evaluation*. Madison: University of Wisconsin Press, 1968. Pp. 97-115.

Sarbin, T.R. Ontology recapitulates philology: The mythic nature of anxiety. *American Psychologist*, 1968, **23**, 411-418.(b)

Sarbin, T.R. Schizophrenic thinking: A role theoretical analysis. *Journal of Personality*, 1969, **37**, 190-206.(a)

Sarbin, T.R. The scientific status of the mental illness metaphor. In S.C. Plog and R.B. Edgerton (Eds.), *Changing perspectives in mental illness*. New York: Holt, Rinehart and Winston, 1969. Pp. 9-31.(b)

Sarbin, T.R. On the misuse of proverbs in identifying "thought disorder." Unpublished manuscript, 1970.

Sarbin, T.R. Contextualism: The worldview for modern psychology. In A.W. Landfield (Ed.), *Nebraska symposium on motivation: 1976*. Lincoln: University of Nebraska Press, 1977. Pp. 1-41.

Sarbin, T.R. The root-metaphor of metaphor: Application to psychological problems. Unpublished manuscript, 1978.

Sarbin, T.R. & Allen, V.L. Role theory. In G. Lindzey and E. Aronson (Eds.), *Handbook of Social Psychology*. 2nd Ed.) Reading, Massachusetts: Addison Wesley, 1968. Pp. 448-567.

Sarbin, T.R. & Juhasz, J.B. The social psychology of hallucinations. *Journal of Mental Imagery*, 1978, **2**, 117-144.

Sarbin, T.R. & Mancuso, J.C. Failure of a moral enterprise: Attitudes of the public toward mental illness. *Journal of Consulting and Clinical Psychology*, 1970, **35**, 159-173.

Sarbin, T.R. & Mancuso, J.C. Paradigms and moral judgments: Improper conduct is not a disease. *Journal of Consulting and Clinical Psychology*, 1972, **39**, 6-8.

Sarbin, T.R. & Scheibe, K.E. *The transvaluation of social identity*. Unpublished manuscript, 1970.

Sarbin, T.R., Taft, R., & Bailey, D.E. *Clinical inference and cognitive theory*. New York: Holt, Rinehart, Winston, 1960.

Sarbin, T.R., Wenk, E.A., & Sherwood, D.W. An effort to identify assault-prone offenders. *Journal of Research on Crime and Delinquency*, 1968, **5**, 66-71.

Saretsky, T. Effects of chlorpromazine on primary-process thought manifestations. *Journal of Abnormal Psychology*, 1966, **71**, 247-252.

Schaeffer, H.H. & Martin, P.L. Behavioral therapy for "apathy" of hospitalized schizophrenics. *Psychological Reports*, 1966, **19**, 1147-1158.

Scheff, T.J. The role of the mentally ill and the dynamics of mental disorder: A research framework. *Sociometry*, 1963, **26**, 436-454.

Scheff, T.J. The societal reaction to deviance:Ascriptive elements in the psychiatric screening of mental patients in a mid-western state. *Social Problems*, 1964, **11**, 401-413.

Scheff, T.J. *Being mentally ill*. Chicago: Aldine, 1966.

Scheff, T.J. *Mental illness and social processes*. New York: Harper & Row, 1967.

Scheff, T.J. *Labelling madness*. Englewood Cliffs, N.J.: Prentice-Hall, 1975.

Schmidt, H.O. & Fonda, C.P. The reliability of psychiatric diagnosis: A new look. *Journal of Abnormal and Social Psychology*, 1956, **52**, 262-267.

Schneider, D.J. Implicit personality theory: A review. *Psychological Bulletin*, 1973, **79**, 294-317.

Schneider, S.J. Selective attention in schizophrenia. *Journal of Abnormal Psychology*, 1976, **85**, 167-173.

Schofield, W. & Balian, L. A comparative study of the personal histories of schizophrenic and non-psychiatric patients. *Journal of Abnormal and Social Psychology*, 1959, **59**, 216-225.

Schooler, C. & Silverman, J. Perceptual styles and their correlates among schizophrenic patients. *Journal of Abnormal Psychology*, 1969, **74**, 459-470.

Schwartz, S. Do schizophrenics give rare word associations? *Schizophrenia Bulletin*, 1978, **4**, 248-251.

Scott, W.A. Conceptions of normality. In E.F. Borgatta and W.W. Lambert (Eds.), *Handbook of personality theory and research*. Chicago: Rand McNally, 1968. Pp. 974-1006.

Shakow, D. Psychological deficit in schizophrenia. *Behavioral Science*, 1963, **8**, 275-305.

Shakow, D. & Jellinek, E.M. Composite index of the Kent-Rosanoff Free Association Test. *Journal of Abnormal Psychology*, 1965, **70**, 403-404.

Shands, H.C. *Semiotic approaches to psychiatry*. The Hague: Mouton, 1970.

Shearn, C.R. & Fitzgibbons, D.J. Theoretical orientations of mental health professionals as a function of professional discipline and length of experience. *Psychological Reports*, 1971, **28**, 230-238.

Sherman, J.A. Use of reinforcement and imitation to reinstate verbal behavior in mute psychotics. *Journal of Abnormal Psychology*, 1965, **70**, 155-164.

Shields, J. Genetics in schizophrenia. In D. Kemali, G. Bartholini, and D. Richter (Eds.), *Schizophrenia today*. New York: Pergamon Press, 1976. Pp. 57-66.

Shimkunas, A. Reciprocal shifts in schizophrenic thought processes. *Journal of Abnormal Psychology*, 1970, **76**, 423-426.

Shimkunas, A. Demand for intimate self-disclosure and pathological verbalizations in schizophrenia. *Journal of Abnormal Psychology*, 1972, **80**, 197-205.

Siegler, M. & Osmond, H. Models of madness: Mental illness is not romantic. *Psychology Today*, 1974, **8**, 71-78.

Siegler, M. & Osmond, H. Aesculapian authority. *The Hastings Center Studies*, 1973, **1**, 41-52.

Silverman, J. The problem of attention in research and theory in schizophrenia. *Psychological Review*, 1964, **71**, 352-379.

Silverman, J., Berg, P.S., & Kantor, R. Some perceptual correlates of institutionalization. *Journal of Nervous and Mental Disease*, 1966, **141**, 651-657.

Singer, C. *A short history of scientific ideas*. New York and London: Oxford, 1959.

Skolnick, J. *Justice without trial*. New York: Wiley, 1966.

Snyder, S.H. Dopamine and schizophrenia. In L.C. Wynne, R.L. Cromwell, and S. Matthysse (Eds.), *The nature of schizophrenia*. New York: Wiley, 1978. Pp. 87-94.

Snyder, S.H. *Madness and the brain*. New York: McGraw-Hill, 1974.

Snyder, S.H. Amphetamine psychosis: A "model" schizophrenia mediated by catecholamines. *American Journal of Psychiatry*, 1973, **130**, 61-67.

Snyder, S.H., Banerjee, S.P., Yanamura, H.I., & Greenberg, D. Drugs, neurotransmitters, and schizophrenia. *Science*, 1974, **184**, 1243-1254.

Sokolov, Y.N. *Perception and the conditioned reflex*. New York: Macmillan, 1963.

Sollod, R. & Lapidus, L.B. Concrete operational thinking, diagnosis, and psychopathology in hospitalized schizophrenics. *Journal of Abnormal Psychology*, 1977, **86**, 199-202.

Sommer, R., Witney, G., & Osmond, H. Teaching common associations to schizophrenics. *Journal of Abnormal and Social Psychology*, 1962, **65**, 58-61.

Spence, J.T., Goodstein, L.D., & Lair, C.V. Rote learning in schizophrenic and normal subjects under positive and negative reinforcement conditions. *Journal of Abnormal Psychology*, 1965, **70**, 251-261.

Spence, J.T. & Lair, C.V. Associative interference in the verbal learning performance of schizophrenics and normals. *Journal of Abnormal and Social Psychology*, 1964, **68**, 204-209.

Spitzer, R.L., Endicott, J., & Robins, E. Research diagnostic criteria: Rationale and reliability. *Archives of General Psychiatry*, 1978, **36**, 773-782.

Spitzer, R.L., Endicott, J., & Robins, E. *Research diagnostic criteria (RDC) for a selected group of functional disorders*. New York: New York State Psychiatric Institute, 1978.

Spitzer, R.L. & Fleiss, J.L. A re-analysis of the reliability of psychiatric diagnosis. *British Journal of Psychiatry*, 1974, **125**, 341-347.

Spitzer, R.L, & Klein, D.F. (Eds.). *Critical issues in psychiatric diagnosis*. New York: Raven Press, 1978.

Spohn, H.E., Thetford, P.E., & Woodham, F.L. Span of apprehension and arousal in schizophrenia. *Journal of Abnormal Psychology*, 1970, **75**, 113-123.

Spohn, H.E. & Wolk, W.P. Effect of group problem solving experience upon social withdrawal in chronic schizophrenics. *Journal of Abnormal and Social Psychology*, 1963, **66**, 187-190.

Spohn, H.E. & Wolk, W.P. Social participation in homogeneous and heterogeneous groups of chronic schizophrenics. *Journal of Abnormal and Social Psychology*, 1966, **71**, 147-150.

Steadman, H.J. Some evidence on the inadequacy of the concept and determination of dangerousness in law and psychiatry. *Journal of Psychiatry and Law*, 1973, **1**, 409-426.

Steadman, H.J. & Cocozza, J.J. *Careers of the criminally insane*. Lexington, Massachusetts: D.C. Heath, 1974.

Stein, M.I. Creativity. In E.F. Borgatta and W.W. Lambert (Eds.), *Handbook of personality theory and research*. Chicago: Rand McNally, 1968. Pp. 900-942.

Strauss, J.S. Diagnostic models and the nature of psychiatric disorder. *Archives of General Psychiatry*, 1973, **29**, 445-449.

Strauss, J.S. A comprehensive approach to psychiatric diagnosis. *American Journal of Psychiatry*, 1975, **132**, 1193-1197.

Strauss, M. Behavioral differences between acute and chronic schizophrenics: Cause of psychosis, effects of institutionalization or sampling biases? *Psychological Bulletin*, 1973, **79**, 271-279.

Strauss, M., Foureman, W., & Parvatikar, S. Schizophrenics' size estimations of thematic stimuli. *Journal of Abnormal Psychology*, 1974, **83**, 117-123.

Streiner, D. Effects of task complexity and verbal evaluation on the learning of normals and schizophrenics. *Journal of Abnormal Psychology*, 1969, **74**, 606-611.

Stromgen, E. Genetic factors in the origin of schizophrenia. In H.M. vanPraag (Ed.), *On the origin of schizophrenic psychoses*. Amsterdam: DeErven Bohn B.V., 1975. Pp. 7-18.

Sturm, I.E. "Conceptual area" among pathological groups: A failure to replicate. *Journal of Abnormal and Social Psychology*, 1964, **69**, 216-223.

Sullivan, H.S. The language of schizophrenia. In J.S. Kasanin (Ed.), *Language and thought in schizophrenia*. Berkeley: University of California Press, 1946. Pp. 4-15.

Szasz, T.S. *The myth of mental illness: Foundations for a theory of personal conduct*. New York: Hoeber and Harper, 1961.

Szasz, T.S. *The manufacture of madness: A comparative study of the inquisition, and the mental health movement*. New York: Harper and Row, 1970.

Szasz, T.S. *Schizophrenia: Sacred symbol of psychiatry*. New York: Basic Books, 1976.

Temerlin, M.K. Suggestion effects in psychiatric diagnosis. *Journal of Nervous and Mental Disease*, 1968, **147**, 349-353.

Thayer, G. & Silber, D. Relationship between levels of arousal and responsiveness among schizophrenic and normal subjects. *Journal of Abnormal Psychology*, 1971, **77**, 162-173.

Thornton, C. & Gottheil, E. Social schemata in schizophrenic males. *Journal of Abnormal Psychology*, 1971, **77**, 192-195.

Tobias, L.L. & MacDonald, M.L. Withdrawal of maintenance drugs with long-term hospitalized mental patients: A critical review. *Psychological Bulletin*, 1974, **81**, 107-125.

Torrey, E.F. Doctors with nothing to doctor. *San Francisco Examiner and Chronicle*, Sunday Punch Section, October 20, 1974, p. 2. (a)

Torrey, E.F. *The death of psychiatry*. Radnor, Pennsylvania: Chilton, 1974. (b)

Trachtman, J.P. Socioeconomic class bias in Rorschach diagnosis. Contributing psychological attributes of the clinician. *Journal of Projective Techniques and Personality Assessment*, 1971, **35**, 229-240.

Treisman, A.M. The effect of irrelevant material on the efficiency of selective listening. *American Journal of Psychology*, 1964, **77**, 533-546.

Treisman, A.M., Squire, R., & Green, J. Semantic processes in selective listening? A replication. *Memory and Cognition*, 1974, **2**, 641-646.

Turner, R.J., Dopkeen, L., & Labreche, G. Marital status and schizophrenia: A study of incidence and outcome. *Journal of Abnormal Psychology*, 1970, **76**, 110-116.

Ullmann, L.P. Behavior therapy as a social movement. In C.M. Franks (Ed.), *Assessment and status of the behavior therapies*. New York: McGraw Hill, 1968. Pp. 495-523.

Ullmann, L.P., Forsman, R.G., Kenny, J.W., McInnis, T.L., Unikel, I.P., & Zeisset, R.M. Selective reinforcement of schizophrenics' interview responses. *Behavior Research and Therapy*, 1965, **2**, 205-212.

Ullmann, L.P. & Giovannoni, J.M. The development of a self-report measure of the process-reactive continuum. *Journal of Nervous and Mental Disease*, 1964, **138**, 38-42.

Ullmann, L.P. & Krasner, L. *A psychological approach to abnormal behavior*. New York: Prentice-Hall, 1967.

Ullman, L.P. & Krasner, L. *A psychological approach to abnormal behavior*. (2nd ed.) New York: Prentice-Hall, 1975.

Ullmann, L.P., Krasner, L., & Collins, B.J. Modification of behavior through verbal conditioning: Effects in group therapy. *Journal of Abnormal and Social Psychology*, 1961, **62**, 128-132.

Ulrich, R., Stachnik, T., & Mabry, J. (Eds.). *Control of Human Behavior*. Glenview, Illinois: Scott, Foresman, 1970.

Vale, S., Espejel, A., Calcameo, F., Ocampo, J., & Diaz-de-Leon, J. Creatine phosphokinase. *Archives of Neurology*, 1974, **30**, 103-104.

Venables, P.H. Input dysfunction in schizophrenia. In B.A. Maher (Ed.), *Progress in experimental personality research*. Vol. I. New York: Academic Press, 1964. Pp. 1-47.

Vestre, N.D. The effects of thorazine on learning and retention in schizophrenic patients. *Journal of Abnormal and Social Psychology*, 1961, **63**, 438-439.

Vieth, I. *Hysteria: The history of a disease*. Chicago: University of Chicago Press, 1965.

von Domarus, E. The specific laws of logic in schizophrenia. In J.S. Kasanin (Ed.), *Language and thought in schizophrenia*. New York: W.W. Norton; 1964. Pp. 104-113.

Wagener, J.M. & Hartsough, D. Social competence as a process-reactive dimension with schizophrenics, alcoholics, and normals. *Journal of Abnormal Psychology*, 1974, **83**, 112-116.

Wahl, O. Monozygotic twins discordant for schizophrenia: A review. *Psychological Bulletin*, 1976, **83**, 91-106.

Walinder, J., Skott, A., Carlsson, A., & Roos, B. Potentiation of metyrosine of thioridazine effects in chronic schizophrenics. *Archives of General Psychiatry*, 1976, **33**, 501-505.

Ward, W.D. & Carlson, W.A. Autonomic responsivity to variable input rates among schizophrenics classified on the process-reactive dimension. *Journal of Abnormal Psychology*, 1966, **71**, 10-16.

Warnock, D.G. & Ellman, G.L. Intramuscular chlorpromazine and creatine kinase: Acute psychosis or local muscle trauma? *Science*, 1969, **164**, 726.

Warr, P.P. & Knapper, C. *The perception of people and events*. New York: Wiley, 1968.

Watson, J.B. The place of the conditioned reflex in psychology, *Psychological Review*, 1916, **23**, 89-116.

Weber, M. *The Protestant ethic and the spirit of capitalism*. London: Unwin, 1930.

Weckowicz, T.E. Shape constancy in schizophrenic patients. *Journal of Abnormal and Social Psychology*, 1964, **68**, 177-183.

Wegner, D.M. & Vallacher, R.R. *Implicit psychology*. New York: Oxford University Press, 1977.

Weidenfeller, E.W. & Zimny, G.H. Effects of music upon GSR of depressives and schizophrenics. *Journal of Abnormal and Social Psychology*, 1962, **64**, 307-312.

Weinberger, E. & Cermak, L. Short-term retention in acute and chronic paranoid schizophrenics. *Journal of Abnormal Psychology*, 1973, **82**, 220-225.

Wenger, D.L. & Fletcher, C.R. The effect of legal counsel on admission to a state mental hospital: A confrontation of professionals. *Journal of Health and Human Behavior*, 1969, **10**, 66-72.

Wenk, E.A., Robison, J., & Smith, G. Can violence be predicted? *Crime and Delinquency*, 1972, **7**, 198-205.

Werner, H. & Kaplan, B. *Symbol formation*. New York: Wiley, 1964.

White, H. The forms of wildness: Archeology of an idea. In E. Dudley and M.E. Novak (Eds.), *The wild man within*. Pittsburgh: University of Pittsburgh Press, 1972. Pp. 3-38.

White, H. Interpretation in history. *New Literary History*, 1972-1973, **4**, 281-314.

White, R.M. & Johnson, P.J. Concept of dimensionality and optional shift performance in nursery school children. *Journal of Experimental Child Psychology*, 1968, **6**, 113-119.

Wiggins, J.S., Renner, K.E., Clore, G.L. & Rose, R.J. *The psychology of personality*. Reading, Massachusetts: Addison Wesley, 1971.

Wilensky, H. & Solomon, L. Characteristics of untestable chronic schizophrenics. *Journal of Abnormal and Social Psychology*, 1960, **61**, 155-158.

Williams, B.E. Deductive reasoning in schizophrenia. *Journal of Abnormal and Social Psychology*, 1964, **69**, 47-61.

Wincze, J.P., Leitenberg, H., & Agras, W.S. The effects of token reinforcement and feedback on delusional verbal behavior of chronic paranoid schizophrenics. *Journal of Applied Behavior Analysis*, 1972, **5**, 247-262.

Wing, J.K. Social influences on the course of schizophrenia. In L.C. Wynne, R.L. Cromwell, and S. Matthysse (Eds.), *The nature of schizophrenia*. New York: Wiley, 1978. Pp. 599-616.

Winkler, R.C. Management of chronic psychiatric patients by a token reinforcement system. *Journal of Applied Behavior Analysis,* 1970, **3,** 47-55.

Winkler, R.C. A theory of equilibrium in token economies. *Journal of Abnormal Psychology,* 1972, **79,** 169-173.

Wise, C.D., Baden, M.M., & Stein, L. Post-mortem measurement of enzymes in human brain: Evidence of a central noradrenergic deficit in schizophrenia. *Journal of Psychiatric Research,* 1974, **11,** 185-198.

Wise, C.D. & Stein, L. Dopmain-B-Hydroxylase deficits in the brains of schizophrenic patients. *Science,* 1973, **181** 344-347.

Wyatt, R.J. & Bigelow, L.B. A survey of other biologic research in schizophrenia. In L.C. Wynne, R.L. Cromwell, and S. Matthysse (Eds.), *The nature of schizophrenia.* New York: Wiley, 1978. Pp. 143-147.

Wyatt, R.J., Schwartz, M.A., Erdelyi E., & Barchas, J.D. Dopamine-B-hydroxylase activity in the brains of schizophrenic patients. *Science,* 1975, **187,** 368-370.

Wynne, L.C., Cromwell, R.L. & Matthysse, S. (Eds.) *The nature of schizophrenia: New approaches to research and treatment.* New York: Wiley, 1978.

Yaffe, P.E. & Mancuso, J.C. Effects of therapist's behavior on people's mental illness judgments. *Journal of Consulting and Clinical Psychology,* 1977, **45,** 84-91.

Yarrow, M.R., Schwartz, C.G., Murphy, H.S., & Deasy, L.C. The psychological meaning of mental illness in the family. *Journal of Social Issues,* 1955, **11,** 12-24.

Yates, A. & Korboot, P. Speed of perceptual functioning in chronic nonparanoid schizophrenics. *Journal of Abnormal Psychology,* 1970, **76,** 453-461.

Youkilis, H.D. & DeWolfe, A.S. The regression hypothesis and subclassifications of schizophrenia. *Journal of Abnormal Psychology,* 1975, **85,** 36-40.

Zahn, T.P., Rosenthal, D., & Shakow, D. Reaction time in schizophrenic and normal subjects in relation to the sequence of series of regular preparatory intervals. *Journal of Abnormal and Social Psychology,.* 1961, **63,** 161-168.

Zanna, M.P. & Cooper, J. Dissonance and the attribution process. In J.H. Harvey, W.J. Ickes, and R.F. Kidd (Eds.), *New directions in attribution research.* Vol. 1. Hillsdale, New Jersey: Lawrence Erlbaum Associates, 1976.

Zarlock, S.P. Social expectations, language and schizophrenia. *Journal of Humanistic Psychology,* 1966, **6,** 68-74.

Zaslow, R.W. A new approach to the problem of conceptual thinking in schizophrenia. *Journal of Consulting Psychology,* 1950, **14,** 335-340.

Zigler, E. & Levine, J. Premorbid adjustment and paranoid-nonparanoid status in schizophrenia: A further investigation. *Journal of Abnormal Psychology,* 1973, **82,** 189-199.

Zigler, E. & Phillips, L. Psychiatric diagnosis and symptomatology. *Journal of Abnormal and Social Psychology,* 1961, **63,** 69-75.

Zigler, E. & Phillips, L. Social competence and the process-reactive distinction in psychopathology. *Journal of Abnormal and Social Psychology,* 1962, **65,** 215-222.

Zlotowski, M. & Bakan, P. Behavioral variability of process and reactive schizophrenics in a binary guessing task. *Journal of Abnormal and Social Psychology,* 1963, **66,** 185-187.

Zuckerman, M. & Grosy, H.J. Contradictory results using the mecholyl test to differentiate process and reactive schizophrenia. *Journal of Abnormal and Social Psychology,* 1959, **59,** 145-146.

Author Index

Subject Index

About the Authors

THEODORE R. SARBIN (Ph.D. Ohio State University, 1941) has served on the staff of the University of Minnesota and the University of California at Berkeley and Santa Cruz, in addition to working as a clinical psychologist in private practice. At various times, Sarbin has held fellowships from the Social Science Research Council, the Center for Social Science Theory (Berkeley), the Guggenheim Foundation, Oxford University (Fulbright), the Center for Advanced Studies and the Center for the Humanities (Wesleyan University). His bibliography includes more than 150 titles dealing with the social psychology of deviance, hypnosis, role theory, jurisprudence, clinical inference, and psychological theory.

JAMES C. MANCUSO (Ph.D. University of Rochester, 1958) has held positions as a psychologist with the United States Veteran's Administration, in public schools in western New York, and at Lehigh University. In 1961 he joined the Psychology Department of the State University of New York at Albany. He is a senior fellow of SUNY Albany's Institute for Humanistic Studies where he has helped conduct the 1980 conference on Thomas Szasz.

Pergamon General Psychology Series

Editors: Arnold P. Goldstein, Syracuse University
Leonard Krasner, SUNY, Stony Brook